THE DREAM BOOK

We have been catching fireflies
when all the while
the stones are glowing

—GIOIA TIMPANELLI,
Stones for the Hours of the Night

THE DREAM BOOK

An Anthology of Writings by Italian American Women

Edited with an Introduction by
HELEN BAROLINI

SCHOCKEN BOOKS • New York

First Schocken paperback edition 1987
10 9 8 7 6 5 4 3 2   87 88
Copyright © 1985 by Helen Barolini

Library of Congress Cataloging in Publication Data
Main entry under title:
The Dream book.
Includes bibliographical references and index.
1. American literature—Italian American authors.
2. American literature—Women authors.   3. American
literature—20th century.   4. Italian American
women—Literary collections.   I. Barolini, Helen.
PS508.I73D7   1985   810'.8'09287   84-23503

Designed by Richard Oriolo
Manufactured in the United States of America
ISBN 0-8052-3972-3 (hardcover)
ISBN 0-8052-0832-1 (paperback)

Acknowledgments for all copyright material used are given on pages
389-393, which constitute an extension of this copyright page.

This book is dedicated to
Linda Lucia, Susanna, and Nicoletta,
my daughters

Contents

Preface

Paths are made by walking. Books are made by questioning.

My questions—long dormant—surfaced when I was invited to speak at a conference for Italian American women.[1] I was asked to speak about the women of Italian American background who were, and are, writers.

Who are they? I wondered. To be able to call up the few names I knew was the same, really, as not knowing any—not enough to wipe out the prevailing notion that there are no Italian American women writers as there are, so notably, Black women writers, Jewish, Asian. In histories, sociological tracts, bibliographies, learned conferences—the names mentioned as Italian American writers are those of male authors, just as the achievers in other areas are also male; it is a totality of male presence that effectively undercuts the importance and witness of women in the Italian American experience.[2] And as I wondered about the unnamed women, there echoed in my mind something a reader of my novel *Umbertina* had written me: "When I first saw your book I was drawn to your name, a novel by a woman with an Italian surname is rare."

1. The Italian American Woman: Challenging and Maintaining Tradition, a conference presented by the Italian American Institute to Foster Higher Education on April 17, 1982, at Marymount Manhattan College in New York City

2. Exceptionally, it was in Professor Andrew Rolle's *The Immigrant Upraised* (Norman: University of Oklahoma Press, 1968) that mention was first made of a "lost" woman writer, Antonia Pola.

I knew she was right, but why? Who were the others? Why have I never heard of their work? Why is it that though we exist, we are not perceived? Before I had many answers, I addressed the conference with a talk called "Breaking the Silence," more a statement of hope than of fact. But I had started on a path. The rest came from walking.

There had to be other writers, I felt; I would have to look for them. Where were the writings that would remedy the lack of our voice in the literature? Why do we not have the record of their experience from these women? For if we do, it is not generally known. Why are we, it seems, so isolated and few? Daniela Gioseffi, a feminist poet and novelist I was to meet later, calls us all the real "Women of the Shadows."

From my own experience, and what I have learned from others, the loneliness of seeming marginal is something well understood by the Italian American woman with literary aspirations. We stand alone, seemingly unconnected to any body of literature or group of writers—anomalies, freak occurrences, nonrepeaters, ephemera.

Being Italian American, being female, and being a writer is being thrice an outsider, and why this is so is partly in the history and social background of the Italian women who came to this country, partly in the literary mold of the country itself.

A more difficult question, though, was not only why we are isolated and few, but whether there was any reason to suppose that, if grouped, we formed something cohesive and had, in fact, a specific resonance as Italian American women writers. I believe it to be so. I believe that the super-abundant tradition we derive from has given us identity, has bequeathed both strengths and inhibitions, has presented problems as well as passions. No matter how encompassing our themes or broad our views, overtones of who we are and how we feel, as formed by our values and history, show up in our work.

I couldn't get rid of the questions, nor could the questions get rid of me. They reverberated in the words of the women I was seeking out: Why was it all but impossible to find writing in which we could recognize the transcultural and transgenerational complexities of who we are, where we've come from, and what the journey has been? Sandra M. Gilbert (née Mortola), who is well known as a literary theorist and writer about women, but perhaps less known as a poet of strong, indeed passionate Italian American identity, stated the problem very precisely: "I am always struck by how few people have written about what it meant to be *us*!"

Yet we have qualms about being too narrowly defined. Barbara Grizzuti Harrison said in a panel discussion once that she did not think of herself as an Italian American woman writer, but as an author who is all of that and more. And I agree. It is not the qualifiers that are important, it is the writing. But it would be disingenuous to deny the ethnic factor. I was impressed, when interviewing Cynthia Ozick some years ago, that although Ozick repudiated with extreme distaste the term "woman writer," she did affirm herself a Jewish writer. Black women writers are equally affirming of their heritage and distinctiveness. Cannot Italian American women find strength in solidarity, and cannot solidarity itself be a means to visibility and voice?

It is not as a separation from the mainstream of literature, but for purposes of historical and cultural perspective, that the writers in this volume are identified as having some connection with *italianità*, for I am always aware that as individual writers, each transcends the limitations of qualifiers. There is a great range among the contributors—of age, education, geographical provenance, occupation, experience as writers, and literary reputation. Some have a remote Italian connection, others were born in Italy; the degree of generational distance from Italy, and even the part of Italy one's people came from have definite influences on these writers. There are perceptible differences in style—from the vivid, oral stories of the unlettered Rosa Cassettari to the intense, linguistic control of Ree Dragonette or the esoteric surrealism of Leslie Scalapino—denoting huge distances and changes. It indicates a complexity denied to the popular image of the Italian American woman.

Although I met many of them—in person, in correspondence, in their work—others are unknown to me, deceased, or "lost." I think of someone like Antonia Pola, who was silenced before she was formed, and her work— so tentative, so unpolished, so pathetically little and yet so forceful in her woman's voice crying out for help long before the woman's movement loosed our tongues. There are women even more lost than Pola, because she left a book while others are unpublished, unrecorded.

So, I have wanted to "name the names," as much as I have been able, and to put on record a part of our national literature which has been overlooked or thought unworthy of attention. This collection, which dramatist Karen Malpede wrote me "feels like coming home," does not claim to be exhaustive; the obscurity of many Italian American women writers and the limits of my personal resources made a complete investigation into literary writing quite impossible. But perhaps the fact of this volume will occasion others in which additional voices will join those here included.

I must express gratitude to Catherine Ruocco, organizer of the Marymount conference; her goading forced me finally to articulate the questions which were the genesis of this book. And I am most appreciative of the support given me by the National Italian American Foundation through its Executive Director, Dr. Alfred Rotondaro, and the advocacy of Dr. Maria Lombardo, Director of Educational Programs for NIAF.

For their help in finding the writers and shaping the thoughts that are expressed in the Introduction, I would like to express appreciation to the learned people whom I met along the way and with whom I spoke and exchanged ideas. They were sociologists, psychologists, teachers, journalists, librarians, and writers, and I thank them all.

I am indebted to the Immigration History Research Center in St. Paul, Minnesota, which offered me hospitality and assistance in the use of their archives, where I found my first sources for several of the older writers included here.

Finally, I should like to acknowledge the cooperation and goodwill of the writers who contributed to this book. They were, in many cases, very generous in bringing to my attention other writers: Rosemarie Santini and Kathryn Nocerino told me about the too little known works of an extraordinary poet, Ree Dragonette; Karen Malpede introduced me to the playwrights Rosemarie Caruso and Michele Linfante. Theresa Vinciguerra identified Sandra M. Gilbert's Italian American background. And so it went.

It was Dorothy Bryant who led me to Alma Rattini Vanek, a seventy-eight-year-old former student from Bryant's creative writing course. I went to see Alma on the heights of Berkeley where she and her husband live with orange trees in the front yard and rear-window views out to the Bay. Alma's Italianness was reawakened by my search for women writers of that background, and it came in an outpouring of memories which she shared with me. She told of being born in a mining camp at Telluride, Colorado, where her parents had immigrated from the Trentino-Alto Adige region of Italy, on the border with Austria, at the beginning of this century.

And then she put into my hands an old, yellowed, linoleum-covered manual she called the dream book. I opened the ragged-edged, loose-paged book. On a front page, in awkward, uphill handwriting was the Italian notation of one Angela Zecchini who, with many misspellings and an incorrect date for the inception of World War I, recorded this terse account of her life: "I was born in 1884 in the commune of Folgaria, district of Rovereto. Departed the old places the day of May 7th. Arrived in Telluride June 12th and on July 20th [sic], in Europe, there erupted a powerful war of the European powers. Written October 7, 1914."

That handwriting was the first I had ever seen of an immigrant Italian woman; and the book itself was the first piece of immigrant "literature" I had ever encountered. It was, Alma told me, a book the Italian women of Telluride used constantly, the Baedeker of their dreams. For each dream could be interpreted by consulting meanings in the alphabetized subject entries, and looking up dreams gave them explication for the strangeness around them and a clue to their *destino*. I tried it, too, for that very morning my daughter Linda had told me her dream: she dreamt of my holding a baby in my arms. I myself had dreamt of stacks and stacks of white paper. In the dream book I looked under "*bambino*" and "*carta*." The reading was of an auspicious beginning for a creative venture. I took it for the sign of this anthology I was beginning, and from it came its title, *The Dream Book*, and its meaning.

The original tattered and much-thumbed dream book was the companion of those displaced women in Colorado, giving them hope or warning, speaking to them of their hidden longings, fears; it was their counsel and guide, as, in another society, the Bible was for the English pilgrims.

Alma related how those isolated women shared any popular Italian novel which might find its way to them. Her mother, and the others, craved those Italian stories which embodied their other lives in the language of their birth. A *romanzo* would circulate among all of them until it fell apart from sheer reading and rereading, satisfying in part their need to transcend their lives. But that was the rare occasion.

For everyday, they had their book of dreams. The men, the rough miners, might laugh at them, but the women knew the power of dreams. They charted their ways through the unknown with the help of divinations from the dream book. It had to serve until the day came when their daughters and granddaughters would be mistresses of the new language, able to lay out lives and signs in their own words in order to make sense of them, and understand the past.

Judith Rossner, explaining the provenance of her novels, touched on this: her material, she said, came from the substrata of her unconscious and was the same stuff dreams are made of. And Paula Gunn Allen, the poet of Native American remembrance, affirms:

> The key is in remembering, in what is chosen
> for the dream.

Yes, in that moment, in Alma's home, as we looked at the old dream book, it seemed to me that all of us women of Italian American background who are writers are engaged in composing the body of another dream book. And often, uncannily often, what we write of, where we start, is with our grandmothers. With those old women, most often illiterate or very little schooled, who had only their dreams, premonitions, and feelings to read.

The new dream book exposes the signs and symbols, the auguries and directions of lives which were—and are—subject to great ambivalence, to dual pulls from opposing cultural influence, to dual vision.

The new writers assign meanings through their poetry, novels, stories, essays, and plays. In the written word, now—*their* written word, finally—

the instructions and directions for lives and futures can be found. Their book interprets the experiences of our collective past and brings into view what had been inexplicable, painful, dubious, conflicting. We shall consult one another in order to know ourselves.

I owe a great deal of personal enrichment to my contacts with many of the women represented in this book, who enlarged my thinking; who moved me by their stories; who broke, by their presence, the confinement of isolation and oddness in which we singly struggled. They brought the warmth and sharing of personal revelation to this work, the joy of their enthusiasm, and the answer to the question, Where are the women? I wish them well in their work. In the truest sense this book is theirs.

THE DREAM BOOK

Introduction

The Historical and Social Context of Silence

As I began this exploration of silent women, the words of a cultural envoy from Italy to the United States rang insistently in my ears. My mention of Italian American women writers had been met with words of impatience directed at their lack of celebrity status: "Who *are* they? "Why aren't they stronger? . . . more important? Who has ever seen their books on racks at an airline terminal?"

Even in a time of hype in which values have been debased to a standard such as whether one has been interviewed on television or not, it was a dispiriting display of lack of historical and humanistic understanding; and of the elitist attitude still lingering in the mother culture which asks testily of its descendants abroad, why aren't you better than you are?

The why is in our history.

And it is not negative history, a litany of ineptness or missed opportunities; quite the contrary: given the many adverse factors to overcome, the Italian immigrants of the late nineteenth and early twentieth centuries, coming mainly from the extreme deprivation of the south, did, in large part, translate their hard work and canniness into successful American terms. They secured an economic foothold in their new environment. They also secured a sense of double alienation; Italian immigration to this country was preponderantly by people who were not wanted or valued in their land of origin, then found they were not wanted or valued here when they aspired to more than their exploitation as raw labor. Some of this still sticks in the Italian American psyche regardless of material success.

That literary arts would lag behind pragmatic ones is no mystery.

Italian Americans cannot be conveniently generalized; they are differentiated by a multitude of variables, including class, education, political activism, religion, number of generations in this country, their Italian provenance, and the subsequent area of settlement in America.

But, by and large, the women have a commonality.

They are women who, with rare exceptions, had never before been authorized to be authors (of themselves, of the word)—not by their external world, nor again by their internal one.

They came mostly from forebears without the ingrained custom of learning as the Jews had; they came speaking regional dialects and most did not read or write any language; they came without a literary tradition; they came from a male-dominant world where their ancillary role was rigidly, immutably restricted to home and family; they came as helpmates to their men, as mothers of their children, as bearers of the old cultural ways. The creativity went elsewhere—into managing the homes, growing the gardens, making the bread, elegant needlework. Though they brought native strengths—sharp wits, tenaciousness, family loyalty, patience, and courage, which are skills for survival—they did not acquire until generations later the nascent writer's tools of education, confidence of language, the leisure to read, and the privacy for reflection.

When you don't read, you don't write. When your frame of reference is a deep distrust of education because it is an attribute of the very classes who have exploited you and your kind for as long as memory carries, then you do not encourage a reverence for books among your children. You teach them practical arts not the imaginative ones.

A conversation with Dr. Marie Badaracco-Apolito, a psychoanalyst, was most illuminating in the area of language and meaning. We were both speculating, from experience, on how little value Italians attach to exact meaning and the literalness of words. *Parole femmine*, they say in Italian: words are feminine, words are for women, frivolous and volatile. Deeds are masculine; men engage in action which is concrete, real. This is unlike the Jews, people of the Book, or Fundamentalist Christians, believers in the Word, who implicitly trust words and honor them. Italians are more skeptical; it is as if, numbed by the rhetoric which continually whirls about them, inured to the conventional formulae and empty *complimenti* of discourse, they tend to lose all notion of words as conveyers of anything "real." What is real is life in the piazza, the marketplace, the family at the dinner table.

Words themselves are meant for fanciful approximations, artificial conventions; they are relative and circumstantial, illusory and masking, but not for relying on. Even more distrustful of words, then, are those who cannot read or write them; all of which creates distancing from that most abstract act with words, the writing of them into imaginative literature.

The first survey of the literary activities of Italian Americans was compiled by Olga Peragallo and published in 1949. Her study lists fifty-nine authors (with an amiable leniency that includes Nicola Sacco and Bartolomeo Vanzetti), eleven of whom are women. In his preface to that work, the late Italian critic, author, and professor emeritus at Columbia University Giuseppe Prezzolini observed that at that time there were, by census count, 4,574,780 Italian Americans in the United States of whom 3,766,820 still declared their mother tongue to be Italian. "This leaves," he wrote, "only 827,960 who spoke English at home; that is a very small minority from which one could expect writers to come forth. . . ." He also noted of the fifty-nine authors that "the amount and value of their literary output would certainly be greater if the members of the first generation had come to America endowed with a culture of their own and if they had been able to absorb also the culture of the United States. They found two barriers: the language and the social background . . . Since these families were driven from Italy by poverty, the ghost of poverty followed them throughout their lives and influenced the education of their children."[1]

Those children, including any hypothetical aspiring authors, were but one or two generations away from ignorance of the English language in any way, let alone as a literary vehicle; they were not book readers. It was their American schooling which provided the beginnings of relating to literature, a literature not of their own world nor of their own experiences, but of Anglo-American models which fed their sense of alienation.

And though, by the early years of this century, some men of Italian American background had begun to write and publish books, for the women it was to be a much longer and later development. There are two notable exceptions, lone beacons which serve to render even deeper the void around them.

Sister Blandina Segale, a teaching nun of the Sisters of Charity, whose letters describing her mission to the Far West from 1872 until 1893 were published in book form as *At the End of the Santa Fe Trail*, is the earliest author. She was of Northern Italian stock and arrived in this country in 1854 at a time when Italians were so few and far between that there was no developed prejudice against them. She was educated and bilingual; her letters show a cultivated person who delighted in arranging a Mozart Mass for Christmas in a mining town, who made knowing allusions to the *Com-*

1. Olga Peragallo, *Italian American Authors* (New York: Vanni, 1949), p. xi.

media, and who taught the quartermaster's daughter Italian by reading *I promessi sposi* with her in the Santa Fe outpost. Sister Blandina was a civic influence in the Western territories, and a social activist who was instrumental in ending lynch law.

She wrote, as she says, in scraps of time, on scraps of paper, throwing them into her desk for a moment of leisure when she could piece them together into her journal. She had the resourceful and adaptive qualities of pioneer women. But the lack of personal written recollections from immigrant Italian women in the form of diaries, memoirs, or letters is only minutely filled by her singular voice. Sister Blandina was far more autonomous than other women of her day, and many generations ahead of the later-arriving Southern Italian immigrants among whom she would return to work in Cincinnati for the rest of her long life.

The second exception is Frances Winwar, born Francesca Vinciguerra in Taormina, Sicily, in 1900 (and unrelated to Theresa Vinciguerra, also in this collection). She came to the United States as a child and, fortunate in parents who had themselves been educated, her own education was encouraged and she became a precocious learner. At the age of eighteen she published her first work in English. She went on to become a most successful and prolific writer, not unhelped by the Anglicization of her name, which, she has related, was a condition to the publication of her first book, *The Ardent Flame,* published in 1927.[2]

In my search for authors for this work, I asked the curator of a large collection of books and manuscripts by American women if it included any works by women of Italian American background. "No," she told me, "this collection represents just la crème de la crème. For instance, if Christina Rossetti were American, not English, she'd be represented." I asked about Frances Winwar. "Oh, yes, of course," was the answer, "but I never thought of her as Italian."

The historical and social context of literary silence, and the clues to the missing women writers, can also be understood in Italian family mores. It is a story of conflicting cultures, alienation, unschooled parents' fear of the American school which they sensed, rightly, was taking their children from their authority, the growing resentment of American children toward their Italian parents, the resulting split in loyalties and personalities, the passing of the old ways, and the painful rites of passage into the new culture.

Italian women who came to this country did so as part of a family—as daughter, wife, sister; or, "on consignment," chosen, sometimes by pic-

2. Frances Winwar, in *Twentieth Century Authors,* ed. Stanley J. Kunitz and Howard Haycraft (New York, H. W. Wilson, 1942), p. 1536.

ture, sometimes by hearsay, from an immigrant's hometown to be his wife. But always in context of a family situation. There was no pattern of the independent Italian woman emigrating alone to better her lot as there was, for instance, among the Irish. For an uneducated Italian woman could not exist, economically or socially, outside the family institution which defined her life and gave it its whole meaning. She came, almost an indentured servant, bonded to her traditional role. The story of Rosa Cassettari, told in her own magnificent and vibrant words, is the story of these women.[3]

She had little choice but to put herself under the protection of a man. Women outside the family structure were scorned as deviants from the established order; they were either wicked or pitiful, but certainly outsiders. Unmarried or widowed women, who were thought, in their singleness, to be consumed with envy toward women with men, and full of spite, were thus commonly held to be the prime casters of the evil eye. In Grazia Deledda's novel *The Mother*, filled with the intensity and superstitions of the harsh Sardinian interior, a mother watches her son, a priest, fall under the spell of a woman who, being "rich, independent, alone, too much alone," was outside normality and thus a threat to all around her. In a patriarchal society, any female whose life was not defined by a man's would be suspect.

Even today it is a rare woman who could say as does Lena, a character in Rosemary Terango's play *Her Mother's Daughter:* "I'm a thinker—I thought myself right out of getting married." But then Lena's place in society is adjusted when she becomes a mother to her young orphaned niece and nephew, redeeming her womanhood and removing suspicion of egocentricity from her life.

A model of the Old World Italian woman who was resourceful, strong, and able to live by her wits and hard labor when it was demanded of her (as it was when her husband preceded her to America and often was gone for years at a time without any word) appears in Lucinda Mays's *The Other Shore*. There, the mother must pit herself against the elements, poverty, and outside hostility in order to survive. She keeps herself and her child alive by her unremitting sacrifice and strength until the long-awaited ticket to America arrives. Mays goes on, then, to have the child, Gabriella, find for herself that the long-dreamt-of street of gold is actually the American public school. She will redeem her life from her mother's through education and self-direction, providing an elevating though historically uncommon ending.

---

3. Marie Hall Ets, *Rosa: The Life of an Italian Immigrant* (Minneapolis: University of Minnesota Press, 1970).

For this much is certainly true of Italian women: they have resources of strength which are denied in the stereotype of them as merely submissive and servile creatures to their men. Back at the beginning of this century, Jacob Riis, who photographed and wrote of the immigrants in their tenement life on the Lower East Side of New York, noted, "There is that about the Italian woman which suggests the capacity for better things." Did he mean her strength, her endurance, her grace under pressure, her faith? They are qualities her daughters and granddaughters cherish and will retain, adjusted to new uses.

There are certain mindsets, however, endemic among the Italian immigrants, which are taking generations to reshape. Self-denial was the psychological preparation among peasants for survival in regions where *la miseria* was the norm of life and there was no chance of a better one. Therefore, one denied oneself aspirations and one's children education because both were futile. When the poor did leave to better themselves in this country, they brought their ways intact, including the old *miseria* mentality.

The ingrained suspicion of education was expressed in the saying, "*Fesso chi fa il figlio meglio di lui*"—it's a stupid man who makes his son better than he is. In America schools were not always regarded as the road to a better future; more often they were seen as a threat to the family because they stressed assimilation into American ways. Reading was ridiculed as too private, too unproductive, too exclusive an enjoyment—free time should be spent with the family group. Learning gave one ideas, made one different; all the family wanted was cohesion.

Here, as in Italy, the top goal was still survival of the family as the chief bulwark against an alien society. This commitment to family was placed solidly upon the shoulders of women, and because of their service to it, it was they who were most denied educational opportunities. As recently as the October 1983 conference on the Italian American Experience held at Columbia University, it was pointed out that though the number of Italian Americans in college has doubled since the end of World War II, Italian American women lag behind both Italian American men and other women when it comes to higher education. It was suggested that the Italian American woman's prime role in the family continues to operate against her involvement in the world outside.

At best women are getting a mixed message: Yes, better yourself, but don't get better than your family; do better economically, but not in your mind and spirit, which would then take you away from us. A film of 1970, *Lovers and Other Strangers*, reiterated the theme of not growing beyond the old style of doing things, when the father in an Italian American family confronted a son who was contemplating divorce: "What do you mean you're not compatible? What do you mean divorce? What are you—better than me? Look at me, do I have to be happy to be married! What makes you think *you* got to be happy? Why do you think we keep families together?— for happiness? Nah! It's for *family!*" Thus is the dialectic set up—there is resistance to change, but change is inevitable.

Even now, education is conceived not as an aid to autonomy but in the narrow, practical sense of helping one earn more money. In the very title of Louise DeSalvo's essay, "A Portrait of the *Puttana* as a Middle-Aged Woolf Scholar," is the recognition that an educated woman was (is) looked on with deep suspicion: the emancipation of the mind put her outside familial control, beyond male authority, and that had to mean untolerable license. The psychological warfare between the family and its progeny is still in fierce engagement.

In commentary on the Southern Italian woman, Valentine Rossilli Winsey, a professor of anthropology and herself one of fifteen children of Italian immigrant parents, writes, "Her religion, her extreme poverty . . . predisposed her to find comfort in the rich lore of communal superstitions. Her heritage of fatalism was inescapable—one's life was predetermined by one's *destino*. . . ." Women knew what to expect; it was all preordained in the traditional way of life: "From birth her duties and responsibilities as future wife and mother had been so impressed upon her that she obeyed almost instinctively the centuries-old rules of proper female behavior."[4]

The Italian woman comes from a patriarchal view of the world in which her life was always dependent upon a male—her father, brother, husband, and, eventually, if widowed, her sons. Family was the focal point of her duty and concern, and, by the same token, the source of her self-esteem and power, the means by which she measured her worth and was in turn measured, the reason for her being. Historically, the woman's role as the center of family life was crucial because of the importance of the family over any other Italian institution.

Within Italian culture, reinforcement of the woman's role and definition in the family was gained through the strong cult of the Madonna—the Holy Mother who prefigured all other mothers and symbolized them. Motherhood, worshiped in the Madonna figure, is here expressed in a verse by Rosa Marinoni, an indefatigable poetaster of some years ago:

4. Valentine Rossilli Winsey, "The Italian Immigrant Woman Who Arrived in the United States Before World War I," in *Studies in Italian American Social History: Essays in Honor of Leonard Covello*, ed. Francesco Cordasco (Totowa, N.J.: Rowman & Littlefield, 1975), p. 203.

I Am a Woman

Not because I have loved,
Not because I have wept,
Not because I have sinned,
But because I am a mother,
I am a Woman.

Professor Andrew Rolle, who has made a unique contribution to the psychological understanding of Italian Americans, observed, "The Madonna had been a mother but scarcely a wife."[5]

Richard Gambino points out in *Blood of My Blood* that it is not to God that Italians cry out in their need but to those interchangeable female figures, the Madonna or *mamma mia*. Gambino, whose book is important to an understanding of the background of the Italian American experience and the present dynamics of it, has described well the positive qualities expected of the female who was to become wife and mother; she was socialized at an early age to be serious, active, sharp, and practical; in a harsh environment, she was recognized as life sustaining by being the central pivot of the family in a way every bit as concrete as the Navajo's traditional hogan, which is built on four poles named after female deities, so that the support of the home literally rested upon the female.

However, in the chapter Gambino devotes to women, his espousal of "*La Serietà*—The Ideal of Womanliness" becomes a too idealized vision of woman's place. In Rolle's psychohistory, she is seen reducing the importance of sexuality and taking on the mater dolorosa role. True, she was the center of life of the whole ethnic group; true, it was she who expressed the emotions of the men; true she must be useful to her family, for her value is based on practical usefulness; but it is less true to women than to men like Gambino that this ideal of *serietà* was the be-all and end-all of a woman's life.

"I have it like heaven now," says the widowed Rosa Cassettari at the end of her life; "no man to scold me and make me do this and stop me to do that . . . I have it like Heaven—I'm my own boss. The peace I've got now it pays me for all the trouble I had in my life."[6] Even unlearned and unlettered women like Rosa had a sense of there being something more to their lives than family service.

The one thing, then, a woman must not do was change. Since everyone leaned on her for support, she was supposed to be permanently accessible and permanently unchanging. She could not exist as an individual with

5. Andrew Rolle, *The Italian Americans: Troubled Roots* (New York: The Free Press, 1980), p. 111.
6. Ets, *Rosa*, p. 253.

autonomous needs and wishes, for that would have undermined the common good.

A very contemporary use of the self-nullifying theme in Italian American women can be found in Rosemarie Caruso's play *The Suffering Heart Salon,* where the ritualization of women's sacrificial lives is played out in a New Jersey beauty salon and embodied in the line, "You don't like it?—do it anyway!" Caruso parallels women to the sanctified host of the sacrificial Mass, who exist to be consumed by the officiating priesthood of men. In their sacrifice is their blessedness, and specialness. Thus they are revered by those who consume them and they, themselves, feel consecrated by their role. But, in contrast, their daughters assert a need for self-identity and want to free themselves from the past patterns; in their self-actualization they *must* react against their mothers; and in denying the value of the mother's role by their rebellion against it, they lay upon themselves a heavy and terrible conflict.

In the meantime, Gambino has woven an illusion. His model woman does not exist; and, if she did, she is no longer desirable to those educated and socially evolving Italian American males (like himself) who have committed exogamy, fleeing her company and the *miseria* mentality for Jewish or Wasp wives. For one of the most verifiable phenomena of Italian American men is that, in their zest for upward mobility, they marry outside their group. This flight to hypergamy is given popular recognition by the ending of the movie *Saturday Night Fever,* in which the woman protagonist, Stephanie MacDonald, becomes the symbol for Italian American Tony Manero of what is better, achieving, upward in life. He leaves his Brooklyn neighborhood (in a symbolic gesture of change) to cross the bridge into Manhattan following her.

The voices of Winsey's interviews with Italian immigrant women, poignant and patiently resigned, or raised in anger, are different from those imagined by the apologists of Gambino's stoic matron, *la donna seria:* "I was thirteen when I came. After three months I got married. My father found the man . . . I got white hair when I was twenty-six . . . my life was finished . . . my husband and I didn't get along." . . . "My mother say, *you* gotta do and *I* gotta do what your father say to do." . . . "I didn't want to marry." . . . "I would never have come here. I would never have made this life . . ."—the chorus of voices speaks of unhappy marriages, no choices for their lives, and a kind of bewildered regret for what life had been. All that sustains them, as Winsey notes, is their belief in destiny; that it was all foreordained, that they had had no choice, that they did what was expected of them.[7]

---

7. Winsey, "Italian Immigrant Woman," passim.

For the Italian immigrant woman met her duties and responsibilities and showed again and again her strength, her resilience, and her timeworn patience. Indeed, her success in keeping the family together has earned her recognition and tributes from sociologists and other scholars.

But no barricade around the family unit was large enough to keep out the winds of freedom wafted on the New World air. The minute their children set foot in the American school and imbibed the notions that in this land all was possible and each person had the right to be self-fulfilled, something happened to the old bonds. They did not disappear, but they loosened. They allowed for new thoughts, new arrangements.

It became apparent that in Anglo-American life (for the English impress was the dominant ethnic pattern and became the standard by which American society judged all other ethnicities as up to par or not), the family had less importance than political or economic institutions, or even the school system. It was soon perceived that "Americans" valued self-sufficiency over family ties. The value placed on individual success and achievement was more than what was allotted family. As a result, the power of the Italian woman was diminished in the new land—she became old-fashioned and backward; she became the focus of well-meaning social workers who wanted to "save her" from what they viewed as an undemocratic patriarchal system without recognizing that in that very system she had found validation and had nothing, immediately, with which to replace it.

The psychological battering endured by the Italian American woman has been considerable. Winsey quotes the poignant remark of a solitary old immigrant woman reflecting on her experience of life in America, which keeps her children and grandchildren so busy running they have no time for her. "Bread rises," she said "only when it's allowed to stand awhile. The soul, too, has its own yeast, but it cannot rise while it's running. It's certain that I got things here which in Italy I never could have gotten. But I had things in Italy which in America I still cannot find—yeast, yeast for the soul!"[8]

The Italian woman's soul was in her consecration as core of the family, upholder of its traditions and transmitter of its values. In that role her hardships and sacrifices were repaid, her value was inviolate, and this gave her a positive sense of her self and of her power—power that was, however, often manipulative and always relative, confined as it was to the home environment and not used in the world at large. In America she was quickly dethroned into the image of the old woman in the kitchen, stirring the sauce, heartwarming, maybe, but actually a figure of ridicule, a caricature. She and the stern values she stood for were no competition for the seduction of *All the Comforts* (to use the title of Joseph Papaleo's fine novel)

8. Ibid., p. 210.

which beckoned her children away from stern duty, away from tacky self-sacrifice, away from the old way.

Not able to Americanize on the spot, the Italian immigrant woman suffered instant obsolescence (an American invention), and became an anachronism, a displaced person, a relic of a remote rural village culture.

More than for men, the displacement from one culture to another has represented a real crisis of identity for the Italian woman, and she has left a heritage of conflict to her children. They, unwilling to give themselves completely to the old ways she transmitted, end up, in their assimilationist hurry, with shame and ambivalence in their behavior and values. And this pernicious heritage has been passed on; even third and fourth generations feel the remnants of it.

Gambino understands the dilemma of the modern Italian American woman caught in the clash between tradition and her own self-fulfillment. Though as an Italian American male he betrays nostalgia for *la donna seria* and her service-to-family role, as an intellectual he also fully recognizes the conflicted personality which the Italian American woman harbors, trapped as she is between being "American in form, but Italian in substance."[9]

For the modern woman it means that traditional power (based upon selflessness and sacrifice) has been lost in the name of autonomy and self-awareness. She cannot be co-ruler in a family, perhaps, in the old way, but she can have power of choice in her own life and, as upholder of a democratic family style, benefit herself as well. The Old World family style and mother role that developed in response to *la miseria* are no longer relevant in a democratic society nor tolerated in affluence.

There are feminists of Italian American background who look for and find strengths in the old traditional peasant values, in the model of *serietà* which Gambino described. In Gambino's concept of womanliness, the values extolled—assertiveness, commitment to work, activism, and practicality— are indistinguishable from the expectations for all *male* Americans. Utilizing the Old World values of the ideal of Italian womanliness in the service of today's quest for self-enhancement, the evolving Italian American woman must redistribute the focus of those qualities from the exclusive service of others—the family—and onto herself as well. That is her dilemma. The pull toward family is powerful, ineluctable. How to arrive at balance is the theme of much that is being written by Italian American women, and something that Louise DeSalvo has explored with humor and feeling in her essay on the *puttana* as scholar in this collection.

9. Richard Gambino, *Blood of My Blood: The Dilemma of the Italian Americans*, (Garden City, N.Y.: Anchor Press/Doubleday, 1975), p. 175.

To achieve that balance would be a feat of what the sociologists call "creative ethnicity," that is, using one's ethnic heritage as the starting point upon which to build one's own identity in a selective and critical way, as opposed to total and unquestioning acceptance of tradition. There is anxiety in choice. The hardships now are not the primitive ones of survival, but the more complex ones of uncertainty of direction, too much choice, self-expression, autonomy.

Bulletins from the front lines keep being issued. In 1980, the Agnelli Foundation issued a monograph on Italian Americans, deciding it was time for the mother country "to revivify relations with the descendants of emigrants from our shores"; they found it time "that there be a rapprochement between the Italian American world and contemporary public opinion in Italy."[10]

Studying data on Italian American income, education, occupation, and political attitudes, a sanguine conclusion was reached. Italian Americans have achieved success in every field, and that achievement, the report tells us, "is incontrovertible evidence that their families have endowed them with a system of verities and solidarity of inestimable value."

The family is not only alive and well but "it is certainly what makes Italian Americans stand out as most different from other Americans" and "it is to the family and its structures that we must turn for the reason for survival of a specific Italian American identity."[11]

An even more recent release from the Sons of Italy was in the form of "Guidelines for the Treatment of Italian Americans in American History Texts," prepared to help textbook editors revise stereotypical treatment and correct omissions. It is a worthy idea, for American publishers (and not just of textbooks) need all the help they can get in revising their prejudicial attitudes toward ethnic groups.

Yet, I could not help but wonder if the Sons of Italy weren't foisting *their* own stereotypes in place of others. On their *List of Positive Italian American Values to Emphasize*, first place went to that timeworn staple of the old immigrant mentality, "The family is the most important institution." That was followed by four other references to family in a total of sixteen items, and the reiteration of "the mother as the central figure in the family providing warmth, love, devotion."

The listed values do not reflect what is really happening in society and among Italian Americans. They do not reflect the interest of Italian American women in furthering their education and choosing careers over early marriage. Nor does the list consider a startling result of intermarriage: 80

10. *The Italian Americans* (Torino: Fondazione Giovanni Agnelli, c.1980), p. 1.
11. Ibid., p. 45.

percent of Italian Americans born after 1960 are Italian and "something else."[12] Family strength was built on the base of the shared cultural values of an endogamous group. How can you report Italian American family cohesion (wherein repose the received values of the old cultural tradition) when that repository is no longer all Italian and, in truth, even when ethnically intact, cannot ever again be what it historically was because the times and needs have changed?

That strong hallmark of the Italian American family, keeping up ties and contacts between generations, is changing because the young people are leaving home to go away to college, are replacing exclusive family relationships with ones among their peers, and are often getting jobs away from home; in step with their American life-style, they are moving out of the old neighborhoods and, thanks to their new managerial positions, as they follow the pattern of Italian American achievement, they are often subjected to the mobility and rootlessness of corporate American life. Although the Sons of Italy list respect for elders and for law and order among the positive values, young people are less inclined to accept parental authority and guidance over their own wants and needs.

But, most of all, family life, which the Sons of Italy and the Agnelli report see as a rock of solidity in a sea of undermining change, will no longer be able to count on the self-sacrifice of women to support it unilaterally. And then what will happen to that statistic which is cited so proudly, that an overwhelming proportion of aged Italian Americans live with relatives as compared to other ethnic groups? Can it be that this was indicative more of dependence and unpreparedness to act on one's own than of family cohesion? A Pittsburgh study of women spanning three generations among Jews, Italians, and Slovaks showed Italian women far less independent than the other groups. Elderly Jewish widowed women, for instance, while maintaining close ties to their children, preferred to live separately and independently and to respect the privacy of their grown children's lives.[13]

The professors and other professional apologists of the Italian family had better listen to the women and to their literature—to the voices of women writers who are telling it as it is. Home life was never as solid and satisfying as the men said it was; it was what it was for historic and social reasons that are now surpassed.

12. Reported by Professor Richard D. Alba in "Children of the Melting Pot: Patterns of Intermarriage Among Italian Americans," a paper presented at the Conference of the American Italian Historical Association, Albany, November 10–13, 1983.

13. Corinne Azen Krause, *Grandmothers, Mothers, and Daughters* (New York: The American Jewish Committee, 1978).

Contrary to folklore, stereotypes, and compelling portraits of the appealing, traditional Italian woman as pillar of her family, Italian American literature abounds with portraits of other women who are harsh, frequently cruel, crushing, unfeeling. They are embittered and malevolent; and, given the strictures of their own lives, there is plenty of reason why.

There is a dark underside to the bright picture of the compact Italian American family life so extolled by sociologists and onlookers: there are men caught in low-paying, demeaning jobs who vent their frustration and rage on wives and children; there are fathers who have deserted families to go west to seek that illusory fortune they left their land for; there is divorce, cruelty, long bitter marriages, and the brutalization of their children and women by unhappy men, acutely drawn, for example, by Dorothy Bryant in *Miss Giardino*. And there is a heritage of the self-hate theme present in Fran Claro's and Karen Malpede's memoirs.

There are examples in life of angry women, embittered women, passive women—women made susceptible, by the low self-esteem their lives afforded them, to exploitive religions. One such example emerges in the unforgettable portrait Barbara Grizzuti Harrison[14] has painted of her mother, a convert to the Jehovah's Witnesses.

> Like most second-generation Southern Italians, my mother grew up insular and clannish; in the teeth of the sorry evidence, she was instructed to believe that only the family could ever shelter, embrace, nourish. The rest of the world was hostile, menacing, exploitive, threatening, incomprehensible, and not deserving of comprehension. *They* were always out to get you. In fact, the family was the smell of incense, beatings, and swollen, angry voices. The Church was no refuge; the Church was her mother's and, she thought, an old ladies' home. It could never be hers. She looked for Family in my father's family—and found jealousies and rivalries, and there too she was an alien. She could not (this is conjecture) love either her family or the world. She chose a religion; she chose "spiritual brothers and sisters"—who told her, as her family had, that the world was *other* and evil, alien, and cruel. She found shelter. She waited for God to smash the wicked world. All her longing was for the future; all her love was for a jealous, devouring God who promised her rest.

Harrison's mother had come from a home where her immigrant father's rage found

14. Barbara Grizzuti Harrison, *Visions of Glory* (New York: Simon and Schuster, 1978), pp. 28–30.

expression in violent fits of anger directed against his five children—not one of whom survived childhood without a nose broken by him. My mother's nose was broken when he slammed an iron into her face in a senseless, voiceless seizure of unprovoked rage. Her mother never protected her.

My mother left this house, over which the threat of violence always hung (a house that smelled richly—and claustrophobically—of fermenting wine and incense and all the stale, dark-brown smells of poverty), when she was 19, to marry my father. Whether she loved my father I do not know.

Some mothers, as in Jennifer Lagier's poem, "second class citizen," or in Rosemarie Caruso's plays, are portrayed with a humor that nonetheless still betrays layers of apprehension or bleak disappointment in their lives, an edge of rancor toward their lot. Or there is the unsentimentalized portrait of Gigi Marino's "Angelina" who, pregnant again, throws herself down a flight of steps.

But family in all its facets—as benevolent warmth and support in Mary K. Mazotti's charming story "La Ciramella"; as compulsive nostalgia and life ritual for Diane di Prima, who writes about shopping for eels for an Italian Christmas Eve in *Dinners and Nightmares;* or as the pleasant surprise expressed in Maryfrances Cusumano Wagner's poem "Preparations for an Italian Wedding" when she finds, "You will be glad you followed tradition;/ you will at last understand your mother"—is what grips the imaginative powers of Italian American writers and, most forcibly, women because their roles were so enmeshed in that powerful mark of their culture.

Family is so central to the core of belief and identity of an Italian American woman that it becomes an irreducible, illogical yearning. In her essay "*Godfather II*" in this collection, Barbara Grizzuti Harrison expresses a longing for the Italian family that goes beyond reality, and she knows it; her critical faculty is right: there never was that perfect state of warmth, security, emotional support. There was an uneasy balance of trade-offs in which "family" cost "freedom." Yet, emotionally, she is, like a moth, drawn to that tempting flame of warmth that the trope of family *seems* to mean.

For Italian American authors, betrayal was present on both sides—the artist felt guilt in longing for distance from family, but also anger and resentment for the lack of understanding family gave her or him. If one were different, there was *no* supportiveness or family loyalty after all, only emotional blackmail. (Here, in a mild form that sounds like a line from one of her own plays, is what Rosemarie Caruso reported as her mother's advice: "Roe—don't write about it. It's going to start trouble, then I can't go there next Christmas.")

Life, then, was conflict or keeping quiet.

Put Italian American women in the context of their origin, their time and place, and the collective psyche which formed and held them, and it becomes comprehensible why they have not been writers. Their experience of literature and language was too new, the old family culture too strong.

Seeds of Doubt: The Internal Blocks

In America, the Italian newcomer faced the cultural imperative of the dominant society: to "pass" you had to lose your distinguishing identity and somehow become a stranger in your own life.

This part of Maria Mazziotti Gillan's poem "Public School No. 18: Paterson, New Jersey" perfectly catches the story:

> Miss Wilson's eyes, opaque
> as blue glass, fix on me:
> "We must speak English.
> We're in America now."
> I want to say, "I am American,"
> but the evidence is stacked against me.

In his novel *Streets of Gold*, author Evan Hunter (who, born Lombino, made the nomenclatural leap into America's mainstream) explored the transmutation of Ignazio di Palermo into Dwight Jamison and his attempt, in this Anglicized persona, to attach himself to the American dream. The realization of the futility of it all comes because, in his self-made Waspness, Dwight Jamison found he did not exist, he was a figment of the American imagination.

It was the myth that failed. The myth that told us we could and should be equally American in the Anglo mold, but forgot to mention that to force people to become what they are not produces not equality but enmity—enmity with one's self. Here is Gillan from her poem:

> Without words, they tell me
> to be ashamed.
> I am.
> I deny that booted country
> even from myself,
> want to be still
> and untouchable
> as those women
> who teach me to hate myself.

By an early age I, too, had a good start on what is a major motif in Italian American writing—the sense of being out of line with one's surroundings, not of one's family and not of the world beyond the family: an outsider. But what really crystallized the inclination I had toward writing was a slim little book of poems called *Seeds of Doubt*. My mother brought it home—a bit put out because she had had to subscribe two dollars toward its publication and how could she refuse since Mrs. Aquilino, the poet's mother, was her friend? It was like giving to the Church, something you had to do though you might not like it.

To me, Alma Aquilino's book of poetry was an extraordinary revelation. All I recall of that long-lost book were the feelings of melancholy the poems conveyed—a delicious sensation in adolescence. But the title made the impact; it reflected my own uneasiness, my own sense of doubt. And even more powerful was the fact—unheard of!—that a female with an Italian name had written a book. My schooling had provided no texts by authors with Italian names, no expectation that people of my background had a rich literature. We were told, instead, of Italian illiteracy. But never that illiterate people have a culture and social systems. Now there is another view of that subject.[15]

No mention of any Italian achievement in social or humanistic arts was ever provided to dispel the message we were getting of being somehow less than the Tom Sawyers and Becky Thatchers around us. This is, as we know, true for all other ethnic groups as well. Feminist writer Vivian Gornick decried what she says is the squashing of ideals present in earlier generations of Jewish social activists and the overlaying of revolutionary goals with the whitewash of Protestant ethics in order to fabricate stereotypes of middle-class virtues. This is possible, Gornick pointed out, because of the overwhelmingly prevalent Wasp models in our schools and colleges.[16]

While schools were busy sublimating minds with the need to Anglicize, we grew up with the look of America—the correct America was imprinted on our minds from Nancy Drew books and Andy Hardy movies. Italian American homes, gardens, names, churches were embarrassing—too ornate, too foreign. It was the pristine, classic simplicity of the white New England church steeple on the village green to which we conformed our

15. "Neither wealth nor literacy guarantees superior sensibility; either can engender a warped set of values, fashionable vulgarity, and callousness toward the disadvantaged. People who are highly literate, like people who are very rich, are tempted to regard literacy or money as the measure of worth." In *Literacy as a Human Problem*, ed. James C. Raymond (University: University of Alabama Press, 1983), p. 12.

16. Vivian Gornick in a broadcast on WBAI in New York, March 6, 1982.

taste, not to the rococo excesses of Catholic sanctuaries—much less the gaudy, overwrought, paganized pageants of saints with which Italian Americans annually annoyed their Irish clergy in some parishes. As Elaine Romaine's poem declares, "You were always Irish, God, in a church where I confessed to being Italian."

For the Catholicism the immigrants found here was a stern, puritanical, inhospitable version of what they had known as their religion. In America everything was tinged by the Protestant ethic: worth was measured by material achievement, visible riches, and success, all of which is quite at odds with the Catholic harmony of everyone having worth in the sight of God and there being a divine plan in everything with hope eternal for salvation. The Protestant ethic stresses competitiveness, anxiety, struggle to succeed, to move up fast and visibly. The Catholic emphasis is on passive acceptance, resignation, and having an internal sense of worth and dignity without the external show of Calvinistic grace which is prosperity. It is the difference between a tolerant, humanistic orientation and the grim judgmental one of evaluation.

"What first struck immigrant consciousness," observed Michael Novak, "was the solitariness of Protestant consciousness. In order to become American, one had to learn to be alone. One had to *value* being alone."[17] Italians had to go against the grain of their very being and most deeply held convictions about life in order to be what America said they should be.

Growing up at odds with ourselves, we found shame even in the taste and smells of our foods—my eldest daughter remembers a school outing at which, while she was relishing her sardines on crusty hunks of Italian bread, the teacher observed, "You certainly are your father's daughter!" singling her out from the eaters of Wonder Bread and peanut butter.

We wanted the look of tweed and tartan and not the embroideries of our grandmothers' Italian bed linens; we wanted a Cape Cod cottage for our dream house, not some stuccoed *villino* with arches and tomatoes in the backyard. Imagine Italians in a Currier & Ives world: sleighing up for Christmas to a cold and isolated farm on a forest's edge instead of strolling through a village where houses are all snuggled one against the other, to mingle in a piazza thick with people and human exchange. It's a different image of the world. The American penchant for being off alone in nature, for being Thoreau, is not part of the Italian humanist mind; it is the American mind. Henry Steele Commager's *The American Mind* views that mind as one in which, it has been pointed out, not a Jew, nor a Black, nor

17. Michael Novak, "'The Nordic Jungle," in *Divided Society*, ed. Colin Greer (New York: Basic Books, 1974), p. 128.

a Catholic are among the major figures presented by him, nor, therefore, their particular sensibilities and visions of what this country means.[18]

Sister Blandina Segale foresaw in her journal that Establishment history, as written by "Mr. Bancroft," would not give the whole picture as to what had been accomplished in American life by minorities. Commenting on how the freedom of conscience edicts enacted by Catholic Lord Baltimore in Maryland were frequently overlooked, she charges, "Yet look at the stream of articles constantly given to the public about Plymouth Rock and the Pilgrim Fathers!" Just as those who decry the Mafia as an Italian import forget that the Ku Klux Klan is an Anglo-American invention.

In its presumption of rightness (which is the other side of provincialism) the Angloconformist society determined that every group but the Anglo-American one was "ethnic." Thus, the disingenuousness, for instance, of John Cheever, who referred to his mother as "an Englishwoman" but denied that his writing, though concentrated on a small world of Episcopalian suburbanites of British descent, was ethnic. "British-Americans simply take it for granted that the customs, language, and school curricula of this country are mainly British-American; this, to them, isn't 'ethnic,' it's natural."[19] This is in part the exigency of having to give a common frame of reference and unity to the many disparate peoples who make up this country. But its elitist and value judgment overtones were something more—a slur against other ways and cultures that was unnecessarily damaging to the peoples who felt its sting.

Fran Claro writes of her mother, who escaped the embarrassment of her Italian immigrant world by immersing herself in books like *Rebecca of Sunnybrook Farm:* "Her heroines were fair-skinned, blond-haired, blue-eyed. She could not identify with them, but their world intrigued her."[20] We all have similar stories of displacement and estrangement—varying in degree by generational differences, but all reinforced by our reading. Our self-image was never in perfect focus, for we could never find who we were—only who the Angloconformist world thought we should be.

It is a delicate question of balance. We internalized English literary culture and were enriched by it, but were denied knowing that our own tradition had, in fact, its own riches and glories. This was the period of American history known as Isolationism and it has passed. We are no longer that narrow. But while I grew up there was only one standard of worth, and

18. Peter Schrag, *Decline of the Wasp* (New York: Simon and Schuster, 1971), p. 20.

19.   Michael Novak, *The Rise of the Unmeltable Ethnics* (New York: Macmillan, 1973). p. xvii.

20. Fran Claro, "South Brooklyn, 1947," *UNICO*, vol. 1, no. 1 (1976).

to be measured against it and found different was a source of pain and guilt. Different origins presume differences in temperament and attitudes; it was psychologically impossible for Italian Americans of earlier generations to fit themselves into the Procrustean bed of Angloconformity without maiming a part of themselves.

"As I grow older, I think more and more about my cultural background which I unfortunately denied for many years," playwright Michele Linfante wrote me; she, too, had experienced the seeds of doubt as to who she was supposed to be.

Aside from its existentialist allusion, the importance to me of the book *Seeds of Doubt* was more in its physicality than in a literary worth which I could not judge. (As Virginia Woolf said, in a similar context, "Whether that is literature or not literature I do not presume to say, but that it explains much and reveals much is certain.")[21] *Seeds of Doubt* explained much and revealed much to me—I was no longer alone.

I had thought I was queer not so much because I wanted to be a writer instead of just marrying, as was my *destino*, but because I was Italian American and aspired to be a writer. I presumed I would have to change my name. Just as singers with Anglo-Saxon names used to italianize them to enter the world of opera, it seemed in the world of letters one should have an English name. But I kept both my Italian name and my Italian nose and I will never know if I might have had a more brilliant career otherwise. What I do know is that the Italian patronym is rare among American women writers.

Names are still powerful signalers. "I am really Sandra Mortola Gilbert," Sandra M. Gilbert wrote me, "and my mother's name was Caruso, so I always feel oddly falsified with this Waspish-sounding American name, which I adopted as a 20-year-old bride who had never considered the implications of her actions!"

In fact, as I began to meet some of the authors in this volume, I found we had identical reactions: each had thought herself unique as a writer of Italian American background. And each thought herself alone. None knew of the others. That, unfortunately, seems to distinguish us from any other group of women writers. Wasps and Jews and Blacks are in the elite writers' groups; many minority women have their own particularized networks. In Toni Cade Bambara's words, "What determines the shape and content of my work is the community of writers . . . writers have gotten their wagons in a circle, which gives us each something to lean against, push off against."[22] Italian American women who write have no supportive circle.

21. Virginia Woolf, Preface to *Life as We Have Known It: Memoirs of the Working Women's Guild*, ed. Margaret L. Davies (New York: Norton, 1975), p. xxxix.

22. Claudia Tate, ed., *Black Women Writers at Work* (New York: Continuum, 1983), p. 29.

From the distance of decades, when I think of *Seeds of Doubt*, I wonder about it in a new way: was Alma Aquilino's doubt about whether she could carry on her role as an Italian American woman as well as her aspiration as a poet? Did she doubt that she would be allowed to fulfill herself? Did she write another book, or is the rest silence?

"What is the way out of this dilemma?" asks Sandra M. Gilbert in her fine essay on Sylvia Plath, as she considers the paradox of Plath's (or any other creative woman's) life: that even as she longs for the freedom of flight, she fears the risks of freedom. Knowingly or unknowingly, Gilbert states the terms of that double bind in language of the Italian American sensibility: "How does a woman reconcile the exigencies of the species—her desire for stasis, her sense of her ancestry, her devotion to the house in which she has lived—with the urgencies of her own self? I don't know the answer."[23] Nor do I; but the exploration of it is, indeed, the stuff of literature, as, for Italian American women, will be the probing of those seeds of doubt that have kept our numbers few.

Dr. Mary Lanna Gottesfeld, a psychoanalyst, is a third-generation Italian American who, in her practice, has observed that even when an aura of empathy has been achieved through the similarity of an Italian American patient's background to her own, there is an entrenched need to hold back family "secrets." Gottesfeld has noted how a powerful family closeness makes preservation of the family network more important than the fate or goal of the individual. She writes, "Unlike the Jewish experience, which is extensively articulated in an authentic way in literature (Roth, Bellow, Malamud, Mailer, etc.), the Italian experience has not been similarly developed. I believe this fact to be part of the defense to maintain what is 'ours.' "[24]

I believe, also, that there is an internal dialectic, a clash of opposites, going on in Italian Americans which is not only a personal condition but one that is reinforced from the outside by external factors of subtle discrimination and rejection.

Emerging from the powerful fortress called Family, Italian Americans are understandably reluctant to share with outsiders, to make their lives accessible and knowable; there is a strong cultural bias against looking too closely at "secrets." It is not difficult to find the parallel with Italian Ameri-

23. Sandra M. Gilbert, "A Fine, White Flying Myth," in *Shakespeare's Sisters*, ed. Sandra M. Gilbert and Susan Gubar (Bloomington: Indiana University Press, 1979), p. 260.

24. Mary L. Gottesfeld, "Countertransference and Ethnic Similarity," in *Transcultural Health Care*, ed. George Anderson and Martha Primeaux (Menlo Park, Calif.: Addison-Wesley, 1981).

can women writers: the necessary distancing from family that writing demands sets up intolerable conflicts within women who have been reared in the cultural tradition of *omertà*—the conspiracy of silence which sees nothing, hears nothing, tells nothing, and thus betrays nothing. Writing is an act of assertiveness and Italian American women, with few exceptions, have not been reared for public assertion.

Italian American women writers are, in fact, women of the shadows, standing not only on the edges of light cast by the luminaries—Oates! Ozick! Jong! Welty! O'Connor! Morrison! Didion! Walker!—but also in the inherited one of their traditional womanly reserve. Italian American women tend to keep out of public view. They have not liked to put themselves forward. They come from a background of negative injunctions: don't step out of line and be noticed, don't be the envy of others, don't attract the jealous fates who will punish success. Italian American women are not brought up with the confidence that makes Jewish women such splendid social activists, such demanding wives, and such able promoters of themselves; nor have they had the long experience of self-reliance and expressivity in the English language (oral as well as written) that Black women have had. They are not incited and brought together by ancient wrongs as are the Native Americans and Chicanos.

They are, instead, susceptible to the idea that excelling, drawing attention to oneself, is not womanly, not good. This notion is prevalent in a society in which belief in *malocchio*—the evil eye—is present on all levels. One mustn't disconnect from one's immediate group, as a writer must in order to get perspective and unique vision: and, one mustn't try to see too much—either into oneself or into others; all such would bring upon oneself the curse of separation.

It is not unlikely that the subtleties of these attitudes have helped reinforce the reticence of Italian and Italian American women and it is not improbable that residues still remain of the very prevalent *malocchio* fear. The taboo is against being seen as excelling in anything, or in that close seeing which is self-knowledge; for the mysteries must be kept. Those who see too far—Tiresias, Milton, Galileo—go blind.

Lawrence DiStasi, who has written about *malocchio*, says the concept of it is deep in the bone: "That beauty and excellence attract the eye, and that the admiring eye thus attracted, no matter how benign it may appear, is *mal*, is evil, and capable of causing harm."[25]

Italian American women have had a hard time overcoming inner blocks to creative expression because they were not empowered, as female chil-

25. For fuller discussion, see Lawrence DiStasi's *Mal Occhio* (San Francisco: North Point Press, 1981).

dren, to be independent. Of course, even as I say this, I know that, as in all things Italian American, there are exceptions: journalist Jean Grillo wrote[26] of a childhood with her five sisters which was as free as a boy's: they grew up wearing jeans, working with their father, handling money, developing a sense of responsibility, and knowing they were appreciated for themselves. She also recognizes that her parents were exceptional—her father, from Spoleto, was not an immigrant but an émigré, i.e., a person of some standing in his home country who had to leave, not from *miseria*, but for political reasons, and her mother was a union organizer. They prized education for its own sake, insisted on their daughters' having independence and drive, "pumped them full of the American dream." Provenance, political activism, class, and education are the variables that make the exceptions that prove the general rule.

More typical are women who have had to disengage themselves from internalized messages of unworthiness. Kathy Freeperson, née Telesco, changed her name to indicate her changed perception of herself after leaving her father's tyrannical household. "Shut up—you're not a boy" was what she and her sisters heard growing up female. Many Italian American women have heard the same message: "What right have you got to think?" or, "Girls can't have opinions."

Other Italian American writers have undergone a de-ethnicizing influence in higher education and have rejected their own experience (too often portrayed in film and TV as backward and ignorant) in pursuit of the "universal" values which are, transparently, Anglo-American ones. It is absurd to think that one can universalize only from Anglo-American models and not Italian American, Black American, or whatever American. Jewish writing in America has disproved this.

Professor Pellegrino D'Acierno feels that in their zeal to take on a monolithic American identity, Italian Americans have let the prevailing culture deform their own life experiences. "Italian Americans," he said, "have been colonized by the American dream," and have failed to make the most of their identity crisis and to use the experience as the crucible for artistic production. "The maintenance of two identities, two cultures, two languages," he said, "should make us dissentious within ourselves, should make us into artists."[27] I would add that such duality is also advantageous—to draw upon two identities, cultures, and languages is to draw riches as well as dissentiousness once it is recognized in a positive way and so used.

26. "Arrivederci Kitchens," *I/AM*, November 1976.
27. From the transcript of the Conference on Contemporary Fiction Writing in Italy and America, held at Columbia University, October 14, 1981.

What prevents this positive use is defensiveness which, Richard Gambino explained, "prevents one from achieving a creative and productive vision of oneself and one's relationship to others. It imposes a psychological burden of intolerable weight." An exacerbated sense of chauvinism and defensiveness is what prompts those who cry out, "We are being defamed!" when mention is made of the Mafia. Giuseppe Prezzolini, who had to sit through years of celebratory Columbus Day dinners, said they revealed the emotional effusions of a badly treated minority trying to bolster a sense of pride through the recitation of names—from Dante to Garibaldi—that the boosters seldom, if ever, know anything about.

It results in what I think of as the Pinocchio personality—so much emphasis and energy are given to being transformed into conventionalized "good guys" that life is distorted and the real heroicness of the Italian American experience is whitewashed into some bland picture of Pinocchio in reverse: real live people who have become dummies of virtuous platitudes. Pinocchio is a paradox: he is "alive" and daring and full of goals and the desire for change until he gains conventional life. It is as a good boy that he becomes a real puppet of conventionality, a wooden stereotype. Defensive people often do this.

Like Mrs. Grundy, their spiritual *comare*, psychologically unresolved Italian Americans unfortunately reinforce in the American mind the image of an unsophisticated, priggish, insecure people. It recalls the defensiveness of the Irish when Joyce wrote of them in *Dubliners* and they ostracized him for it. He held the mirror up to them not to defame them, but for them to know themselves, to become free of the disabling phobias of the past.

Whereas the desire to read about the Jewish experience has been an element of cohesiveness among Jews, the Italians have heretofore not wanted to read about themselves. To write for public knowledge the intimate facts of family life—can one imagine an Italian Portnoy or Isadora Wing?—is the ultimate betrayal, one that is taken at the risk of exclusion from the family.

The very solidity of the Italian American family, which is its success, makes it hard to break away from; and to be a writer means breaking away and taking distance from where one came in order to see it better, more truly. This puts the Italian American woman writer in a precarious position: that is, do you keep close to family, enjoying its emotional warmth and protectiveness, and lose your individualism; or do you opt for personal independence? Do you go against the grain of your culture to embrace the American concept of rugged individualism? Do you choose loneliness over denial of self for the family good?

This is an issue of separating, present in all human beings; the process of individuation by which one becomes him- or herself. The working out of independence/dependence factors is critical in the development of both men and women and for people of all backgrounds. But some cultures, in effect, demand too enormous a ransom to release the individual from benevolent captivity.

If this is a dilemma for all Italian Americans, it is more so for the writer, and utmost for the writer who is a woman. For it is the woman who, at the core of the family, is the transmitter of its traditions and upholder of its values. Can *she* defect from the one institution Italians believe in, the family? Can she at least redefine the ancient laws for her advantage?

This is the paradox: Italian American women are the core of their families and they are the ones who have most subordinated themselves to the well-being of the total entity. Family above self. But, being at the heart of things, it is they who, breaking the silence imposed on them by family loyalty, are best suited to make literary use of the material implicit in family struggles. What provides the thematic material is, ironically, the greatest obstacle to the writing. For that old sanction of *omertà* both defies creativity and instigates it.

Anaïs Nin, whose diaries have been published in several volumes, put it this way: writers make their lives public so that others are enabled to articulate their own. It is interesting that Italian American women are not diarists, nor journal keepers. They are not used to intense self-inspection, only to the condoned relief of the confessional, in which a male figure exonerates and blesses them.

But now the phenomenon of rising expectations has reached everyone. Italian American women have a generation or more of higher education; family economic stability has been reached; the woman's movement has been an enabling force toward assertiveness, self-reliance, and opting for independence.

Self-birthing is well known to women of ethnic minorities who, lacking models, have created their own. Joy Harjo, a Native American poet, defines it: "As I write I create myself again and again . . . We have learned to only touch so much. That is why I write. I want to touch more . . . it frees me to believe in myself . . . to have voice, because I have to; it is my survival."[28]

Tina DeRosa, in a passionate statement of identity and duality, takes on the dichotomy which many educated young women of her background are experiencing in the conflict between their past and the Italian family of origin, and their future as educated American women: "I know now that where I belong is with myself, knowing, that I don't really belong any-where. That is the inheritance . . . You say partially goodbye to one world,

28. Joy Harjo, "Bio-Poetics Sketch," *Greenfield Review* 9, nos. 3 and 4 (1981): 8–9.

partially hello to another, some of the time you are silent . . . then you
write about it . . . Don't let anyone tell you who you are. You will know."[29]

And Alice Walker, a triumphant and gifted Black writer, affirms this deep
need for the true image of self, not the surrounding society's concept of
what one should be, in an essay in which she tells of Toni Morrison's
response to the question of why she writes the kinds of books she does:
because, she said, they are the kind of books I want to read.[30]

Thus, says Walker, expanding on Morrison, "in my own work I write not
only what I want to read—understanding fully and indelibly that if I don't
do it no one else is so vitally interested, or capable of doing it to my
satisfaction—I write all the things I should have read."[31]

Italian American women have long been denied the possibility of finding
themselves in literature. Where are our models, the voices that speak for
and of us? How can we affirm an identity without becoming familiar with
the models by which to perceive ourselves? We are what we read, but, in
the case of Italian American women writers, we can seldom read who we
are.

Therefore, Tillie Olsen in her splendid book *Silences* says to all the silent
women: create yourselves. There is much that is unwritten that needs to be
written. Bring into literature what is not there now.

It is unfortunate that Grazia Deledda is so little known here, for she is
someone Italian American women might well emulate. Strong, relevant, a
highly recognizable model embodying Italian tradition, Deledda is also of
international significance. She is a magnificent figure of the self-motivated,
achieving woman who accomplishes her life's mission. Born in the most
backward and isolated part of Sardinia in 1875, she received only three
years of schooling, but continued to teach herself and set herself the task of
making her country live in literature. She not only produced a steady
stream of literary work (thirty-three novels, eighteen collections of stories,
and other writings), in the face of great odds, but was honored with a Nobel
Prize for Literature in 1926 for her accomplishment.

Not to be underestimated is the equal achievement of Deledda's having
combined, in her life, family and art. Grazia Deledda was not in the Anglo-
American style of the childless great women writers like Jane Austen,
George Eliot, Emily Dickinson, Willa Cather, Edith Wharton, Virginia

29. Tina DeRosa, "An Italian American Woman Speaks Out," *Attenzione*, May
1980, p. 38–39.
30. Alice Walker, "Saving the Life That Is Your Own," in *The Third Woman*, ed.
Dexter Fisher (Boston: Houghton Mifflin, 1980), p. 154.
31. Ibid., p. 157.

Woolf; she had the backing of her Northern Italian husband for her writing career. He and their sons, and family life as a whole, were the necessary sustenance to her art. She needed both.

The name and story of Grazia Deledda were not in schoolbooks as I was growing up, but that is hardly surprising; what *is*, is that even with the new surge of interest in women writers and the resurrecting of old and forgotten authors, Deledda is all but a forgotten woman. Ellen Moers's *Literary Women*,[32] for instance, is a thick compendium of the great women writers, concentrating mainly on some sixty English, American, and French women of literature, with textual and bibliographic references to worldwide women authors. Grazia Deledda is omitted; the only Italian authors mentioned are in the back-of-the-book appendix: a line for Renaissance poet Vittoria Colonna, two for contemporary novelist Natalia Ginzburg.

It amazes me, too, that the first book-length account of Deledda's life written in English, a fine study by Carolyn Balducci called *A Self-Made Woman*,[33] should carry on the book jacket the recommendation "for ages 12–up." By sidetracking this important work into the graveyard of Young Adult Books, the publisher has, in effect, denied it the general distribution and recognition it deserves, making it more than likely that it has been, and will be, overlooked.

Balducci writes of a recording that Grazia Deledda made shortly before her death from cancer in 1936 in which she said, "I have had all the things which a woman could ask of her destiny." Deledda did not, in fact, ask anything; she herself fashioned her own destiny to become what family and evidence had told her was impossible: a great writer. And she did it on her terms. Unlike Christina Rossetti, who wrote from an internal agony of renunciation and made her art the bitter fruit of a masochistic abnegation, Deledda did not deny herself. She said she believed in only two things, the family and art for its own sake; these were the only beautiful and true things in life.

That this striking figure should be so little known, so missing from the consciousness of Italian American women writers who need precisely and desperately the kind of validation she gives, is just another of the instances of silence in which we have seemed to struggle alone without models, without inspiration.

Another not-much-heard-of Italian author is Sibilla Aleramo (1876–1960), who wrote *Una Donna* at the beginning of this century, anticipating feminism and women's liberation by many decades. It was in this autobiographical novel that the word "feminism" was used for the first time, and

32. Ellen Moers, *Literary Women* (New York: Doubleday, 1976).
33. Carolyn Balducci, *A Self-Made Woman* (Boston: Houghton Mifflin, 1975).

the author's personal suffering was seen as part of a total condition of women. *Una Donna,* widely known in Europe, has been translated into English[34] and is a gripping account of the psychological anguish of a creative woman's marriage to a small-minded and stultifying oppressor, and her liberation at great personal expense. It is a story of courage in a time and place that made her action and subsequent book utterly remarkable. But Aleramo, too, is missing from our reservoir of models.

The silences Tillie Olsen speaks of come not only from male critics who overlook women authors, but sometimes from feminist critics, editors, publishers who engage in a great deal of "vertical" expansion with still more diaries and autobiographies of unknown "American housewives and writers," predominantly of Anglo-Saxon origin, and always documenting the same experiences, but make little attempt to go horizontally into truly new areas to find other voices and to reach into experience that is not the Anglo-American one, not the established one.

In the wake of the feminist movement, the silenced women writers of the past were exhumed, explained, exhibited as lost treasures. They were reprinted, for example, by The Feminist Press, and compiled in the volumes of *Notable American Women* and other sets. Examples of Anglo-American women predominated, as is natural, but why are Sister Blandina Segale or Renata Brunorini, an actress and playwright of the beginning of this century,[35] or novelist Mari Tomasi, for example, not represented when many more marginal women of Anglo-American background are?

And in Annis Pratt's introduction to her *Archetypal Patterns in Women's Fiction,* she acknowledges having done, for that study, "close readings of more than three hundred women's novels."[36] None of these novels—not one—is by an Italian American woman. Writing on the novel of development, Pratt says that in women's fiction it is more often the story of women "growing down" rather than "growing up." Yet Italian American women are writing of rising expectations and the quest for self-realization. One of these is Dorothy Bryant, whose novel, *Ella Price's Journal,* is a classic example of the novel of growth—in this case, not of a young male, but of a middle-aged wife and mother.

Bryant's married name, under which she writes, cloaks her Italian American background; and her character—Ella Price—is an Anglo-Saxon Everywoman; but just as the outsider experience is heightened when told

34. Sibilla Aleramo, *A Woman,* trans. Rosalind Delemar (Berkeley: University of California Press, 1980).

35. I am indebted to Dr. Emelise Aleandri for bringing Renata Brunorini to my attention.

36. Annis Pratt, *Archetypal Patterns in Women's Fiction* (Bloomington: Indiana University Press, 1982), p. 5.

from the point of view of the double outsider (the Black, or the Jew), so, too, the woman's experience of being stifled in a male world could have been made even more compelling, I feel, if Bryant had used her own Italian American background from which to create the story of a woman's growth toward autonomy. Because of her tradition, the Italian American woman is more conflicted in moving out of marriage toward autonomy than the more assertive Anglo-Saxon or Jewish woman. I wonder if Bryant felt her theme would be taken as less universal if she had written from the Italian American viewpoint. That is a restriction that is subtly felt, perhaps subconsciously heeded.

Diana Cavallo's sensitive and introspective novel, *A Bridge of Leaves*, is written in the first person also, but as the reflections of a young man whose thoughts and memories record his inner journey from an early self-contained world to full immersion in the world of others that brings him to the crisis and resolution of his maturity. It is a true *Bildungsroman*. And yet, I wonder, why was the novel not told in the female voice?

Non-Wasp writers have come to the fore brilliantly—Jewish women writers, Blacks, Native Americans, Chicanas—all have been collected, given critical attention, and, thereby, given presence. The Italian American woman writer belongs nowhere—not minority, not mainstream as Jewish and Black writers now are, she remains silent as a group, without champions or advocates. Why is the Italian American woman's story less worth telling than any other?

The Study of Women[37] contains a section called "Breaking the Silence of Women," but that silence is made relevant only to Anglo-American women. The Italian American woman writer, by default, is stranded in a no-woman's-land where there is small choice: either follow the omnipresent models that do not speak to her own particular experience, or write of her experience and know that it will be treated as of no importance, too "different" for critical attention. Alice Walker asked the right question: why should anyone require more of a reason for the existence of *Sula* (or *Rosa*) than for *Jane Eyre*?

A revolutionary concept could be based on the fact that Italian American women, by preference or not, have traditionally worked at home—taking in lodgers, making artificial flowers, doing piecework and embroidery, cooking for others, and even, like the heroine of Antonia Pola's novel *Who Can Buy the Stars?*, making bootleg whiskey. Why not, then, work at home as writers? This would be revolutionary in admitting intellectual and artistic endeavors as "work," especially since they seldom produce immediate income. But the *miseria* mentality would finally have been overcome.

---

37. Eloise C. Snyder, ed., *The Study of Women* (New York: Harper & Row, 1979).

Whereas English and French women writers have always been strong, the tradition of women writers in Italy, noted by critic Sergio Pacifici, is relatively recent (notwithstanding those Renaissance exemplars who are often cited to prove that Italian women have long had voice and stature as authors but prove only that women writers in Italy were an isolated class phenomenon, not a national trend). The emergence of nationally known women authors coincided in the late nineteenth century with the unification of Italy as a nation, and the limited social emancipation of women. The liberated postwar Italy of the late 1940s, and the later feminist movement, saw an increase of notable women writers and, says Pacifici, "Their increasing popularity with the public and the critics represents a significant cultural phenomenon that may well herald a new era." Previously, relatively few women attained literary distinction and this, Pacifici asserts, was not surprising in a country where the social order was shaped so exclusively by men. The lack of critical attention he ascribes "less to an objective question of artistic merit than to critical negligence or a pronounced prejudice against female talent."[38] This is true no longer in Italy, where some very notable women have attained critical acclaim, but it is notoriously true of Italian American literary men, who not only do not accord any attention to women of their background who are writers, but are not even familiar with the names of these women.

It is a special problem: Italian American women have not had the critics or literary historians who would attempt to probe their background and unlock the reasons for silence. The women in English and American literary tradition who have been acclaimed were both well educated (some, like Margaret Fuller and Elizabeth Barrett Browning, very precociously), and passionate readers—e.g., George Eliot, Emily Dickinson, Virginia Woolf. They also had self-centered lives—with few exceptions they were not in the position as wives and mothers which Dickinson termed the "soft Eclipse," i.e., the stifling of creativity by marriage.

It is interesting how many English or American women turned from the Anglo tradition and toward the *idea* of Italy as a freeing of their human qualities and an enriching of life. The Brownings went off to live in Florence; Margaret Fuller, in her thirty-seventh year, arrived in Italy as the leading American woman writer and intellectual of her times and found love and motherhood there, writing later, "Italy has been glorious to me." And Emily Dickinson, from Amherst, thought of Italy as the loosening of trammels, some absolute freeing of the spirit:

38. Sergio Pacifici, *A Guide to Contemporary Italian Literature* (New York: Meridian Books, 1962), pp. 133–34.

Our lives are Swiss—
So still—so Cool—
Till some odd afternoon
The Alps neglect their Curtains
And we look farther on!

Italy stands the other side!
While like a guard between—
The solemn Alps—
The siren Alps
Forever intervene!

Jean Feraca is one of a growing number of Italian American women who have lived in Italy and brought the unique vision of the American Italian to bear on the ancestral land. Her poetry collection *South from Rome: Il Mezzogiorno* is a strong evocation of an unromanticized, deeply felt archetypal Italy as veritable motherland, not an outsiders' pleasure land.

Even the relatively few literate and educated Italian women who emigrated to this country would have brought few models of women writers from their culture and few incentives to imitate them. This lack has presented a significant problem to Italian American women. Yet I think that of all the American models available, it is probably to the Black woman writer that the Italian American woman can feel most affinity. "That's where all the life is," Toni Morrison says of Black writing.

Alice Walker relates that in her story "The Revenge of Hannah Kemhuff," she "gathered up the historical and psychological threads of the life my ancestors lived, and in the writing of it I felt joy and strength and my own continuity." Walker was noting the influence on her of another, hitherto unknown, Black woman author, Zora Neale Hurston. In researching her story, Walker had found only white collectors of Black folklore until, "in a footnote to the white voices of authority" she found the great treasure of Hurston, the Black woman who was to be her model.

For there are differences in approach and outlook between Black and white models, between Anglo-American models and the ones Italian American writers will create. Models are important inasmuch as they connect the present writer to her past, provide a continuity that makes a shared culture a valuable resource; one's own culture is important to the spirit of the writer and to the writing itself.

Part of the intensity between Italian American mothers and daughters is somewhat explained by the lack of cultural models in the literature and their having only immediate female family to base themselves on. But, being unable to follow the ways of their mother's generation, they try, instead, to make over the mother, to improve and uplift her, as in Rosemarie Caruso's *The Suffering Heart Salon*, so that the daughter will have a *worthier* model. It never works. What might work, instead, might be some reworking of the Demeter/Persephone myth with its Sicilian locus as the ultimate in the powerful mother-daughter bond. A critical appraisal of Daniela Gioseffi's powerful woman-focused poetry is entitled "The Return of Demeter" and explores Gioseffi's insistence on the "revival of the archetypal female consciousness as giver of life, nurturer of living things, and maker of life-giving arts,"[39] and her celebration of the Good Mother.

Italian American women need models cut to their own needs, from their own cultural cloth. If not a New England nun like Emily Dickinson, perhaps Saint Catherine of Siena? Caterina Benincasa (1347–1380), a disputatious mystic, a diplomat, the center of a spiritual revival, the patroness of Italy, and a Doctor of the Church, knew how to take on the men. She was also famous for her *Letters*. We might remember that George Eliot's Dorothea Brooke, the heroine of *Middlemarch*, modeled herself after Saint Theresa of Avila.

For there is an Italian American pattern in writing that is quite similar in some points to Black women's writing: the patient strength, tolerance, earthy attitudes, and concern with life-force. Gioia Timpanelli, high priestess of the Italian oral tradition, feels an affinity, thereby, to the oral tradition of the Blacks. I myself can identify more readily with the Black woman writer than with other authors. Both Black and Italian American women write from passion and emotional commitment, not stylistic chic. Both are reaching for life and positive affirmations. A quest for self-actualizing forces is what characterizes the personages of Italian American writing. Those they write about are afflated with hope, with the sense of change, with inspiration. They are not in the Ann Beattie or Joan Didion "deflation" period of emptiness and futility. Theirs are not the wispy, stylish voices of women who have for long periods been attenuating their stories to reflections on minutiae. They write from the passion of the outsider experience; they write, finally, as women who must be heard, whose time has come.

Italian American women who write are in the process of redefining themselves, of redefining family patterns, while all the time they value and hold on to tradition. They are writing to create models that were never there; they are writing to know themselves. They are emerging, not receding, writers. Italian American writers are recombining two cultures into some-

39. Harold Schechter, "The Return of Demeter: The Poetry of Daniela Gioseffi," *Psychocultural Review*, 1976, pp. 452–57.

thing which is of neither one world nor another, but, belonging to both, forms a third realm of consciousness and expression. These new women identify their Italian background and American foreground, thereby doubling their perceptions. There is an Italian American identity because they have an awareness of it and this has brought very definite emotional overtones into their work.

Italian Americans, male and female, in their literature, as in their lives, are obsessed with family. It is their theme much more than such "American" ones as Didion's angst, Beattie's bleakness, personal ambition, spiritual struggle, or the hard working out of the clinical sex relationship.

Families are everywhere in evidence. In Gian-Carlo Menotti's *The Saint of Bleecker Street*, there is a poignant passage in which Michele, the saint's brother, cries out to a family gathering:

> "I know that you all hate me.
> For you I was always the rebel and the
>   cursed one.
> Since I was a child you've always hated me,
> because I never asked for love, only understanding."

For, in fact, families will give love—a love that is wild and strong, and blind—but not understanding to those who are different or defiant of family ways.

Donna DeMatteo, a dramatist of talent unaccountably overlooked by Broadway, has shown in her play *Rocky Road* the way out for her woman protagonist: Lynn, who has suffered a nervous breakdown, chooses to recover on her own, away from her family, and to find strength in herself, by herself. In *The Silver Fox*, DeMatteo depicts a successful self-made businesswoman who takes over the traditional male role as head of family and rules just as tightly until the myth she has created around her son-in-law collapses and her daughter reverses the power position.

The working out of mother-daughter relationships and the working out of understanding between the two generations as roles and expectations change is present in Michele Linfante's humorous and touching one-act play *Pizza* in this collection. Other women writers have dealt with family themes by going back to explore strong ties with grandparents as Diana Cavallo did in *A Bridge of Leaves* and Tina DeRosa in *Paper Fish*.

All is not family; it is a dominant theme, but we have riches well beyond it. We have the same theme of alienation in a hostile and uncomprehending society that has been so well used by Black and Jewish writers. Uprooting, resettling, cultural dichotomy, divided loyalties, self-hate and self-doubt, the problems between generations, the problems between the sexes as men and women search for new roles—the Italian American experience has it all, and it has all to be told.

When I worked in the library of Sarah Lawrence College, I processed books and into my hands would come the splendid, fierce Jewish consciousness of Cynthia Ozick, Grace Paley, or Adrienne Rich; or the rich Black awareness of Maya Angelou, Alice Walker, or Toni Cade Bambara. They are the defenders and champions of what hurts the most—their Jewishness or their Blackness.

Using the springboard of their own tensions, Italian American women can now fashion out of them the literature that will stand because it speaks to all people of a fundamental predicament and a universal search. This is a strongly creative moment for them—not only in life, but in art as well. American literature needs a corrective view of women by women—it is peopled with male concepts of women, false images of wounded and wounding creatures that have filled a great body of American fiction with "indignity and assault . . . loneliness and terror" in "a world deprived of full-fledged, mature women."[40] That assessment was written almost twenty-five years ago by literary critic Leslie Fiedler. Since then the women's movement has unleashed a flood of writings that upgrade the image of women. To this outpouring, Italian American women have contributed little, and that little unnoticed; they have yet to give the fullness of their experiences to the expansion and revitalization of the national literature.

In a very true sense, the Italian American woman writer has to be a self-made person; lacking a literary tradition, she works in isolation without models and interpretive critics, struggling against inner doubts and outer odds to become an author, sustained only by the need and impetus of what she is doing.

Why this is so has to do not only with the inner blocks of her tradition, but very much, also, with the external obstacles of the society and the barriers of the prevailing literary hegemonies.

Literary Hegemonies and Oversights: The External Blocks

It is usual to hear that there are no Italian American writers of any value; established critics say it by not noticing them, academic professors of American literature say it in defense of why Italian American writing is

40. Leslie Fiedler, *Love and Death in the American Novel* (New York: Stein & Day, 1966), p. 24.

never presented in course work; Italian American authors of some promi-
nence, like Gay Talese, say it in the confidence of being the exception; and
people who read say it for the simple fact that except for Puzo's *The Godfather*, no other work is perceived; no author—no John Fante, no Diane di
Prima, Ferlinghetti, Sorrentino, Innaurato—is familiar enough to come to
mind. It is easy to dismiss what one doesn't know.

The spurious and circular reasoning is this: if there had been any Italian
American first-rate authors one would have heard of them. But once that
was said of women as a group, too; women writers and women's experience
were by definition minor—the male experience was presented as the universal human one. Now we know more.

It is not that Italian Americans have not written work of value; it is that
the dominant culture, working under its own rules and models, within a
tight network of insiders—editors, agents, reviewers, critics—is not eager
to recognize and include in its lists that which does not reflect its own style,
taste, and sense of what is worthwhile. Italian American novelists are not
generically "second-rate"; they handle different material and handle it with
the newness, and perhaps rawness—but also passion—of the just-born and
self-made writer. Literature is not only in the great and practiced writer. It
is also in the new voices which add to the store of human experience; in the
voices which, by enriching and extending the national literary achievement, become of permanent value.

Ethnic writing was not given entry to the cultural mainstream of the
American literary world but existed, at best, in some backwater of folklore
and curiosities. Thus, John Fante's inspired production (*Wait until Spring,
Bandini!*, 1938; *Ask the Dust*, 1939; and *Dago Red*, 1940), or a fine novel
like Michael DeCapite's *Maria*, got published, but not really noticed or
taken up in any way.

For it can be claimed, fairly, that Italian American writing *did* and *does*
get published, that there is no concerted effort to keep Italian American
authors from appearing in print. It can be said, also, that there is no concerted conspiracy of silence on the part of reviewers or literary critics to
exclude mention of Italian American writing. How could there be!—to
maintain a conspiracy would imply recognition of that body of literature,
would imply critical awareness of Italian America.

The Italian American novel, when written by an Italian American author,
is all but invisible, while authors of other backgrounds, using that material,
have received attention.[41] An extreme case is the Arno Press reprint of

---

41. Some examples are: *The Immigrants* by Howard Fast; *The Little Conquerors*
by Ann Abelson; *Principato* by Thomas McHale; *Household Saints* by Francine
Prose.

Anna C. Ruddy's 1908 novel, *The Heart of the Stranger*, in The Italian American Experience series. Published in 1975, that thirty-nine-volume set includes nine novels, of which Ruddy's is the only one by a woman and a non–Italian American; *The Heart of the Stranger* is an embarrassing, sentimental depiction of Anglo-American ladies ministering to the immigrants of Little Italy. It is weird in its attempt to duplicate Italian talk, its banalities, its condescension, and is, quite simply, unfit to represent the Italian American experience from a woman's perception or anyone else's. That such a travesty is perpetuated at the expense, say, of not reprinting Mari Tomasi's novel of Italian American granite workers, *Like Lesser Gods*, is only one item in a long list of grievances and exclusions.

In a country this size, comprised of such rich and varied strains, there should be room for all facets of literary expression and familiarity with them. But that is not the case. There are hierarchies and hegemonies which, consciously or unconsciously, promote and decide what is literature and what is not. The facts of literary life are elementary: it is not simply publication, but what come both before and after that counts.

An interesting example of this is the instant elevation to celebrity status of Mary Gordon with the publication of her first novel, *Final Payments* (1978). Gordon is represented in this collection with an early piece of published writing, a memoir of her partially Italian American background which was recognized as of literary value by UNICO National, an Italian American service organization which has been encouraging and annually publishing young authors of Italian American background since 1976.

Gordon, a new young writer of promise, was backed by older established authors who add to their own luster with their literary discoveries. Mentors are significant: Gordon studied with prize-winning poet Philip Booth; critic Elizabeth Hardwick advised her on her manuscript; respected novelist Margaret Drabble wrote the prominent jacket blurb; reviewer John Leonard consecrated it. Thus, an instant network. Gordon became an instant wonder, the most celebrated young writer in the country at the moment of publication, whose whole career has gone forward on that initial momentum. *Final Payments* was nominated for the National Book Critics' Circle Award and named by *The New York Times Book Review* one of the outstanding books of the year. She has, in turn, become a reviewer and critic of merit. By the time her second novel, *The Company of Women*, came out, she needed no further jacket endorsement. Her name is instantly recognizable, her celebrity status secure, her literary achievement confirmed by an entry in the *Dictionary of Literary Biography*.

At a symposium of Critics and Book Reviewers sponsored by the Authors' Guild and held April 21, 1982, Gordon appeared on the panel and heard copanelist Jonathan Yardley, editor of the *Washington Post Book World*, mention how advance talk works to get new books immediately noticed: "There is an obvious case at this table," said Yardley. "Mary Gordon's novel of 1978, *Final Payments*, which was given a remarkable advance promotion effort by its publisher, making clear to reviewers that this was a book of seriousness that had commercial possibilities but needed to be dealt with seriously."[42] Later, Gordon herself said, "Reviews have a tremendous impact on book sales . . . books which are not reviewed are buried."[43]

And that is exactly what happens to the overwhelming majority of books which are published without special advocacy: if they are not signaled for attention by powerful names, they die.

Harvey Shapiro, former editor of *The New York Times Book Review*, and also a panelist at that symposium, revealed a dismaying statistic: *The Times*, which does more reviewing than any other publication in the country, can mention only about 8 percent of all books published in a given year. Even so, between the daily edition and the Sunday book review section, it manages to give double reviews to some books (all too predictable) while the vast number are not reviewed at all. Too bad, says Shapiro, but that's how it is.[44]

Books that are not reviewed are not picked up elsewhere along the tightly linked chain of literary life. Literary achievement is gauged by appearance in required reading lists, literature course outlines, textbooks, anthologies, critical appraisal, book reviews, and bibliographies. All things that Italian American writers have been largely excluded from—not by design, but because they lacked prominent names and advocacy.

When I was in school, American literature was identified regionally—the New Englanders, the Southern school, the expatriates, Western Expansion. Jules Chametzky, a scholar of cultural pluralism as reflected in American literature, has written about literary regionalism. It became, toward the end of the nineteenth century, "a strategy for ignoring or minimizing social issues of great significance. These issues concerned race and class and the new money-power; an upheaval in American ethnic composition; far-reaching challenges to older American social assumptions and mores. Such matter called for serious literary treatment; but such matter deeply explored could upset notions of unified national culture."[45] Local color and regional literature could be accepted by the dominant public and leading editors, but only insofar as they reinforced notions of a basically homogenous rather than a conflicted nation and culture.

42. *Authors' Guild Bulletin*, September–October, 1982, p. 16.

43. Ibid, p. 23.

44. Ibid., p. 25.

45. Jules Chametzky, "Our Decentralized Literature," a paper presented at John F. Kennedy-Institut fur Amerikastudien, Heidelberg, June 4, 1971, and published in *Proceedings*.

And I remember that Pietro Di Donato's powerful 1939 novel, *Christ in Concrete*, burst onto my consciousness as something absolutely unique—something that came from no school but its own searing, mind-opening Italian American background. Di Donato was launched by the Jewish-Socialist circle he frequented in New York, which got him recognition and lionized him as had never before happened to an Italian American author. Though not a popular author in the sense of Mario Puzo with *The Godfather*, Di Donato was a critical success and a Book-of-the-Month Club choice, and is still the only known and respected novelist of Italian American background for many academic and intellectual readers.

Katherine Newman, a scholar and critic, has proposed discarding many of the old theories of American literature "since they were fitted to a specific body of literature: that of the Anglo-American seaboard culture."[46] Taking a wider view of the whole oeuvre, other characteristics can be discerned, and she sees one characteristic of American literature (particularly relevant from the ethnic perspective) as eccentricity, in its exact meaning of being off-center, asymmetrical, irregular, uneven. That explains, to me, the uniqueness and marvelous strangeness of *Christ in Concrete*. That explains, also, other facets of Italian American fiction, with its "extraneous" material, distortions of character (I am thinking now of Marietta in Antonia Pola's *Who Can Buy the Stars?* or the raging father in John Fante's *Brotherhood of the Grape*), eccentricity of style and language, and the often ambiguous attitude of the implied author. That is not to be wondered at: Newman quotes other studies to show that implied authors of ethnic novels tend to be schizoid, that is, in conflict between the values of their ethnic groups and those of the majority group.

This very off-centeredness (and it is relevant, here, to note that Barbara Grizzuti Harrison's book of intelligent, perceptive essays is aptly entitled *Off Center*) of Italian American literature should be valuable in itself; ethnic literary scholarship stands for understanding material that, before, in a policy of Literary Apartheid, was often excluded because measured by nonapplicable standards. Like the feminists, ethnic literary scholars opt for a humanist criticism that transcends narrow views of what people are or should be. This should breach the old fortress that Mario Puzo set out to gain admittance to by writing *The Godfather*. For it was when he made the deliberate effort to embrace condoned formulas of "American" writing that Puzo was admitted to the club of visible writers.

Following Puzo's example, Gloria Vitanza Basile, a former screenplay writer, set out, in 1976 (with a book called *The Godson* and now reissued as

46. Katherine Newman, "An Ethnic Literary Scholar Views American Literature," *Melus*, Spring 1980, p. 6.

The House of Lions), to match his mass market success. And she did, becoming, according to promotion copy, "unique among the male-dominated ranks of hardcore action novelists." Her commercial success is a distinct anomaly among Italian American women writers.

Rose Basile Green, in her comprehensive study, *The Italian-American Novel*, devotes more space to Mario Puzo than to any other of the seventy-five authors she considers (seventeen pages for discussion of *The Godfather*, two pages for *Christ in Concrete*); she applauds Puzo, who had written a very fine but previously little-noticed novel, *The Fortunate Pilgrim*, for playing the American game, finally, with *The Godfather:* "An Italian American novelist, Mario Puzo, has pried open the box that has secreted the sacred blackballs of the American literary club."[47] And he has done so, she says, in an acceptable way; he has not only presented the Don as a self-made man in the best American rags-to-riches tradition, but he has dressed the Italian American novel in a cloak of violence attesting "to a basic American disposition that crime is an accepted method for achieving power, even as transgression is the occasion of the salvation of the soul from sin."[48]

A pragmatist, Green declares, in effect, that if commercialism is the way to get one's previous (but unnoticed) writing appreciated, then that's the way to go. It is not a convincing argument for the long view; nor is her other thesis, that the basic optimism of Italian American writing will eventually win it success and a place in the American showcase of literature.

For it is hard to square a kind of mindless optimism with the hard psychohistory of the Italian American experience. Andrew Rolle's *The Italian Americans: Troubled Roots* deals not so much with past hardships, upward mobility, and great achievements as with the underpinnings of Italian American emotional life—the subsurface ambivalence in Italian American lives. For *that* is the reality. There are depths of bitterness, frustration, rancor, repression, and disappointment behind the surfaces of those warm and humorous portrayals of family life written by Jerre Mangione, Marion Benasutti, John Fante, or Marie Chay, as those authors indicate.

It is that factor of internal conflict, and not the deliberate commercialization of the story or pandering to violent themes, that relates Italian American fiction to the American mainstream.

For that is another characteristic of American literature that Newman cites as deriving from the pressure of pluralism: "It is *choice-making*, value-seeking, repudiating the superficialities of our society. . . . The greatest

47. Rose Basile Green, *The Italian American Novel* (Cranbury, N.J.: Fairleigh Dickinson University Press, 1974), pp. 367–68.

48. Ibid., p. 386.

American theme is *not* the fulfillment of 'the American dream' of material success, but rather the selection of a cultural mode which will satisfy the spiritual and emotional needs of the individual. The chief preoccupation of our writers is *the necessity* of choice."[49]

The necessity of choice—the old ways or the new? one's loyalty to family or self?—has always been implicit in the main thrust of Italian American writing. Italian Americans are laden with conflicted choices in loyalties and roles, with contradictions within the tradition, with ambivalence in life. It is not always a cause for optimism—seeking resolution of conflict is painful—but it *is* affirmation, it is using one's native strength and wit, it is autonomy. And that seems to be the direction toward which Italian American writing is propelled.

When, twenty-five years after Olga Peragallo's compilation of Italian American authors, Dr. Green did her notable critical study, it far outstripped in material, analysis, and complexity Peragallo's work. It is interesting that among Italian Americans it was two women who did the pioneering work in this field; yet, in Green's study of seventy-five Italian American authors, only four are women and Green does not address the question of why there are so few—it's almost as if it were assumed that women were not to be the poets and novelists and dramatists of their lives, that they were, indeed, in literature, as in life, only to be defined by men.

The few women authors of Italian American background who have dealt with their ethnic material have been the ephemerids of literature, fated to have a creative life-span as brief as the mayfly's. They are born, in a literary sense, already out of step by virtue of their themes. They are given no notice by reviewers, which means they go out of print swiftly and recede into the silence from which they came without having made a ripple in the mainstream of American writing. It is a demoralizing and chastising experience. A writer must be given the opportunity to publish at least two or three books in order to have a substantial voice, a presence. Many Italian American women never get beyond the first one because the lack of response and attention makes a publisher unwilling to risk further. Because she has been dismissed or discouraged, frequently her whole artistic life-span has not even had a chance to be documented.

Lacking encouragement, notice, and the impetus to continue writing which comes from having been heard, that primary act of courage, constituted by the will to be an author and to overcome a heritage of female self-denial, is without resonance for the woman of Italian American background and at great psychological cost to her. This condition persists to the very present. The 1981 edition of the *Harvard Encyclopedia of American*

49. Newman, "Ethnic Literary Scholar," p. 10.

Ethnic Groups carries an entry on Italian Americans which, in the space dedicated to literary achievements, makes no mention of any woman.

Literary history is falsified if it doesn't record all voices and give access to these voices by publishing, keeping in print, and making part of study courses those writers who aren't only the prominent ones of the dominant tradition. As Newman says, the critical function is to examine works on their own aesthetic terms, to relate them to the entire corpus of American literature, and to overcome the internalized stereotypes and cultural myths that have caused critical myopia.

Can critics determine what is literature (as Virginia Woolf said *she* could not) by saying what they think it should be, over and above what it *is*? Emilio Cecchi, and other Italian critics from the aulic tradition of the grand names, failed to understand and to empathize with the fresh eccentric vigor of the newly literate Italians in America; it was not until the 1940s when insightful younger authors like Elio Vittorini and Italo Calvino were translating and introducing American authors to Italy that some attention was given to a few authors, notably Pietro Di Donato and John Fante. But by and large, Italian critics do not relate to the Italian American experience and are very latecomers into that area. American critics, likewise, did not much like Italian American material unless it was made humorous (defanged, as it were) and charming as, for instance, with Jerre Mangione's *Mount Allegro,* an appealing novelized memoir which, published in 1943, has managed to stay continuously in print, the only Italian American work to do so.

Publishers have been cool to the reception of Italian Americans outside of the safe stereotypes of a warm people with funny behavior (*Mount Allegro*) or Mafia criminals (*The Godfather,* Talese's *Honor Thy Father*) or poor laborers exploited in their work (*Christ in Concrete*). They are cool to the complexities of human nature portrayed in minority or ethnic groups—they prefer racial tensions for Blacks, gangsterism and family solidarity for Italians, and complicated emotions or angst only in Wasps or Jews. Genevieve Belfiglio, publisher of *Real Fiction,* explains that she founded that publication of short stories out of frustration, because her experience was that "major publishing firms attempt to mainstream fiction, at the expense not only of writers, but readers as well since only a narrow range of experience and style is acceptable."[50]

Publishers say they cannot afford to be crusaders. But Black writer Zora Neale Hurston replied that she refused to be humbled by second place in a contest she never designed, and she identified what comes out of safe, marketable publishing as candidates for the American Museum of Unnat-

50. *Real Fiction,* vol. 1 (November 1982); see unpaged introduction.

ural History, i.e., a weird collection of stereotypes—nondimensional figures that can be taken in at a glance, as, the expressionless American
Indian, the shuffling Negro, the inarticulate Italian, etc.[51]

To perpetuate the literature of the winners and the celebrities, the publishing industry has come up with a new way to categorize authors—by
whether or not they write "midlist" fiction. This is the dumping ground for
novels that sell between 7,000 and 20,000 copies and has become the
euphemism for what is dismissed out-of-hand as second-rate. That is, the
rating of fiction is now assigned by number of copies sold within an arbitrary
range. Someone has come up with the magic numbers: evidently, when
sales reach 20,000 copies the publisher gives the go-ahead to promote a best
seller; under 7,000 copies, it must be quality stuff since it's not moving. In
between is the midlist of the untouchables, where practically all of Italian
American writing would fall.

One novelist's manuscript was continuously rejected because it didn't
"seem right"—in this case, the Italian American woman character was the
achiever and her Jewish lover was not; the author was told this appeared
anti-Semitic and it was suggested that the roles be reversed. Of course!
Then the formula would have been observed—the same one that John
Sayles used in his film *Baby, It's You,* which is the story of two high-school
lovers: he's an Italian greaser who takes woodwork and she's a Jewish
princess who's the president of the Drama Club and headed for Sarah
Lawrence. She, it's understood, will get over her transitory sexual attraction to Sheik (his nickname derives from a condom) because she is going to
be someone and he isn't. Hardly anyone of Italian American background
hasn't encountered the use of that stereotype in real life, as when a teacher
remarked to Dorothy Bryant (who was then Dorothy Calvetti and at the top
of her class), "You can't be Italian, where were your people from?" Near
Turin, said Dorothy. Then, said the teacher, relieved, they're of Germanic
origin.

Italian American characters are not allowed to be individuals, to be complex, to be alive and contradictory, subject to the pulls of tensions and defeats
of doubt, subject to losses and gains and changes. Instead the cultural myth
perceives them in very rigid, demeaning stereotypical dimensions.

That Italian American women writers have been underpublished is unde-
niable; just as exclusionary, however, is that the few who are published are
not kept on record and made accessible, even bibliographically, in libraries
and in study courses. Not only do Italian American women writing their
own stories publish with great difficulty—write an Italian cookbook, author

51. Zora Neale Hurston, "What White Publishers Won't Print," in *I Love Myself*
(Old Westbury, N.Y.: The Feminist Press, 1979), p. 109.

Nives Cappelli was told when she tried to market an ethnic novel, but don't write about Italian Americans because they don't read—but once in print, they must confront an established cadre of criticism that seems totally devoid of the kind of insight that could relate to their work.

New York Times reviewer Michiko Kakutani noted that to be an author, to her, meant "writing a novel that was important enough to be included in a series, or short stories memorable enough to be collected in an omnibus volume."[52] It is notoriously difficult for short stories to be published in book form: for Italian American women it is almost total exclusion. "Authors," thus, are those who are reprinted and collected, or those with names, a fashionable style.

But even the stylish writers have their doubters: literary historian John W. Aldridge is quoted as saying, in his *After the Lost Generation,* that young American novelists "have been constantly handicapped by the emptiness of the characters and situations about which they have been obliged to write."[53] And Anatole Broyard in one of his *New York Times* book review columns pondered on how critics choose to praise novels for perverse reasons: Joan Didion for her bleakness, Ann Beattie for her disaffection, Toni Morrison for her unforgivingness . . . others for their tough disdain, bitterness, despair, chilling unflinchingness. Authors of indictments, accusations, arraignments, and exposés of human inhumanity are congratulated on their courage. (And they are all reviewed in *The New York Times.*)

There are those in the publishing world who maintain that the answer to why some writers are known and others aren't is exposure, or denial of exposure, in the country's largest newspaper book review outlets. In fact, it has been said, the answer to the all-embracing question concerning the Italian American woman who writes—"Why are we not known?"—can be summed up in a few words: *The New York Times.*

It is not only in reviews, but also in feature articles and in letters it chooses *not* to print, that *The Times* ignores authors. For instance, in the magazine section on May 1, 1983, drama critic Mel Gussow wrote an article entitled "Women Playwrights: New Voices for the Theater." It was grand to see women spotlighted, but where were the names of Donna DeMatteo, Karen Malpede, or even Nina Faso, the producer of *Godspell?* Why hadn't he investigated two Italian American theaters, The Forum of Italian Ameri-

---

52. *The New York Times Book Review,* February 6, 1983.

53. Richard J. Margolis, in a review of *The American Novel and the Way We Live Now,* by John W. Aldridge, in *The New York Times Book Review,* June 19, 1983, p. 18.

can Playwrights and Il Teatro del Rinascimento, where women like Rosemary Terango and Adrianna Tregianni are showing notable work? A letter of
inquiry which asked those questions was never run in *The Times*. The
following week, in the book review section, there appeared a piece called
"Brooklyn, Borough of Writers"; a lot of names appeared but not those of
Barbara Grizzuti Harrison or Daniela Gioseffi.

Multiplied inexorably, year after year, author after author, and never
redressed—never even acknowledged—these kinds of oversights add up to
veritable ostracism.

The New York Times best seller list is another tool in the service of that
ostracism: "Today one list, that of *The New York Times*, dominates the
hardcover book trade. It is offered to us without explanation of how it was
compiled; it is posted prominently in stores from coast to coast, as if it were
carved in marble; and it is in itself a powerful instrument of promotion for
the books it lists, a kind of self-fulfilling prophecy."[54]

After the reviewer, it is the critic who takes the long view and decides
what becomes part of the official canon. And that, Bernard De Voto wrote
some time ago, is *the* literary fallacy—i.e., believing that what the critics
present and perpetuate as the National Literature is the measure of a
culture.[55] What they actually do is present their ad hoc list of winners.

Next in the ring of exclusion, editors of collections and bibliographic
works, like the powerful H. W. Wilson Company, close admittance into
those bibliographic retrieval tools to writers who have not been reviewed in
the publications which the Wilson Company chooses to scan.

Without listings in Wilson's *Short Story Index, Fiction Catalog, Book
Review Digest, Standard Catalog for Public Libraries,* etc., the nonre-
viewed author is, indeed, buried—impossible for a teacher to find and
select for a reading list or studies course. Nor, of course, do compilers and
anthologizers pick up these "lost" authors. When teachers, editors, compilers consult the Wilson volumes for, say, the names of authors who are
writing about Italian Americans so that they can be included in syllabi,
presented at conferences, studied and commented on, they are naturally
led to the conclusion that there are pitifully few Italian American authors.
In the eighth edition of the *Fiction Catalog,* in nine entries for books about
"Italians in the United States," seven of the authors are of other ethnic
background and include Jimmy Breslin, Bernard Malamud, Howard Fast.
This means that books like Octavia Locke's *A Cup of the Sun,* Nancy
Maniscalco's *Lesser Sins,* or Dorothy Bryant's *Miss Giardino,* all of which

54. John Brooks, "Bookstore and the Spirit of Publishing," *Authors' Guild Bulletin,* Winter 1982–83, p. 10.
    55. Bernard De Voto, *The Literary Fallacy* (Boston: Little, Brown, 1944).

are about Italian Americans, will never be picked up by a reader, teacher, or researcher looking for material in that subject area. It is, again, like never having been published at all except for that minute inner circle of friends who may have heard personally of the event—certainly such work is not "published" in the true sense of being made public and accessible. It's as if the writing of Italian American women were some fastidiously secret pursuit, a distilling of a rare liqueur.

It is a dismal fact of life that in addition to all the inner blocks to creativity an Italian American woman has, there are formidable external blocks, built into the system, as well. Dorothy Bryant, a well-thought-of author who experienced all the frustrations of the publishing world when her first two novels were published by major houses, decided that not only could she do better on her own, but she could keep herself in print as well. She founded her own publishing house, Ata Books, and with the help of her husband publishes only her own work, keeps it continuously available, and even makes a profit. But that takes an initial investment and some kind of partnership and is not something that all authors could or would want to do.

When I worked in a college library, I became aware of a few areas of bibliographic oversight in regard to Italian American women writers; I am sure there are many more.

1. No Italian American novels are listed in the category of family chronicles in the bibliography of *American Historical Fiction*.

2. Not until the fourth revised edition (1974) of the *Literary History of the United States* is mention made of a few authors of Italian American background. Before that, only Mozart's librettist, Lorenzo Da Ponte, had been cited, as if Di Donato, Fante, Tomasi, Winwar, Mangione, DeCapite, etc., had never written.

3. The four-volume *Library of Literary Criticism*, a compilation of critical writings about American authors, includes no author of Italian American background.

4. *Contemporary Literary Critics* (New York: St. Martin's, 1977) lists 115 American and British critics. Missing, along with Bernard De Voto, is any other Italian name.

5. *The Book Review Index* includes only fiction that has been reviewed in at least four journals on Wilson's approved list, which effectively excludes practically everything written by Italian American women. In effect, the reviewing media, not the book itself, is being judged.

6. In *The Ethnic American Woman*, a collection of writings of ninety-five women authors from twenty-four ethnic groups, the Italian

American group is represented by one entry, the non-literary writer of a scholarly paper, as compared to dozens of Black or Jewish literary writers.

These items demonstrate the self-perpetuating myth on the part of readers, editors, professors (and the demoralizing perception among Italian Americans themselves) that Italian American literature *is* second-rate because if it weren't, it would be included in the Wilson publications and other collections; would be issued in paperback or series; would be anthologized, collected, selected, recommended, discussed, analyzed, and put in course offerings.

Unfortunately, like the victim who blames him- or herself, exclusion leads Italian American writers to the Kafkaesque conclusion that their writing is not worthy of being included. To get out of this dismal swamp we need reviewers, the critics who will explicate our experience and relate it to the dominant culture, and teachers who will promulgate the work because they need it and want it but have to know *it is there*!

Professor Robert Viscusi, who is director of The Humanities Institute at Brooklyn College, taught a course there in the Italian American novel, and he says the answer is that *we* must become the critics of the Italian American novel because "the role of the critic—who perceives and establishes the quality of novels by the quality of his/her readings [of them]—is essential . . . we will need critics to show us how to see what is there, how to find the model that the novel . . . offers, how to lift its layers, manifold and delicate as they are, ever so gently, not destroying as we go but always searching."[56]

Among the minority groups, Jews have become excellent critics, literary scholars, tastemakers. And the Blacks have benefited by the critical attention of liberal Wasps and Jews, set on righting the wrongs of racism. Women, with the revival of feminism, have set up their own presses and gone back to find the women who have hitherto been neglected, remarkably without ever having found an author of Italian American background to reclaim and put back into print.

The other minorities—Chicanos, Asians, and Native Americans—are doing some of the most interesting work that is being published today. They have been championed by the Before Columbus Foundation, have started their own anthologies and collections on the accurate premise of being "other sensibilities"—i.e., outside the criteria and self-perpetuating themes of the Establishment molds.

56. Robert Viscusi, from an address to the Panel on the Italian American Novel at the Conference of the American Italian Historical Association, October 1980.

In the college library where I worked, there passed through my hands myriad collections reflecting the awakening of various ethnic groups in this country, and their collective voice was wonderful: not only fiction, poetry, essays, but excellent finding tools that assured that the women of these groups would always remain accessible, that they had not written in vain. The autobiographies of Black women are annotated and compiled; Yiddish women poets are the subject of new research; *The American Indian in Short Fiction* is an important locating tool and contribution to the cultural studies of that group. Other titles abound: *Give Birth to Brightness: A Thematic Study in Neo-Black Literature; The Jewish Woman, 1900–1980: A Bibliography; The Third Woman: Indian, Black, Chicano and Asian Women Writers of the United States; The Golden Land: A Literary Portrait of American Jewry; Aiiieeeee: An Anthology of Asian American Writings.* And on and on. There is nothing comparable for Italian Americans.

Even the general comprehensive studies like *Women in American Theater*, or *Women and Literature: An Annotated Bibliography of Women Writers*, or *Revelations: Diaries of Women* omit the Italian American voice. Lina Mainiero, editor of the four-volume set *American Women Writers* published by the prestigious publisher Frederick Ungar, was predisposed to include Italian American women in that collection but said there were none that she could find; unless writers had won awards, been carried in anthologies, or mentioned in literary criticism, there was no way to know who they were. Thus, again, we see Anita Bryant listed as a notable American author, but not Dorothy Bryant; Diane Wakoski, but not Diane di Prima; a batch of Anglo-American women called Aunt Fanny or Cousin Kate, but no Sister Blandina Segale.

The difference between neglect and respect can be the network of support which one has: in the academic world, in the publishing industry, with reviewers or people in the media; recommendations for writers' colonies, panel appearances, grants, readings all count. It is almost virgin territory to Italian American women writers, who clearly need a support system other than the family.

When readers happen upon our books in secondhand bookstores, or in someone's personal library, it is always with the shock of revelation that we hear from them ("Thank you for writing your book—there is so little on our experience that one would believe we don't exist")—in those words, or in variations, does the proof come, both of our tenuous existence as authors, and of the need for our existence.

A further answer to "Where are the women?" is that the record is incomplete and therefore distorted.

The cycle of neglect has to be broken. Until then the Italian American woman's voice has not yet been heard.

Affirmations

There is an answer. If others will not take the subject of Italian American writing seriously, we will, in Professor Viscusi's words, take it seriously ourselves. We will become not only the writers, but also the teachers and critics of our experience. That is what Black women writers have said and done. And that is what our own tradition counsels us; in the Sicilian version of the Noah's Ark story, after the Lord chose two of all His creatures to go aboard the ark, the fleas found they had been forgotten. So they slipped on by getting into Noah's beard. As the Sicilians say, "We are like fleas; if the Lord forgets us, we must use our own wits."[57]

A new form of literary criticism based on the theories of psychoanalyst Karen Horney could be most appropriately applied to developing Italian American writing, for Horney had a humanist approach to experience, and proceeding from her studies of alienation, her work focused on the unblocking of neuroses which hindered growth of personality and the full development of a person. Her concrete focus, coupled with Abraham Maslow's theory of basic human needs, is extremely relevant to the analysis of realistic literature. Dr. Bernard Paris, in his *A Psychological Approach to Fiction* (Bloomington: Indiana University Press, 1974), is the chief developer and applier of these psychological theories to the study of literature.[58]

Horney offers the most systematic account of self-alienation—an area very pertinent to the feelings of unworthiness, low expectations, self-hate, and self-doubt experienced and revealed by Italian American women. What Bernard Paris calls Third Force psychology is beyond Freudianism and behaviorism in that it recognizes a third principle—the evolutionary and constructive force in human beings, the drive toward self-actualization rather than repression. This seems extremely applicable to the growth-oriented direction and force of Italian American writing which proceeds from a sense of alienation and is reaching toward a newly articulated self-development.

But, more, this kind of humanistic psychology can also be valuable, according to Dr. Paris, in another sense: "Third Force psychology . . . permits us to evaluate cultures, therefore, in terms of a universal norm of

57. I am indebted to Lucia Chiavola Birnbaum, a strong Sicilian woman, for this tale.
58. See also his "Third Force Psychology and the Study of Literature, Biography, Criticism, and Culture," *The Literary Review* 24, no. 2 (Winter 1981): 181–221.

psychological health which has nothing to do with the quite possibly misguided values of individual societies. Those things are good in a culture which satisfy the basic needs of its members and foster their full human growth, while those things are bad which frustrate the basic needs and induce self-alienation."[59] This is an important tool of criticism in understanding the values and beliefs of that entity which Viscusi calls Italian America.

Indeed, Carol Bonomo Ahearn has shown the potential of this method in her analytical essay, "Definitions of Womanhood," included in this collection and based on Maslow's criteria.

Among the theoretical questions that Katherine Newman poses for a critical framework by which to evaluate ethnic literature is this: what are the causes that bring about the production of literature by writers of an ethnic group?[60] To that I think that Italian American women could answer: the need to know ourselves; to create our models, to write the stories that need telling, and to make available the books that need reading.

In the broadest sense, that is the function of literature. Literature gives us ourselves.

As a group, Italian American women have angles of vision and particular perceptions which can be uniquely revitalizing factors in this country's literary heritage. We can use the same strengths our grandmothers had, but now for artistic rather than economic growth.

Perhaps the first step is the keeping of journals, the writing of autobiography or memoirs. In the volume *Women's Autobiography*, there is a chapter entitled "In Search of the Black Self," along with much material by Anglo-American and Jewish women; there is not, however, a single entry by an Italian American woman. A reference work, *Italian Americans: A Guide to Information Sources*, published in 1978, has a surprising paucity of autobiographical material in the subtopic "Reminiscences and Autobiographical Narratives" and some dubious inclusions, including an Irish teacher's patronizing account of teaching the children of Italian immigrants in Boston's North End entitled *'Scusa Me, Teacher*.[61] A few glossed-over, self-published, congratulatory accounts of material success in America are included but they are not the stuff of true-life histories; quite missing, as yet, are the honest and revealing stories of women's inner lives.

Material can be found: the Immigration History Research Center in St. Paul, Minnesota, has resources which include Grace Spinelli's manuscript

59. Paris, "Third Force Psychology, p. 221.

60. Newman, "Ethnic Literary Scholar," p. 5.

61. Francesco Cordasco, ed., *Italian Americans: A Guide to Information Sources*, vol. 2 in the Ethnic Studies Information Guide Series (Detroit: Gale Research Co., 1978).

"Roots and Wings," an oral history by journalist Clara Grillo, and the complete documentation of the extraordinary story of Rosa Cassettari. In San Francisco I happened upon Genevieve Altieri's charming memoir, *The House on Grant Street;* in New York, Il Teatro del Rinascimento gave a performance of *I Remain, Your Uncle Ambrogio,* based on the letters of her uncle collected by Gene Mangiapelo Horwitz. Recently, a compelling book, *The Nurse's Story,* by Carol Gino, touched tangentially on her Italian American background while presenting an honest and moving portrayal of a young woman's life choices. Older women are writing of their past, and eighty-four-year-old Tia Talamini has a collection of autobiographical stories that deserve to be published. There are human documents—oral histories, letters, diaries, memoirs—which, rare as they are among Italian Americans, have to be searched out and preserved more fully than has been done up to now, because therein would be those authentic voices of women so missing as points of contact with our past.

Black women have realized the importance of the personal voice as part of the long, united march toward recognition. Black autobiographies, they say, help rend the veil of white definitions that misrepresent a person to him- or herself and to the world. Creating a new identity can create a new literature.[62]

Italian American women want to plumb the sense of who they are, echoing Viscusi's "We want to become what we are." As Sandra M. Gilbert put it, "My Italian-American 'identity' has always been important to me, partly I imagine, because (since I don't speak Italian) it's been such a baffling part of my life, so crucial yet so mysterious, and partly because . . . the experience of Italians in America has been so vivid to me and yet it seems, by most people, to be neglected or misunderstood."[63]

Redefining the self not as mirrored by society's expectations but in one's own authentic terms is essential for an integrated literary expression. Autobiography, when it is honest and not a camouflage, can be a powerful declaration of selfhood and a positive step toward establishing an incontrovertible voice.

When I examined the papers, notebooks, and diaries of Diane di Prima in the Special Collections at Syracuse University, I found in them a rich evocation of the counterculture life of the 1950s and 1960s. And the thread of her Italian Americanism—her preoccupation with the children, the meals, the ritual of the eels for Christmas Eve—holds it all together in a

62. Regina Blackburn, ed., *Women's Autobiography* (Bloomington: Indiana University Press, 1980).

63. From a letter to Helen Barolini.

strong personal way and gave it a nostalgia I found very moving. It is the vein from which her wonderful, intense poetry flows, and it is in that kind of writing—the intimate revelation—that Italian American women will probably most powerfully express themselves.

Indeed, almost all of the literary creation done by the women in this collection seems to have grown out of autobiography—from Nancy Maniscalco's picaresque version of a Queens childhood, to the poetry which celebrates Italian kitchens, gardens, and grandparents. Most explicit is Karen Malpede's evocation of her childhood and its juxtaposition with a highly transformed mythical scene from a play. What exists in the genre of autobiography as such has hitherto been written by men, but Barbara Grizzuti Harrison's poignant and harrowing story of her experience as a Jehovah's Witness is the very best of the autobiographical form as it traces the inner development and growth and change of a person.

Summary

Finally, the exclusions have been so great, so close to total, that the depressing futility that I felt actually reversed itself into exhilaration; instead of continuing outrage, an almost paradoxical sense of euphoria begins to prevail—rather than go on pointing out omissions, neglect, discrimination, I found myself thinking, And now, for the first time ever, I present . . .

But this is not the first time ever in print for most of these authors; it is the first time, though, that we have kept company together and been associated, in an anthology, by our tradition. A tradition that may be passing? Some refer to the waning of ethnicity; already the academic practitioners of the Italian American experience have begun to refer to its twilight. In Italy the Twilight Poets, *I crepuscolari*, of the beginning of the twentieth century heralded a new poetry, not just the waning of the old. Just so, we could imagine, it might be now, even as ethnicity, as such, approaches its dusk.

Italian American women writers are late in coming to the fore of expressivity, as we have seen; but, in a sense, the American odyssey has allowed them to turn things upside down. Women, notably, have taken the strong role in the fiction of the immigrant saga. There is by now a whole gallery of such literary portrayals—the strong woman has become part of a tradition and lives in such characters as Fortuna of Julia Savarese's *The Weak and The Strong;* in Marietta of Antonia Pola's *Who Can Buy the Stars?;* in the matriarchs, Annunziata of Ann Abelson's *The Little Conquerors* and Lucia Santa of Mario Puzo's *The Fortunate Pilgrim;* and in my own *Umbertina*. She lives in this last verse of Maria Gillan's previously quoted poem:

Remember me, ladies,
the silent one?
I have found my voice
and my rage will blow
your house down.

Women are becoming the voices of the Italian American experience, and
it is not surprising that they have taken this long. If there have been great
omissions previously it is because before notable work can happen, there
must be readied ground, there must be preparation and receptiveness in
the living culture. And the emergence of Italian American women is, for
most, just now happening, is incredibly new. In language that is particularly suited to Italian American women—with their plantings, and gardens,
and patient cultivation—Cynthia Ozick, in her essay on feminism "Women
and Creativity: The Demise of the Dancing Dog," says, "Cultivation pre-
cedes fruition. It will take many practitioners of an art to produce one great
artist."[64]

A start has to be made and then, like reverberations, one work will set off
another: each new literary work responding to a previous one, provoked
into being by having to answer something left unsettled in the other work
and, in turn, provoking new responses to itself. Each writer stands on the
shoulders of another. We all need each other and the larger the community
of talent, the better for each individual.

What must happen for Italian American women to become the writers of
their material is for them to see themselves as writers in the first place, and
then to practice and develop their art. "The duty of a writer—the revolutionary duty, if you like," says Gabriel García Márquez, "is simply to write
well."

It is new and exciting for women of the Italian patriarchal society (and
their American descendants) to see themselves as writers; before, they saw
and valued themselves as upholders and transmitters of a precise culture
through their precise roles as wives and mothers. To evolve from that old
and potent image has taken at least the century that has passed since the
inception of the great migrations. But it is beginning. The seeds have been
planted—not the old seeds of doubt, but the ones that bear fruit.

As Iris Sangiuliano brought out in her very wise book, *In Her Time*, it is a
false dilemma for a woman to choose between family and career; she can
have both. Life, she finds, unfolds not predictably, but in "great surges of

---

64. Cynthia Ozick, "Women and Creativity: The Demise of the Dancing Dog," in
Woman and Sexist Society, ed. Vivian Gornick and Barbara K. Moran (New York:
New American Library, 1971), pp. 431–51.

billowing change; and it is the unpredictable which is the seminal female ingredient for change: conflicts + contradictions = change." "Women," Anne Sexton said, "are twice born."

Thus, women are in the unique position of being able to use the dichotomy of two cultures as the crucible for artistic production. The Black women writers have been particularly fine at this: "Our alienation is our great strength," says Nikki Giovanni.[65] This lies at the base of Italian American women using strong themes; they are using the paradox of their lives, which has militated *against* expressivity, *in* expressivity. As Barbara Grizzuti Harrison said regarding her own submersion as a Witness, "Women are good at turning their desolation to their advantage"; from waiting comes intensity of focus, words straining to be heard, passion, conviction, an inner voice.

Grazia Deledda set out to write the literature of Sardinia because there wasn't any. In doing so she created a universal oeuvre. Italian Americans have a similar task: to chronicle, before the end of this century, the story of the great journey of the Italian people to this country. It is an epic theme and it has not been dealt with in Italian literature, and not sufficiently from the woman's perspective in American literature. But its time has come. My eldest daughter, a scholar of medieval Italian literature, reminds me that the opening words of the *Decameron* of Boccaccio, that essential storyteller of all time, are *Umana cosa*—"Something human." And that is, for me, a summation of the Italian American woman writer's particular sensibility—very human, the stuff of life. Italian Americans tilt toward life, bringing realism, vigor, specificity, humane understanding of the emotions, and respect for the human verities to their material.

Few of us are self-consciously writing "ethnic"; we are American writers, writing in the fullness of our exposure to, and experience of, American literature. Yet as Tina DeRosa commented when her *Paper Fish* was published, "It has only recently been pointed out to me that I am an Italian American author." I shared that surprise when *Umbertina* was published and I suddenly became an Italian American author as I hadn't been in the previous decade.

This brings to mind another curious pigeonholing: in the academic world the works of Italian American authors have, by default, been shunted off into the departments of Italian, sociology, ethnic history, or Italian American studies; it is certainly a mistake to link Italian American literature with Italian literature, and crucial for the validation of Italian American writing that it be recognized as what it is, an unquestionable part of American literature.

65. Tate, *Black Women Writers at Work*, p. 70.

I believe that the writers represented herein are writers who transcend gender and ethnic group; some have a specific Italian American frame of reference; for others it is much more attenuated. But since, at some point, they all derived from a common tradition, one in which woman had so strongly defined a role, it is, I think, important to see them in that cultural context in order to see them whole and in order to hear the particular cadence of their voice. That is not to relegate them to some separate ethnic drawer in the bureau of American literature, but to identify them as an important source of writing which has been overlooked.

Once the missing pieces have been fitted into the national literature, the unheard voices listened to, the contributions of a large group of American life attended to, the emphasis on ethnicity, per se, will have been transcended.

This is, for the moment, a partial record of the voice of Italian-descended women in America; this is the documentation of their special tone, their special strengths, their unique vision. In banding them together, they are given focus and weight. Once grouped, they are then free to be themselves, to be what they first and foremost are: writers in their own right.

MEMOIRS

Sister Blandina Segale

A nun of the order of the Sisters of Charity, Sister Blandina was born Rosa Maria Segale on January 23, 1850, in the Northern Italian village of Cicagna, near Genoa, and arrived in the United States as a young child with immigrant parents who settled in Cincinnati. There, at the age of sixteen, she entered the novitiate of the Sisters of Charity motherhouse, followed by her sister, who took the name Sister Justina and to whom the letters of Sister Blandina's journal of correspondence are addressed.

As a young nun, Sister Blandina was sent by her superiors to Trinidad, in the Colorado Territory, and she spent the next twenty-one years on the Western frontier recording her mission work among the Indians, the founding of schools and hospitals, the overseeing of everything from construction to Christmas programs, and the continual giving of herself, as she said in her final journal entry, "to meet emergencies as I saw them," which included stopping lynch mobs or standing up to Billy the Kid.

Her journal was originally published in installments in a Catholic magazine, but received attention for its historic value and was then first published in book form, in 1932, as *At the End of the Santa Fe Trail*. It is a rich record of the vigor and accomplishments, the dedication and joy, which men and women of Catholic religious orders gave to building up the West. They were workers, builders, believers . . . but, at the end, Sister Blandina, with her characteristic straightforwardness and clear sight, had the premonition of being expendable. In fact, she was relieved of her public school teaching duties at the school she had helped start in Trinidad, when she refused to discard her religious garb, as the secular authorities demanded.

After twenty-one years in the West, Sister Blandina was recalled to Cincinnati, where she and Sister Justina then worked thirty-five years ministering to the needs of the numerous, inpouring Italian immigrants. She lived until the age of ninety-one.

These excerpts are from the beginning of Sister Blandina's journal as she sets out on her Western mission and arrives in Trinidad, to a period of time in Santa Fe under the authority of the revered Bishop Jean Baptiste Lamy, whom Willa Cather was to immortalize in *Death Comes for the Archbishop*. Cather's novel disregarded the nuns and emphasized the civilizing influences on the frontier of the French-born bishop. Sister Blandina's journal, however, records the names and deeds not only of the dedicated Sisters, but of the Italian Jesuits and Franciscan Brothers who spent their lives working in the West, foreseeing, correctly, that Establishment history would not give the whole picture as to what had been accomplished by those generally overlooked groups: Catholics, minorities, and women.

---

from At the End of the Santa Fe Trail

On Train from Steubenville, Ohio, to Cincinnati. Nov. 30, 1872. My Darling Sister Justina:

How interestedly you, Sister M. Louis, and myself read Eugénie de Guérin's Journal and her daily anxieties to save her brother from being a spiritual outcast! This Journal which I propose keeping for you will deal with incidents occurring on my journey to Trinidad and happenings in that far-off land to which I am consigned.

The Journal will begin with the first act. Here is Mother Josephine's letter:

> Mt. St. Vincent, O.
> Nov. 27, 1872.

Sister Blandina,
Steubenville, O.

My Dear Child:
    You are missioned to Trinidad. You will leave Cincinnati Wednesday and alone. Mother Regina will attend to your needs.

> Devotedly,
> Mother Josephine.

This letter thrilled us both. I was delighted to make the sacrifice, and you were hiding your feelings that I might not lose any merit. Neither of us could find Trinidad on the map except in the island of Cuba. So we concluded that Cuba was my destination. I was to leave Steubenville quietly so that none of my obstreperous pupils might cause the incoming teacher annoyance. Hence I went to Sunday Catechetical class as usual—2 P.M. I was to take the 3 P.M. train for Cincinnati. I said to my hopefuls, "Instead of catechism, I'm going to tell you an Indian story today." The schoolhouse roof was not disturbed, though the hurrahs were loud enough! The moral of the story was "Indian Endurance." Dismissed them at two-thirty without one word of goodby except the daily one. You remember how surprised I was to see a crowd at the station to wish me "Godspeed"; I thought I was to slip away without anyone's knowledge except our own. Mr. Tait and Mr. McCann wished to speak to me alone. Both had been in the West. "You will have a long travel on the plains," they said, "before you reach Trinidad."

"Where is Trinidad?"

"A little mining town in Southwestern Colorado." So then I knew my destination, which of course, I would have been told at Mt. St. Vincent. Both gentlemen said they have traveled on the plains on the Santa Fe Trail, and they seemed to have made it a matter of conscience to inform me on the subject of cowboys. This in substance was their conversation with me:

"Sister, you may be snow-bound while on the plains." I looked my assent, I knew I could not stop the snow.

"Travelers are sometimes snow-bound for two weeks, and you are alone. This, though, is not the greatest danger to you."

Mentally I was wishing both gentlemen somewhere else.

"Your real danger is from cowboys." I looked at the speakers.

"You do not seem to grasp our meaning. No virtuous woman is safe near a cowboy." Both gave up trying to make me understand what they considered danger. Why should snow or cowboys frighten me any more than others who will be traveling the same way! So you see, dearest, I'm not going to so long a distance as we thought. At three o'clock A.M. the baggage checker came through our coach. I looked to see how much the pocketbook contained—just twenty-five cents. If I used it to ride to the Good Samaritan I'd be minus the fare to Mt. St. Vincent, so I made up my mind to skirt around from the Little Miami to the Good Samaritan Hospital.

At four A.M. I rang the front doorbell—no response. I sat on the stone steps and waited till I heard the rising bell, then I waited another fifteen minutes when again I rang the doorbell. Sister Anthony came.

"Why, child, where did you come from; how did you get here? I'm sure you are cold." I said I came from Steubenville.

"Oh, yes! dear Father Bigelow died there. He was good to this hospital. Last year he sent a barge of coal to us." I said he was good to anyone in

need. He died possessed of three dollars and fifty cents. His hand was
always open to any kind of distress.

I did not mention to Sister Anthony that I walked from the Little Miami
Station.

After Mass, breakfast and smiles of sympathy and "God Bless You" from
the Sisters at the Good Samaritan, one of the nurses accompanied me to
Fifth and Vine Streets, where I was to take "Barney's Bus" for Mt. St.
Vincent. The bus was to leave at ten A.M. I waited till three P.M. then asked
one of the clerks if he thought Mr. McCabe would run the bus that day.

"I fear no bus will run to-day. There is an epidemic—epizootic among the
horses." I asked if Mr. Segale's place of business was anywhere near. He
pointed to Wood's Theater and I started to the place indicated. Brother
Henry managed to find a "hack" to send me to Mt. St. Vincent. On the way,
between the first ascent of the hill and the Seminary, I met Sisters Gabriella
and Delphina walking in the slush and cold on their way to the Orphan
Asylum. I stopped to take them in. They returned with me to Cedar Grove,
from there the driver was to take them to the Asylum in Cumminsville.
Sister Gabriella said to me, "I would gladly go where you are going instead
of shouldering this heavy burden." Sister is to be mother to three hundred
orphans, taking Sister Sophia's place.

The Sisters are showing great sympathy. I heard Sister Benedicta say,
"She does not mind going so far and alone—I've not seen her shed a tear."
Nor will you, my dear Sister. The tears will flow where none but He and
myself will know. Still, I'm delighted to go. I did not tell you, dearest, that
one year ago last November I wrote to Mother Regina saying I envied the
sacrifices the Sisters were making who were sent far away to do God's work.
I've received my answer with compound interest. You know that up to date
the Sisters going on distant missions were consulted and none were sent
who had parents living. I am pleased that that record is broken in my case.

Mother Regina told me to spend a day at home.

Dear Lord! Give me strength. I anticipate a scene.

I spent Wednesday, December 5th, at our old homestead. Mother kept
open house all day. Friends came in groups. Mr. Leverone and bride, his
mother and the bride's mother, Mrs. Garibaldi, the Misses Gardelli and a
host of others. Mrs. Garibaldi threatened to take off my habit. I said,
"Hands off! Have you any right to detain Mary if John wishes to take her to
California?"

"Oh, that is different."

"Yes, as different as heaven and earth. I have chosen my portion, Mary
has chosen hers, each abides by her choice."

John Leverone's mother acted most sensibly all day. She was soothing oil
to all the protests made to my going. Our dear mother kept quiet. When we

were permitted a lone interview she asked, "Do you want one of your sisters to accompany you?" I answered, "I prefer to do just as my superiors have told me."

"Well, then I will give you a thousand-dollar check so that in case you desire to return you will have the wherewith."

"No, no, dear mother, I fully realize the responsibilities I assumed. As you are aware, I realized them from the first day I entered the Novitiate."

Mother replied: "And I want to tell you I never doubted your vocation. I agree to your sacrifice, my dear child, keep on serving God, I will never interfere. Now that I have your explicit answer, friends cannot urge any logical reason to prevent your going."

All day the visitors reminded me of a disturbed ant hill. When mother and I were alone she spoke the Genoese dialect. It was like hearing sketches of a favorite opera. Wednesday at 2:00 P.M. I went to visit our Ecclesiastical Superior. The Most Rev. J. B. Purcell offered me several gifts. But St. Francis Xavier is my patron, so I'm not going to possess any superfluous article. I only regret I could not pass our home without going in, as St. Francis Xavier did. If I aim high I surely must reach some upper strata of detachment in His service. One thing I take with me, the impressive blessing given me by His Grace, part of which rings clear—"May angels guard your every step." He was extremely sympathetic at my having to go alone.

I went to confession to Rev. Dr. Callaghan. You may recall how we enjoyed his lecture on the "School Question" delivered in Steubenville. After mother had a short interview with me, father managed to see me alone. He took hold of me and asked, "Have I ever denied you anything?"

I signified no.

"You have never disobeyed me in your life?"

I assented.

"Now I command you—you must not go on this far away mission! Are you going?"

"Yes, father." He let go the hold on my arm and walked toward the door. Not without my seeing his tears falling fast. He did not realize his hold on my arm gave me pain—not to speak of the heart-pain for him.

In the railway station at St. Louis between train time, I got off to purchase a pair of arctics. I saw several Italian women selling fruit. One of them had a daughter standing near. I asked the mother if she would permit her daughter to accompany me to the shoe store, which was in sight. The mother looked at me earnestly then said to her neighbor peddler, "How do I know who she is, she looks like a *monaca* (sister) but she might be a *strega* (witch)." I thanked the true guardian of her daughter and went to make my purchase alone. I spoke English to the peddler.

If good Sister Benedicta who thought I did not mind—because I did not cry—had seen me during the greater part of last night she would but too truly have said, "That heart is human in every fiber." That I succeeded in dignifiedly getting away from home is Thy Grace, oh, my God!

Forty-two persons accompanied me to the train, among them friends of old, but my purpose never faltered, not even in shadow. Such tactics as I executed yesterday! I see one trait strong in me, the straight service of God. Not the father whom I had never seen cry, nor the most patient, dearest mother whose heart is crushed at my being sent alone, much less the friends who used every argument to make me say I would not go—could elicit the faintest trace that I was not more pleased at my going alone than if I had had a dozen with me.

Sisters Antonia and Gonzaga came to the waiting room. I asked the company to permit me an interview with the Sisters. When going toward them, one of my dear old friends said, "Look, we cannot doubt she is happy." This was not intented for my hearing, the noise caused the speaker to raise her voice. Sister Antonia asked me how I had spent the day. I narrated some incidents. "I'm an ancient religious, but I could not have gone through the ordeal as creditably as you did." What if I had mentioned all the heart sighs I had witnessed! When it was time to board the train I asked that my last interview be with my mother. Cannot you picture her sad, endearing look of appreciation? I'll skip the last talk with mother— some of it was in silence.

Trinidad
Dec., 1873

We are preparing for Christmas. The Vigilant Committee now composed of ten in the senior class is making secret preparations to supply a Christmas surprise for certain families and children who only know of Santa Claus by hearsay. In my turn, I suggested to the pupils not on the Committee to surprise the Seniors. Clothes and shoes are put in new dress suit cases. Candy boxes are hung on the Christmas tree. The young ladies of the Academy gave their last season's dresses, which are almost new. These will be sent to some families that have been reported as "Needy." Two of the convent girls each received diamond clustered rings and, because the diamonds were not set to their liking, they discarded them. I could not refrain from saying, "I hope I will never see the day you would be glad to possess them."

After the Vigilant Committee has distributed the prepared boxes to the different families, all our pupils will assemble in the Christmas tree room and receive their surprise. Then those who have to go to confession will do so. Those who remain will contribute Yuletide facts or legends.

Then preparations for midnight Mass. The choir will render Mozart's 12th Mass; organ, harp, and first violin will accompany. Quite a change from the time of an untuned instrument and nasal singing. As you will notice, we are progressing rapidly, though Trinidad is not yet on the map.

What came to my mind just now is: "Will the frontier missionaries in the South and West, Franciscans and Jesuits, fare any better in public records than did the first missionaries who staked all to bring the knowledge of God to those who inhabited the newly discovered lands?" True, Mr. Bancroft did narrate in his History of the United States some of the hardships and heroic sacrifices made by the first Jesuits, but I have been told on excellent authority that bigots are determined to have Mr. Bancroft omit the praise given the first Indian missionaries when he issues the next edition. If he does so, I predict that he, with his history, will sink in the estimation of every honest reader of history, and the result will be a change of Bancroft's U.S. History in many of the schools now using it.

How much is there made of Lord Baltimore giving freedom of conscience to those who lived where he controlled! Yet look at the stream of articles constantly given to the public about Plymouth Rock and the Pilgrim Fathers! "Oh, Justice, where art thou!" . . .

Santa Fe
Spring of 1877.

My dear Sister Justina:

The last entry made in the journal I'm keeping for you gave a brief description of the journey of the first band of our Sisters form Cincinnati to Santa Fe Territory, New Mexico. They traveled by rail, water and stage. The second band of our Sisters, traveling by caravan, had some stirring encounters as novel and dangerous as any experienced by Kit Carson, or Uncle Dick Wootton.

Both these men have been intelligent guides to avoid warring with the roving Indian tribes. Kit Carson was, for a time, General Fremont's "Power behind the throne" in scouting and guiding over trails, and places where foot of civilized man had never trod. He acted in the spirit of a Free Lance. Military discipline must have been galling to him. Carson saved the life of General Fremont on two occasions, and the General saved Kit Carson's life at least once. Is that not cementing friendship for life? Mr. Wootton (Uncle Dick) is an entirely different character from Mr. Carson. Mr. Carson is astute and daring; Mr. Wootton is kindhearted and depends much on "Luck," as he terms it. I am acquainted with all his children, and have often met Uncle Dick. His life at present is very quiet. His present occupation is keeping the tollgate near the dividing line between Colorado and New Mexico. He still has enough excitement to live on. "Wootton's Place," as it is called, is a refuge for many outlawed characters. Not that he wants it so, but it is the inevitable consequence of present conditions.

The second band of our Sisters left Mt. St. Vincent May 10, 1867. They were Sister Augustine Barron and her sister, Sister Louise Barron. At the time Sister Augustine was missioned to Santa Fe, she was assistant-Mother of the Community. Previous to this time, she had had charge of two of our largest establishments, so you can at once surmise the middle post of life had been passed. Sister Louise is two years younger.

In the fall of 1866, the beloved Bishop Lamy stopped at Mt. St. Vincent and pleaded for an addition to our Sisters already doing mission work in Santa Fe. He wanted to establish some industry by which the native girls might, in time, make a living for themselves. He strongly emphasized "Industry for the Native Girls." He was then on his way to France, where he hoped to find recruits from the seminaries and financial aid from friends. He returned in the spring of 1867 with a reinforcement to help him carry out plans approved by the Holy See for the betterment of the inhabitants of his vast diocese. Twenty-six souls accompanied him.

When, at some future day, the Church in New Mexico will find a historian, no greater names will be written than the heroes of this pioneer band: R. Rev. J. B. Lamy, Rev. D. M. Gasparri, S.J.; Rev. M. Bianchi, S.J., and Rev. M. Leone, S.J. The life of each of these pioneers was made up of self-oblation and heroism so sublime by the side of which the most notable characters in Tasso pale as meteors before the sun.

Rt. Rev. Bishop Lamy wrote from France to have the Sisters meet him in St. Louis. Three Loretto Sisters and our two Sisters proceeded in company with the Rt. Rev. Bishop Lamy and his twenty-six recruits to Leavenworth, Kansas. In Leavenworth, the Rt. Rev. Bishop manned a caravan of about one hundred covered wagons and started on his famous journey on the Santa Fe trail on the 14th of June. On the 18th, the caravan reached St. Mary's of the Potawatomis. The Jesuit Fathers and students came several miles to meet the travelers. Sunday was spent at St. Mary's, from which the caravan left June 24th.

On the 29th, the Feast of St. Peter and St. Paul, the caravan camped a few miles from Junction City. At noon four Indians visited the camp. This did not portend any good. After a consultation with some of the experienced drivers, the Bishop gave orders to return to Leavenworth at which place all the mules attached to the caravan were sold and replaced by oxen, as having more endurance.

From Leavenworth the Bishop ordered a detour from the Santa Fe Trail. The Kiowas—the most rapacious Indian tribe of the plains—had sent scouts to visit our travelers when camping near Junction City. The Bishop who understood Indian tactics and Indian warfare, changed the animals and the route, in hopes that the Kiowas would be thrown off the scent. The caravan continued its slow travel until the latter part of July. The eagle eye of the Bishop was constantly on the watch for any sign which might indicate the near approach of Indians. The Comanches and Apaches had also free scope on the plains, but the Kiowas were feared the most. When victorious in their attack on white men, they were most ferocious. The men were first scalped, then killed, the children were also killed; the women were made prisoners—a fate far worse than death.

On the 30th day of July, without any apparent reason, the Bishop ordered a corral to be made. Every wagon in the caravan was arranged to form a circle; the oxen were driven inside the circle. The travelers and teamsters ran inside the circle none too soon, for the Kiowas' death whoop preceded the sling of hundreds of arrows which fell harmlessly for some time. This was kept up until sunset, when the Indians retired. The order from inside the circle was: "Be on the alert, hands on guns, no fires to be lighted."

The day's travel had been arduous for want of water. All were suffering from thirst, and, though the water of a river could be seen distinctly not more than a few rods from their improvised corral, to attempt to satisfy their thirst, or to water the oxen, would be certain destruction to all. The Sisters prayed their beads and the men kept a vigilant watch, not to be surprised by a night attack from the fierce Kiowas. At daybreak it was discovered that cholera had broken out in the caravan! Soon after the Indians renewed their attack! Word was circulated that one of the Sisters of Loretto had the cholera! Whether it was cholera or fright the victim gave up her soul to God. Meanwhile, the Indians flung their arrows in quick succession. The travelers were well protected by the circle of wagons, from which vantage ground their guns carried death to some of the attacking Indians.

Some kind-hearted messenger came to Sister Augustine and said: "A young man under a wagon on the opposite side of the circle has the cholera and is pitifully calling for his mother." The words were scarcely uttered when Sister Augustine said, "I'll go at once to render what help I can."

Sister Augustine crawled under from one wagon to the next, while arrows were thickly showering above her, and some arrows fell near her, but lost their force by striking either wagon hub or cogs. When speaking of this to me, she said, "I could only compare the flying of arrows around me to a disturbed beehive." Sister Augustine reached the dying young man and tried to soothe his last moments as his mother would have done. So he and the dear Sister of Loretto were buried, strangers in every way. Months afterwards, all efforts to find their resting place were unavailable.

Meanwhile, the Indians continued the aggressive fight. The weather was intensely warms, all needed water. The Indians had the advantage. The cholera was doing its work, but no more victims succumbed to death.

It is said that one of the leaders of the party called a few of the men with well balanced minds and gave them his orders: "If the Indians continue the attack for twenty-four hours we are doomed. Make no mistakes in the directions I now give you, but let no man act until I give the order. When I see death is inevitable for us I will give the signal. Then you, Mr. ———, shoot Sister Louise, you, Mr. ———, shoot the elder of the Loretto Sisters, and you, Mr. ———, shoot the younger Sister of Loretto. I will shoot Sister Augustine."

Some people, many hundred miles away, asserted the man could not morally give such an order. This is true, but knowing the treatment of women prisoners in the Kiowa tribe, I would have preferred to have been shot rather than to have been made a prisoner.

The sun was declining. The Kiowas disappeared. The leader of the party asked: "Are any of you men willing to practice strategy by wading the stream and land some boxes of provisions and a barrel of liquor on the other side of the stream? Apparently, it is taking your life in your own hands, although I see no danger. My only regret is to use such means to save ourselves." The freight was safely landed on the other side of the stream. As the sun disappeared, the freighters discontinued their work.

The Indians fell into the trap. They suddenly appeared from nowhere and rushed for the barrel of whiskey. They soon chopped off the top of the barrel with a tomahawk, and each, with scooped hands eagerly drank the liquor.

Word was quietly passed to "Start fires an hour later." By this time the Indians had their fill and were dropping off in a dead sleep. Our travelers, like the Arabs, "Stole silently away." The caravan was safe and on its way to Santa Fe. The men and large boys of Santa Fe and surrounding villages formed a cavalcade and met their beloved Bishop about fifteen miles from Santa Fe and escorted him to his adobe cathedral. Meanwhile the Sisters, priests and seminarians arrived in Santa Fe and all proceeded to the cathedral, the *Te Deum* was sung, with what heartfelt gratitude you may imagine. This was the 15th of August. Since our Sisters left Mt. St. Vincent on May 10th, it is evident it took them three months and five days to reach their destination. The details of the journey on the plains have been omitted. The attack of the Kiowas on the caravan was interpreted in the states as that all males were killed and all females made prisoners. You remember the anguish the news caused our Sisters East, especially Mother Regina.

Albuquerque
1886.

"Vanity of vanities and all is vanity."

Fortunately for my peace of mind, dear Sister Justina, neither praise nor unjust criticism affects me. At this period, it is praise. What does it all amount to? If the laudation is given actions performed and those actions are accompanied by single-mindedness, and the direction is straight to God—He will be the recompense. If flaws are found—may the mercy of Christ cleanse them.

As complicated as is the frontier life (and I've lived it fourteen years—from Kit Carson to Trinidad, Colorado; to Santa Fe, New Mexico; to Arizona—by trips) yet I have never turned aside from the purpose for which I was missioned to the Southwest, viz.: to teach and meet emergencies as I saw them. "To meet emergencies as I saw them" is my interpretation of the Superior's wishes.

Rosa Cassettari

The great outpouring of Rosa's marvelous oral memoirs was fortunately collected, preserved, and published by Marie Hall Ets, a social worker at the Chicago Commons settlement house, where Rosa cleaned, who was the recipient of Rosa's stories. In Mrs. Ets's book, Rosa is given the surname of Cavalleri.

A foundling, Rosa was brought up by a foster mother in the silkmaking village of Bugiarno in the north of Italy, near Milan. When Rosa was just fourteen she was pressured into an arranged marriage with a brutal older man who soon left to work in the iron mines of Missouri. Sometime later he sent for her and, though it was against her will, her foster mother encouraged her, telling her that in America even the poor, like her, got smart. Rosa arrived in America in 1884. Eventually she left the husband who beat and demeaned her and went to Chicago, where she remarried, had children, and found work. As Professor Rudolph Vecoli says in his introduction to *Rosa: The Life of an Italian Immigrant,* Rosa's "journey from Bugiarno to Chicago was for her a high adventure in which even the hardships are relished for their bitter flavor. Rosa's zest for life which permeates these

pages triumphed over adversities. In the end she can tell it all, without a
tear in her eye or a tremor in her voice."

---

from Rosa: The Life of an Italian Immigrant

The year my Leo was born I was home alone and struggled along with my
children. My husband went away because he was sick—he went by a doctor
in St. Louis to get cured. That doctor said he must stay away from his home
one year and gave him a job to do all the janitor work around his house for
five dollars a month and his board. So me, I used to go all around to find the
clothes to wash and the scrubbing. The city hall was helping me again in
that time—they gave me a little coal and sometimes the basket of food. Bob,
the sign painter downstairs, he helped me the most. He was such a good
young man. He used to bring up a big chunk of coal and chop it up right in
my kitchen and fix the stove.

I was to the end of my nine months, but the baby never came. So I went
by one woman, Mis' Thomas, and I got part of the clothes washed. Then I
said, "Oh, Mis' Thomas, I've got to go. I've got the terrible pains!"

She said, "You can go when you finish. You've got to finish first."

"No, I go. Otherwise I'll have to stay in your bed." When I said that she
got scared I would have the baby there, so she let me go.

I went by the midwife, Mis' Marino, and told her to come; then I went
home. When I saw it was my time, I told Domenico something and sent him
with all the children to the wife of Tomaso. I told those people before, when
they see the children come they must keep them all night—it's my time. It
was really, really my time, and I had such a scare that I would be alone a
second time. So when I heard a lady come in the building—she lived downstairs—I called to her. She said, "I have no time." And she didn't come up.

I was on my bed all alone by myself and then I prayed Sant' Antoni with
all my heart. I don't know why I prayed Sant' Antoni—the Madonna put it
in my mind. And then, just when the baby was born, I saw Sant' Antoni
right there! He appeared in the room by me! I don't think it was really Sant'
Antoni there, but in my imagination I saw him—all light like the sun. I saw
Sant' Antoni there by my bed, and right then the door opened and the
midwife came in to take care of the baby! It was February seventh and six
below zero. There I had him born all alone, but Mis' Marino came when I
prayed Sant' Antoni. She washed the baby and put him by me, but then she
ran away. She didn't light the fire or nothing.

Oh, that night it was *so* cold! And me in my little wooden house in the alley with the walls all frosting—thick white frosting. I was crying and praying, "How am I going to live?" I said. "Oh, Sant' Antoni, I'll never live till tomorrow morning! I'll never live till the morning!"

And just as I prayed my door opened and a lady came in. She had a black shawl twice round her neck and head and that shawl came down to her nose. All I could see was half the nose and the mouth. She came in and lighted both the stoves. Then she came and looked at me, but I couldn't see her face. I said, "God bless you!"

She just nodded her head up and down and all the time she said not one word, only "Sh, sh."

Then she went down in the basement herself, nobody telling her nothing, and she got the coal and fixed the fire. Pretty soon she found that little package of camomile tea I had there on the dresser and she made a little tea with the hot water. And that woman stayed by me almost till daylight. But all the time she put her finger to her mouth to tell me to keep still when I tried to thank her. And I never knew where that lady came from! I don't know yet! Maybe she was the spirit of that kind girl, Annina, in Canaletto? I don't know. I really don't know! I was *so* sick and I didn't hear her voice or see her face. All the time she put her finger on her mouth and said, "Sh, sh." And when the daylight came she was gone.

About seven o'clock morning my children came home. And Mis' Marino, that midwife, she came at eight o'clock and said, "It's so cold I thought I'd find you dead!"

Then here came the city hall, or somebody, with a wagon. They wanted to take me and my new baby to the hospital. But how could I leave all my children? I started to cry—I didn't want to go. And my children cried too— they didn't want me to leave them. So then they didn't make me. They pulled my bed away from the frosting on the wall and put in the front room by the stove. And my baby, I had him wrapped up in a pad I made from the underskirt like we do in *Italia*. But that baby froze when he was born; he couldn't cry like other babies—he was crying weak, weak.

My Visella was bringing up the wood and the coal and trying to make that room warm. But she was only a little girl, she didn't know, and she filled that stove so full that all the pipes on the ceiling caught fire. I had to jump up from the bed and throw the pails of water so the house wouldn't burn down. Then God sent me help again. He sent that Miss Mildred from the settlement house. She didn't know about me and my Leo born; she was looking for some other lady and she came to my door and saw me. She said, "Oh, I have the wrong place."

I said, "No, lady, you find the right place."

So she came in and found out all. Then she ran away and brought back all those little things the babies in America have. She felt sorry to see my baby banded up like I had him. She didn't know then, Miss Mildred, that the women in *Italia* always band their babies that way. And she brought me something to eat too—for me and for my children. That night another young lady from the Commons, Miss May, she came and slept in my house to take care of the fire. She was afraid for the children—maybe they would burn themselves and the house. Oh, that Miss Mildred and Miss May, they were angels to come and help me like that! Four nights Miss May stayed there and kept the fire going. They were high-up educated girls—they were used to sleeping in the warm house with the plumbing—and there they came and slept in my wooden house in the alley, and for a toilet they had to go down to that shed under the sidewalk. They were really, really friends! That time I had my Leo nobody knew I was going to have the baby—I looked kind of fat, that's all. Those women in the settlement house were so surprised. They said, "Why you didn't tell us before, Mis' Cavalleri, so we can help you?"

You know that Mis' Thomas—I was washing her clothes when the baby started to come—she wanted a boy and she got a baby girl right after my baby was born. When I went there the next week to do the washing I had to carry my baby with me. When she saw him she said, "Well better I have a girl than I have a boy that looks like your baby! He looks for sure like a monkey!"

In the first beginning he did look like a monkey, but in a few weeks he got pretty. He got so pretty all the people from the settlement house came to see him. After two or three months there was no baby in Chicago prettier than that baby.

When the year was over for him, my husband came home from St. Louis. He didn't send me the money when he was there—just two times the five dollars—so he brought twenty-five dollars when he came back. Oh, he was so happy when he saw that baby with exactly, exactly his face and everything—the same dark gold hair and everything—and so beautiful. But he saw that baby was so thin and pale and couldn't cry like the other babies. "Better I go by a good doctor and see," he said. "I've got twenty-five dollars—I'm going to get a good doctor." So he did.

But the doctor said, "That baby can't live. He was touched in the lungs with the cold. Both lungs got froze when he was born."

And sure enough he was all the time sick and when it was nine months he died. My first Leo and my second Leo I lose them both. Oh, I was broken-hearted to lose such a beautiful baby!

I have to tell about another good thing the settlement house did for me. That winter my Leo died we were still living in that little wooden house in the alley. All my walls were thick with frosting from the cold, and I got the bronchitis on the lungs, with blood coming up. So one of those good ladies from the Commons, she arranged and sent me to a kind of home in the country where people go to get well. They had the nice nurses in that place and they cured me up good. I had a good time there too—I was all the time telling stories to entertain the other sick ladies.

In those two weeks I was gone, Chicago Commons helped my husband take care of the children, and my family moved into a good building. That building in front of where we were living had the empty rooms good and dry. But when my husband asked the manager, he said, "No, I don't let no Italians in!"

So Dr. Taylor, he went himself downtown, or someplace, and saw the owner to that building. The owner said yes, the manager has to let my husband in. The rent was no more, and there we were in a nice dry building. I was no more sick after then. We were the only—or almost the only—Italian family in the neighborhood that time, and the Germans and Norwegians were afraid to let us come in their buildings. But Chicago Commons took care of us. In that time all the streets by the Commons were the Norwegians and the Lutherans. And on the next street were all the Irish. But then the Italians came and the Norwegians moved away. Most of those Italians, they were not Italians—they were Sicilians. Oh, the Irish and the Sicilians they didn't get along together! They were all the time fighting. The Sicilian downstairs put out the tomato sauce to bake in the sun—all the yard covered up with those boards for the tomato sauce—and the Irish upstairs she hung up her clothes above with the paper between so the cord don't dirty the clean white shirtwaist. When she took off the clothespins, the paper, and sometimes the pillow case, went in the sauce. Then they both got mad and started the fighting.

Pretty soon after my first Leo died that darling Miss May got me a job to come every day to do the cleaning in the settlement house. Then Gionin got the good job sweeping the floor for the electric company. And after not long we got to be the janitor in that building where they didn't want the Italians. I had to scrub down the stairs once a week and do a little work like that, and we got the rent for half. We went along good that way. But I had a lot of worry too, because I was all the time gone to my work and my children were alone on the street. My Visella was eight or nine years old and she had to be the mother to the other children. And I had more trouble because the landlord in that new building was so mean. He was all the time beating the children. One day he kicked Visella and beat her terrible because she was playing house in the back alley and moved some boxes he didn't want moved. I was afraid to tell Gionin because he would start fighting with that boss. But I was crying one day when Miss May came in my house. I said, "If only I can have a little house of my own so those men can't lick my children."

She said, "How much do you think it would cost, Mis' Cavalleri?"

I said, "Oh, it costs lots—about a thousand dollars!"

The next week she came back and she said to me and my husband, "If I borrow you the money to buy a little house do you think you can pay me back like rent?"

"Oh, no!" Gionin said. "That much money I can't take for a debt!"

And I said no too. I can't sleep with the debt. But she meant it, that good Miss May. She trusted us and wanted to do it. She was a rich lady but she used to love me. She was the one who slept in my house the time my Leo was born. And later she'd give me much pleasure when she'd come in my house and eat. She'd come in and see the onions and she'd say, "Oh, Mis' Cavalleri, I just love the onions! I want an onion sandwich." And she'd go out and buy a lot of butter and some bread and come back and eat with me.

The residents in the settlement house now are not like in those old days. Now they all have their own work and go their own way. They're all pleasant and nice. They come in the kitchen Sunday night and say, "How you are, Mis' Cavalleri? If we help with the dishes will you tell us a story?" But it's not like in the old days when everyone was one family.

Me, I was always one that liked to entertain the people. So every noon I used to tell a story to the other cleaning women in the Commons when we were eating our lunch in the kitchen. In that time I didn't talk much English but I acted those stories so good that they understood anyway. I made those women bust out laughing when I told some of those funny stories from the barn in Bugiarno. One day Mis' Hill, the housekeeper, came in and heard me telling. She was so crazy for the way I told the story, she went and told Dr. Taylor. Then Dr. Taylor found me one night and said, "Come in the parlor, Mis' Cavalleri, and tell the story to the residents."

Me, I felt like one penny the first time I went in before all those high-up, educated people, and I had to talk half in Italian. But I was so reverent and acted the story so good that when I was the sister seeing the Madonna come alive all those residents raised up from their chairs with me. And oh, I wish you could see how they laughed when I told the funny stories! After then I all the time had to tell the stories to everybody—to the Woman's Club, to the man's meeting, to the boys' party, to the girls' party, to everybody. Sometimes when they had the big meetings in Hull House they would tell me to come there. One time that university in Evanston made me come there and tell stories to those teachers who were going to school to learn the storytelling. I went everywhere. But always some resident—one of the teachers from the Commons—had to go with me, because I didn't know how to go alone. I loved to tell the stories. I never said no.

Gionin, oh he was glad when I told the stories. So for practice I used to test them on him first. If he listened good—if I made him laugh or made his tears fall, then I knew I said them good. Sometimes he went with me to those parties in the settlement; but when I went up to tell the story, he went out of the room. He couldn't stay in, he was so afraid I'd make a mistake. He was more excited than me. But then after a while sometimes he used to stay in too. And he was proud how the people were enjoying to hear me tell.

Me, I was always crazy for a good story. That's why I love so much the dramatics. If somebody says to me, "Leave the supper and take the show," I'll take the show every time and let the eating go. I just love the drama! After I got the job to go every day to the settlement for the cleaning, and Gionin had the job with the electric company, we got along better. My children got bigger too. So then I used to hide a little money from the food so I can go to the shows. That one afternoon in the week I had home from the scrubbing I hurried up and did my washing and prepared the supper; then I'd run. But sometimes the show was long, and I'd see it start to get dark. I'd have such a scare I'd run all the way to get home before my husband came. I was going in the front door and quick put on the apron, because Gionin came in the back door—from the back street through the alley. Once he caught me. It was that time he was working in the night. As soon as he started for his work, I put on my shawl and I beat it. The snow was to my knees, but I didn't care, so long as I could see the show. But Gionin came back again—he forgot his little knife. He said, "Where's Ma? Where's Ma?"

Visella said, "Oh, she'll be right away back. Probably she ran to the store."

I used to go to the drama on Clark Street. I walked way out on Clark Street near Grand Avenue. The first drama I saw was *Hamlet*. I always did like that drama. Laura Alberta, she was the actress that made all those dramas in that New America Show on Clark Street. She used to play good plays—only good plays. Oh, all the shop girls were going behind by the stage door and watching to see her come out. And she used to talk nice to those poor girls. Then she used to come to our church. Sunday morning after the mass the people were outside waiting and looking, like she was God coming out.

Once I begged Gionin so much to take me to a show, and I was doing this, and doing this, and everything he liked to please him and make him go. So when we came out it was late, and I was hustling up so we can get a good seat. He said, "To other places you can't walk, your leg hurts you so much; but to the show you can run."

The Folding of the Flag—something like that—it was a kind of a war show, we saw that time. But my husband was not like me; he didn't care so very much for the show. In that show they had beautiful scenery—beautiful! I remember they had all that paper scenery. Now no more. After that big fire the government won't allow it. Me, I took my Visella and went to see that big fire—the Iroquois fire, where the theater burned up. We didn't see the fire but we saw after, when they were shoveling the dead people on the wagon. And then we had the nerve to go right away to the show on Clark Street. (I'd like to know what they did with that New America Show. It's not there anymore.)

Yes, I was always a friend with the shows. I used to go over on Milwaukee Avenue and see the nickel show. Oh, I remember one little bit of a place with two rows of chairs and no air—but that was later when they made the moving pictures. After five or six years the police found out it was not a fit place to go in, and they locked it. Some of those other places where I used to go the police came and closed too, because they were dangerous for fire. Then there was one show near the settlement house that was not right. There were some Italian men that came out on the stage and said jokes to make everybody laugh. But they said wrong things too—all kinds of dirty things that the men like. Two of those teachers from the Woman's Club they told me one day to come with them to that place. They wanted me to interpret so they know what it was. They thought it was not right, but they had to know it to tell the government to shut it up.

But me, I didn't want to snitch. Those men were Sicilian, but they were Italian people anyway, and I was thinking maybe they didn't want to say those bad things—probably they had to say them to get the living for their children. So I said to those ladies, "Better you take somebody else, because those men are talking the Sicilian, and I don't understand very much."

So then I went to that Maurice myself—he was the boss of the show—and I told him he'd better look out and stop those dirty jokes. But he kept on just the same, and the government came and closed his show.

That Jew man that has the little moving-picture show across from my house now, he's good to me. When it's a nice picture he comes by my house and says, "You want to come tonight or tomorrow night, Mis' Cavalleri? It's a swell picture." And when he sees me come, he lets me buy the ticket and go right in the door ahead of everybody. He knows I can't stand in that line of people with my bad leg. When it's a bum picture, he doesn't tell me to come. He never tells me to come to those pictures where they won't let the children in. In those pictures I have to close my eyes almost the whole time to not make a sin.

Fran Claro

Fran Claro is a free-lance writer who also works as managing editor of *Scholastic Scope*, a magazine for teenagers. Her husband, too, is a writer and they live in the Little Neck area of Queens, New York, where they have raised a family of five children. Her reminiscence was one of the prizewinning essays of 1976 published by UNICO National, a service organization interested in encouraging the literary work of young Italian American authors, and, she says, it is for the women of her family. She plans to expand the piece reprinted here into a novel.

South Brooklyn, 1947

My mother's name was Mary. Maria Luisa was her given name. It was a beautiful name—it could have been contracted to Marisa—a very fashionable name for girls today.

Instead, she chose to call herself *Mary*—good old American *Mary*. I remember my father singing to her:

Mary . . . Mary . . . plain as any name could be . . .

My mother delighted in the song, until she heard the lines:

But with pro-pri-e-ty,
So-ci-e-ty
Will say Mar-ie.

Then she'd say, "Oh, I hate that 'Marie.' My name is *Mary*."

When we went to the stores, she'd meet her old classmates. "Hello, Marie," they would say, because this is what the nuns in school used to call her.

When she started elementary school, she spoke only Italian. She was the oldest child in the family, and she would eventually be responsible for overseeing the education—and the Americanization—of five younger brothers and sisters.

Her introduction to formal adult English started when she was about 11. Those were the depression years, and she would translate into Italian for my grandparents all the letters they received from the bank.

Years later, she remembered reading them the letter which told them that their mortgage had been foreclosed.

She escaped from her Italian world by reading. *Rebecca of Sunnybrook Farm* became her favorite book. For long hours—after she finished helping my grandmother with the younger children and the sewing homework— she would sit and read. Her heroines were fair-skinned, blond-haired, blue-eyed. She could not identify with them, but their world intrigued her.

She wanted to absorb the culture of these American heroines. Because her parents were not educated, she grew up listening to Italian soap operas and being entertained at street festivals. She rebelled against this gaudy, flashy brand of entertainment. As she grew into adulthood, her childhood dreams of American respectability grew into a determination to separate her children from a culture she had learned to despise.

She would never allow her children to get involved in any of the activities which were dear to her parents' hearts. Their culture, she believed, was not one to pass to a new generation.

I remember the Saints' days, especially the parades and the feasts. Early on a Saturday morning, the band would line up outside the church, and the marchers would assemble.

"Open the window!" I would call to my brother. "Quick, I hear the parade coming!"

My mother would say, "Run, get a pillow for my elbows."

We were safely aloof in our second-floor apartment. So my mother could join us in watching the parade, without feeling that she was taking part in it.

As the band passed, my brother would sing along:

> *Oh, the monkeys have no tails in Zambawanga,*
> *In Zambawanga . . .*

"Ma, look! The girls with the collection trays!"

"Hurry," she'd tell my brother, "get some change. No, not a quarter, a dime."

She'd thrust the money into my hand. "Here. Throw it out the window."
I'd toss the coin and yell, "Look, Ma, she got it!"

The girl would look up and smile. She was always a little too fat for the
blue rayon dress she wore.

We never watched the parade from the curb. If you were there, you were
expected to give a dollar. The maids on the Saint's float would pin the bills
to the sash on the statue and give you a holy picture.

My brother and I concentrated on the parade. My mother watched,
keeping her distance. She was safe in our little apartment.

The committee came first. These were the men who collected money all
year to pay for the affair in honor of St. Lucy—St. Michael—St. Ann—it
depended on the province they came from.

They wore red, white, and green sashes and a lapel pin printed with the
word COMMITTEE. The median age of the committee members was 65. The
parish's Italian-speaking priest walked with them.

The band played. (There were many tubas.) After the band came the
float, pulled by the strongest—and, often, the most simple-minded—young
men in the neighborhood.

Of course, it wasn't called a float. It was The Saint. Ripe young virgins in
cheap party dresses pinned the money on the overpainted statue amid a
setting of fake grass and fake flowers. It was a living Woolworth's window,
decked out for Mother's Day.

The widows followed The Saint. They were dressed in black, with black
rosaries wrapped around their hands. When they caught your eye, they
would perform an elaborate sign of the cross, kiss their fingers, raise their
eyes, and point the kiss in the direction of The Saint.

In the row of committeemen, I would see my grandfather, his face
flushed, sweating, and proud. This was *his* parade. His good grey suit—
with the COMMITTEE pin prominently displayed—was used for this one
time every year.

Oh, how I wanted to be part of that parade. I wanted to be on that float. I
dreamed about pinning bills on The Saint. But my mother was becoming an
American.

"That's not for you," she would say. "Even when you're old enough,
we're not gonna let you do that."

My father did not interfere. He deferred to her in all decisions about
raising us.

My father was the local high school graduate, and he took some pride in
being a man of letters. He could be counted on to fill out alien registration
forms and to address the tags for the packages everyone sent overseas.

"Mike, you got any boxes?" my mother would ask the grocer. "I'm making a package for Italy. I need a box."

These packages were not "for the relatives," or "for home." They were *for Italy*.

I used to think that a man stood on the dock in Naples and gave all my old clothes to everyone in Italy.

My father worked very hard, but I was never impressed with his civil service job, or even with the time he spent in Korea during World War II. All of it never impressed me the way my grandfather's work did.

My grandfather—and almost all his friends—*dug*. I was never really sure just what they dug, although I knew it had something to do with buildings.

At five o'clock, my brother and I would walk the six blocks to meet him at the subway. His heavy shoes would be caked with mud and plaster. His hands were hard and brittle, like plastic. His complexion was almost Indian red. On the way home from the subway, he would joke with us, half in English, half in Italian.

As soon as we got to his house, we would bring him hot coffee with milk and sugar. We would sit on the window sill in his kitchen, lean out on the fire escape, and see the back of our own apartment.

My grandfather smiled most of the time. He liked to play with us, and he felt proud when we walked with him. We loved being with him.

But what I found charming about him, his daughter—my mother—found embarrassing. It was to please him that she had to attend the feast that followed the parade.

Oh, the feast.

The street from avenue to avenue festooned with curlicues of colored lights and Italian flags. In the middle of the block, a bandstand erected on a level with a second-story window.

The smell of the grease, fried, refried, and refried.

The Saint's dais—a storefront where the statue stood, guarded by members of The Committee.

"*Zeppole, calzone, salsiccia forte!*" shouted the vendors.

My mother, in her patented stage whisper: "Don't eat from those stands! Look, they're filthy! He just blew his nose! Oh, it's disgusting!"

This was her litany, as she unwillingly soiled herself by dragging us through the crowd on a Saturday night.

"Please, Ma, let us stay a little while," my brother would beg.

"Only until we see your grandfather. So he knows we came."

"Here's a dime," my father would say to my brother. "Go try that game."

"No, you do it, Dad." My brother stepped aside so my father could wind up with the small, soft ball.

My father, the almost-ballplayer, winding up. For a minute, he forgot he was 27 and the father of two. He was 16, and trying out for the high school team. He made the team, but he never played a game. He had to work after school.

"C'mon, Dad!" my brother cheered.

The man with the greasy black change apron: "Here, Mister. Pick your prize."

"Take the snake on the stick!" my brother said.

The snake was black and silver and white crinkled paper with one rhinestone eye. It twirled around a skinny dowel. We waved it at each other.

"Ma," I said, "I'm hungry."

She hesitated. Then, "All right. When we walk up the street, we'll get a lemon ice. At least it's clean in the pasticceria."

"*Canta, canta Napoli,*" beseeched the voices of the widows, who brought folding chairs to set up under the bandstand. The music followed us up the street.

If we slowed down, my mother tugged at us.

"Don't dirty your dress. Watch out for that hot grease."

"Look," my father said to us, "there's your grandfather."

"Grandpa, Grandpa, look what we won!"

"*E bello,*" he beamed at us. He turned to his friend. "*Luigi, questo mio nepoti.*"

"*Una bella ragazza,*" Luigi said.

"*Maria,*" my grandfather said, "wait. *Zia* Caterina is coming."

"No, Pa. The kids want a lemon ice. Tell her I'll see her next week. Good night, *Cumpari*. Good night, Pa."

On the way up the street, we met the priest. My mother looked as if she might die. She felt naked. She had come to the feast to please her father. Now she had to face the Irish priest.

"Hello, Mary," he smiled.

"Hello, Father. The kids wanted to walk down and see what was going on," she said, blushing. Under the lights, I could see a tear in her eye.

I felt her stiffen and grab my hand. To herself, she was saying:

> Good Irish father, forgive me, but my children don't know what they're doing. You can be here because you're not one of us. You can be here because *Cumpari* Sal will put a table and chair from his bar at the curb for you and bring you a free cold beer. You can be an observer. But my kids, they want to listen to the music and eat the food and play the games. And my father, he's proud. He thinks this stinking, filthy display will do honor to a saint.

She continued to blush and smile at the priest.

"Well," he said, moving on to greet others, "I'll see you all at the nine tomorrow."

"Good night, Father," we all said.

The walk up the street to the pasticceria was my mother's Gethsemane.

My father met an old bachelor friend. "Hey, Frankie," my father called, "is Sonny here with you?"

"Yeah. He's over there with *Cump' Angelo*. You and Mary leaving already?"

"Yeah, well, you know—the kids. Tomorrow's church and all." My father was embarrassed.

Cumari Amelia, Frankie's mother, approached my mother. "Maria, you see *Cumpa* Giuan? He's with your father, no?"

Just being talked to here was humiliating for my mother. "They're over there, *Cumari*, by The Saint."

Didn't these people realize that she had to get off this street? She didn't belong here. Her children must not enjoy this!

"Listen," Frankie said, "don't forget stickball tomorrow at 11 on 18th Street."

"Yeah," my father answered. "I'll be there after we stop up and see Nana."

"G'night, Mary," Frankie said. "G'night kids."

My mother said, "Good night, *Cumari*."

"*Sta bene, Maria.*"

Finally, we arrived at the pasticceria. My father bought nickel cups of lemon ice, just for the kids. He and my mother would take only a taste.

The mixture inside the pleated, slightly waxed cup had a snowy-granular-sour-sweet taste. As the ice softened, you squeezed the cup, and the delicious lemony flavor came into the corners of your mouth. It made you lick the corners of your lips.

"Should we stop at your mother's on the way home?" my father asked.

"No, my brother's bringing his girl over tonight. We'll just go home." She sounded very tired.

The lemon ice got softer. If you folded the cup vertically in two and bit down on the waxy cup, the syrup dribbled down your throat.

My brother tried to grab the snake from me.

"C'mon, let me hold it for a while."

"Hey, stop fighting with your sister." My father rolled the snake around the stick and tucked it under his arm.

"Next year," my mother said. "we're not going anywhere near that feast."

The music became vague and distant as we neared home. But I could still hear the voice singing:

Mama . . . Mama . . . solo per te la mia canzone vola . . .

The next morning, my father—the usher—led us to our pew at the nine o'clock Mass. It was a front row seat. My mother sent us to Catholic school so we would be allowed to sit in the front of the church on Sunday. Years earlier, she had been forced to sit in the back, because she went to public school.

She was going to Americanize her children primarily through the church. She wanted her children to become Rosarians, to join the Holy Name Society and the Sodalities.

Her children would never walk the streets soliciting contributions for a saint's feast day. But every Tuesday, they might "help the pastor out with Bingo."

The "fine ladies" of the Rosary Society impressed my mother as being modern, secure, and attractive. She thought the way they let their ice cream melt in their coffee was very stylish. She admired their appearance, so different from her very dark and very Italian beauty.

She admired them without stopping to realize that she was in awe, not of Ladies of the Manor, but of Brooklyn Irish Catholics.

The church did its Americanizing well. By the time I was ready for high school—having lived through the Irish nuns under the direction of an Italian pastor—I had no real identity. I acted like all my Irish classmates, dressed like them, and excelled over most of them in grades.

But no matter what I did, I just didn't *look* like them. All the Peter Pan collars and washing granules in the world could not erase my Italianness.

In college, I started thinking about why my Italianness bothered me. Gradually, I came to realize that it bothered my mother, and not me.

I became interested in the language and the music. I learned a lot that I should have learned years earlier, and I talked to my mother about what I was learning.

My mother—because she revered education—began to listen seriously to what I was talking about. She came to realize that there could be beauty in Italian music and elegance in Italian food.

She learned that there was charm and joy and zest in the enthusiasm my grandfather shared with his friends in planning a feast.

After my brother and I became the adults she wanted us to be, she stepped back and took a long look at us. She realized that without the feasts and the church and the dozens of relatives, we would not have been the same people. After all those years, she was ready to learn about and enjoy her own culture.

She had decided to become an Italian.

Karen Malpede

Born in Wichita Falls, Texas, of a Jewish mother and Italian American father, Karen Malpede is a feminist playwright, an editor of works on theatrical history and criticism, a teacher of theater at Smith College, and cofounder of the New Cycle Theater in Brooklyn, where she now lives. Her notable anthology *Women in Theater: Compassion and Hope* is being reissued in paperback.

Malpede has said that a doubly alienating mixed background meant she did not fit any group, and that has helped her write drama that is free-ranging. For this collection she offers a most revealing and moving autobiographical introduction to a scene from her play *A Monster Has Stolen the Sun*. This unusual juxtaposition gives an unequaled insight into how a mythical Celtic play grew from the very concrete circumstance of a heritage that was part Italian American and part Jewish and, for that, conflicted and subject to violent emotions.

Malpede's "Celtic play about childbirth and parenting" is linked to vivid childhood recollections of, she says, "how it was that my father's fathering led to this moment of this scene."

Introduction

One year before my child was born, I took the plane from London to Milan to visit Judith Malina and Julian Beck, old friends whose Living Theater troupe was performing a new play in an old flower market turned into a theater for the people by the artistic wizard Dario Fo. It was almost Passover, festival of freedom, time of pogroms for Jews world over, a time of year I had learned to dread quite early in my life without knowing why. Growing up in the white, Presbyterian, affluent northern suburbs of Chicago, Passover was a holiday I had scant knowledge of. I did know that every year at spring, while my little friends were filling Easter baskets and showing off new patent leather shoes, my Italian Catholic father would escalate his rage at his beautiful Jewish wife and their two unbaptized children, and my house became, once more, a frightening place to live.

"The Last Supper was a Seder," my mother used to whisper to us as we were growing up, "and Jesus was a Jew." "Our greatest rabbi," Judith Malina, devout daughter of a rabbi, would many years later confirm. As a child I knew neither Passover Seder nor Easter Mass; I did not know it had been decreed my mother's people had killed my father's God and so I could not begin to understand the roots of the abuse he hurled at us.

Now the small charter plane bumped onto the runway. Its steel doors slid open and I walked down the metal stairway toward the Italian land. "You got cancer, Joey, because you married out of your religion," my Italian grandmother told her dying forty-two-year-old son. He was dead fifteen years by the time I landed in Milan, long enough for the wounds of those early years to mend, long enough for me to have exorcised the wild girlhood love I bore for this hurt and hurting, impassioned man. The airport was lined with young Italian soldiers bearing rifles. Fitting, I thought, to be met by the state's show of violence against its rebellious children, "Terrorists," they're called, terrorizing the terror makers with their wanton, futile acts.

Then my feet touched the ground. And the tears came, followed by the wish, which was a physical impulse, an involuntary muscular desire, to lay my body down upon the ground and kiss the good Italian earth. My father's home, though he, himself, never had set foot here and did not know the name of the town from which his grandparents had come. In the thirty-third year of my life, without meaning to, while traveling to see my friends, their play and spend the Seder with them, I had come back to my father's land, come back for him and to him, as the silent sobs which shook me as I walked to the airport bus explained.

In a year, I would bear the grandchild he never lived to see and write *A Monster Has Stolen the Sun,* the play about parenting from which a scene is reprinted here. A little girl would be born to me, a child more beautiful than I who was known to have been a beautiful baby, my father's special pride. "Dad would have liked her, he always liked little girls," my twin brother remarked in that full, kind, sad voice of his. My brother had another story; he knew too well about our father's inability to parent boys. "Your husband hates this baby," the Black nurse told my mother, a young and frightened army wife in Texas, about the sickly boy-child in the crib whose arm was nearly broken by the father's rage. And in the years of growing up, very little but ridicule for the son escaped the father's lips.

Last summer at my mother's sister's house, she told me that whenever my mother's phone calls were delayed, my aunt assumed we had all been murdered by my father, or had died in the car which he, drunken and distressed, had crashed somewhere along the freeway speeding from his mother's house to ours on Sunday nights. In his mother's house there was one book, the Bible, lying on the marble-topped round table with its white-and-gold-fringed lamp which occupied the center spot in the bay window of this second-floor brick worker's flat. Every house on the street had such a table and a lamp visible between heavy fringed curtains as we drove up. My father's father worked on the assembly line at the dairy and had a black, blistered nailless thumb never healed from an accident at the plant. He grated Parmesan cheese on the *Chicago Tribune* and swore about the stupidity of the "goddamn White Sox." My father's mother wore black shoes, stockings, dress, a small diamond cross at her neck, her gray hair neatly curled at beauty shop appointments, her one adjustment to the fashion of the New World. She looked ancient to me, always, yet lived only to be sixty-six, dying two weeks to the day before my father did. And his broken father, who lost wife and only son so quickly, turned to us and asked us not visit him again. We reminded him of Joe, he said, or of Joe's transgression, and he didn't want to be reminded.

In my early youth, I idolized these two, the dairy worker and his wife, and thought they had a wisdom of simplicity no one in the affluent suburb where I lived could know. They had been on relief all during the Depression. According to my father, he had eaten mainly prunes and worn one ugly maroon sweater. My liberal mother thought it strange that her in-laws and her husband still hated Roosevelt and always voted Republican.

As a child, I loved my grandparents' scrubbed kitchen with its big pots of sauce, the white bakery boxes full of cookies and the endless relatives who drifted in and out, big Rosa, little Rosa, big Joey and little, and Uncle Tiny who weighted three hundred pounds. A sprawling Chicago Italian family, the younger generation all wore hot jewelry and drove hot cars, some had connections to the Mafia, and no one but my father spoke correct English, as my artistic, upper-middle-class mother could not keep from pointing out. No one spoke fluent Italian, either; most had come as children to this land. "All Jews cheat, don't you think so," my grandmother turned to my mother in the presence of company and asked. And she toilet-trained my father by burning him on the penis with a fireplace poker. That was a story he told my mother in dark nights when their passion for each other and each other's hurts had brought them close.

America, how cruel you are to immigrants, ripping away culture, language, land, roots, and whatever sense of self, dignity and kindliness these things provide, all for the lure of wealth, for a chance one's only son might work his way through college and become a C.P.A.

It was brave what my parents did, breaking class and religious lines to marry in 1943. Two despised peoples, consolidating burdens in their rush to assimilate. Because he had been abused himself and had suffered poverty and prejudice, my father became the abusing male. We know now that the battering of women and children cuts across class and religious lines, but Wasps are quieter about brutality, as they are about most things, and in the Wasp suburb where we grew up no one lived in such a tumultuous house as we.

Never since have I heard such hideous language as he used, screaming at his family over fried chicken and mashed potatoes which we forced ourselves to eat so we would not have to look up and meet his eyes. Sometimes my brother would break out in nervous laughter, and that, of course, would increase my father's rage. We had learned not to answer back. Now a playwright who produces ritual plays of transformation, written in verse, I grimace at the innocence of those who write swear words for the stage and think they are being realistic; they would not dare imitate the strings of sexual, scatological invectives he hurled so regularly at us. He had a lyric poet's sense of cadence and internal rhyme, an imagist's finesse, he startled and surprised.

Does one speak this way about the dead? Perhaps it was the Catholicism, or the working class from which he came. Perhaps it was his betrayal of both when he married a kind and gifted Jewish woman and worked his way through college to become an executive. He was in too much pain to live. The cancer which ate him from the inside out seemed fitting in its horror, a gruesome metaphor suddenly run amok.

He went back to the Church a few years before he died. I used to go with him to Midnight Mass on Christmas Eve. Still in Latin, then, the Mass was a great show, and only dimly did I understand his pain, as he knelt alone with me while everyone else filed slowly to Communion and was absolved of sin. Buried, irony of ironies, on Yom Kippur day, the priest intoned, "Joseph Malpede died for his sins," and we three mortal ones sat in the first row, the Jewish wife and two unbaptized children. Once while he was dying, he sat bolt upright in his hospital bed and told us each how much he loved us and how hard he had always tried to show us love; he asked us to care for one another, and spoke like a noble man, a father, about his coming death. But the rages never ended, and once, too, a weak shadow of a man, he came screaming naked through the house brandishing a knife.

When he died, I stopped writing fiction for eleven years, and when I wrote again, it was a play about women wresting their lives back after the deaths of men like him.

I have never met a man more passionate, a man who held more fire in his soul, a man who cried as easily or seemed to love as fiercely as he raged. Without him, I would never have known so clearly the glory of the human soul which hides beneath the gaping scars life makes.

Is this knowledge visible within the scene from *A Monster Has Stolen the Sun* which is reprinted here? In it, a man is put under a spell in which he dreams he has given birth. He dances with the newborn child; he speaks the words to his small son I felt in my heart when my daughter first appeared to me. In this small bundle which he holds, work of his own loins, he sees no rival nor successor but his own great vulnerability revealed, and he does not shrink from what he sees, does not seek to murder it, does not attempt to break its arm, does not scream at it with hate. For a moment, the father comes clear to us as, potentially, a man of love, of warmth, dreamer, poet. Then he wakes from his spell, and smashes his imaginary infant hard against the rocks.

This long play is set in Celtic Ireland, a mystic culture I found because childhood had alienated me from both my Italian and my Jewish roots. But the play's central tales of father/son, mother/daughter, and the fight between women and men belong to me, my father, my mother and my brother. The play ends eighteen years later when the father gives up his power over others and rocks his grown son in his arms, in the sort of birthing motion lived out which is but dreamlike in the scene printed here. My father had this birthing motion in him, driving him; for fear of it, I think, he died. And this is my song of praise for all he was but could not be. And this is my song of praise for that part of him I would have live.

---

from A Monster Has Stolen the Sun

---

*Scene 2 (*BRIGIT, *the midwife, and* OWAIN, *the king of a small kingdom, or tuath, approach an ancient burial spot, which is marked by a dolmen, rising up out of the rocks)*

BRIGIT: Once I carried you, slung between my breasts,
    and danced here through the night.
    Now the rocks pierce the soles of my feet
    and the wind reminds me of death.
OWAIN: Once we danced together in this spot,
    our breath billowing up.
    We were the crystal waves that lept
    from the depths of the sea
    to shatter in brilliant shapes
    for the sake of eternity.

BRIGIT: This much we know, but much is lost,
  So I have brought you here as if to dream
  the future of some unbegotten race.
  This much is known, and not much else:
  how I caught you from your mother's heaving womb
  to bear you at my breast. How you stood
  shaking with desire when I aroused your sex,
  then journeyed to the center of the earth
  to spill your virgin seed into that scared cave.
  How life and death seemed one to you that once.
  All this is known, but nothing else,
  so I have brought you here as if to dream the future
  of an unbegotten race.
OWAIN: Once I knelt in awe before your shape

  (*He kneels.*)

  I stared at the weight and motion of your breasts
  and felt my own shape change.
BRIGIT: Now a passage into yet another form is asked.
  The hungry child sucking at my breast,
  the long-haired youth delighting in the dance
  have grown into a man whose time to father
  the unknown is come.
OWAIN: Is Etain already due?
  These many months have seen me turn from her.
BRIGIT: I have watched. I have not said a word.
  Etain kneels in prayer on the cold stones; she follows
  the bird's flight with her eyes. The young girls
  you chase have grown wise. You have remained as you were.
OWAIN: Etain grew large and quiet and unknown before my sight;
  she changed and, yes, I felt myself remain the same.
  So I turned from what I could not understand.
BRIGIT: And sought a new love out.
OWAIN: As you sought me when you, too, felt a need
  to bond with something vibrant and untouched.
BRIGIT: I have watched and have not said a word.
OWAIN: You know the charm that would
  have kept my love for her alive.
BRIGIT: Three things only do I know:
  The love of the life that is over and gone;
  the love of what was and will never return;

the torturous love of the unborn.
This last I would share with you.
OWAIN: Come to me for one moment out of time,
    let us be once more as we were,
    a girlish youth gasping with wonder
    and the wise woman he lay under.
BRIGIT: Back, further back in your heart,
    search for what was and has been forgot.
OWAIN: Take me back beyond that midnight spring
    when the moon lay open and full
    to a time I lay snug in your arms
    when the world was an orb of milklike flesh
    and milky smells.
BRIGIT: Back, further back in your heart.
    Back beyond time or regret.
    A creature unborn is all that is left of what was.
    I have brought you here to dream that new change through.
    You will lend your flesh and your bones
    to the greed of what is unborn.

OWAIN *squats on the ground. He feels himself to be pregnant and begins to move in the rhythms of birth.*

BRIGIT *sings the song of the solitary birth and the chorus of crows emerges from behind the dolmen to accompany her.*

BRIGIT: On a windswept hill on a mountain plain
    washed by the salt of the sea and the rain
    a solitary creature, deer, cow, pig, mare, goat,
    woman alone, squatted down to give birth.
    How many times has this story been told,
    how few the listeners. How many times
    has the labor been made to the sound
    of the wind and the song of the birds.
    And she who brought forth the unknown,
    how many times did she shiver and shake,
    caught in the moment of death, the effort that knows
    one release, form out of form, fear birthing love.
    When the lonely work was done, when she had licked
    the infant clean, who was there on that lonely plain
    to marvel at what had been made. A bandy-legged calf,
    a sniveling runt, an unwanted puck, a son to be feared,
    a daughter scorned. The lonely one and the newborn work
    of her heart rage at the welcoming wind.

OWAIN wakes. He sees the "babe" he has birthed. He cradles and welcomes the "child" he imagines is there.

OWAIN: Hello, little babe, little beast, little one.
Where have you been? Where have you come from?
A moment before you were only the faith
that the effort would end and a child would be born.
Your wet head slithers across my chest.
Your fingers grasp at my flesh.
Your eyes blink open and stare.
You are life looking up, crawling up out of your well.
You have come from the mud, from the ocean's dark you have come.
A beast flung down from the sky, heaved up from the earth's dark cave.
How did you dare to trust a love I never have known
would anchor your heart in my own?

OWAIN begins to rock the "child" when, suddenly, the crows begin a piercing, jeering call.

OWAIN: What is that sound? The crowd, the world
that calls me from the task of birth. Away,
away, away, you flat-beaked crows.
away, I am not weak.
Stop your screeching, jeering song.

(He wakes from his dream.)

What monstrous trick is done that you would lead me
through this hurt, this fear, this great exultant
effort of the heart, to leave me face-to-face
with mocking sky and barren rock.

(He chases after the crows.)

Be gone, you evil tribe of birds.
Be gone, you stinking, ugly things.

(He chases them behind the dolmen, out of sight.)

Leave me as I was,
a man whose mute and shuttered loins
hold fast against unknown, unwanted things.

(BRIGIT emerges from the dolmen, as herself.)

BRIGIT: Hush, Owain, hush. Before the rage
  which is all you can remember now,
  lived an image barely touched, inside you still:
  a wild delight at birth which turned to fear.
  Upon the sudden thought birth takes all you are,
  rips and uses you while the small thing born demands
  a love more pure than any such a torn and shattered thing
  can give.
  Owain, awake, you have been to the source,
  turned and fled, but the source of that devouring
  delight will one day claim you for her own.
  Not the birth, but love of the birth,
  Not the child, but awe of the child,
  Not the effort, but reverence before it,
  are yours.

The dawn has come. A bird's song is heard and MACHA *answers it. She is
seen in the distance, heavy with child, a burden carried on her back. She
is leaping across the rocks.*

OWAIN: Who is that?
BRIGIT: It is Macha, the poor shepherd's wife.
OWAIN: She strides with the grace of the wind or the wave
  yet her belly is heavy with child.
BRIGIT: She is half-tamed.
  She sings with the wildest of birds.
  She runs with the hind and the fox.
OWAIN: Why have I not seen her before?
BRIGIT: Her strength bids her keep to herself.
OWAIN: Where is she from? She is not of this place.
BRIGIT: She came down from the mountain last year;
  to ease the poor shepherd, who lived alone.
  She grew fond of the one she had found;
  now she carries a child under her heart.
  Come, the dawn has played itself out.
  Macha is gone from our sight. I am called
  by the light of the sun back to the tasks of the day.
OWAIN: Go by yourself back to the house,
  I would seek out that poor shepherd's flock.

Louise A. DeSalvo

Louise A. DeSalvo spent the early part of her childhood in Hoboken, New Jersey, with her parents, Louis and Mildred Sciacchetano, both children of Italian immigrant parents. An associate professor of English at Hunter College, she teaches students many of whom, like herself, are the children of working-class parents. After earning her Ph.D. from New York University in 1977, she published *Virginia Woolf's First Voyage: A Novel in the Making* and *Melymbrosia*, an edition of the earlier version of Virginia Woolf's first novel; and has co-edited *The Letters of Vita Sackville-West to Virginia Woolf*. DeSalvo has just finished her own first novel and is working on a feminist reading of the works of Nathaniel Hawthorne. She lives in Teaneck, New Jersey, with her husband, Ernest, and their two sons.

from A Portrait of the *Puttana* as a Middle-Aged Woolf Scholar

The year is 1975.

I am thirty-two years old, married, the mother of two small children, a Ph.D. candidate, on a charter flight to England with a friend to do research on Virginia Woolf at the University of Sussex in Falmer. This is the first time in my whole life that I am going away by myself. I have no idea where Falmer is, except that it is near Brighton. We have no hotel reservations. We have no idea how we will get to Brighton. But we are gloriously drunk on our third sherry, free from the responsibility of our children for a while. (We have already had enough sherry so that each child can have her or his own little sherry bottle as a souvenir when we return home.) We are, at long last, grown-ups, going to do *real* research. The next generation of Woolf scholars, in incubation. We are formidable.

I come from a family, from a cultural heritage, where women simply don't go away to do things separately from men. That is not to say that men don't go away to do things separately from women. They do. And often. But in the land of my forebears, women sit around and wait for their men. Or they watch their children and wait for their men. Or they work very hard and watch their children and wait for their men. Or they make a sumptuous meal and they work very hard and watch their children and wait for their men. But they don't go anywhere without their men. Or do anything for themselves alone without their men. Except complain. To their children or to anyone else who will listen to them. About their men and about their bad luck in having been born female.

A few years ago, I decided, like everyone else, to explore my ethnic roots. It lasted a very short time. I bought a pasta machine. Learned how to combine the ingredients for pasta, to roll out the dough, and cut it. Word got out that I was a terrific pasta maker. Then I began to realize that you pretty well know how enslaved the women of any country are by the kind of preparation their traditional foods require. Any recipe that begins, "Take a mortar and pestle . . ." now drives me into a feminist frenzy. Well, pasta making is something like that. Women who really care about their families make it fresh every day. Purists insist that if the sacred pasta dough is touched by metal pasta machines (i.e., twentieth-century labor-saving devices), it becomes slightly slippery—a quality in pasta that is akin to infidelity in wives. Oh yes, I now remember what women who do anything without their husbands are called. *Puttane*. Whores. I remember hearing stories in my childhood about how women like that were stoned to death in the old country.

Well, given a background like that, you can imagine the way I felt as we flew high above the Atlantic. There I was, a *puttana*, alone at last.

Early on in my work on Virginia Woolf, I thought that I would devote the rest of my life to carefully considered scholarly essays and books on every aspect of her life and art. Those were the heroine worship days when I blanched at the sight of her manuscripts, when I did not dare to think that she had an outhouse, much less that she and Leonard used the typescripts of her novels instead of toilet tissue, that she could be hardy enough or human enough to walk across the Downs in her beloved Sussex. I saw her as an earlier generation of critics had painted her for me—frail, weak, crazy, tortured, looking out of windows, vacant, probing the inside of her troubled psyche. . . .

I loved the sight of myself, briefcase in hand, walking up the steps of The New York Public Library, past the lions Patience and Fortitude (I would have preferred lionesses), thinking that the kid who grew up on the streets of Hoboken, New Jersey, was now walking past the painting of Milton's daughters taking down the immortal words of his verse, now walking down the third-floor corridor to the Berg Collection, now pressing the buzzer. And they were actually letting me into the sacred recess where I would soon sit next to all those famous literary scholars whose work I had read and do work of my own.

The American Dream.

And as I sat there, beginning my work, I thought that if only I could have the good fortune to be able to sit over a glass of sherry at the Algonquin, or even over a cup of coffee at Tad's Steak House down the block, with someone really famous to talk about Virginia Woolf, life would be so sweet, so very sweet, and I would ask for nothing more in this universe.

I got into Woolf scholarship quite by accident. (Or so I thought at the time.) When I was in graduate school at New York University, I took a course with the Woolf scholar Mitchell Leaska. He was in the throes of his work on *The Pargiters,* his edition of the earlier draft of *The Years.* I was enthralled with his classes. I'll never forget the day that he brought in his transcription of Woolf's holograph, the handwritten draft of that novel. I changed my mind about what I would be doing with my scholarly life in the moments it took him to read to us from Woolf's earlier version of *The Years.* Here was a more political, less guarded Woolf. I had never known that earlier versions of literary texts were available. It had never occurred to me before that one could inquire into the process of the creation of a novel and learn about the writing process and the process of revision in so doing. It sounded like detective work. It was meticulous. It required stamina. Drive. It was exciting. I too would be working with manuscripts. I think I understood that I required a grand consuming passion in a project.

I soon decided to work with the manuscripts of *The Voyage Out,* Woolf's first novel, because I wanted to catch Virginia Woolf in her beginnings where I thought she might be least guarded.

The Voyage Out is about Rachel Vinrace, a young, inexperienced woman, who accompanies her father on a trip to South America. On her father's ship, the *Euphrosyne,* she resumes a relationship with her aunt and uncle, Helen and Ridley Ambrose, and she meets Richard Dalloway, a former Member of Parliament, and his wife, Clarissa. Rachel becomes involved with two parental surrogates—Helen and Clarissa—but the relationship with Clarissa is complicated because Rachel is sexually attracted to

Richard. During a storm at sea, Rachel and he embrace. That night she has a dream that she is being pursued.

Later, when she is at Santa Marina, a South American port city, she meets Terence Hewet, who is spending his holiday there. They fall in love and decide to marry. But both are extremely reluctant lovers. Rachel dies of a mysterious illness before the couple can marry.

What I had no way of knowing when I decided to work on *The Voyage Out* was that I would have enormous difficulty keeping the problems that I was having in my life separate from the issues that Woolf was discussing in the novel. I had reached that moment of sexual reevaluation that often occurs at about thirty. Although I was married, I went through a time when I identified with Rachel so strongly that I believed I shared her distrust of intimacy. It was simpler for me to see myself in terms of Woolf's character than it was to look at my own problems. I vacillated between thinking that Rachel—and by extension myself—were typical of all women, and thinking that her hesitations (and mine) were pathological. It took many years for me to separate myself from Rachel Vinrace. It took many years for me to understand that part of the reason for Rachel's hesitation was her submerged rage at the misogyny and brutality of the men in her life—all disguised through the artifice of civilization to be sure, but there nonetheless. In the process of separating myself from Rachel, I learned not to make disparaging judgments about Rachel's behavior—or mine—but to look for the causes of that behavior in familial and societal histories. I also saw that I was letting this very close identification with Rachel hold me back, keep me in check, because my work was making me feel very powerful. And I was terrified of feeling powerful.

I wake up in the middle of the night from a dream. The dream is easy to describe, difficult to comprehend. Ishtar—the many-breasted goddess— with a face vaguely like that of Virginia Woolf but resembling my mother, in profile, has placed her hands under my armpits and has picked me up. Her face is impassive. She does not look at me, does not recognize me, stares past me. She begins shaking me—not violently, but powerfully and rhythmically. As she shakes me, all the things that define me as a woman fall off. They form a pile beneath my feet. As she continues to shake me, still staring beyond me, impassively and without emotion, what is left of me begins to shrivel into the baby doll that I remember having in my childhood. The only openings I have, now, are the hole in the middle of the little red mouth that you put the toy bottle in and the one where the water runs out, between the legs. I begin saying, in the doll's voice that I remember, "Mama, mama." Ishtar stares impassively ahead. But she stops shaking me.

Working on Woolf's composition of *The Voyage Out* was my first long project. One that would take years. It terrified me and it thrilled me. Sometimes I would feel immensely powerful, feel that I, single-handedly, might change the course of Woolf scholarship. Or I would feel impotent, wondering how I could make any contribution to our knowledge of Woolf.

I learned what it is humanly possible to do in one day; what one cannot do; that one must trust the times when no work is getting done, because it is in those fallow periods that the unconscious mind is working. I had to change the way I thought about time. I had to scale down my expectations to a human level. All of this was very hard for me to do. Every time I sat down to the project, my infantile power fantasies reared their ugly heads. I always thought that I would get more done in one day than it was possible to do. Then my feelings of potency would turn into feelings of powerlessness and despair. I slowly learned that the work could only proceed as quickly as it could proceed. (I have not entirely learned that lesson yet.) I learned that I have the same trouble that anyone else has in working, in writing comprehensible sentences, in revising them, but that if you work every day, the work will get done. I gradually realized what working on *The Voyage Out* for seven years must have been like for Virginia Woolf. I too was working on a project that was taking a very long time. There was the temptation, too, to work constantly, without interruption, to get it done more quickly. There was the temptation to work incessantly—days, nights, weekends—at the mountain of manuscripts, at the letters, diaries, and journals that Woolf had written while composing the novel.

From time to time, my husband reminds me of a moment in the days preceding our marriage. He was off at work. I was at our apartment. The place was filthy. I was trying to clean it so that we could move in. All the stores in the neighborhood were closed because of some holiday. I decided that I would clean all the tiles in the bathroom. The only thing I had that would do the job was a toothbrush. So, instead of waiting for him to come back to help me, instead of waiting for the next day to get a scrub brush which would speed the work, I took the toothbrush to the tiles. When he came to pick me up, I was exhausted and miserable, but also triumphant because I had finished.

Much of my work on Virginia Woolf's composition of *The Voyage Out* at the beginning was like that day with the toothbrush. . . .

As I recorded the progress of Virginia Woolf's days in order to figure out what she was doing as she was writing *The Voyage Out*, I started realizing that this was one hell of a woman, filled with incredible energy, so different from my original impression of her. Reading about her life in London, her visits to the British Museum, the books she read, the jaunts down to Sussex on weekends, the trips to St. Ives, to Wells, to The Lizard, to Lelant, Cornwall, the walks, the work, the lived life, fruitful beyond my wildest imaginings, her engagement with the most important political and social issues of her day, her teaching of working-class people, I began to revise my picture of her and my hopes for myself. I decided that it would be foolish of me to spend endless days alone inside libraries working on Woolf when the great woman of my dreams had spent no small portion of hers walking around the countryside, cultivating important relationships, particularly with women, taking tea, learning to bake bread, teaching, getting involved in politics, becoming an essayist, a novelist, integrating work and pleasure, and having, what seemed to me, in contrast to my boring scholarly life, a hell of a good time.

That's when I bought my first pair of hiking boots and started walking, first around the lower reaches of New York State and then, at long last, through her beloved Sussex and Cornwall, and later through Kent, Cumbria, Northumbria, Yorkshire. I retraced the trips she took while she was writing *The Voyage Out;* visited the places she visited; read the books she read; began having important friendships of my own with Woolf scholars; started teaching; began writing essays; started writing poetry; wrote a novel. . . .

I am thirteen years old. I have begun my adolescence with a vengeance. I am not shaping up to be the young woman I'm supposed to be. I am not docile. I am not sweet. I am certainly not quiet. And, as my father has told me dozens of times, I am not agreeable: if he says something is green, I am sure to respond that it is orange. I have mastered every conceivable method of turning my household into turmoil. I have devised a method of looking up at the ceiling when my father lectures me that instantly drives him into a frenzy.

In the middle of his fairly frequent outbursts, I run out of the house, feeling that I am choking, the tears hot on my cheeks. It is nighttime. I have no place to go. But I keep running. There are welcoming lights a few blocks away. It is the local library. I run up the stairs. I run up to the reading room with its engulfing brown leather chairs, pull an encyclopedia down from the shelf, and pretend to read so that I won't be kicked out. It is cool and it is quiet. My rage subsides. I think that if there is a heaven, surely it must resemble a library. I think that if there is a god, surely she must be a librarian.

It is 1957.

I am fourteen years old, standing behind the window of the bakery where I work to earn my spending money. Inside the bakery, I have to control my appetite or I will eat everything in sight and become grotesque and obese. You can't let yourself do that because boys only like attractive girls and attractive girls are always slim. What I do inside the bakery is fold paper boxes before I put the pastries and the cakes inside. And then I tie up the boxes with the red and white string that always tears into my flesh. What I'm doing is putting my appetitive self, which I am afraid will run out of control, into neatly packaged, antiseptic, pure boxes—containing it and tying it up.

Across the street, through the window, I see my friends playing endless games that involve laughing, touching, rolling on the grass. I am behind the plate-glass window, looking at life, looking at them having fun, locked away, earning money by putting buns in bags and cakes in boxes.

On Halloween, children come and paint the plate-glass window. They paint witches and goblins in black and in primary colors. Now I can't even see what is going on in the park across the street. But I still put the buns in boxes. It never occurs to me to even fantasize breaking through the window while I'm working or to wash the paint away. Or, more simply, to open the door and cross the street to the playground. Work is work. And work permits no play. I have to work. That is the way it is. Opening the door to let in the sound of laughter while working, crossing that street to the playground after work, learning to enjoy work and learning to be able to play took many years. And psychoanalysis. And work on Virginia Woolf.

Autumn 1963.

I am a senior at Douglass College. In 1963, Douglass College is the kind of school a bright young working-class woman can afford. Douglass, I think, is filled with brilliant women, and I have never seen brilliant women before. I have studied Shakespeare with Doris Falk, the novel with Anna Wells, philosophy with Amelie Rorty. I now have Twentieth-Century Fiction with Carol Smith.

Carol Smith is lecturing on Virginia Woolf's *To the Lighthouse*. She is talking about the relationship between Mr. and Mrs. Ramsay in "The Window" section of the novel. I have never in my life heard such genius. I am taking notes, watching her talk, and watching her belly. She is very pregnant. She is wearing a beige maternity dress. I take down every word, while watching to see when the baby she is pregnant with will kick her again.

I learn to love Virginia Woolf. I observe that it is possible to be a woman, to be brilliant, to be working, to be happy, and to be pregnant. And all at the same time.

Granddaughters

One of the richest mines of the Italian American imagination is the grand-parent—mythical, real, imagined, idealized, venerated, or feared. The grandparent embodies the whole tribe, the whole heritage for that—in overwhelmingly the most cases—is as far as a present-day Italian American can trace his or her descent. After the immigrant grandparent, or great-grandparent, there are just faceless hordes stretching back into the past—unknown, unvisualized, unnamed. Many Italian Americans embody the paradox of coming from very ancient roots of an ancient civilization and culture, but knowing their past only as far as a grandparent. Most often there are no written records beyond the grandparent to tell us more of our ancestry; there are no photo albums in velvet Victorian covers. In our grandparents is incorporated all of the past, all of tradition and custom, and, we imagine, some archetypal wisdom and native intelligence. We start from the people who came here.

Over and over again, in the writing, there is mention of a grandparent. Sometimes it is a dream, as in Rosemarie Caruso's vision of her grand-mother walking down to her from the moon—a benevolent vision where the harsh reality never enters—and which inspired Caruso's interesting explo-ration of tradition between mothers and daughters in a play called *Shadows of the Morning Moon*. In a poem called "the dream," which was published in *Sinister Wisdom*, Michele Belluomini writes:

> back in the old neighborhood
> cautiously picking my way among
> abandoned houses and broken sidewalks
> I am trying to follow my grandmother
> but clumsy, I fear I will fall
>
> she shouts encouragement to me in Italian
> she climbs a rope ladder to the attic
>
> words float from her mouth like water

The veneration, the awe, the wish for the strength of the grandparent is an enduring topos, ineluctable and omnipresent, a referential for every writer represented in this collection. The following two pieces, poetry by Gigi Marino, and prose by Mary Gordon, stand for the rest.

Gigi Marino

Gigi Marino is presently based in Houston, Texas, where she is employed by Exxon and works as a deckhand merchant seaman on oil tankers, saying she's "been writing steadily since being out to sea." She plans to return to Pennsylvania State University to finish her degree in English. In 1980–82 at Penn State she won several poetry prizes and while still in high school put together a collection of student writings about their coal-mining heritage entitled "Mining Folk."

Angelina

My grandmother used to buy
chickens for a quarter apiece
from the people on the hill;
she'd twist their scrawny necks
painlessly with leathery
quick olive hands
then whack off the head
with a thick-bladed hatchet
she sharpened weekly on her
grindstone in the dank,
dug-out cave cellar where
we kept drainpipes stuffed
with paper and rags
so that rats from the creek
wouldn't sneak in at night.

Saturdays we washed clothes
there in the wringer in that
low-ceilinged stone-hole,
far from a child's paradise.
Upstairs noodles dried
on clean white sheets
draped over beds and chairs;
we blessed a huge tub of dough
with the sign of the cross,
then punched it down
and turned it into bread.
For supper she served
broiled knobbly chicken,
a few potatoes, dandelion greens,
and always: bread.
We sweated all day for Sunday,
a clean house and spaghetti.
She'd start the sauce before Mass,
then made sure we ate it all:
"*Mangia, mangia,*" she crooned,
"Tank God you don't got no tb."

My grandmother was always old.
I have a picture of her young,
maybe thirty, in the 1920s.
Already she'd started shrinking,
sitting outside on a footstool,
thin legs tightly pressed,
hands clasped, Mona Lisa lips,
eyes dipped with sadness.
Five babies too many,
not enough time to sew
the aprons that she sold
door to door, saving pennies
to buy the house where
she spent the first month
picking roaches off the walls.

My father, she didn't want—
she punched her belly, as if
dough, threw herself down steps,
still he stayed inside her;

she visited a doctor, with
Nicky, a small boy then, at
her skirts; the doctor said,
If I kill the one inside you,
I have to kill this one first.
Gramma never said that was sin;
but, "Don't let no boys
look under your dress."
That was a sin as bad as stealing—
Gramma called thieves "Black hands,"
men who waited by the tracks
behind her house for men
on payday on their
way to the beer garden.
Booze was sin too, worse,
because her husband drank,
but yearly her kitchen filled
with wine air of boiled grapes
that she grew and picked—
gallons of dago red she jugged,
and let go to vinegar
hidden in the dark cellar.

Her eyes went bad first,
suddenly, glasses, no good,
"I know your voice,"
then she knew everyone,
stopping people in the streets
to hear their voices, to hug
them and say, "I love you,"
to every stranger she met,
swearing it was 1944 yet.
She quit planting gardens,
but the ground, so fertile,
sprang to life each year:
roses, poppies, garlic,
tomato, pepper grew side by side.
Still she knew which was the
flower to place in the vase
in front of the plaster Madonna.
The fig tree out back
quit blossoming, her grape vines

fell, she didn't notice,
tv did her no good, those
voices, senseless to an old woman.
But children's voices she
understood, those, ageless.
She remembered her family's names,
Pearl Harbor, some broken Italian.

Daily she tracked miles,
to church, to town—
towards the end, sometimes
wearing only a slip, coat, boots.
People in church gasped,
called my father to come get her;
she smiled all the way.
My parents finally dressed
her in street clothes each night
never knowing when and where
she'd go, nothing stopped her.
Until the day they laid her
in a strict hospital bed.

The day I visited her
she asked if she was in church;
she looked like an angel misplaced;
her hair, long undone, all silver,
the sanitary hospital smock
floating over her thin body,
she, knowing somehow that I
knew, ran her thin hands across
my face and felt the
tears she couldn't see.
Two days later, my father
walked into the room,
she was screaming,
the angel had flown—
and left the body,
small, calm, smiling.

I waited each night at the wake
for her thin hands to grab me,
hold me close to her, hugging.

But when I touched the fingers,
stiff, like tough roots
growing above ground, I
knew their movement done.
But even as my sisters and I
carried the casket, I thought
she'd jump out, demand to
walk that church aisle by herself
as she'd done for the last
fifty years, stopping
at each pew to tell
strangers, "I love you."

I bless my dough each time
I make bread—
four hands punch it down:
Mine, young and strong,
and two old, skinny ones.

Mary Gordon

Surely the least known of Mary Gordon's outstanding literary achieve-
ment is her publication in the first issue of UNICO National's *A New
Day*, the literary magazine featuring award-winning authors of Italian
American heritage. In addition, she has published stories in *Ms.*, *Redbook*,
Mademoiselle, and *Virginia Quarterly Review*, and received the Emily
Clark Balch Award for Fiction. Her first novel, *Final Payments*, was widely
acclaimed and nominated for the National Book Critics' Circle Award. Her
second novel is *The Company of Women*, which critically established her as
"her generation's preeminent novelist of Roman Catholic mores and manners." Mary Gordon was born and raised on Long Island of a father who was

a Jewish convert to Catholicism and a mother of Italian-Irish immigrant stock. She has a daughter and a son born of her second marriage, to Arthur Cash.

Zi'Marietta

My grandfather was always afraid of Zi'Marietta, his youngest sister, and he passed his fear on to the rest of the family. Nevertheless, all the stories in the family canon that revolved around her were told to make her look foolish, carping, trivial, or vain. My grandfather never told any of these stories himself; neither, however, did he prevent their telling by his wife and children. The burden of feeling inferior to a younger sister was thus relieved guiltlessly. If his own children could laugh at his sister, grandpa's thralldom was only a temporary one: it would end with his death; it was a private, terminal weight, and not a legacy. For Zi'Marietta represented to my grandfather refinement, distinction, elegance, gentility, and these were a difficult baggage for the catch as catch can America he had moved into. Still, Grandpa valued the idea of Zi'Marietta and what she stood for, and he would never allow his wife or his children to contradict or criticize her—to her face, that is.

By the time I knew Zi'Marietta, she was in her late sixties, a small woman who always wore black and indicated, by her posture and her tone of voice, genteel but final defeat. It was difficult for me to associate this small, aged lady with the virago of the family stories.

"You have small feet," she said to me. "That is the sign of a lady. No one else in your family has small feet." She offered me old pairs of her shoes, worn, but well made. This was the '50's, however, and the demarcations between the shoes of old women and the shoes of fashionable girls were clear and final. But I accepted the shoes with the guilt and anger of the young who receive what they do not want from the old: guilt that I did not want these gifts, anger that I felt forced to take them, anger, too, at an old woman who did not know the right things to give. I have always felt the pressures of politeness, and I kept the shoes in the bottom of my closet until I left home, long after Zi'Marietta had died.

"If you read," said Zi'Marietta, "read the things that a cultured gentleman likes to talk about. Don't read things that no one likes but yourself. That will only keep you lonely."

I never asked her to explain; I don't remember the titles of the books she read in the room that was always in semi-darkness. I didn't listen to what she said about my nails and my complexion, about what one could indicate to a man by a tilt of the head or a turn of the ankle. She died in 1964, while I was away at college, priding myself that I was above all these tricks, these valueless and illusory skills that women had depended upon for centuries. The style then was to affect no style, and what did Zi'Marietta stand for but style, with all its bald implications?

And besides, I had heard stories about her. She was not a good woman, they had said. There were dark tales about what she had done to *Nana*, her mother. My grandmother said that *Nana* had begged to come and live with her son, even though his wife was not Italian, could not even speak the language, because of what her daughter had done to her. The family said that after *Nana* could no longer walk, Marietta sat her on the toilet in the morning and wouldn't let her move until it was time for bed. Marietta had driven her husband away from her, had killed him with her demands, they said Uncle Arturo, called Uncle "Toot" had had the loudest laugh in New York until he married Marietta, they said. Everyone loved him; he would give the shirt off his back, they said. He worked on the docks and died of a strangulated hernia. Everyone said it was Zi'Marietta's fault, and I didn't understand why. The family said I would understand when I was older, when I could see how a woman could empty the life out of a man with looks, with silences. And she had killed her daughter, they said, poor Rose who was always so sad, who ran herself down to wait on her mother, who was given nothing but abuse for her pains. All the pictures I saw of Rose showed a girl who had been born old, who had dark circles under her eyes even as a child. She had not had the freedom or the time to be even wistful, which might have been her salvation. She looked ill-fed, wearied, not from a great sorrow, but as though her feet had always bothered her. Now, they said, it was well for Marietta to say what a good daughter she was, now that she was under the ground.

I couldn't bring myself to believe that this failed, but glamorous old woman, with her perfectly manicured nails, her thick, coiffed hair, had caused such misery. It was easy for me to ignore her, to visit her in the old people's home at Christmas, to say I would come back soon, and then to forget until the next Christmas. It was easy for me to take part in the family jokes, to use the family expression, "She's pulling a Zi'Marietta attitude," to mean that someone was being high-falutin' or putting on airs. It was easy for me to think of her ornate crystal and elaborate silver as "old country" and irrelevant, like the rest of the family. It was worse than that, they said (and I went along); it was hypocritical, for everybody knew Zi'Marietta had nothing, had been supported by my grandfather since her husband died.

My grandfather had never wanted Zi'Marietta to work. He was a jeweler, proud of his craft, proud of his ability to pay a year's worth of bills in one day at Christmastime, when the rich bought their jewels. He paid for Marietta and *Nana* to come to New York from Sicily in 1905. He had been here three years and had a place for them to live in West Hoboken, New Jersey.

Zi'Marietta was content to stay home for a while, but then she became bored and restless. This was America, she wanted to make money; she wanted to go into the city to work. No, said my grandfather, he was the head of the family; even though their father was dead, he could provide for his sister and his mother. Behind his back, though, Marietta went to work for the local dressmaker, and then went to New York to work for Macy's. My grandfather worked long hours; he never knew that Zi'Marietta went into the city all day, and *Nana* did not betray her daughter's secret. Zi'Marietta kept all the money she earned in her jewelry box, along with the diamond earrings my grandfather had made for her eighteenth birthday. The truth came out, however, when my grandfather had to deliver a bracelet to Macy's, and saw his sister. He was a gentle man, but he felt he had been deceived by his little sister, and so he was furiously angry, Not at all penitent, either for having disobeyed her brother's wishes, or for having lied to him, Marietta assumed a wounded posture. My grandfather, stricken with guilt, said she could continue to work, as long as she kept the money for herself, and allowed my grandfather to pay her expenses and her carfare. She agreed, and my grandfather was relieved that his sister had forgiven his vicious temper with such grace.

It was through Zi'Marietta that my grandparents met. Marietta made friends with an Irish girl whom she worked with at Macy's. My grandmother was a strapping woman, twice the size of the delicate Marietta, and people laughed when they walked together on the street. But my grandfather did not laugh; he fell in love, proposed marriage, but asked for a long engagement so that he could break the news to his mother and sister, the news that the girl he was going to marry was not Italian.

Nana accepted the news, if not happily, with loving resignation. Zi'Marietta retired to her bedroom and did not join the family for three days. She would have to quit her job, she said; her health was deteriorating; she was beginning to have fainting spells again. And so, my grandparents put their wedding off for two years, until Zi'Marietta married Uncle Toot and moved to Brooklyn. My grandmother deeply resented this, and remembered it for the rest of her life, as she remembered that Marietta had called her a peasant, and told my grandfather that he was marrying a girl who had spent most of her life with cows. Grandma was clever enough, however, never to express her opinion of Zi'Marietta in direct ways that my grandfather could directly counter.

The most famous Zi'Marietta story presents my grandmother as hero of the cold war with her sister-in-law. Besides the unfortunate Rose, Zi'Marietta had a son named Joe, a repulsive child who grew into an even more unpleasant adult. Joe was his mother's darling. He had been born, to Zi'Marietta's everlasting guilt, with a club foot. He had been spoiled before his father's death; afterwards he was doted upon with obsessiveness common in, if not peculiar to, widowed mothers of only sons.

My Uncle Nick was the same as Zi'Marietta's son Joe, and to bring them together was to guarantee bloodshed, or at least major destruction of property. They were both twelve this day, and they were juggling with oranges. My grandparents and Zi'Marietta sat near them, watching the two boys laconically as they drank coffee. There was the predictable crash. Joe had sent an orange through the windowpane. My grandfather rose, and as if by reflex, took off his belt and thrashed his own son. Nick didn't murmur; he accepted his unearned punishment in dignified and wounded silence, and disappeared discreetly out the back door.

It was obvious to everyone that Nick had been unjustly punished. Zi'Marietta told Joe that he shouldn't pay attention to Nick when he suggested rough play. Joe, she explained to my grandmother, was a delicate boy, and couldn't allow himself to become over-excited. At this point, Joe dissolved in tears, and told his mother he wanted to go home. Zi'Marietta finished her coffee slowly, put on her gloves, and rose to leave. My grandfather said that my grandmother would be glad to drive her home. Zi'Marietta said they would have to go quickly, because both she and Joe had to have a nap in the afternoon; he for his health, she for her beauty.

My grandmother placed the coffee cups in the basin and quietly walked out of the door toward the car. My grandfather stood at the kitchen door waving, waving, as his wife, sister and nephew drove away. Zi'Marietta stared down at her gloved hands; Joey sniffled in the back seat.

When my grandmother came home, my grandfather was contrite, but silently so. He told my grandmother to tell Nick not to encourage Joey to roughhouse.

In silent rage, my grandmother closed her hand around a coffee cup, breaking it in two. She cut herself badly from fingertip to wrist. Blood spurted into the sudsy water in the sink. My grandfather went pale, and bustled to get iodine and bandages. He filled a basin with water and put it on the kitchen table.

"Come here, *cara*," he said to my grandmother, "let me bathe your hand."

My grandmother walked silently to the table, with the solemn dignity a smaller woman could not have brought off. Still silent, she sat next to her husband and let him bathe and bandage her wounded hand. Her husband kissed her bandaged hand in wordless contrition.

They never spoke of what had caused my grandmother to break a cup in angry frustration. It was much later that the incident became a family joke, an example of Zi'Marietta's meanness, my grandfather's fearful impetuosity and husbandly tenderness, my grandmother's Northern and stoic restraint. No one one ever wondered what it was about Zi'Marietta that inspired my grandfather to punish his own son rather than embarrass her, that inspired my grandmother to wound herself rather than criticize her sister-in-law to my grandfather. What remained was the image of Zi'Marietta looking down at her hands in the car, not even waving to her brother, who stood at the kitchen door. No one realized that my grandmother was implicated in this nexus of anger, fear and silence—it was simply a funny story to illustrate the differences in people's tempers.

When Zi'Marietta died she left me her silver-backed brush and comb. "Brush your hair five-hundred strokes a day," she had said, "and put olive oil on your hair after you wash it. American girls kill their hair. Your hair is alive; it is your glory as a woman."

For many years, I kept the comb and brush in its box, shoved away in the back of a drawer. Now I have begun to use them, not often, but at those times when I most need to feel like a beautiful woman who has come from a line of beautiful women. When I most need that weight, Zi'Marietta's heavy silver comb and brush are there for me.

And this is important: what the family forgets when they talk about Zi'Marietta is that she was a beautiful woman, that she turned heads on the streets of New York for thirty years, that Arturo Cavalcante had married her for this reason: she was the most beautiful woman he had ever seen. This was what gave her her airs: she wanted manners that would make her difference clear, that would preserve her distinction when age had destroyed it. Her plan had worked, but not in the way she wanted. She did have distinction, but it was the distinction of the lonely, not the distinction of the revered. Why did it go wrong? There are a million considerations—of time, of economics, of geography—of the factor that Americans never want to admit is determinative: luck.

The silver comb and brush lie on the top of my dresser, heavy, archaic, ornate as history, singular as heritage. When I raise my arms to brush my hair, I can only go on for a little while. In another time, women brushed their hair for hours with these, the instruments of their craft. These women, like Zi'Marietta, gave their lives, their precious, precious hours, to beauty. I have never had enough hours in my life. I brush, count to one hundred, stop and move quickly to something else. How could I go on longer?

NONFICTION

Frances Winwar

Born Francesca Vinciguerra, May 3, 1900, in Taormina, Sicily, she became the writer Frances Winwar in 1927 upon the publication of her first book, the historical novel *The Ardent Flame*. Her parents had immigrated to America when she was still a child and she began very soon to write in English; at eighteen she was sending her work to Max Eastman's *The Masses*, and later reviewing books for the *New York World*, and subsequently *The New York Times*.

With the publication of her first book, she settled into a career of biographical writing, specializing in the nineteenth century with a series on the great English literary figures of that time. Among those works, *Poor Splendid Wings*, a biographical narrative study of the Rossettis and their Pre-Raphaelite circle, is especially noteworthy for having won in 1933 the important Atlantic Prize of five thousand dollars for nonfiction. The list of her ensuing publications is very long and includes fiction, translations from the Italian, and history for juveniles, but she is chiefly known for her biographies of famous people told in an engaging narrative style which conveys the authenticity of the period, the complexities of the lives she is dealing with, and the excellent rendering of the many famous personalities with whom her subjects were involved.

Frances Winwar was married to Jerome Roman, by whom she had a son, and whose name she used at the beginning of her writing career when she signed herself Francesca Vinci-Roman; subsequent marriages were to Bernard Grebanier, Richard Webb, and Francis Lazenby. She now makes her home in Florida with her son. She is the only writer of Italian American background listed in *American Women Writers*.

from Poor Splendid Wings

When the four Rossetti children were still young, on the evenings when the paternal sitting room had been too noisy with the polyglot oratory of the Professor's visitors they would go to the boys' garret and spend together the hours before bedtime. Sometimes Maria, the eldest, read aloud, while Gabriel and William colored stage prints, and Christina, the youngest, listened, her grave eyes fixed on her sister's lips. Sometimes they would peep into some formidable tome, always whispered of as *sommamente mistico*, over which their father, with his long-peaked cap shading his face, pored for hours at a time. They would shut it with a gasp of awe at the mountains of black-letter and furrows of small type covering the bottom of the page. Their favorite pastime was working out sonnets from end-rhymes, at which Christina excelled. There were nights, however, when the thunderous company overstayed, and serious amusements palled. On those occasions the children played cards. Through some quirk of fancy they had come to identify themselves with the four suits: Maria with the clubs, Gabriel the hearts, William the spades, and Christina with the diamonds. In three cases, at least, the choice was prophetic.

Christina at eighteen showed nothing of the hard, glittering quality of the diamond. James Collinson, tame and shrinking, had not been awed by her, though she did so much resemble Gabriel's Mary, Virgin, for which she had sat,—

> As it were
> An angel-watered lily, that near God
> Grows and is quiet.

Outwardly Christina was soft and womanly, her rare gayety lighting briefly the meek gravity of her face. But within, where Collinson had not the sight nor the understanding to see, there was a keen, white sharpness, protecting, like a coat of armor, something she held above the treasures of the world. Not that she did not yearn for the gifts of life. Her lips were arched and full for the luscious fruit, though ready to tighten at a whisper from within. The wide-winged nostrils, like Gabriel's, sensitive to the fragrance of living, quivering with the breath of her being, betrayed a struggle the set face would not reveal. To Collinson, as to those who saw her with her brothers, she was a good girl ripe for marriage, who would make a virtuous wife and a dutiful mother. That, her household duties over, she would steal away to her room and write verses, such as had already appeared in print, need not have frightened an eligible groom.

Indeed, any fond grandfather with a printing press in the shed of his garden would have done as much for a pretty niece with a penchant for versifying. In 1842 old Polidori had printed a translation of Maria's; two years later the press in the Regent's Canal garden had produced Gabriel's *Sir Hugh the Heron*, which he would not now hear mentioned. Then had come Christina's turn. But Grandpa Polidori had had nothing to do with the publishing of Christina's poems in the reverend pages of the *Athenæum* in 1848.

From the day Gabriel had introduced Collinson to his family there had been a tacit understanding that Christina's affections were engaged. James came of a solid family, Christian and respectable. He attended the same church as the Rossetti women, and in behavior was devout and mild. Nothing could be said against him except, perhaps, that he had none of Gabriel's dash or William's good sense. He seemed too easily led—but then, that was not always a fault.

By the time the *Germ* was talked of, Christina and Collinson were looked upon as betrothed. William had even visited at the Collinsons' for a number of weeks, during which he had indited much informative correspondence to Christina. Nothing stood in the way of the future marriage.

Collinson, meanwhile, roused by his love out of congenial torpor, did what he could to please Christina. He worked long at his portrait of her, in emulation of Gabriel's, but the two paintings were as unlike as if two different women had posed for them. Gabriel's, lit with spiritual beauty, gazed out "strong in grave peace"—the soul itself painted. Collinson's was a simple English girl, gentle, but not burdened with intellect. He saw her, he wanted her, that way—and as Leonardo painted himself in Mona Lisa, Collinson drew a self-portrait in Christina.

Perhaps in those hours when he saw her clearly he may have felt a sense of want in himself; perhaps the activity of his companions stung him to rival them. At any rate, when the brethren were all enthusiasm in the preparation of their magazine, he wrote a long, blank-verse poem, and illustrated it. Gabriel acclaimed both poem and etching. The stunner had at last done himself justice. Christina would be proud of him.

Christina was proud; but also saddened. For some months her love had given her little happiness. James had changed, and she knew what caused the change. It was not that he loved another; that Christina would have understood, and in herself the image of him would have been treasured as an unalterable relic. It was the image itself that had altered, superseded by the reality of the man. He was a weakling. Though she had long hidden the truth from herself, averting her eyes to fill them with the pleasanter aspects of his talent and manhood, she could do so no more.

Again she read over the script of his poem, the "Child Jesus":—

> Joseph, a carpenter of Nazareth,
> And his wife Mary had an only child,
> Jesus . . .

She had loved it because James had written it, and because it was beautiful; but the reading of it gave her pain. Brought up as she had been in the Church of England,—though with Puseyite leanings,—she had no sympathy, however, with anything that hinted of Rome. Collinson had strong tendencies in the direction of ritual and mysticism. Lately he had forsaken her church. Again, he had confessed to her that before their meeting he had been converted to Catholicism, but that upon learning that the difference of their worship would have stood in the way of their understanding, he had returned to his former faith. Christina was a devout member of her church. Religion was the one thing in which she would neither make, nor accept, compromise. Scrupulous to bigotry in her morality, she had already given up the theatre and the opera, arguing that since actors and singers were of easy virtue, it was one's Christian duty to discourage their performances. How much more was one to discourage laxity in faith!

She read James's description of what had been their dream of home—an English home, though he laid it in far-off Nazareth:—

> A honeysuckle and a moss-rose grew
> With many blossoms on their cottage front. . . .

Blossoms like those at her maiden aunts' at Holmer Green, where she had spent heavenly weeks in her childhood. She could see with James

> The orange belted wild bees when they stilled
> Their hum, to press with honey-searching trunk
> The juicy grape; or drag their waxèd legs
> Half buried in some leafy cool recess
> Found in a rose. . . .

He must have watched those bees in the garden of his home. Yet at the very time Collinson had been writing of flowers and bees she had been describing another dream land, in a dirge for an imaginary girl she had wept for in her heart.

> Where sunless rivers weep
> Their waves into the deep,
> She sleeps a charmèd sleep:
> Awake her not.
> Led by a single star,
> She came from very far
> To seek where shadows are
> Her pleasant lot.

Again and again, then when she had loved most and seemed most happy, she had written of that one who died in sorrow. In the abundance of a brooding imagination, she decked bier and funeral chamber with the flowers of her art. Sometimes she recognized herself in that corpse.

> The curtains were half-drawn, the floor was swept
> And strewn with rushes, rosemary and may
> Lay thick upon the bed on which I lay.

And once, in suffering for which she would confess no reason, she had written with trembling hand, pressing her breast against the washstand in her room,—

> Have patience with me, friends, a little while:
> For soon, where you shall dance and sing and smile,
> My quickened dust may blossom at your feet.

Why that gloom at the height of her happiness? Why the incessant mourning for that unhappy maiden of her imagination? Sometimes when her mother had tried to look too searchingly into her thoughts, she had turned away. To *her* she could not have lied as she was lying to herself. Had she borne that gaze longer, she would have had to avow that all those dead girls were dead selves, selves that she had wished dead, rather than in love unworthily. Yet she did want to love. She had given James love that was neither for mother nor brother. What had come to threaten it? Inquire as she would, she did not know. Not with her mind. But there were many things she felt, and in her feeling she had glimpses of clues to which she hastily shut her eyes.

She was attached to her mother. In that household, the head of which the children never remembered as other than elderly, Mrs. Rossetti was the teacher, the guardian, and, in all mildness, the playmate. When Professor Rossetti came home, his chair would be waiting for him by the fireplace, the Dante tomes open where he had left his abstruse researches. There he remained for hours unmolested. Occasionally a volume in Italian would appear, bearing his name on the title page. Profound, and of recondite learning, the Professor's studies on Dante were as far removed from Victoria's England as the works of some obscure monk in the thirteenth century. Only Maria would read them, admiration in her eyes. However, when not bent over his books or entertaining his nondescript revolutionists, the Professor was a doting and tender father, whom his children treated with the same respect his pupils had for him at King's College.

Gabriel and William had been sent to school, like other boys. Maria and Christina were taught entirely by their mother. By a tacit understanding the girls followed their mother's faith; and, since the Professor was in no sense religious,—leaning rather dangerously toward freethinking,—the male members of the family were left to make their choice. Nevertheless Mrs. Rossetti watched zealously over them all, and, if one of the boys seemed in danger of straying,—as when Gabriel stood accused of reading such immoral books as Shelley's,—she pulled him back firmly to wholesome pastures. It had never been necessary to play tithingman over Christina. Her mother's word was law; her look, command—not that Mrs. Rossetti had ever had to command her younger daughter, the most devoted of her devoted children. It was enough for Christina to give her pleasure. She was eleven years old when she wrote her first poem—to her mother, on her birthday.

Except for rare absences, when the girls took places as governesses to sustain the family budget, mother and daughters were never parted. Separation was torture to Christina. She worshiped her brothers, Gabriel especially, though she felt more comfortable with William, nearer her age. Gabriel had always been looked upon as the hope of the family whom the others might approach but never overshadow. In Christina's mind standards were set by Gabriel's accomplishments and by William's virtues. She had had few opportunities for measuring other youths against her brothers—or, indeed, other men, outside the odd friends who came to see the Professor. Her life was bounded between home and her family, the church and her mother.

It was like the discovery of a new realm for her when her brothers began going out into the world. At first she glimpsed it in reflection, through the mirror of their reports; little by little she set a timid foot in their domain, though with her eyes turning backward for maternal guidance. Sometimes that world was brought to the decent drabness of Charlotte Street, and the drabness colored through its magic. But it was not for long. Instead, the world claimed Gabriel, who from then on came home, in the young girl's eyes, as a voyager bearing strange and wonderful tales of places that were not hers to behold. She lived vicariously through his adventures, and if at times her cheeks flushed before her mother's gently lifted brows, her lips were quickly humbled to silent apology.

Then had come Collinson and the other young men. They trooped to Charlotte Street—a jolly, well-mannered crew, converting the bare living room into a gay agora alive with youth and ideals. That happened seldom, and then it ceased altogether. Gabriel, however, took to inviting Christina to his studio, where she sat for his paintings. She loved it there; for, even when he drew away to the apartness of his work, life filtered in as persistently as light through his windows. At times she had been at the studio scarcely ten minutes before it was ringing with the voices of as many friends. James came oftenest.

In the beginning she had not been drawn to him. He was retiring in his ways, dull in his speech. Beside Gabriel with his bluff manliness, James seemed weak and pale. But then, few of Gabriel's friends could measure up to him. Millais might be handsomer, in a conventional sense, but he did not possess that fire from within that lighted her brother's face as he spoke and lent warmth to his actions. Woolner was uncouth in his speech: she was a little afraid of him. Hunt she found difficult of approach. Obsessed by his mission, he had little thought for anything else. Collinson was always at hand, with touching, if awkward, attentions. He was hopelessly plain. She had to admit that, whenever she looked from his to Gabriel's sensitive face with its spacious brow and fine, speaking eyes. Yet she took kindly to him, and whenever Gabriel spoke well of him and his work, her lids were moist with gratitude. She was content when she did not make comparisons, and it was then she allowed the joy of love to come into her life.

Unused to the precious gift, at first she had contemplated it in secret, dandled it, treasured it jealously, sharing it with none.

> My Mother said: "The child is changed
>> That used to be so still;
> All the day long she sings and sings
>> And seems to think no ill;
> She laughs as if some inward joy
>> Her heart would overfill."

But as the months wore on, an inexplicable melancholy possessed her, and she had no more pleasure at the thought of her love. That something, perhaps in James, perhaps in herself, robbed it of bloom. Oddly, when she was definitely promised to him, she wept for love as dead, made it a grave among the flowers and laid a stone at its feet. Setting the scene for herself and James, she wrote even the words they might say of the present, become past.

To few chords sad and low
Sing we so:
Be our eyes fixed on the grass
Shadow-veiled as the years pass,
While we think of all that was
In the long ago.

"When I am dead, my dearest, sing no sad songs for me," she could say, envisioning the ultimate sundering.

She had to confess disillusionment; but she could not blame James wholly. It was no fault of his if he was timorous and weak; no fault of his if he could not ever approach Gabriel. His home was not the home that could be hers. His mother—what angel could ever take the place of her own? The fledgling dove she had brought out to see the sun shrank back and was afraid. The tremulous wings folded closer to the nest.

Yet her heart mourned for James and for herself. She loved him as much as she could ever love any man not her brother; but that love was not sufficient. She dreamed of a hearth and children of her own; still, the maternal breast was sweet, the home nest safe. Passion stung her, wakening her virgin senses; the curb of devotion to her mother and her faith pulled her away. The months were eternities of struggle that left her weary and with her problem unsolved. Only in the haunting vision of death, with rest at last in the lap of earth, she found appeasement.

Barbara Grizzuti Harrison

Born in Brooklyn, New York, Barbara Grizzuti Harrison again resides there with her son and daughter after travels which have taken her to India, Libya, Guatemala. Her articles have appeared in many important publications and some of her essays were published in the collection *Off Center* (1980). She is also the author of *Unlearning the Lie: Sexism in Schools* (1973), *Visions of Glory* (1978), and a novel, *Foreign Bodies* (1984).

Godfather II: of Families and families (1974)

When my radical friends cottoned to the fact that I was a *Godfather I* junkie, I was quick to anticipate and disarm criticism by arguing that while it was possible for a *lazy* audience to understand from *The Godfather* that Mafiosi went around knocking off only one another in internecine wars, making offers that couldn't be refused only to other pestilential pigs, leaving the rest of the citizenry to go about their God-fearing ways in peace, an *intelligent* audience could easily extrapolate the truth from Coppola's film— which is that the Mafia ruins small lives, destroys innocent grocers as well as rival dope-dealers. *The Godfather,* I said, bore witness to the bitter truth: evil, hydra-headed, renews itself and triumphs in the end; in America, the Corleones win.

To which my radical friends said, *Bullshit:* "Don Corleone and Sonny and Michael were all so damned attractive. They were killers, but one liked them just the same. Their evil was mitigated by their charm." And my brother said, "You liked it because you're Italian." And of course my friends, and my brother, were right. I had not, after all, seen *Godfather I* six times for the pleasure of witnessing the triumph of Evil over Good. I saw it because, in spite of its celebrated violence, it was perversely comforting and warm; it had a uniquely tender, cradling quality. Each time I saw Don Corleone die his rose-garden death, I was set squarely in that fabled place where families honor, respect, support, and protect one another, *touch* one another, forgive one another their sins. Viscerally I understood the Corleones better than, say, the Louds (and I liked them better, too). *The Godfather* nourished the notion that there was someone, some force, who could absolve guilt and make all the hurt go away, someone whose accepted authority could gentle and sustain us.

"Heresy," my feminist friends snorted. "You are talking about patriarchal families who have no remedy for pain, families that smother you, that protect you because you're their property. Step out of line and see what they do for you." My critical intelligence—and my own experience as a third-generation Italian—told me they were right. And yet I returned, as if on a pilgrimage to an atavistic part of my nature, to the courtliness of Don Corleone, to the sanguinity and vivacity of Sonny, to the magnificent reserve of Michael—that eloquent stillness that promised everything, that promised absolution. *Godfather I* created a world analysis could not sour. I felt embraced by the film, and not just because I so rarely see the pungent gestures and rich rituals or hear the rude songs, the lyrical-vulgar dialect of my childhood, reflected in literature or art: I have a vestigial yearning to believe, damn it, that there is a safe, redemptive place, a landscape where everyone knows his or her place, where one follows, with benediction and grace, the yellow brick road to the shrine of approving family gods.

And then Coppola, in his extraordinary sequel to *The Godfather*, did more to challenge my cherished conviction that the family can be a Salvation Army than did all the harangues of my radical friends.

Consequently, *Godfather II* gave me an attack of spiritual indigestion similar to the heartburn I invariably suffer after Italian weddings. I return, always, from a family wedding blood-warm, warmed by "the blood." I think of the extravagant assurances we have all ritualistically exchanged: "You are our blood," we tell one another, "We will love you whatever you do, we are here for you." And then I think of the work some of those men with whom I've danced the tarantella and exchanged blood-love do in the world (it's not pretty); and I marvel at my capacity to be seduced by the passion and authority and vigor and charm of men whose work I cannot love. And I think—looking at their wives, who have reaped the traditional rewards of traditional lives—What would have happened to those warm, smiling women if they had chosen separate identities, if their paths had violated the ethic of *la famiglia*? Would, in fact, their men have been there for them? And then I think of my brother, who is a just and generous man, whose authority I *do* accept, who can outcharm Sonny any day of the week, who *is* always there for me, who stills my restlessness and makes me feel safe, as no one else in the world can make me feel safe. And I think of my gentle father, who has learned painfully to love his maverick daughter, who defends me even when he finds my life incomprehensible. And then I think of a few bitter women, sitting outcast and alone, who are tolerated merely because they are "the blood," but who are not protected, not loved, because in some way they have violated the sacred rules of this large, lusty family composed of good men and bad men, of strong women and selfless women. I think of the strength of Italian women, of strength perverted and strength preserved. And I am painfully confused. I want all of these people to love me, to comprehend me; I want none of them to constrain or confine me. And I know that what I want is impossible.

I would be surprised if Coppola were not also a victim of the hopelessly ambivalent feelings about family—about the bonds that both heal and mortify—that all second- and third-generation Italians suffer. I think *Godfather II* must have been a painful film for Coppola to have made.

Politically, *Godfather II* is as explicit and forthright as *Godfather I* was elliptical. It bludgeons us with what its predecessor hinted at. It says, with a specificity that leaves little room for a gentler interpretation, that we are one nation under capitalism, and that under capitalism, the Enemy is One—and the enemy includes corporate business, members of the United States Senate, organized labor, and the Mafia. It is, as Pauline Kael has aptly said, "an epic vision of the corruption of America."

Psychologically, *Godfather II* is kaleidoscopic—some have said muddled. But its confusions are *our* confusions, its malaise *our* malaise. *Godfather I* was an almost elegiac film. *Godfather II* is an ice bath. After three and a half hours spent inside the second-generation Corleones' conspiracies and psyches, I felt as if I'd been savaged, betrayed, cheated. I've spoken to Italian friends and they agree: Coppola, who gave us in *Godfather I* the romantic family idyll we all craved, forced us in *Godfather II* to test all our own troubled, troubling feelings about family. What he gave us was not entertainment, not a mythical romance that released us, briefly, from the oppression of our singularity and aloneness, but necessary pain.

There was a kind of golden aura about Brando's Don Corleone, even as he was plotting to destroy half the population of Harlem. He was a luminous goon. There, but for a few wrong turns of fate, one felt, goes a real sweetie pie of an Italian poppa. One could imagine being caressed by his caring; he was the prototypical daddy of our nursery dreams—the powerful man of the world who wipes the tears from the eyes of his babies and acts always, and only, to protect his cherished family. He was, literally, the God/Father. Don Corleone was a rock against whom one might lean. The Michael of *Godfather II* is a defoliator, a glacier. There is, about Michael, everything dark, dank, and pernicious. Charity is inimical to his nature; he feeds on the blood, not only of his enemies, but of his family. He kills his dopey older brother Fredo, destroys the womanhood of his sister Connie, and shuts his wife, Kay, out of his heart and his life and robs her of her children. As *Godfather II* ends, he is absolutely powerful and absolutely evil, locked in the solitary confinement of his own corruption, without warmth and without pity.

How well Coppola knows that in Italian families the blood calls to the blood; how devastatingly he deals with the fact that a sister needs, above all things, the approval of her brother to remain whole. When thrice-married Connie approaches Michael (on her knees) and says, with palpable self-loathing, Everything bad I have done to myself I have done to hurt you because you killed my true husband and turned me into a whore, she begs to be allowed to return to the family, *to take care of Michael*, in order *to redeem herself*. Now, for one brief (shameful) moment, I felt my heart leap: the family is back together again! Reunion! Fortunately, I was sitting next to my sister-in-law, who has lived through enough Italian melodramas and vendettas not to be so easily gulled. She introduced a note of raucous sanity into mindless sentimentality: as Connie groveled and Michael bestowed his icy benediction, my sister-in-law yelled, *"Right? There's always some woman around to pick up the pieces!"*

I would like to have seen a woman like my sister-in-law protrayed in *Godfather II*—a strong Italian woman, that is, with a built-in bullshit detector. I'm sorry that the woman who *named* Michael (who pronounced him evil) was the quintessential WASP Kay. When Kay can no longer pretend to herself or to Michael that she is innocent so long as she is ignorant, when she aborts Michael's dynastic successor, her bitter reproach is couched in words I find unacceptable: "I won't," she says, "be part of your two-hundred-year-old Sicilian thing any longer."

My Calabrian chauvinism notwithstanding, I wish Coppola hadn't allowed Kay to imply that Sicilian families have particularly bad odor. Clearly *Godfather II* tells us that crime Families stink to heaven. But what about our need for *family*? Coppola's film says brilliantly and unambiguously that the end preexists in the means—that a single small maggot of corruption, given enough filth to feed on, becomes a devouring multiheaded dragon: I gave you Don Corleone, Coppola says, and I permitted you to love him; but you should have been smart enough to know that evil breeds greater evil, and that the end result would be Michael, would be devastation.

But does Coppola not believe that families can heal? My brother and my father—who are good men—inspire me to believe. Does Coppola? I don't know. I don't know because *Godfather II* doesn't tell us. It tells us about a killer Family; its ambiguities spring, I think, from the fact that the bleakness of its vision cannot wholly disguise Coppola's need to believe. But the need to believe is not the same as belief itself. There is a tension between the need and the conviction. *The Godfathers, I* and *II*, reflect that tension, that anguish.

One thing is certain: Coppola understands the terrible hunger of second- and third-generation Italians. Caught in the limbo between the old ways and the new ways, we all want what we are quite sure we cannot have: we want to suckle forever at the family breast. I think he also understands the hunger of all Americans to believe in the goodness of human nature. What Coppola says to that is, Forget it. Bad people are bad people.

What men do in the world resonates in their bedrooms. If one's work in the world is evil, one's "love" for one's family turns into something obscene. The Michael Corleone who has a prostitute butchered to compromise a defiled and defiling senator is incapable of loving *any* woman. The protection the Corleone men offered their women was predicated on the ignorance of those women; and those women, who cultivated blindness, reaped their own destruction. The price they paid for being sheltered was the loss of their souls. I have known women like that. As long as they remain mute and unprotesting—as long as they care more for pasta than for politics—they are happy. As one is happy in a dream. The Corleone men created a dreamworld for their women; they locked them into pink and pretty closets. The closets were roomy—there was space enough for laughter and lust and love and fun. I know those closets; I know that it is possible to stay in them forever. But, for most of us, eventually the world impinges. Mama Corleone, who never questioned, never stepped outside her defined and defended world, died relatively happy in her Skinner-box closet; but even she, at the end, had a glimmer of recognition that her acquiescence had helped to produce that which Kay called "unholy, . . . an affront to God."

If *Godfather II* has a moral, it is that you cannot feed evil men and expect to be nourished by them. Evil men are never "good family men." The myth that Italian-Americans have helped to perpetuate ("Joey Gallo brings his mama roses every Sunday") an Italian-American has helped to destroy. Americans have found that myth irresistible; in these lean and hungry times, when people huddle together for warmth, when robust folk heroes are the vivid symbols of our weary desires, audiences may find Coppola's iconoclasm unforgivable.

Carol Bonomo Ahearn

Carol Bonomo Ahearn was born in the Italian section of Greenwich Village in New York City. She now lives in Providence, Rhode Island, with her two children. She is an educator and writer, and has published poetry, articles, and book reviews. She received her M.A. in English from Brown University and has received grants from the Danforth Foundation of Higher Education and the National Science Foundation for Medical Education. She is active in community affairs, serving on the board of directors of UNITAM (United Italian Americans), and as a state committeewomen.

Definitions of Womanhood: Class, Acculturation, and Feminism

With the rise of interest in ethnicity which characterized the seventies (especially with the publication of Richard Gambino's impressive and ground-breaking work, *Blood of My Blood*),there is a danger for some to carve in stone a fixed definition of what it means to be an Italian American man or woman. I wish to focus specifically on definitions of Italian American women to suggest that the range of role definitions are myriad, that a woman must know herself as an individual to determine what is best for her, and that she must also know the socioeconomic and historical context of her Italian American tradition, so that she can resolve apparent conflict between the pull of the family and of her individual desires.

I intend to use two novels, Mario Puzo's *The Fortunate Pilgrim* and Helen Barolini's *Umbertina*, to trace definitions of Italian-American womanhood from the perspective of class, acculturation, and feminism, for all three forces operate in the lives of contemporary Italian American women.

The Fortunate Pilgrim and *Umbertina* are worth looking at in tandem, because taken together they form a whole in the experience and evolution of the contemporary Italian American woman. These two novels present a range of role models, so that informed decisions can be made amidst an abundance of riches rather than a dearth of choices, thus allowing us to pick and choose as our needs change.

For purposes of clarification, I have devised a construct of four dominant stages in the acculturation process. They are by no means definitive or rigid, allow for some fluidity, and are certainly open to refinement. The first stage is the immigrant stage of trust and hope—trust in one's cultural values—and hope for a better life in a material sense; the second stage gives way to shame and doubt about one's heritage, and a vague desire for new goals in life. This stage gives rise to the third stage of role confusion, where the goals of one's heritage, one's personal goals and the goals of the new culture (in this case America) all seem to be irrevocably at odds with each other; and the last stage which I call integrated autonomy, in which all three forces are resolved in a personal manner satisfactory to the specific individual.

Lucia Santa and Umbertina exemplify the immigrant stage of trust and hope; Octavia and Carla are both beset by shame, doubt, and a vague desire for new goals; Marguerite is an example of role confusion because she fails to discover the significance to herself of her Italian American heritage; and finally Tina who integrates her peasant origins on her mother's side, her intellectual upbringing as the daughter of an Italian poet, her personal goals and her American formation.

1

Briefly *The Fortunate Pilgrim* chronicles the life of Lucia Santa Angeluzzi-Corbo and her six children through their many travails. Lucia Santa Angeluzzi, so poor in Italy that she could not even afford the traditional nuptial linens, leaves for America to form a new destiny for herself by marrying an Italian American. She is widowed while carrying her third child and eventually remarries. Her second husband, Frank Corbo, goes insane, her oldest daughter, Octavia, marries a non-Italian, her son Larry becomes a member of a protection "union," another son, Vinnie, commits suicide, and a third, Gino, who had been a ne'er-do-well, upon Vinnie's death accepts his role in life, namely to work to support his mother and the two remaining children.

At the beginning of the story, we are introduced to Lucia's reality in her first marriage:

> Her feeling had been the feeling of millions of women toward *improvident* husbands. That men should control the money in the house, have the power to make decisions that decided the fate of infants—what folly! Men were not competent. More—they were not serious. And she had already begun the struggle to usurp his power, as all women do.[1] (Italics added)

The passage is interesting not only from the perspective of what it tells us about Lucia and her view as the wife of a poor man, but also from the perspective of style. It is typical of Puzo's blending of interior monologue and narrative voice into almost one voice, and that narrative voice is female in its total understanding and acceptance of and sympathy with the immigrant woman's point of view. The message is that it is up to these women to do what they must do for the sake of their children. This biological bond gives them a fierce strength. We read that "She had an enormous strength, not unusual in women, to bear adversity." (p. 14) "It was always the men

1. Mario Puzo, *The Fortunate Pilgrim* (New York: Lancer Books, 1964), p. 33. All subsequent references shall be made in parentheses in the body of the paper.

who crumbled under the glories of the new land, never the women." (p. 115) If some heroes in Italian-American literature are Christlike and draw upon the symbols of Christianity for their world view, Lucia is Madonna-like, strong in her role of suffering and by enduring triumphing.

Only once—and momentarily at that—does Lucia allow herself to doubt and ask a philosophical question. She is thinking of the deaths of three of Teresina Caccalitti's sons in one year during World War II. Teresina, who was capable of any treachery for her own advantage, was not able to control this fate. "Did nothing help then? Was there no escape for anyone? For if evil cannot prevail against fate, what hope is there for the good?" (p. 282) We can be tolerant of Lucia's musing no more than this. Greater minds than hers have grappled with this age-old problem. Milton in *Comus* shows us that in the struggle between good and evil, evil often triumphs because it uses methods that the good will not allow themselves. Shakespeare, in his emphasis in so many of his plays on blind chance operating in our lives, has in his acceptance of its operation anticipated Lucia's query. But if Shakespeare accepts blind chance or fate, the narrative voice in *The Fortunate Pilgrim* cautions that in the face of the cruelty that fate deals each of us, heroism for a cause greater than self is sheer foolishness. We are told that Dr. Barbato's father, upon learning of his son's heroic exploits during World War II, had a stroke "from sheer exasperation at his son's foolishness." (p. 284)

Although a tragic view of life, namely a desire to do great things and suffer for it, pervades Lucia's *thinking* (she thinks of optimism as dangerous [p. 276]), a comic view of life to do great things and endure informs her actions. Though "she was pessimistic about life . . . she lived like a true believer in good fortune. She rose in the morning with gladness . . . Her hope was a physical energy replenished by her love for her children and the necessity to do battle for them." (p.166)

Lucia defines this "physical energy" which enables her to "do battle" for her children as *the* necessary ingredient in a mature woman. Octavia's expressed desire to be happy brings Lucia's contemptuous, raging retort, "Thank God you are alive." (p. 17) For all Lucia's wisdom, her reality puts enormous boundaries on her role definition of woman, so that the knell is struck for the tension that will exist between the generations. The older generation, because of their personal history of dire poverty, has, using Abraham Maslow's hierarchy of needs, only the first three levels satisfied, i.e., the most basic needs of food, clothing, and shelter, next safety and security, and lastly love, affiliation, and self-esteem. And *all* of them are satisfied through *family* ties.

But the next generation, again using Maslow, wants the higher need of self-actualization (as opposed to family-actualization), loosely described by them as "happiness" and involving an individuation unknown and impossible to the immigrants. We can also infer from the novel that it is an individuation that is also impossible for the second generation of Italian Americans. Vinnie, who commits suicide, cannot even name what it is he longs for; Octavia wants "happiness," but she needs security too much to venture forth and fulfill herself by becoming a teacher. She does not believe in her mother's values, but she also has not developed a coherent value system of her own, so that she feels an "overwhelming sadness—not specific, but general, as if her stepfather had suffered some fate common to humanity and that some judgment waited for her, too." (p. 197) It is not only Lucia but also the second generation who lacks a structure with which to comprehend these amorphous desires. However, unlike the young who feel a longing for self-actualization, Lucia feels a fear of what she cannot understand. Instead of the "general sadness" that Octavia experiences and a vague fear of the future, Lucia, born to the immediacy of reality, projects her fear onto a specific thing. Since life for Lucia *is* a *physical* battle every day (a battle for food, for cleanliness, for health, for freedom from accidents), she creates a deadly opposition between the physical and the mental. "They who read books," she says, "will let their families starve." (p. 216) Only her way of hard physical labor is comprehensible to her. She fears that the young "finding life painful will evade battle duty." (p.216) She cannot comprehend that books might enable the young to do battle in this New World, for their battle in life is more complex than hers had been, and needs more thought—the work of the mind—than physical work to succeed. She cautions that youth with its struggles ahead "should not poison its will with fairy tales and dreams that enchanted them from paper pages they turned and turned into the night." (p. 217) Lucia, like all peasants the world over, is excluded from the world of books. We read, "The mother wondered, What could be in these books that stunned her daughter into some magic oblivion?" (p. 150)

Octavia's desire to be a teacher is discouraged. It is something new and the new, being unknown and having no conceptional framework in which to be understood, is frightening to Lucia. Better to tread the familiar path and remain a seamstress. Security is the preferred mode; risk-taking for the sake of self-actualization is incomprehensible to Lucia, unattainable for Octavia, who has also been formed by the financial insecurity of her past and needs economic security above all.

Lucia only knows that a woman's place *is* the home. She "had the power of life and death over the human beings nearest to her . . . She had her duty to her children, big and small. She dismissed love that was personal, an emotion of luxury, of uncomplicated lives." (p. 123)

If this is her definition of a woman's role in life and of her relationship to her husband, her definition of a man's role equally emphasizes duty and responsibility to the family. We read of "husbands, protectors of children, of life and fate, creators of their own world, acceptors of life and fate who let themselves be turned into stones to provide the rock on which their family stood." (p. 235) Gino, like all her sons, is instructed in this lesson, first by Lucia and Octavia and then by his oldest brother. "He had to think of the family . . . he had to stop doing whatever he felt like doing." (p. 268)

Gino's acceptance of his role is poignant. "Trembling," Gino "promised to become another Vinnie, work in the railroad, marry, live in the tenements along the Avenue, wait at trolley stops with a child in his arms, chain himself in the known, lightless world he had been born in." (p. 272)

Obviously the role definitions of these men and women are based on their economic situation in society. They are just entering the working class. In her relationship with her children Lucia accepts as a given that she must be their "boss," an interesting use of a capitalist metaphor in regard to one's children. In *Umbertina* Marguerite will comment on the similar use of capitalistic metaphors to describe family relationships.

Lucia definitely acts in a manner which psychologists would call the "overinvolved" parent. And Lucia would probably even understand this criticism. But, she would counter, she doesn't have the economic luxury to act otherwise. At the end of the book Lucia, for the sake of her own economic security, tacitly colludes with Larry, in his immature relationship with his wife: *Lucia* will be company to his wife while he pursues his affairs. This is the great sadness of Lucia's mode of relating to her children, for she has only created a little boy, not a man, one who will suffer all his life from what is currently called the Peter Pan syndrome.

Unlike the generations who are to follow, Lucia is unconflicted about her values. She knows with surety what she knows. For example, when Lucia learns that Larry has slept with a married woman, she goes to the woman to nip further impropriety in the bud. Children "sleep under my roof," she says, "until they are married. My children do not become drunkards . . . or go to jail, or go to the electric chair." (p. 75) Lucia continues painting vividly the somber reasons for stressing obedience. "He must obey. Am I right? Does a son show respect to his mother or not?" (p. 74) she adds rhetorically.

As in most things, Lucia is no fool. She knows why she must act as she does. If financial ease were her lot in life, perhaps obedience and respect would be lesser values in parent-child relationships. As a matter of fact, Lucia can even let go of some of her deepest values if it is in the interests of her children to do so. For example, she is secretly pleased that her daughter has not married an Italian. She thinks what mother who had suffered under the masculine tyranny could wish on her tender daughter those guinea tyrants . . . who locked up their wives at home, never took them out except to a wedding or funeral; who made an uproar . . . if spaghetti was not steaming . . . at the precise moment their baronial boots crossed the doorsill; who never raised a finger to help their pregnant wives. . . . Thank God Octavia was marrying a man who . . . might show mercy to womankind. (pp. 217–18)

Octavia shares her mother's view of Italian men, and marries a Jew who, like her, likes to read. The most acculturated of all Lucia's children, Octavia has purchased her measure of independence at a great price. She rejects a central value of Italian American womanhood, and decides not to have children. She views children as that which enslaves women and precludes individuation. Octavia doesn't wish to repeat her mother's life, so that at the end of the book, Octavia, pursuing her career, has risen from seamstress to forelady.

On the other hand, Lucia wants her sons to marry a "good Italian girl who knew from the cradle that man ruled, must be waited on like a duke, fed good food that took hours to prepare; who cared for the children and the house without whining for help." (p. 217) What is not included in this definition is a significant as what is.

Implicit in the first statement is the lack of appreciation of some Italian men for the unpaid work of their wives in the home, a "he who pays the piper calls the tune" type of tyranny. The implications of the second statement are even more interesting. Lucia cannot imagine a different sort of relationship for her sons to their wives. Certainly she must hope that her sons will be benevolent tyrants, a more humane type, where service springs from love and appreciation, instead of despotic tyranny. However, the harshness of poverty cannot really give rise to gentler conceptions and definitions of relationships, no less cause different actions. As a matter of fact, since the economics of the working class allows for little individuation, and prizes adherence to role division and function, the concept of emotional intimacy between husband and wife, as stated earlier, is absent from Lucia's world view, and perhaps explains her total emotional fusion with her children. It is a fusion which serves well the parent willing to make a lifelong commitment to emotional nurturance in exchange for economic survival, but it does not serve well all children. For the child wishing to individuate beyond the family and its definitions, and risk losing the security gained from such fusions, attempts at separating can be more difficult than need be. And even for those working-class families who have risen beyond their working-class roots (as we shall see in *Umbertina*), a devotion to total dependency upon family, beyond economic need, remains. Even with a better economic situation, new definitions of familial relationships and role definition are slow to be born in such a cultural environment.

Perhaps there are more than just economic reasons that make new definitions difficult for both Italian-American children as well as parents. Perhaps still operative is the ancient Roman concept of *damnatio memoriae*, namely that the worst punishment for a Roman was to have his memory erased from future generations. Anyone who visits the ancient Forum can still see the arch from which Geta's name was erased. Septimius Severus had the arch built for his two sons, Geta and Caracalla, and had their names inscribed on it. After Septimius's death, a power struggle arose between the two brothers. Caracalla triumphed; he had workmen use water to "wear away" Geta's name from the stone. This was thought of as the most terrible aspect of the power struggle, because, by erasing Geta's name, his memory was also erased from future generations.[2] Perhaps the Roman concepts of family, existing within its structure, and being held in esteem by it down through future generations still operates, causing conflict and inner turmoil in the lives of Italian Americans when it comes to dealing with the concept of autonomy.

The larger meaning of *The Fortunate Pilgrim* involves Lucia's view of America as a metaphor for a "blasphemous dream." (p. 286) The blasphemy echoes a Blakean theme and involves Lucia's wanting the dream without recognizing the realities of the human condition, i.e., that with every gain there is a loss. "America . . . blasphemous dream . . . why could it not give everything?" (p. 286) She had wanted all this, i.e., "enough food and money for an old age surrounded by respectful and loving children" without the suffering, the guilt, the sorrow, "without fear of death and the terror of a judgment day. In innocence." (p. 286)

As a child, Lucia's wildest dream had been to "escape the fear of hunger, sickness and the force of nature . . . No one dreamed further. But in America wilder dreams were possible and she had never known of their existence. Bread and shelter were not enough." (p. 286)

Lucia is the fortunate pilgrim, because her pilgrimage through life did not include "wilder dreams" which would have put existential demands upon her. These are demands that challenge Gino and Octavia and those who follow, because an old dearly held value, namely that of identification of self through family, will need to be challenged and new resolutions, balancing self, family and work, forged.

---

2. A dear friend, Isabel Pingree, relates a story about her family which corresponds to the Geta story. When her father emigrated to the United States from Italy, he carved his name on the church door, as did all the immigrants, so that posterity would not forget them.

2

Umbertina by Helen Barolini traces the role development of the women of one Italian American family. Umbertina is the founding mother, as it were, of the family. She is of the immigrant generation, corresponding to Lucia, and possessing the same strength and courage that Lucia has. Like Lucia, Umbertina has a sureness about her values and her task in life. Although Umbertina knows that she has left behind failures as well as successes, she is too stubborn to regret them. She too has risked all for her children.

As far as role definition is concerned, Umbertina more nearly takes on the man's role of earning money,[3] first by making sandwiches for her husband's fellow-workers, and then by expanding the business to a full-fledged grocery store.

Umbertina and the family pool their labor and their resources and they expand into other lucrative business ventures. Although Umbertina hates waste and is totally utilitarian—there is no room for beauty or even for angst—she "could not tolerate stinginess and was an abundant provider [of food] to her family."[4]

Though Umbertina directs her energies on establishing her own economic independence as contrasted with Lucia, who relies solely upon her children for her financial security, Umbertina, nonetheless, like Lucia, takes on the functions of provider, protector, and worker, having inherent within them the survival and prosperity of the family unit as the priority value. By working together, in imitation of agrarian structures, they will all succeed.

One of Umbertina's daughters, Carla, corresponds to Octavia. Carla's desire to attend college is not taken seriously. Instead, she is pressed into service as a bookkeeper for the family business. Despite the Longobardis' economic success, there are only accidental rather than essential differences between Octavia and Carla. Materially Carla can have whatever she wants—with one big proviso—so long as she maintains the close family bonds. Although there is no economic need for Carla to work for the family, the code still persists, probably due to distrust of anyone outside the family and the tradition of total reliance on the family.

The suggestion, as in *The Fortunate Pilgrim*, is that Carla and Octavia's

3. A Calabrian sociologist tells me that Calabrian women are known to work "like a man." As a matter of fact there is a town in Calabria where role reversal has occurred with the women the merchants and the men caring for the children.

4. Helen Barolini, *Umbertina* (New York: Seaview Books, 1979), p. 96. All subsequent references shall be made in parentheses in the body of the paper.

generation cannot really act in terms of satisfying anything but the most basic of needs. In Carla's case, Umbertina's judgment that Carla's desire for college is a romantic whim is just, for in marrying, Carla chooses not the intellectual non–Italian American suitor but rather the good provider from her own background, evidencing, like Octavia, the great need for economic security. Carla vaguely knows there is more, but she doesn't have a structure to give it definition, and her problem languishes in romanticism.

Since Carla, the youngest of her mother's seven living children, experienced less of the struggle than the others, it is she who asks if Umbertina had been in love with her husband. Again the immigrant generation in the person of Umbertina blames books for such foolishness. Carla connects happiness with romantic love, which Umbertina denounces: "dreams of love and happiness, as if such things could come bound in any one man." (p. 139) Umbertina knows that happiness isn't a prize that is given and that you can hold on to, but rather a "feeling of satisfaction that receded or advanced according to each day's design." (p. 139)

The novel goes beyond Carla and Octavia's generation to explore definitions of womanhood by focusing on Carla's daughter, Marguerite, and her daughter, Tina, named for her great-grandmother. It is Marguerite, Carla's daughter, who finds herself attracted to Umbertina, "that mysterious old woman with whom she couldn't even speak." (p. 150) Umbertina functions as the silent Buddha on whom Marguerite projects all wisdom.

And Marguerite is in need of searching out an inner wisdom that will clear away her confusion about her life, its meaning and her future. If Carla and Octavia have never been able to formulate the right question in order to find an answer appropriate for each of them, Marguerite is capable of formulating the question to the consternation of her parents: the initial questionings surface as a criticism of them, their way of life, and what they have not been able to give her.

As a child, she is thought of as too serious for a girl, because she reads serious books and finds her parents' life of ease, "the American way of progress: college fraternities, Rotary Club, country clubs," empty. (p. 153) Marguerite's parents, Carla and Sam, only want her to be happy, but they have only the definition of happiness that their generation can have: economic ease, marriage, respectability achieved through acquiring the accouterments, "just show" (p. 154) and without substance, or emotional connections, as far as Marguerite is concerned.

As each generation must define itself anew from the previous one, so must Marguerite, who ultimately achieves what Octavia and Carla only indistinctly feel a desire for, namely autonomy from the family.

Marguerite makes an early attempt at separation from family and at individuation which is dramatic and predictable, yet futile. She meets Lennart Norenson, a Dartmouth student, at her brother's wedding reception, and elopes with him that very night. She felt he understood her when he asked what she was doing alone in that big house with her parents with nothing to do. (p. 157) She takes a route common to middle-class women of her generation in an attempt to discover themselves. If nothing else, marriage is the sanctioned way for a daughter to leave her parents' house. In a week she returns home, having discovered that Lennart had to drink to function, and her parents quickly move to have the marriage annulled.

She goes to England and has an affair with a man who introduces her to Alberto Morosini, a poet, whom she marries. She does what her mother could not bring herself to do. She opts not for riches of the world, but for riches of the spirit. She thinks that by marrying Alberto, twenty years older than she, and from an old Venetian family, she can learn from him, mistakenly thinking that happiness would come from his informed and caring guidance, instead of through her own sense of direction.

Marguerite generally has enjoyed their life together partly in Italy among Italian writers and partly in Washington, D.C., among government officials. But we meet Marguerite when she is in her forties, her children almost grown, and she is questioning the meaning of her life and her marriage. Unlike Lucia Santa in her forties, who leaves Manhattan with her two youngest children for Long Island to live in a two-family house with her son, his wife, and her grandchildren, looking forward to the economic security that they have achieved, Marguerite is in the throes of a midlife crisis.

Marguerite has left Alberto in Rome and decided to take "the immigrant's route," seeking her "fortune in the New World." (p. 201) She moves from the feeling of a few months before of not existing and of being detached from people to feeling acknowledged and seen for herself as she talks to people about doing translations in the future. Marguerite tells her family of origin of her decision to divorce Alberto and, in facing them, makes a mature separation from her parents. In a converse of the immigrants before her, whose physical separation from their parents forced psychological separation and autonomous action, Marguerite must return to her parents to declare her autonomy from them and from Alberto.

Marguerite, however, must make one more realization before she can return to Alberto. She goes to Florence looking for a teaching job, and meets Richard, a minister in his forties, who has not followed the bright career back in America that his background destines him for, but rather who serves in this outpost. Realizing that there will be no physical love between them, Marguerite thinks about their coming to an arrangement. And yet Marguerite demands to know of Richard if this is all there is to be had. Richard answers with a quiet fixity that this *is* it. His answer reassures her, for she realizes that part of his attraction is that he has the nerve to

accept the human condition. And yet this acceptance is not enough of a
basis for a relationship. Ultimately Richard's vapid socializing exhausts her.
"To be Mrs. Wareham instead of Signora Morosini when it all comes to the
same thing without, however, Alberto's warming physical need of her" (p.
219) seems the height of foolishness. "I can do as I feel" (p. 221), she thinks.
She doesn't have to stay in Florence, she doesn't have to prove that she can
work and take care of herself, she doesn't have to arrange a new "classy
marriage," she doesn't have to prove to her parents that she is as hardwork-
ing and practical as her brothers. She doesn't have to be her father or what
he wants her to be. She doesn't have to be "the man of the family—alone, or
with Richard." (p. 222) She can simply be herself.

This passage marks a freedom to define herself which, for reasons already
noted, the Italian American women of the first generation, such as Lucia
and Umbertina, did not possess, and the women of the second generation,
such as Octavia and Carla, stuck in security, could not utilize. (Actually the
first generation were freer to define themselves than the second. However
their definitions were to a large extent determined by economic forces.)
Coupled with Marguerite's own unique persona, class, acculturation and
feminism have come together to make new choices possible for her. But this
greater freedom in which Marguerite identifies more with the values of the
New World than with the peasant values of *la via vecchia* brings greater
problems.[5]

Although Marguerite knows who she is not, she does not yet know who
she is, and shortly after returning to Alberto, who understands her confusion, she has an affair with Massimo, a man of literary ambition, as an
attempt to find herself. Although Marguerite tries again to define herself
through a man, Massimo, even if he weren't married, will not allow her to.
She wants to give meaning to Massimo's life. She wants Massimo to need
her and thus create meaning for her own life. Though she works on her
photography, which Massimo encourages her in, Marguerite has not received the assignments she had imagined, so that she sees working for the
recognition of Massimo's novel as her way of giving meaning to her life.
Unlike Umbertina, Marguerite did not focus early enough on defining herself. She dully recognizes that she has "relapsed into emotional dependence
upon a man who would always survive without her." (p. 274)

5. Actually Marguerite is a richly complex character who is also defining herself by
separating from the stasis and deadness of Old World intellectuals with whom she
and her husband socialize. However, that aspect is beyond the scope of this paper.
Nonetheless, it would make an interesting study coupled with the experiences of and
writings about Italian Americans living in Italy as they mold their self-definition,
especially as Sartrian existentialism touches on issues of freedom, belief, choice, and
life's meaning.

In her diary that her daughters find, we learn that Marguerite was pregnant with Massimo's child, and that the auto accident in which she dies was a disguised form of suicide.

Carla, of course, has no knowledge that her daughter probably committed suicide. Her grief is voiced in these words:

> Her face and shoulders sagged with the burden of being too late to make it up to the daughter she had not understood or approved of, or even, at times, liked. As if speaking to herself, Carla added, "What did she want? What was she looking for? . . . All that moving around. All those homes she set up and then tore down. And moving those girls around so they had no normal life at all . . . What was it all for? To punish us?" (p. 286)

Even with Marguerite's death, Carla has only one way of looking at Marguerite's life, namely from the perspective of her own value system of *la via vecchia*, of roots, family, stability and security. It is almost as if the uprooting of the immigrant generation magnifies the longing for and emphasis on roots of the second generation to the exclusion of everything else. Yet we are told that when Marguerite returns to America to declare her independence, there is an unacknowledged look of envy in Carla's eyes. The illogic of Carla's last remark in which she muses that Marguerite's actions might have been prompted by a desire to punish them almost obscures the sadness of her total incomprehension of her daughter and of the concept of individual autonomy which respects differences.

If Carla's limited acquaintance with other life-styles prevented her understanding Marguerite, Tina, Marguerite's daughter, is the beneficiary of the evolution of role definition among the Longobardi women. Tina has just broken up with Duke, with whom she was living. When she learns after leaving him that she is pregnant with his child, she does not commit suicide like her mother, nor does she return to Duke, but rather she avails herself of the choice to abort the fetus. She also learns from her mother's inability to define herself early (Tina reads in Marguerite's diary how in college, unlike the girls who knew who they were—one of them is descended from Thomas Edison and Marguerite is the only Italian American there—and where they were going—on to become writers, doctors, etc.) to focus on what she wants to do vocationally, and to undertake an odyssey to find out who she is before involving herself permanently with a man, in her case a Wasp named Jason.

Being of the next generation, Tina does not have certain liabilities that her mother had. For example, Tina knows that her mother couldn't achieve autonomy because her family wasn't supportive of that concept. Autonomy represents the luxury of the American tradition of individuation, of life, liberty and the pursuit of happiness. Jason says, "I think too much is made of this whole family business. After all, once you're grown you can live where and with whom you choose and have the life you choose." Tina responds:

> "Yes, sure, but maybe the point is you can't grow up to get out *for good* if the family isn't supportive in the beginning. A strong base is like a launching pad. But a weak one is just a swamp. I think that's why my mother never got wholly away—there was no push upward from behind her. She was meant to fizzle out." (p. 319)

Tina also recognizes that Marguerite existed mainly to provide "life-systems for the men and children" (p. 358), and, feminist that Tina is, she sees clearly that this was not enough for Marguerite at this stage in her life.

Tina also comes to understand why her grandparents couldn't give Marguerite what she needed. They were too caught up with the task of their generation, i.e., of trying to be middle-class American, and this included imitating the vocational idleness of middle-class women of that historical time. Tina is free of trying to be middle-class American. She simply was born into that station in life and is receptive to American feminist concepts. On the other hand, her grandmother, Carla, can instruct Tina.

> "Your mother . . . never knew what she wanted. But you're more like *my* mother, the Umbertina for whom you're named. She was a strong person and she stuck to her guns." (p. 398)

Tina learns how to blend the good from each of the forces of her life. Initially she had ignored her mother's side of the family, because culturally they weren't "up" to her father's side. But once she starts along this search, going back to Castagna, and finally to the Museum of Immigrants display at the Statue of Liberty, Tina receives her epiphany. In a passage that arouses deep emotion within the reader, we learn that, unknown to Tina, she in fact sees on display Umbertina's very own bedspread, which poverty forced her to sell. We read that

> Tina stood entranced at the spectacle of a magnificent bright-hued gloriously woven bedspread that bore the motifs of Calabrian design . . . "Look at that . . . isn't it gorgeous?" . . . Tina stood before the glass drinking in the beauty and warmth of the old spread. Its colors irradiated her spirit; the woven designs of grapes and tendrils and fig leaves and flowers and spreading acanthus spoke to her of Italy and the past and keeping it all together for the future. (pp. 407–8)

The gutsiness of those first immigrants has saved Tina from what might otherwise be the sterility and enervation of her father's intellectual Venetian background. Tina realizes that through doing what she loves (her scholarship) and by understanding her roots, she will be strong enough to be herself.

Because Tina knows who she is, she can quickly still musings which Marguerite prolonged and face the future with optimism.

> Was there more merit in being self-contained, reserved, unemotional, reticent in the Anglo-Saxon way of the Jowerses, and of Jason? Or in her Latin excessiveness of emotion, her flights of fancy, her intensity of feeling?
>
> It was a silly argument, she thought. Comparisons are odious. And futile. (p. 422)

Any life is a personal odyssey, lived out within a particular cultural and historical perspective. These two novels set this odyssey within an Italian American framework and idiom, giving a familiar ring, as it were, to the personal quest which all people must make to become autonomous. I hope that my remarks, in relating the personal quest to the Italian American experience, do not obscure the universality of the themes of these books.

I would also like to emphasize that the four stages of acculturation not be thought of as stages which all Italian American women go through. A slower acculturation process and/or an acculturation process which on an individual basis never reaches the stage of the arts and the intellectual world would not share the role confusion of the third generation. As long as one followed the traditional path of economic upward mobility, there would be no need to resolve the disinterest of a heretofore utilitarian and a-intellectual Italian American heritage, an a-intellectualism which I suspect is rooted more in economic necessity rather than disregard for the intellectual per se.

Rosemarie Santini

A professional writer, Rosemarie Santini was born in the Greenwich Village section of New York City and still resides there. Her published work has covered every area of writing and her articles have appeared in many publications, including the *Daily News Sunday Magazine,* to which she is a regular contributor. Her books include *The Secret Fire* (1977) and *Abracadabra* (1978). Santini has also taught, edited, and worked in television.

An American Dream

"Where are the children?" Ida Rinaldi asks as she breaks one egg after another into a large mound of flour, first breaking each egg into a glass and inspecting it for any discoloration. It is a process learned in the old days, in the tenements on Thompson St., when the eggs were often bad and destroyed whatever they were put into. "My mother taught me how to do this," she says.

Resting on the tablecloth that covers her kitchen table is a large, wooden board on which she begins to knead the mixture. On the counter nearby, other necessities for her Italian cuisine are in evidence: tomatoes, canned, of course, in Italia, tomato paste from the same country—very expensive— beef meats, and stale bread mixed in milk, all ready to be rolled into large meatballs. She enjoys her chores, part of a process which will take hours. She is preparing fettucine as her Neapolitan mother taught her. "Let's see, eight people, eight eggs," she counts with peasant logic.

It is hot in the kitchen this August day, and she puts her hand to her forehead, smearing her tanned complexion with white flour. "Where are the children?" she asks again, although there is no one to answer.

At 67, Mrs. Rinaldi does not fit the popular picture of an Italian Mama. She is chic, petite, and slender. She wears the tight pants of the '70s, a shell blouse and tiny gypsy earrings. On the left finger of her right hand are a diamond engagement ring and a wedding band in an antique setting. They are not the original ones. In 1931 when she married, she was given no engagement ring and her wedding band was of plain silver.

Other things were different then, too. Now her house is a three-story brick-attached house in a lovely section in Queens. A backyard, a porch, a lawn are her proud possessions. Her apartment on the second floor could be featured in *The Sunday News* interior decorating pages. It is modern and sleek, and the only signs of her Italian heritage are tiny Botticelli angels in antique gold, which liven up the living room.

In 1931, her wedding home was an unheated, three-room tenement apartment in the Italian section of Greenwich Village. There, while working as a dressmaker, she raised her family, keeping the small apartment spotless, cooking on an old stove, cooling her groceries in an ice box; a living-room couch was her children's bed. Enduring these hardships, Ida Rinaldi and her husband worked and saved for the fulfillment of their American Dream, a house of their own. Finally, when their daughter Kathleen married and had a family, the Rinaldi-DeGiovanni clan moved from the tenements to the surburban splendor of Queens.

Here the brick houses all stand in a row, attached but separated by fence lines announcing ownership in this working-class neighborhood. Most owners, like the Rinaldi family, spent their entire life savings on the down payments. Only the electrical wires, hanging like kite lines over the pretty streets, mar the vista of this lovely neighborhood, an effect which the homeowners add to by stringing up clothesline in the backyards, probably a hangover from tenement days. Although most houses have washer-dryers, old habits die hard, and the Italians prefer their clothes bleached and dried in the sun, a custom inherited from ancestors who washed clothes in the village brooks of Italy.

Other neighbors have planted tomatoes in their gardens, but not this family. In the Rinaldi house there is a *House Beautiful* quality of floors polished almost too clean, of furniture oiled, of dustlessness, and in the duplex below, where the DeGiovannis live, the same cleanliness dominates all.

The other dominating interest in this household is "What's for dinner?" Today, it is the egg fettucine specialty, hand-rolled, to be served with a thick meat sauce. Mrs. Rinaldi explains that she is spending so much time on this delicacy as a treat for the children, her two grandsons, teenagers

Paul and John, who were, of course, a major reason for the Rinaldi-DeGio-vanni move from Greenwich Village. But where are the children?

Kathleen DeGiovanni brings her mother the news. Her two sons have baseball games to play. After that, they are going to the DeGiovanni beach club for a swim and a party.

Mrs. Rinaldi's eyes look sad. "What about the egg noodles?" she asks.

"Can we keep them?" her tall, brunette daughter suggests.

Sighing, the older woman cuts the dough carefully in strips, then carries the long, thin pasta into the extra bedroom. "Well, no one's using the extra bedroom. We can lay them out here," she says, laying the pasta carefully on the bed.

Afterwards, she pours a cup of expresso. "It's all changed," she says. "When we first came here, our life was more centered in this house. It was the '60s, and we were so glad to get out of the tenements. This seemed like a good place for our grandchildren to play and grow up. Now, everyone is going this way and that. I guess that's life."

She spoons three sugars into her tiny demitasse cup. "I hope it doesn't get damp. Noodles are impossible to keep separate when it gets damp." As she sits, her hands move with infinite patience and care, a habit from another era when hands were important for darning, sewing, crocheting, knitting, making pasta.

Does she miss the old style of living in the Italian section of Greenwich Village? "I loved it, but now everyone has either died or moved away. When I walk down the streets, I don't know anyone." But weekly, she does walk down the streets, riding the bus and subway into the city to have her hair done, buying ricotta and mozzarella in the old cheese store across the street from the church, the same store where she shopped as a young bride whenever she could afford it. Once in a while, she runs into an old neighbor or a friend who tells her how terrible living in the Village is nowadays.

Sometimes she wonders whether her life has really improved, although they have more room and more conveniences. Later, her daughter Kathleen comments on this: "I grew up sleeping on a living-room couch. Here, my sons have a bedroom to themselves. We moved into a brand-new area where everyone was mostly Italian and mostly friendly. When the kids were small, I could leave them on the front lawn and not worry about them."

But the kids were no longer small, and Kathleen and her husband spend most of their time working in the city, going to church and school meetings, chauffeuring the boys to baseball games, grabbing a moment or two at the beach club, where a swim, a game of tennis give them much pleasure, not returning home until it is time to sleep.

The boys do not even mow the lawn nowadays, even though their weekly allowance from their grandfather should influence them to do so. Their major interests are sports, dancing, music, visiting more affluent neighborhoods, attending rock concerts, meeting new girls. John and Paul, 15 and 17, are tall, solid, muscular young men who say they want to live farther out on Long Island, near the sea, in a house complete with a boat moored at a dock, an office nearby in town, and lots and lots of privacy.

Dark-haired, studious Felix DeGiovanni agrees with his sons. "My parents were immigrants, born in Europe. They didn't have any choice on how to live when they arrived here. I had to compromise, too, and live in Queens, instead of farther out, because I work in the city."

Although Mr. DeGiovanni likes suburban living, he feels that his boys have been too much sheltered. "I learned all about life very young, on the city streets. I was working in the neighborhood pasta store after school when I was 13. My kids will be put through college without having to work. They have everything they need. They don't know how to take care of themselves, and I'm not sure that's good for them."

Mr. DeGiovanni earned his M.A. in engineering by going to night school and working as a draftsman during the day. Because his children do not have to struggle, he feels they are not as mature as he was at their age. Also, he reiterates a familiar parental theme, questioning whether his sons have any respect for authority.

Grandfather Rinaldi agrees that life is very, very different from the time he came over on a boat from Italy. "Then we worked hard and respected our parents and our family." White-haired, retired from the U.S. Post Office, Mr. Rinaldi sits on the porch in his rocking chair, pensively smoking his pipe as he watches the comings and goings in the neighborhood, talking about how different his life would have been if his parents were not immigrants.

If he had stayed in Italy, he might wander down to the town's square where he would find the other older men sitting and pondering the past and would argue with them, raising his voice in melodramatic splendor. If he had remained in Greenwich Village, he might walk over to the private men's club where Italian men play bocce and pinochle and talk about politics. But in Queens there are only a few senior-citizen centers for this kind of social interchange, and Mr. Rinaldi says the people there are too old.

Still, he is happy that he has at last attained his idea of a successful life: a house he owns out of what he considers the city, a safe place far removed from tenement living. Yet, there is a bittersweet element to his satisfaction, as if now he has everything, what does he really have?

"When we lived in Italy, I felt superior," he explains. "My parents were respected. We lost all that when we came to America. For years, I couldn't speak the language properly. Other kids from the neighborhoods called me names. I had to fight a lot, and I didn't understand the ways of living here.

It took me a long time to get accustomed to America. That's why I worked so hard to better myself. To get what I had dreamed of all these years."

What is this dream anyhow, and has it worked for these former city dwellers in their effort for a better life? There is a lack of primitiveness here on these residential streets, so far from the tumultuous streets of their youth in the city . . . a sterility, almost a disease of cleanliness, where a speck of trash spills over onto their private thoughts and peaceful existence. Yet the neighborhood concepts which most of these former tenement dwellers grew up with are still in evidence. There are eyes in every second-story window, observing any stranger on the streets in minute detail, and visitors are associated with this house and that. There are pleasantries on the street, greeting of neighbors and friends.

Then, suddenly, the streets are empty. It is 5:30, dinner time in an Italian working-class neighborhood. The men have walked or driven home from their jobs. The children have stopped playing. In the Rinaldi-DeGiovanni home, the beautiful homemade noodles lie on the bed in the guest bedroom, uncooked, waiting for the meat sauce and imported, expensive cheese.

In the kitchen of the top floor apartment, the Rinaldi grandparents are eating vegetables in garlic oil with fresh Italian bread, waiting for the third generation of the family to be available from their busy life. This third generation is swimming in the beach-club pool, clowning with friends, listening to rock music, drinking soda pop, eating frankfurters, oblivious to the lifetime of dedication and hardship represented by the plates of rare and delicious fettucine in marvelous sauce that await them.

Gioia Timpanelli

Gioia Timpanelli is a poet and storyteller in the tradition of her ancestral Sicily, where the women kept the culture and handed it down in the oral threads of legend. She has performed with Robert Bly and Joseph Campbell in telling stories from folktale, Arthurian, Christian, and Sufi sources, traveling throughout this country and Canada. As a producer, writer, and broadcaster for educational TV, she has received two Emmy Awards. *Stones for the Hours of the Night* is the title of a collection of her published poetry. She has lived in Italy and the following excerpts record some Italian travels.

Italian Traveling

WEDNESDAY

Saint Lucy, Saint Lucy
Flame of our Flame
Saint Lucy, Saint Lucy
Light of our Darkness
Saint Lucy, Saint Lucy
Light of our Light

We miss the mountain road twice and twice we wind up on the superstrada to anywhere. At the same point in the highway, we pass the same sign pointing to a medieval cluster of buildings. When I make the same mistake again, I figure, "Enough! I'll get off this road, see if I can get a cup of coffee, buy some dog cigarettes and start again." Once off the strip highway, I'm on a small rubble road that no one has bothered to pave. The asphalt ends abruptly and my car falls off it with a start. It's like opening up a dream door to discover a place that one has never walked but somehow knows well. It wouldn't have surprised me to meet some old friend crossing the square. But no one is crossing the square; it is empty. The only place that looks public, with its dangling salt and cigarette sign, is closed. Since there is no one to ask, I start to back the car up, look in the mirror and see something moving: It is a large black dog crossing the square. He stops just beyond the car, finding a grease spot to lick, bobs his head up and down in satisfaction. Remembering last night's dinner, remnants still wrapped carefully inside my bag, I get out and give him all my cache. The dog never looks up so I never see his face. Yet, something draws me out. I walk to the other side of the car, look around, and then I spy her, standing so still in a small rounded doorway. How long has she been there staring at me? She is a very, very old woman, entirely black wrapped; her form fills the rounded doorway and for a second I doubt that I am seeing her. Maybe it is a shadow, but no, she is there, her intense round eyes looking directly into mine. I feel like stepping toward her but something stops me. "Signora," I call out softly, very softly. "Yes," she answers, waiting in her place as I take some steps toward her and stop. "Signora, would you help me? I need a place to stay." Now, another woman, younger by thirty years at least, dressed in dark green, appears in the doorway. "Follow us," she says as both of them disappear into the low, stone building. We all three enter an enormous cavelike room: cold dark stone room with a slight smell of old hay. They face me and when I walk up to them, I notice we are in a small circle. There is only one light bulb hanging from the ceiling so far up I don't have a sense of its beginnings. A large wooden table is directly under the light. The rest of the room is in darkness. "I'll write it down," says the green woman, and with that she walks directly behind the table, takes out a piece of paper from a notebook. While she is writing, I see that next to her crooked writing finger, lying on the table, is a delicately cracked egg, not in a box or on a plate but just lying there, balanced on the dark table. She taps her finger. I look again and see that just out of the light is another egg and next to this one there is a nest of folded paper cradling five eggs and next to them is a low paper box and in it are more eggs, small and lightly placed one on top of another. I look down and am surprised to find boxes of eggs not more than a few inches from my left foot. . . . And then I know that everywhere in this dark cave there are eggs: eggs in boxes, eggs in wooden crates, eggs in giant glass jars, eggs on the floor, covering almost every foot, eggs on shelves, on every wall, right up to the ceiling. Eggs, eggs, and more eggs. An egg cave. Eggs everywhere.

The green woman hands the slip of paper to the old one, who hands it to me. I read on the slip carefully written Valino Martini Alberto, and at the exact same time the two women look at me and say, "You should stay at Martini (says the older) at Alberto (says the younger)" and as if they had said the same words, satisfied, we all smile and I bow my head.

"Thank you and good day." There is no further discussion as I leave the place carefully and step out into the gray autumn light; a light rain is beginning to fall as I walk to the car. The dog is gone, the piazza empty again except for my car. I get in, but before I start it I read the paper again. Now, finally, I know where I am going.

AUTUMN: SATURDAY

Leaving home one goes into the wilds
There is no place between

The highway turns into a provincial road, the provincial road turns into a town road, the town road narrows into a dirt road which soon is a cart lane, and that becomes an old donkey trail which falls abruptly to a footpath and finally even this becomes so overgrown the dried brush scratches and taps at the car as we make our way up into the mountains and finally stop. We can go no farther in this machine. Zia Dina (Alberto's aunt is called "Zia" by every young villager) gets out of the car quickly, looks around squinting and nodding, points to a fallen thatched shelter and says, "That's where the shepherds live in summer, up here on the mountain. A casino. Did you know it is called a casino? They are the only ones who come up here anymore. Shepherds and sheep. Well, Mario and I and a few others are here." Her eyes widen playfully and she laughs as she says the last.

She turns and walks across a mountain field and I follow her to an ancient rock pile, white and gray rubble, one story high. From somewhere a teen-age boy appears and Zia Dina takes one of the large bread loaves that she is clasping to her breast and hands it to him. He disappears as quickly as he appeared. The way it takes time for the eyes to get accustomed to the dark before they can see what is there, it takes my eyes time to see this old place. What seemed at first only rock ruin now becomes a marvelous old town: small attached stone houses with a stone front step, small stables and hand-carved stone archways now appear. The street is so narrow that the projection of an architectural detail on one side shadows a part of the doorway on the other. The town seems to have no piazza, no separate church building; here even the Mother and Son have gone back to the land, rocks, to the great sky itself. We walk through the deserted street, no doors open, no voice calls out; toward the end of the street we are suddenly face-to-face with three white cows who come ambling toward us slowly. In the narrow street the five of us fall automatically into single file, making room for each other carefully. The first cow looks me in the eyes as we pass each other and when, for no particular reason, I look back, I see she, too, has turned to look back at me. No one else comes and Zia Dina does not even mention this event. The chickens everywhere get the afternoons to scratch in the fields, the cats at night roam far, and the young dogs travel out from early morning, and so in this town it is natural to find cows free walking the streets. They are going for their *passeggiata*—to find that last sweet mouthful of something good to eat, to that ribbon of pasture at the beginning of town where the stones of the village and the stones of the land mix with the earth and bright sweet grass.

I follow Zia Dina as she leads me to the outskirts of the village where the houses end and a purposeful space lined with many paths leads to an old fountain whose font is made of half found rock and half human-hewed rock; some spigots of unceremonious color and shape but instead of one or two there are five pouring forth a strong flow of water. As we come up to the fountain a marmalade cat is lapping, taking a long drink from a lower basin.

She does not run away or even look up nor do we disturb her. Zia Dina takes a tin cup from behind some rocks and asks me with some ceremony, "Would you like a drink from the fountain?" But ignorant of what I had been asked to take and not being at the moment thirsty, I say, "No, thank you." She drinks and we walk on. But I think it strange that I have been asked so formally to have some of the water from this fountain.

In an hour, we have circled around, gone to the four corners of the village. We have looked in all directions, high on the top of the mountain to valleys and farther mountain peaks. We have seen the bare autumn fields ("Mario had the best vegetable garden once. We always had more than we needed. He would give a lot away."), the chestnut woods below, felt the cloud. "This is our old apple tree. It still has good fruit." An old apple tree of autumn, no leaves but shimmering black bark, wet and rough tiny valleys, bark valleys with dark life in them. Underfoot, the wild grasses cover everything so we touch yellow hair as fine as a child's. The grass grows to the edge of the thick mud road. We have circled around and now pass the old fountain and then I remember . . . the place where the bees sing, an ancient village famous since before Roman times for its fountain of healing water that heals both inner and outer cares. The same fountain, in the same place, the water still flowing.

It is cold and a strong wind springs up; we are cloud wet. Zia Dina leads the way back into town, to the doorstep of the house she and her husband, Mario, refuse to leave completely, even though the upper floor has fallen in during the earthquake of two years before. She knocks at the door and Mario answers immediately. He greets us warmly, smiling and showing the way, all the while saying, "Enter, enter . . ." As soon as we cross the threshold I feel it, something in the room. I can't exactly name it but it is the feeling of old spirit and it touches every corner of this ancient stone room. It is like walking into a presence. One feels it always in holy places and that is what I feel in this simple room. Zio Mario has made a great fire in the hearth for us and we each take our place near it, even the black and white cat, Minio, on the left, and the old dog, Fino, on the right. There is a great sense of peace here. We all sit in silence for a long while; nothing needs to be said or done here. We sit around the ancient fire, drawn to it. Finally, after all this traveling I feel I have found something. We are here, deeply warmed in some center, a place of hidden stone where a constant fire burns, formed so long ago it has no name and it burns not only for warmth. We have circled around and around and finally find this hearth where we all live and no place else and since it is where we are born each day again and again where there is even a strong feeling of protection where else can we go? Where else would we be at home? Since this is the fire that starts all others how can they let it go out?

We sit a long while in silence. Then Zia Dina speaks, "The engineers say the house is not good. We never go upstairs anymore. They say we can never come back here and they have given us a small box to live in for the winter. It's nearby; I'll show you. Maybe you understand it and can explain how things work in it. We sleep with relatives now and come back home each day and have our fire and cook a little something for ourselves and for the creatures. We don't mind sleeping in the box." She says this all matter-of-factly. She rests in what she knows.

In these past weeks I have been in many places where life was fully lived but no home had this feeling of holiness about it. This place where the sacred fire burns. Where can they go? How can they give it up? To another fire, we say. We can say that, for our fires have been found in places as we go and we've heard some holy ones talk of this possibility but we know it is not easy and of the two ways, this traveling fire is the harder to find. Zia Dina and Zio Mario are reluctant to leave their ancient hearth but soon they will leave it.

Why THIS fire? This particular one. Zia Dina says, "It is a humble place. We know that." Perhaps, it is the earthquake which has left it so . . . exposed to only this center but whatever it is, the spirit in this room, near this hearth is unmistakable.

FICTION

Mari Tomasi

When the first of her two novels, *Deep Grow the Roots*, appeared in 1940, Mari Tomasi was selected by the American Booksellers' Association as one of the year's ten most promising new novelists. She was born in 1907 in Montpelier, Vermont, and lived all her life there. Her second novel, *Like Lesser Gods*, is the story of the Italian American granite workers in that state. Tomasi worked for the *Montpelier Evening Argus* and, for a time, with the Federal Writers' Project in Vermont. She was an active member of the Poetry Society of Vermont and the Vermont Historical Society, for which she wrote a researched piece, "The Italian Story in Vermont." She died in 1965.

from Like Lesser Gods

Why, she thought bitterly, why should Pietro be cursed with this ridiculous passion for stone, and why could she not make him see the need for finding other work? Her mind so thrummed with these familiar thoughts that she could not concentrate on the card game nor did she hear but snatches of the conversation, which drifted from one subject to another:

"There should be snow for deer hunting next month—"

"With the sanatorium at the top of the hill the taxes will probably be raised. But it should mean a fine sidewalk." And the *maestro*'s chuckle, "Hah, if they are like the Ibena taxes, don't be too sure. Public money, like holy water, is dipped into by everyone."

Someone murmuring, "Eh, Ronato tells us, Pietro, that you are carving a beautiful memorial."

And Pietro's shy supplement, "The best these hands have ever made. Yet, if it were Ronato's work, I would consider it the least of his master-pieces."

Maria snapped to attention. Pietro was saying, "It is a cross, standing just so high." His stubby, calloused fingers indicated a height in the vicinity of his umbilicus. "And it is nearly smothered under vines. The best job I have yet undertaken, and it will be finished next week."

The best job—finished next week.

The words revolved in Maria's mind with the persistence of a catchy merry-go-round tune. Suddenly, their relationship to a former well-remembered threat of Pietro's fired them with potential significance. She well remembered the day when the stonecutter Gateau had been threat-ened with dismissal if his hands again slipped carelessly to spoil the stone he was working. Better still she remembered Pietro's fervid, "If by accident my hand should sometime err, just let my boss give me hell. I would throw the job in his face, and quit."

The best job I have done—I would throw the job in his face and quit.

As clearly and as sweetly as an Angelus calls laborers from their toil and bids them forget fatigue and defeat, so these words dispelled Maria's fruit-less years of begging Pietro to leave the sheds. She must take matters into her own hands: *she must ruin that fine stone of Pietro's, make it appear a careless slip. The boss, Gerbatti, would fume and scold. And against such injustice Pietro would make good his threat. . . .*

Maria's mind was made up. From that moment she directed the even-ing's activities to the success of her plan. "More wine!" she urged her guests, and made sure to pour a brimming glass for Pietro, too. Ronato, watching Maria's face ripen a joyous red, murmured, "Your cheeks, Maria, are as happily red as that dress you wear."

At midnight, Lucia and Ronato were in mellow readiness to say their good nights, yet Maria detained them with a refilled pitcher of wine. Not until Pietro's words stumbled thickly one over the other and his cheeks bloomed a brick-red, did she close the door behind her visitors. And when Pietro's arm lay in leaden embrace around her waist and his deep breathing bespoke a half-drugged sleep, she rose from their bed, dressed quickly, supplied herself with flashlight and chisel, and stole from the house.

That plunge into chilly night air washed away some of the confidence she had enjoyed in the grappa-vaporized room. A palsied moment of indecision held her slippered feet to the porch. She looked right and left on Pastinetti Place, into the silent drama of darkened windows and deep shadows. In the harsh moonlight the Vitleau sanatorium site was a grotesquerie of exhumed maple roots, standing watch over their open graves. Maria's lips tightened derisively. She stepped resolutely across the granite chip walk and ran in quiet flight down the center of the dirt road.

Down Main Street, on the second block, a cluster of lunch-cart habitués was noisily inviting Officer Riley to a hot dog and coffee. She breathed more easily after she had crossed the bridge and tracks to the shadows of Shed Row. A darkened car was parked beneath a sprawling river willow. In its interior a quartet of male and female voices woefully harmonized—"Show me the way to go home—" Maria gained the sheds and kept to their back yards. Under moonglow Maria's practical mind waxed fanciful. The weathered structures loomed gaunt specters. Strewn grout pieces lay on the ground like whiting bones. Here and there oblong blocks of stone became overturned tombstones. She looked defiantly at the moon. Her lips curled their scorn at its eerie attempt to weaken her determination: here beneath her feet was the harsh reality of granite chips; each step was a sharp reminder of what stone could do. . . .

The great front doors of Gerbatti's shed were strongly barred against her. She tried to raise one after another of the high, heavy windows and succeeded only in loosing thick showers of gray dust. She crept around the side to the smaller windows of the office. A wire ripped open her thumb. The muscles of her arms strained to aching agony before a window at last gave an inch. She explored the inside sill with her index finger, and discovered a bent spike holding the window secure. She poked at the spike with the chisel until she could turn it in its pocket and pull it.

The quartet's mournful voices drowned the creaking of the window. Maria climbed into the room. Her flashlight threw a circle of light on the floor and revealed dust-filled cracks between the floor boards. She reflected grimly that even Gerbatti, boss though he was, received his share of the dust. A door opposite her opened into the dark wet room. It was cluttered with giant saws and polishing machines. Wet room, indeed! *Dio*, here was the earthy chill of some subterranean cave. And cloyed with it was a dank smell of rust and oil that constricted her body into a knot of shivers. What was it Pietro said? Ah, yes—the machinists hate water because it rusts their well-oiled machines; and the carvers detest oil because it stains the granite. Yet, in this machine room, water was truly needed. It had to be fed, she knew, in steady, cold streams to prevent the metal saws from melting as they heatedly cut into stone. Ah, if granite could thus torture metal, what, then, could it do to flesh and blood! But stone was not always the victor. Maria's mouth twisted into a sly, determined smile: stone could not reason, stone could not plot as did her brain. . . .

She pushed open another door to the drier, chalky air of the finishing room. And here she was blind to everything but Pietro's favorite corner where his little masterpiece stood under a stiff covering.

Maria wasted no time. She pulled off the tarpaulin, studied the granite cross dispassionately, and set the chisel point to a corner leaf design where a chip might appear to be a slip of Pietro's hand. With an iron bar she hammered at the chisel. The sound struck into the lofty room with a hollow, sepulchral note. Another blow. A small edge of the cross chipped off and fell to the dirt floor. Another blow. The leaf pattern dwindled to half a leaf. Another blow. Another.

She straightened breathlessly. Now that the deed was accomplished, its magnitude temporarily appalled her. Maria's hands trembled; her heart thrashed wildly against her ribs. And for the first time since she entered the spacious finishing room, she looked about her.

A half-dozen memorials stared back at her, stonily, ghastly in the moonlight. On the boxing platform three little markers plainly lettered—ALMA, GEORGE, and ALICE, held her fascinated eyes with their almost human accusation. She uttered a cry that was half prayer, half scorn. She shook her fist at them, and fled back to the office window, clambering out in such haste that when an outside wire caught at her skirt she tugged it away frantically, undismayed at the tear, only eager to put the river once more between herself and Shed Row.

It was not characteristic of Maria Dalli to stint a healthy sleep appetite with worries. Night, she reasoned, was for sleep. It was during the day that one should worry about getting rid of worries. Wasn't it foolishly inconsistent to nourish the body daily with good food, protect it with clothing, veer it from injuries—and at night to undo this good by punishing the body with wakefulness and by teasing a sensible brain into lunacy? And so it was tonight.

She crept noiselessly into the house. Once again beside the deeply breathing Pietro, she promptly fell into profound sleep. But asleep she was no longer mistress of her mind. Before the seven o'clock whistle could awaken her to reality, it became a shrill police call which gathered together hundreds of blue-coated police. They were marching toward her from the four corners of Granitetown. Hundreds of stern police eyes were riveted to her right hand which clutched a chisel and which was hacking away at the lifeless face of the man for whom Pietro was carving a cross. . . .

The sound of Pietro's voice came to her from a great distance. "Yours is a big head, too, this morning?" he was inquiring sympathetically. She heard the words even as she struggled to wakefulness. He sat in his nightshirt on the edge of the bed, tenderly massaging his forehead.

She murmured, "Big head?" It came to her, then, that he was referring to last evening, the grappa fumes, and the wine. She smiled ruefully, "Sì, sì, we were too generous with the wine last night."

As soon as Pietro and his dinner pail disappeared down Pastinetti Place she fed the children and sent them off to school. Mister Tiff left with them; this was the day for mending umbrellas on Willow Hollow Road. Maria did her housework automatically; mentally she was following Pietro step by step. *Now he enters the shed . . . he chats a moment with Ronato and his friends . . . now the shed whirrs with activity, everyone begins work. . . . Pietro draws the covering off his cross . . . he stares at it with disbelieving eyes . . . now comes Gerbatti. . . . Gerbatti gasps, he fumes and storms . . . the workmen gather around curiously . . . my poor Pietro is shamed before them. . . . "Go to hell!" he shouts to Gerbatti. "I quit!" . . . and he walks out of the shed, never again to return. . . .* This dreaming was balm to Maria's heart. She bustled about preparing his favorite dinner, for soon he would be home, dinner pail and all. He would be saddened, perplexed, enraged. She must prepare a good dinner. He would enjoy *salsigi*, and a snappy salad of endive, tomatoes, and onions.

Vetch and Petra ate their noonday meal and left again for school. The *maestro*, she decided, must be at Lucia's table today. But why didn't Pietro come home? Ah, well, he was no doubt fine-combing Granitetown this minute for another job. Sì, that was it. He would find a job, work for a month or two while they made plans for the little store they would have in their house. . . .

It was shortly after four when he came in, his round face thoughtful and his head bent, and she saw that in his preoccupation he had neglected to slap the stone dust from his clothes. She knew he must be grieving at leaving this work he loved, but she felt little pity. *Dio*, if an infant were attracted to the color red, would she not remove a red-hot poker from its reach even though the babe screamed as if its heart were breaking? She waited in vain for Pietro's, "Well, Maria, I did it. Today I quit the sheds." He muttered only with his preoccupied air, "The days are getting too brisk for only a kitchen fire." And in a few minutes she heard him in the cellar cleaning the furnace.

After supper when the children were abed she thought: surely, now he will speak. But he shrugged into his coat explaining briefly, "I promised to help Rossi with his grappa tonight."

She consoled herself: Pietro is Pietro. He will say nothing until he has found a new job. He does not want me to worry. Sì, that is it. . . .

She was alone in the kitchen darning socks when Mister Tiff entered

quietly, the golf bag drooping from a slumped shoulder. He was hanging
back with a strangely hesitant air, ill at ease, uncertain. Despite the cold
evening his high, pink forehead glistened with perspiration. He handed her
a small square of red-and-white checked cambric. He spoke fast, as if to put
an early end to this distasteful mission. "Last night you wore a skirt of this
cloth, Maria; the skirt was whole and pretty. Last night in Gerbatti's shed,
Pietro's stone was mutilated. This morning this piece of cloth waves accusation from a wire outside Gerbatti's office window. And this morning, I
wager, your skirt is minus this little square of cloth—" He shook his head,
sighed.

Maria stood speechless. Her fingers clenched the cambric square until
her nails, cutting into her palm, smarted her to activity. Her voice was
anxious, fierce. "Does Pietro know?"

He shook his head in silence.

"No, no. I chanced to be walking the yard on my way to Willow Hollow
Road. I saw the cloth—and I remembered." He finished compassionately,
"Don't fear, I won't tell."

She gripped his arm in wild hope, and despair. "What happened, *Maestro?* What did Gerbatti say? What did Gerbatti do?"

"Do? Pietro did not tell you?" He was honestly amazed.

"Not one word has he spoken!"

"Nothing happened, Maria."

He felt the trembling of her hands before they fell limp from his arm.

"Gerbatti did not give him hell?" she said tonelessly. It couldn't be true.
Her wretched deed in vain. . . . "Pietro did not rebel and—quit?"

The question was a plea. He understood. There might be thousands of
wives who blessedly resigned themselves to the hazards of their husbands'
work, but it had to be a deeply loving and deeply willful Maria who would
try to take matters into her own hands. She was strong of mind and strong of
heart; and although strength has its own joys and rewards, it is heir, too, to
its own brand of pain. He asked, gruffly tender, "And why should Gerbatti
give him hell, Maria? Anyone could see it was no accident. It was the
intentional butchering of some malefactor. A beautifully worked stone—in
ruin. Gerbatti respects Pietro's love for his work, he had only to see Pietro's
stricken face to know he was innocent."

Her shoulders drooped. Her face shrank, beaten, white. Only her black
eyes were defiantly burning against this defeat. He shifted awkwardly
under their blaze, and he was thinking: if only Lucia could love the poor
Ronato as Maria does Pietro. . . .

She whirled away from him. Never had anyone seen a tear glisten in
Maria Dalli's eyes, nor would she let the *maestro* see one tonight.

He limped up the stairs after her, his heart fluttering with a great fear. If last night Maria, riding her crest of omnipotence, ruined a costly stone, what greater harm might she do on some tomorrow? And to remind her of what the stone cost Gerbatti would make little impression tonight on her stony mood of defeat.

The door to her bedroom was open. He began timidly, "May I speak to you, Maria?" She did not reply, and he continued, "Forgive me if I repeat what I have already told you—that sometimes for a man there is but one job at which he can be happy. I have seen Pietro at his work. It is as if he has two hearts: one that beats for you and his family, and one that beats for his work. Since the very beginnings of family, the husband's lot has always become the wife's. And justly so. Remember the wise Ruth who even made her mother-in-law's lot her own, when she said—'Whither thou goest I will go.' And the Roman bride of antiquity formally promised her husband—'Where thou art, Caius, there am I, Caia.' In the same measure your own promise 'for better or for worse' makes Pietro's lot your lot, and you must accept it if you would keep his love."

She had turned a rigid back on him and was staring, unseeing, through the window.

He gained courage in her silence. "Think how Pietro would feel if he knew his own wife had damaged his stone—"

Her voice carried assurance, and a trace of mockery. "He won't know— unless you tell him—and you won't do that."

He said quietly, "You are right. I won't do that, Maria. But suppose God had not been so generous with you? Suppose Pietro himself had come upon that all-revealing piece of cloth? Me, I think it would mean the end of everything beautiful and honest between you. Hah, Maria, don't you know that a man is but an oversized boy, and he likes oversized compliments and flattery on the work that is near to his heart? And, instead of flattering him you beg him to quit his work! *Dio mio,* haven't you known men as fine as your Pietro who have fled for comfort to the arms of other women?"

"Spare yourself the lecture, *Maestro,* Pietro never looks at other women."

Mister Tiff weighed the prudence of implanting a seed of doubt in her mind, but fearful of its catastrophic outcome in the hands of the willful Maria he reluctantly compromised with a—"No? No?"

He did not see the shadow creep into her face. And he turned away, nursing but little hope that he may have touched upon a vulnerable spot in Maria.

Alone, she crouched stiffly on the granite step beside the bed. She was not pondering the *Maestro's* exact words, but rather the poignant associations they stirred, and which now pummeled her, mind and heart. She,

Pietro, and the children were happy. Except for her persistent fear for
Pietro's health—they were happy. If Pietro ever learned that she had ruined his little masterpiece, how could they continue to love here with the
oneness of spirit and body, and the sweet completion that had always been
theirs.

The dismal failure of last night's trip to Gerbatti's shed was losing itself
now in the vital urgency of preserving the happiness that was hers, Pietro's,
and the children's. Her hands clenched over her knees. "God, please do not
let Pietro find out." . . .

Pietro never saw Peter Michael again. A week after the baby's christen-
ing Petra arrived at the sanatorium for her usual afternoon visit and found
her father napping. She sat beside him for a while, watching the tired lids
quiver over the sunken eyes. Then she slipped out to one of the comfortable
wicker chairs in the sun porch. Her own eyes closed drowsily, and she was
gliding into the tranquil days of childhood when she and Peggy tramped
Vitleau's orchard for the summer's first violets. A hand shook her. She woke
to the urgent words of one of the nurses. "Miss Dalli, your father—"

Petra flew past her down the hall. Gino was attempting, with ice packs,
to prevent the ever-widening of those bright patches of red on her father's
pillow. She knew he was dying. It was added torture to see his soft eyes
humbly pleading forgiveness of her: as if he were saddened at causing her
this grief, yet himself were quite willing to go.

They came quickly from their corners of Granitetown: Father Carty,
Maria, Gabbi, Americo, Mister Tiff. Pietro wished wearily that the white-
tunicked Gino would keep his hands from him and let him die in peace. The
boy's efforts were delaying, only for a few minutes, the great and final
moment of release. This business of dying would be a drifting, not unpleasant sensation, were it not for the grief-ravaged faces around him that tore at
his heart.

Of all the eyes about him only Maria's were dry, bright; her face, an
inscrutable mask. He was proud of her. As strong, as unflinching as granite
she was, he reflected, in his last earthly flicker of humor. The same qualities
in these two he loved. . . .

The faces around him blurred. He was soaring giddily above them, out of
and above himself. He could scarcely see his family and friends; yet in a
strange lucidity he was viewing the complete panorama of Dalli life in Italy
and in Granitetown. He was with his childhood friend, Italo Tosti, in the
hills of northern Italy . . . he stood at Italo's grave in Granitetown . . . and
here he was testily suffering Gino's tireless hands . . . he was embarking
with Maria on the blue Mediterranean . . . he was beside her in their bed

at Pastinetti Place . . . he was here at the Granitetown sanatorium watching
her face grow dimmer and dimmer . . . he plowed brown fields under an
azure Italian sky . . . he hunted mushrooms at Peter's Gate . . . he was in
Gerbatti's shed caressing beauty into stone . . . he and Italo were boys,
pilfering eggs from the hennery of the village priest Don Ricardo. . . .

Redheaded Father Carty, breathless from this hurried sick call, stood
gravely over Pietro. Pietro saw him as another Don Ricardo; and he murmured the deathbed plea of the old world *paesani*, "*Gesù, Giuseppe e
Maria!*"

But his last breath did not come. He was in Gerbatti's shed once more,
his hand guiding the steel into the pattern of a slender cross. He sweated
over his work, eager to finish it before the end of the day's work. . . .

A four o'clock whistle began screeching to Granitetown that stonecutters
were through for the day. In Shed Row, another whistle, and another, took
up the cry. Pietro heard them. A smile settled on his gray face. His head
dropped forward in a nod, and then he was dead.

Antonia Pola

Antonia Pola is the pseudonym of Antonietta Pomilla. She is one of those
legions of "lost" writers of whom nothing is known except the title of
one book, *Who Can Buy the Stars?* (1957) and that only because it was
thought worthy of mention by Professor Andrew Rolle in his own *The
Immigrant Upraised* (1968). The book jacket of Pola's novel carries the
information that she was born in the Piedmont region of Italy, was educated
there, and taught school near Turin. Her home in this country was in
Cicero, Illinois, but no trace of her could be found there, nor was her book
to be found in the Cicero Public Library.

Yet Pola wrote an account of an Italian immigrant woman which is forceful, unsentimentalized, and sharply different from the portraits of submissive women which seemed to be the standard for her time. Her protagonist,
Marietta, comes to America as the "picture bride" of an Italian coal miner.

But he is no match for her intelligence and ambition as she starts a bootlegging business during Prohibition days and begins to earn the money that her husband cannot. Yet it is all futile—money cannot buy back what she left in Italy, nor could she ever return to the impoverished life she had known there. She is left, in the end, with belonging nowhere. Stylistically uneven though the book is, Pola's portrait of Marietta remains imprinted in one's mind.

from Who Can Buy the Stars?

"But, Mother, why didn't you wire as soon as you got to New York? I would have had a party for you."

"That's exactly what I didn't want, Delfina. Besides, the boat docked on the thirteenth. I didn't like the date."

Delfina looked surprised. "Mother! Don't tell me that you've become superstitious all of a sudden! If that's what a trip to the old country does for you—!" She laughed disbelievingly as she bustled about completing her supper arrangements. "I know, it's just that you didn't want any fuss made over you."

Marietta laughed, too, as if in agreement. No need for anyone to know that the thirteenth of the month, from now on, would always hurt her heart.

She had not wanted to get in touch with anyone when she first landed. She had not wanted to see anyone, and she was suddenly, strangely, not quite sure that she would be glad to get home. But she had gone directly from the boat to the railroad station and had taken the first train.

When she got to Indianapolis the next day, she sent a wire home. Andrea and Mario and Gina were waiting for her when she reached Clifton at five o'clock that afternoon.

"Christ, but I'm glad to see you back!" Andrea said. "An old soldier like me needs his general."

Mario hugged and kissed her, so glad to see her that he almost forgot to release her. Gina jumped up and down with joy at the sight of her mother, but Marietta could tell that the child had not missed her much.

Delfina had stayed at home to start the supper, and now, swelled with importance, she urged them all to hurry and sit down, so that they might eat while everything was at its best.

"How good it all is!" Marietta exclaimed after she had tasted the various dishes. "As fine as anything I tasted while I was away."

Delfina nodded, and Minot blushed with pleasure. The two were getting along, thought Marietta, only Delfina had become too conceited; she was almost patronizing. She had never been very bright, but her sweetness had made her a dear. Marietta hoped she didn't lose that, or she would be a colorless woman.

"I asked Minot's mother," the girl said. "She couldn't come for supper, but will be up later in the evening."

Angelina was using common sense; she understood that a mother should have only her family around her, on her return after a long absence. And still, after the meal was finished, there seemed little that Marietta had to say to them, or they to her. The first greetings were over, and she had not yet returned to her familiar place in their daily life.

"I'll go over to see Celeste," Marietta said, "before Angelina gets here."

She walked slowly over to the Gilbertis', taking along the handmade shoulder scarf, of white wool, that she had brought Celeste as a gift from Italy. Jim wasn't at home, and Marietta understood that. She wouldn't want to be home either if Joseph Gaia were to call at her house.

Celeste was very glad to see her, and they visited for almost half an hour. They barely mentioned the breaking-up of the partnership and the Gilbertis' plan to move to Chicago. When Marietta stood up to leave, Celeste looked at her appraisingly.

"You weren't away very long," she said. "Still you have changed."

"What makes you think so?"

"I don't know." Celeste was carefully folding the scarf. She added as an afterthought, "I like you better."

"It's all to the good, then," Marietta said laughingly. But she wondered as she left.

Later, when Angelina came to welcome her back, Marietta felt irritated as usual by the woman's vivacity. There was in her an element of joy and life almost impossible to define. Antonio had come with her, and there was much asking and answering of questions. It was almost like a party, after all, for Delfina had baked a cake for the occasion. It was nice, only the child was giving herself too many lofty airs.

"Doesn't she know that a really nice person acts simply and kindly?" Marietta asked herself.

Then she thought that perhaps it was her own fault. Maybe she should have taken more time from the business to teach her children the good manners that *Nonna* had taught her. Still, Mario had been brought up just the same as the others, and he was always modest and gentle and kind. Mario was born nice.

She hoped that if she had another baby, it would be beautiful and gentle like her first-born. She intensely wanted a baby; that desire, more than anything else, had urged her homeward with the greatest possible speed. It made her glad when the Musis left early, saying they knew that she must be tired after her journey. She wasn't tired, only eager.

Early the next morning, before the girls were up, Marietta waited in the sitting room between the kitchen and the store. Mario had opened the place and would be coming through. She had to talk to him about his plans.

He started when he came in and found her there, but he didn't seem really surprised.

"I know you're anxious to take hold of things again, Mother," he said with a little laugh.

Marietta shook her head. "One day more or less will not matter. I want to talk to you." He sat down, and she noticed that his wrist was bare. "You're not wearing the wristwatch I brought you for a present. I thought that you liked it."

"Oh, I do like it, Mother." He blushed. "But it's too expensive a piece of jewelry to show around Clifton."

"It's paid for. What makes you afraid of letting people see it?" He must have a reason for not wearing the watch, but she knew it wasn't its cost.

"Well," he said, blushing again, "the fellows I go with, they can't afford a Swiss watch, not like the one you gave me anyway. There might be some wisecracks about it."

"What kind of wisecracks?"

Mario hesitated, looked embarrassed, and finally said, "Oh, just wise-cracks. I'll wear the watch when I'm dressed up." Before she could question him further, he went on, "Mother, did you want to talk to me about my going to Chicago?"

"About your staying here in Clifton," she corrected him, smiling fondly. "You know I don't want you to leave me."

"And I don't want to leave you, Mother. But I have to go to Chicago."

His voice was respectful, but very stubborn. Marietta spoke sharply. "Have to? Why do you have to go to Chicago?"

"To learn to be a carpenter. That's what I want to be more than anything in the world."

"All right, I don't object to that. But you can learn here in Clifton. I'll go myself to Erikson—he's the best carpenter contractor in town—and ask him to take you on as an apprentice."

"Please, Mother, don't go to Erikson!" He got up suddenly and walked to the window. Over his shoulder he said, "He wouldn't have me."

"He would if you were to tell him you're willing to work for less than the scale."

Still not looking at her, Mario said, "I don't want to work for Erikson. I know what he thinks of money that is not on the up and up." As if he knew how much that must have hurt her, he rushed on, "In Chicago, I'll stand a better chance at the trade. Jim Gilberti's going to ask his son-in-law to help me get in."

So that was how Gilberti planned to get his revenge! She might have known he would strike at her most vulnerable spot, just as she had struck at him. She forced herself not to think of that, to keep her voice calm and quiet.

"If you stay here, as soon as you're through with your apprenticeship, I'll finance you to go on your own."

"What difference will that make?" Mario cried, turning around. His hands were clenched, his whole body tense. "It will be the same as with the watch."

Marietta looked at him, a question in her eyes. She was afraid she already knew the answer.

"Somebody is liable to remark that only bootleggers could afford such costly things." The words were the ones she had feared, but the tone was almost unbearably bitter. In a softer voice he added, "It hurts to have a tag like that."

"Since when has it been hurting you so much?"

"From the very beginning, Mother. Only at first I wasn't so conscious of it, or I was too young to feel as I do now."

That was true, Marietta knew. He had always objected to the bootlegging, but she never thought it would come to this. She couldn't let him go. She assured him that there would never be any more bootlegging. By and by, the people of Clifton would forget that the Sassos had once sold liquor. All the while she talked, she fussed with her hair.

"We didn't really harm anybody," she asserted.

"But we broke the law twenty-four hours a day." He was still standing at the window, his back to the light. Sitting upright in a straight chair, Marietta waited for him to go on. "Mother, people in general begrudge us our money. I feel like a criminal."

Again Marietta fixed her tresses. From the sudden look of tenderness, almost of pity, on Mario's face, she realized that he recognized how upset she was. But he shook his head.

"Mother, it was such a mistake."

"I wanted us to be rich."

"We could have got along with the store," he said stubbornly. "The bootlegging money meant only unhappiness."

"Who else got hurt?"

"Delfina."

The bell tinkled as someone came into the store. Marietta motioned Mario to go in and wait on them. She couldn't. Her legs were shaking. She was cold all over. God, to have her beloved son accuse her so unmercifully—this was worse than Joseph rejecting her love.

"How much more can I stand?" she asked herself.

But she had to know exactly what she had lost, and what she still had and could save. She closed her eyes, so as to gather strength. When she heard the customers leave the store, she called Mario to come back.

"I want to know about Delfina," she said.

Mario told her then that Delfina had loved Joe Bailey (the ballplayer, Marietta remembered; he had been coming around quite often for a while, and then she hadn't seen him again). Now Mario said that Delfina had lost him because of the bootlegging. (But I never knew, Marietta silently protested. If she had known—if she had . . . ? What could she have done?)

Her son spoke quietly, but she could tell that he had suffered for his sister. And only two weeks ago, he said, Gina had been left out of the birthday party of one of her best friends. The child had cried bitterly.

"What's one party?" Marietta asked defensively. But she knew only too well the heartache her daughter must have felt.

"There are going to be other parties," Mario said, "to which Gina will not be invited. Eventually she'll learn the reason."

Marietta felt like an animal at bay. The dearest things in her life were breaking all around her. She would pick up the pieces. But now, this minute, she must save Mario's love and respect for her. He was the best of all her children.

"Sit down, please." It was as if she were talking to a judge. "You know, I guess, that when I came to America I was only seventeen years old. You must have heard us talk about that."

"Yes." He sat down in a chair in front of her.

"In those seventeen years of life in Italy, I already had suffered all the privations and humiliations of poverty."

"Were you really poor, Mother? Were you hungry?"

The anxious note in her son's voice gave some comfort to Marietta. Again she smoothed her hair.

"We were really poor. I never went hungry, but our meals at home were poor and always the same. I never was cold for lack of clothes, either, only they were skimpy clothes, patched and homemade and faded. Until I was fourteen, I went barefooted on weekdays, all summer long, I've often wondered how my feet kept a good shape after the way I walked without shoes on dusty highways, rutted country roads, and on the cobbled streets of Nuvale."

For a long minute mother and son looked at each other.

"Italy is a very beautiful place to live," Marietta said slowly and soberly. "Still I was deeply grateful to your father because he asked me to come here as his bride. The day I sailed for America I cried, and leaving the Bay of Genoa I swore that I would get rich or there was no excuse for leaving my country and my family. That's why I've done what I have."

Mario shifted his feet and contemplated the pattern of the rug. He didn't want to look at his mother. She went on to tell him how every time a child was born to her, she swore again to get rich. Finally she asked, "You believe me, don't you Mario?"

"Yes, Mother. You looked at money in your own way. To me, it seems the wrong way."

He wasn't saying he was sorry for her. His own present hurt was much more important to him than all her suffering, past and present. She made one more effort.

"You are good and honest. You should be able to make the people of Clifton like you for your own self. I think it's worth trying, Mario."

"I don't have the courage. I'm too easily hurt, and I've been hurt too much."

How cruel he was! She could only hope he would remember this and in time understand the motives behind her actions.

"All right," she said. "I'll have your clothes ready for you; you can leave whenever you want to."

He looked at her, and she saw tears in his eyes. But he got up and left without a word.

After her son was gone, Marietta didn't move from her chair. She was alone, watching her life and her house crumble into ruins. She felt crushed, frustrated.

She turned eagerly as the door opened again. But it was only Andrea. Poor helpless Andrea.

"Anything wrong, Marietta?" he asked. "Are you sick?"

She shook her head, afraid to trust her voice. Then, recovering her poise and self-control, she told him of Mario's determination to go away, and her decision to send Gina to a good boarding school. He was surprised to hear about the school, but he agreed willingly, not caring one way or another. She said that at least one of their children should have the advantages of an education. She didn't want to discuss her real reasons with him—or the reasons for Mario's leaving, either. He never had been enthusiastic about the bootlegging.

Neither alluded to the past night. It was too painful. Andrea was done, finished, and the money he had paid for the doctor and medicines had been useless. There was never going to be another baby. The certainty of that had kept Marietta awake for hours, intensified her feeling now.

"We will be alone and lonesome," she said dejectedly.

"Delfina and Minot are with us. We won't be lonesome."

She didn't bother to point out that Delfina was already on her own, living apart as a stranger. He wouldn't understand. At heart Andrea was a child. Even the tragedy of his lost virility had been tempered for him by his simple good-natured philosophy.

Last night, after a little swearing, he had looked at the bedroom ceiling and told Marietta that he had felt it coming on for years, had been prepared.

"Jesus Christ," he had said mildly, "no use getting sore. We have had four children, more than many men can get. Some can't even go with a woman at all."

Marietta had wanted to cry out that she was only forty years old, but she knew that her protests would be wasted. Her husband was like certain streams of water, wide and deep, and sheltered by friendly trees, that no storm can ever disturb greatly.

Now he looked placidly at her. "And don't worry, Marietta. We won't be lonesome. There will be little ones to play with. I'm pretty sure something is on the way. Did Delfina tell you?"

"No, she didn't. But a few days ago when Angelina was here, I heard her lecturing our daughter about lifting things, wearing high heels, and climbing too many stairs." He pulled at his mustache with pride. "When Angelina left, she was so happy even her back danced up and down with joy."

He laughed, expecting Marietta to do the same. Marietta couldn't. This was, strangely, the hardest blow of all—that there should be a child on the way, but not her child. Angelina, already looking forward to being grandmother, would be the supremely happy one. That woman seemed to know how to reach the stars, while she had been fool enough to want to buy them.

"Madonna!" she said to herself. "What a mistake and what a waste!" But, somehow, she would still get something out of life. She must. If *Nonna* were living, she would want her to. Mario. . . . Andrea. . . . Gina. . . . Delfina. . . . Joseph. . . . She was unable to think clearly. Her heart had received too many cruel blows in succession.

Silently, almost unconsciously, she got to her feet and walked over to the desk in the corner of the room. From the top drawer she took out the ledger where the accounts of the store were carefully marked down, day by day. She sat down and took up a pen.

She must check to see what profit had been made during her absence.

Rose Grieco

Rose Grieco, the daughter of Italian immigrants, has written with warmth and humor of the Italian American world for many years. A three-act comedy, *Anthony on Overtime*, dealing with the conflicts and problems arising out of a double culture and how they can become the vehicles of enrichment, was produced at the Blackfriars Theater in New York during the 1961–62 season to critical acclaim. Her stories and articles have appeared in numerous magazines and several anthologies. Ms. Grieco, a lifelong resident of Montclair, New Jersey, has been given several awards for her continuing interest in preserving Italian folkways in this country and has pursued multiple artistic activities in her community.

The Sunday Papa Missed Mass

My uncles Angelo and Jim came into our family by virtue of having had the good sense to marry my mother's sisters Mary and Lina. I don't mention Uncle John, because although married to Aunt Rose, he always managed to keep a safe distance from our affairs.

With her four daughters married, Nonna turned her thoughts toward keeping them physically close to each other, so that in times of trouble they would not have far to turn. The girls cooperated beautifully by living within one block of each other on the Upper East Side of New York.

However, when children started arriving rather regularly, except in Aunt Rose's case, the women decided that while it meant venturing into new territory, their growing families should be surrounded by space and trees and gardens. Nonna quietly allowed her daughters to convince themselves, because it was they who were going to have to convince their husbands.

The idea of leaving the city was given fresh impetus when a "comare" of ours went to a wake in a place called Montclair in New Jersey, and was charmed by the giant trees and surrounding mountains. Her enthusiasm inspired the women in our family to want to settle there, too.

Aunt Rose, being the oldest, set the migration into motion by explaining to her husband that at the age of twelve their son was totally unfamiliar with fields and gardens. In Montclair, they could plant fig-trees and tomato plants and grape-vines. Now, Uncle John wasn't quite so concerned about fig-trees or tomato plants as he was about his wife's beauty, which caused many men in the crowded neighborhood to cast better than admiring glances in her direction. While pretending to agree for their son's sake, Uncle John was accommodating only because he fervently believed his rose was safer blushing unseen in the country air.

Aunt Mary was next in line, and should have continued the journey into the unkown, but, as usual, waited to see what Teresa would do. My mother had little trouble persuading my father. She had always been the quiet one, and when she talked for an hour about how her poor sister Rose must be sick with loneliness out there all by herself, with no one to turn to in times of illness, or listen to her troubles on worrisome days, my father said he would think about it, which meant yes. My mother could have spared herself the trouble of saying her little piece, because my father liked green hills anyway.

When my mother said goodbye to Mary and Lina on the day of departure, they wept as if they would not meet again till the next world. Nonna quietly observed her daughters' luxurious weeping, for she realized that this abundance of sorrow in act one was necessary for the happy ending in act three.

My parents were not long in Montclair when Uncle Angelo was forced to listen to Aunt Mary's litany of loneliness. He let her talk it out, and when she was talked out she became silent and sad; and when Aunt Mary was sad it was the kind of sadness that could not be borne. Uncle Angelo capitulated as he knew he would, because he missed my father.

And that left Lina. Her job was relatively simple because the spade-work had been done, the forest had been cleared. But since she never allowed any drama in life to pass her by, Uncle Jim had to listen patiently while she described to him the torment of being torn from the arms of her nearest and dearest. If a husband died, another could be found, but where pray could one get another sister?

It has never been established whether this particular brand of reasoning swayed Uncle Jim, or whether it was the lonesomeness he felt on Sunday afternoons when he thought of his brothers-in-law playing cards, with the gallon of wine always within easy reach.

In any case, the family was soon re-united, as the women knew it would be; for their husbands' thinking was clear and uncomplicated. They knew that happy women breed happy children, the sum of which adds up to a happy man.

The first spring in their new surroundings arrived, and with it awoke the ancient urge to plant. Once the fig-trees and grape-vines had taken root, the talk turned to the planting of tomatoes. The problem was, where to get the large branches that would hold the heavy flowering plants when they grew ripe.

My father had taken to walking up into the mountains every Sunday morning before Mass. There were thousands of trees up there, heavy with strong branches. He talked over his discovery with Uncles Angelo and Jim. As usual, Uncle John stayed safely away from the fireworks.

The plan was to go up into the mountains early Sunday morning, before anyone was awake, even the police, and provide themselves with the means for starting their tomato gardens. Then my mother asked the unhappy question; was it legal to chop branches from trees that were not on one's property?

Uncle Angelo immediately took the floor. Who, he asked, was responsible for all those magnificent trees flowering on the mountain-top? God, they answered. Were they children of God? Of course, they answered. Was it conceivable that God would deprive His own children of something He so liberally allowed to fill up His mountains? No, they answered, all but my mother, who was finding it difficult to figure out just how God had got Himself involved in this project. The men, however, satisfied now that the Almighty had a personal interest in the success of their venture, blithely made their plans to strip the trees of the Orange Mountains.

The next Sunday, long before dawn, armed with axes and a gallon of wine, the gentlemen planters walked the long walk up to Eagle Rock. As I listened to the details of this story through the years, I could never understand why, if their project was so righteous, they should have pursued it under cover of darkness.

However, when they reached the mountains and saw the number of strong, healthy branches growing in wild profusion, all doubts quickly disappeared. For they saw a definite purpose in the growing of these trees; they were expressly created so their limbs could be cut off to hold up tomato plants.

Putting the gallon of wine tenderly aside, they took off their jackets, rolled up their sleeves and lifted their axes. Until now, the only sounds heard were the pre-dawn rustlings of animal-life, and the restless cries of birds whose world had been rudely disturbed. Boom! The sound reverberated through the silent mountains like thunder, and awoke any wild-life that still slumbered.

"Shhh!" Uncle Angelo, with his fingers to his lips, cautioned Uncle Jim and my father. "Do you want to wake the dead?"

"What are you afraid of?" asked my father. "There isn't anybody around."

"And if there was," said Uncle Jim, "these trees are as much ours as theirs. They belong to the world and we're part of the world."

"I know . . . I know," whispered Uncle Angelo, who realized that Uncle Jim was simply mouthing the philosophy he had so firmly instilled in him. "Still, this is a new country, and you can never tell what kind of crazy laws they have. Remember, I'm a citizen. If I get in trouble I have rights. But with you, they'll deport you."

"No, they won't," said my father, as he raised his axe. "My children are citizens, so they can't deport me." Boom! Down came the axe, and off came the limb.

Uncle Angelo's eyes almost popped out of his head. "Gently . . . gently . . ." He was afraid to speak above a whisper.

"I'll show you." And Uncle Angelo cautiously, quietly chipped away at a weak limb, while the two regarded him, unbelievingly.

"If you want to stay here till next week," said my father, "all right. But I'm getting back for ten-thirty Mass." Down came the axe, as birds and animals squealed and chirped in outraged frenzy.

"Listen," whispered Uncle Angelo, hoarsely, his eyes wide as saucers.

"What's the matter with you?" said Uncle Jim. "Get to work so you'll have a nice thirst for a glass of wine." *Boom* and *Crash!*

"I thought I heard a motorcycle," said Uncle Angelo, creeping cautiously toward some bushes.

"It's your imagination," said my father, unconcernedly.

The tree-choppers were so engrossed in their work, that of course, by the time they heard it, it was too late. As the two motorcycles approached, they remained frozen to the spot. All the time, Uncle Angelo lay flat on his stomach, one arm around the gallon, not daring to breathe. As soon as the motorcycles left with their Sunday-morning cargo, he peeped out, and caught a glimpse of his brothers-in-law . . . each seated cozily beside a trooper, wearing an odd look of bewildered importance.

I doubt if anyone ever hustled down that mountain as fast as Uncle Angelo, on that brightening Sunday morn. With his axe over his shoulder, and the gallon of wine safely in his other hand, he moved his big body as fast as possible toward our house.

When my mother saw him, standing alone in the doorway, the gallon of wine not even touched, she knew she was in the face of tragedy. She remained calm as he related the unhappy details of the morning, but broke down completely when told that her handsome husband had been taken to police headquarters in a basket. She took a batch of bills from her bosom, and commissioned Uncle Angelo to bring them back at any cost. Then she went hurriedly to Aunt Lina's house, and while they shared their mutual sorrow, their envoy started riding the infrequent trolleys in the direction of Orange.

Needless to say, my father never made ten-thirty Mass.

The embarrassing details of how Uncle Angelo played hide-and-seek with the questioning police-officer, as to how he knew his brothers-in-law were in trouble if he hadn't been in the act too, are best left unrelated.

With money left over, after the fine had been paid, and a violent hunger beginning to consume him, Uncle Angelo calmly ordered a taxi.

At about three o'clock, a rustle of excitement was heard, as curious neighbors gathered outside our house. The waiting women ran to the window and beheld Uncle Angelo holding the taxi door open for the other two as if they were visiting dignitaries. Nonchalantly paying the driver, with my mother's money, he followed them into the house, looking neither to the right nor left.

When the excitement of reunion had died down, Nonna was heard muttering to herself from her rocker by the window.

"What are you saying?" demanded Uncle Angelo, for there was never any love lost between these two. "Anything that is worth saying is worth saying out loud."

"I said," shouted back Nonna, "that if anybody had bothered to consult me, I could have told them this wasn't the day to go. I dreamed of beans last night, and anybody over the age of three knows that means trouble."

Uncle Angelo gave her a long, searching look, and finally tapped the gallon.

Marion Benasutti

For more than fifty years Marion Benasutti has pursued a writing career. As women's editor of Philadelphia's *Italian American Herald*, she wrote news and features and a column called "Speaking Italian" in which she gave her readers insights into that language. She has been most successful in

blending her immigrant background with the American cultural scene, and
her stories and articles have appeared in many local and national publications. Many of her family pieces provided the material for the book about
her family entitled *No Steadyjob for Papa* (1966). Widowed, Mrs. Benasutti
still lives in the Philadelphia area near her son, an attorney.

from No Steadyjob for Papa

Nowhere in Philadelphia will you find a street like the Back street, for it has
since become a wide smooth stretch of asphalt with identical row houses on
either side of it, and unless you had lived there, as we did, you could never
believe that it had once existed.

There was a street called the Front street where the houses stood in neat
squares of green grass, their front porches illuminated at night by lamps on
little wooden posts at the foot of each set of steps. In the dark, the lights
looked like suspended glowworms, the number of each house swinging on a
sign attached to the underside of each elegant little lamp.

The Back street, as far as anyone could recall, had always been there, at
the edge of the city. Both streets had names, of course, but to us one was
simply the Back street and the other the Front street, with a jungle of
overgrown bushes and shaded footpaths between. The streets were like two
separate entities, strangers to each other. The area was known as Goat Hill
because the immigrant Italian families who lived there had kept goats. The
nearest landmark was the Branchtown Hotel on the Old York Road. In 1751
the Branchtown Hotel served as a stagecoach stop for coaches plying the
route between Philadelphia and New York. We knew it only as the trolley
stop on the way to Poplar Street in South Philadephia. From the Branchtown Hotel you walked down a long tree-shaded avenue where the "rich
people" lived until you came to a fork in the road. On one side was the
Episcopal church called The House of Prayer and on the other was the Beer
Saloon. These two buildings faced each other at the top of the hill at our end
of the street.

The Back street was unpaved and it ran up a hill at one end and up a hill
at the other end. We lived in its hollow. The Laceys came to live in the old
farmhouse at the top of the hill at the end of the street, farthest away from
the church and the saloon. After a bad summer storm, the water in the
hollow between the two slopes of the street came up to the windows of the
houses, and the lucky ones, such as we, walked out of our front doors into

delicious swirling water up to our waists. When the waters subsided, little frogs appeared in the mud puddles. Long years afterward, whenever I heard the expression "it rained cats and dogs," I thought of the little frogs in the mud puddles. I remembered the feel of the clean soft rain against my upturned face and the squishy feeling of the mud between my toes.

Although we were the "poor kids" who lived in the Back street, in the long summer evenings in our dusty bare feet we did not think about being poor; we just had fun. In the twilight we played street games, Red Light and Run, Sheepie. We played ring games. We were lean and brown, fearless and strong, and the summers were an endless season of delight and great expectations largely unfulfilled.

Except for an occasional Army truck racing down one hill and up the other, raising horrendous clouds of dust, there was no thundering motor traffic to impede or interrupt the flow of our delight. The doughboys who filled the trucks waved their overseas caps wildly at the kids who waved frantically back, not thinking, or even knowing, that these were soldiers on their way to war, sensing only the immediate excitement.

There were things to hide behind in the Back street: black bushes, mysterious and fearful in the night; tangled gardens; outhouses; wagons, broken and horseless in the empty fields. In the distance, beyond the Front street, we could see the brick towers of the new public school where some of us would go in September. One day there would be rows and rows of new houses stretching from the Front street to the new school and beyond. But because of the war the building had stopped; the abandoned dug-out cellars became thrilling hiding places, treasure troves from which we stole bits of lumber and bricks and bright shiny nails.

At the top of our hill was a great tree. "Under the spreading chestnut tree" meant, for me, that tree, although no chestnuts grew upon it. The tree stood high on the hill, across from the Beer Saloon on the other side of The House of Prayer, its branches spread generously all around. The grass grew right up to its trunk, for it was not like other trees, so jealous of the sun that all beneath them was bare and dead. This was a godlike tree. Under it the grass and moss were thick and green, like the dark green velvet that Mamma made into dresses for the rich ladies of the Tennis Courts, and as soft to lie upon.

Sometimes I would run away from the others and fling myself breathlessly beneath the tree. The voices of the children squealing "Run Sheep-e-e-e-e-e" were an endless echo in the deepening twilight. "One, two, three, Red Li-i-i-ght," came the faint screams from below. Sometimes, lying under the tree, in a dreaming void, I heard music coming softly from the Tennis Courts, beyond the Beer Saloon, where the rich children played. I would feel myself lifted to the sky, a part of the softness, every-

thing soft, the music, my body, languid and still, the darkness closing
down softly.

Sometimes Franz was with me under the tree. He was the German boy
next door, the unhappy German boy who did not like being called Hun, and
who played the violin so entrancingly that Papa said, "Mark my words, one
day that boy will play before the Crowned Heads of Europe!" And immediately in my mind the Crowned Heads of Europe rose rampant, pierced with
jewels and glittering with gold and silver, and I envied Franz mightily.

We picked buttercups in the fields and held them under one another's
chins. If the buttercups reflected their soft yellow glow, we screamed:
"Look! She likes butter!" as though we had discovered a magic formula or a
profound truth.

Sometimes the boys, more daring than the girls, grabbed a bunch of
brash yellow dandelions (we pretended not to hear them call the dandelions
"pee-the-beds") and dashed after us madly. If they tagged us with the
dandelions we knew that the dire prophecy foretold in that phrase we
pretended not to hear would, at some future time, be shamefully fulfilled,
so we ran harder, harder, away from the boys, in a delicious never-ending
race.

On Saturday afternoons we washed the dust from our bare feet, put on
high sneakers, and for six cents, a nickel and a penny, we went in a body to
the movie matinee at the Punk. It was really The New Lyric Theatre but we
had long ago given it the more pungent name. There, vicariously, we hung
over cliffs with the heroine and lived through the horror of being bound
hand and foot in the path of an onrushing locomotive. The rollicky music of
a tinny piano punctured the action while villain's fist met hero's chin in a
fight to the finish, with never any doubt, of course, as to the outcome.
Didn't the good guys always win? But not until the following week, when
the action was resumed. Once we saw, because the manager had neglected
to order the film changed for the children's matinee, a lurid Cleopatra in
the shape of Theda Bara. It was frightfully boring. No cowboys, Indians,
death-defying leaps, forest fires, or fist fights. We walked out in a body.

When all other excitements palled, the cry arose: "Let's go to the Tennis
Courts!" The Tennis Courts, in our minds, were capitalized, in keeping
with their importance. As we ran, the dust of the Back street billowed in
gusts under our feet. By squinting one eye, we could watch the games
through the cracks in the fence. I would stand endlessly, patiently waiting
my turn at a crack. I would push an eye against the crack, squinting so hard
the black and purple whorls came, blinding me, so that the rich children
running around the courts, the girls in their white middies and skirts, the
boys in long white flannel pants, ran together in a great white blinding
circle. Almost the best time of all was when the courts were empty. Then

we scaled the high board fence, yelling like Indians, running into the bushes, burrowing for the lost balls.

In the evenings the grownups came. Music poured from the Tennis Courts and there was the hard smack of ball against racket and the word "love" over and over, and I knew that I had to, one day I would have to, explore farther into this other-world place and that I would do it, alone.

Mamma sewed for the Tennis Court ladies. She had learned her craft well when, as a girl of twelve, she had been apprenticed to a dressmaker in Milan. Nobody sewed like our mother and for so little, too, and the ladies knew this. They came to our house, these fine ladies, stepping daintily over the dust of the Back street. They did not speak to me, nor I to them.

Those first years were the most fun, even though we knew Mamma hated the Back street. She had always been proud, our mother. Not for nothing did she bear the name of Europa, a mythical Phoenician princess. Her other names were Elvira Adele. Papa called her *Donna*, the word that in Italian means woman, wife, but for a long time we thought Donna was Mamma's name as Papa shouted: "Donna! Where 'ta hell's my pants?"

His pants were always exactly where he had dropped them the night before, at the foot of the bed. Mamma could never get him out of the habit of leaving them there, and it was fun to hear Papa shouting in the mornings.

Unlike Mamma, our father enjoyed life in the Back street, as he would have enjoyed living anywhere, natural hedonist that he was. Papa was both happy and wise but he did not, alas, inherit from his maternal Italian ancestors the energy and industriousness that Mamma maintained was typical of the north Italian. As our mother so often said despairingly, "That man! He is lazy as a Neapolitan!" Really, it was sad that Papa had to work for a living. He would have been quite happy puttering about in his garden, tending to his strays, reading *The North American*, and fighting with Mr. Leopoldi, our neighbor, about politics and the Austrians versus the Italians.

But from the beginning Mamma had hated the drab frame house in the Back street with its dim damp parlor, so unlike our sunny green house in western Pennsylvania; the black-encrusted range in the kitchen that never worked properly; the grimy tin-lined sink with its recalcitrant iron pump that was, as our mother so often bemoaned, as temperamental as a prima donna. But more than anything, I think she hated the *feeling* of being poor that the street gave her. It seemed to rob her of her innate dignity; it demeaned her in a way that we, who were happy there, could not wholly understand. For how could she know, as we did, the thrill of pushing bare toes through the hot silky dust of the brown unpaved road; the feel of cool running water to wade in; the thick green grasses in the fields, with only the

sound of insects or frogs to break the dreaming quiet? Mamma knew only
the dirt.

"It is a mean, dirty street," she would complain often, bitterly.

"The dirt of God's good earth," Papa reminded her mildly, puffing on his
pipe, his feet propped comfortably against the door of the hated stove.

But Mamma would move her shoulders expressively, as if to shrug off the
feel of something thoroughly unpleasant.

"Never fear," she threatened darkly. "One day I shall be free of it, of the
dirt and the mud. I shall have *'na bella casa* to live in all the days of my life.
Like your sister," she would end always on a note of envy. Then she would
begin to bang pots and pans about in a fine fury.

"It is the war," Papa said placatingly. "Rents are high. She had no choice,
my sister, for, look you, we had to have a place to live in, quickly. And this
was all there was!"

"*Ma che!*" Mamma said disbelievingly. "Would *she* live here, your sister?
Picture, if you will, your sister and that fine daughter of hers living in this
horrible place. Not for one moment would she abide here. She would not
be dead here, your fine sister! She, with her *palazzo* made of stone, and the
street all paved in front of it. Oh, that ditch! Oh, that monstrous spawn of
the devil!"

When Mamma was really frustrated she took her feelings out on the ditch
that ran alongside our house. When it rained hard the ditch filled up with
water and spilled over into the yard. For us it was just another place to play
in, to run in barefoot after the rain. The ditch had originally been an
excavation for the installation of sewer pipe, but the war had put a stop to
that too.

One day Gran'ma said: "Let us make a *rosaria* over the ditch. It will
please your Mamma."

So we gathered pieces of lathe from the abandoned houses and made
an arch over the ditch and Gran'ma planted little red climbing roses over
the arbor and we had our *rosaria*. Gran'ma had hoped to placate Mamma,
her natural enemy. Mamma pretended not to notice. Nonna planted fox-
gloves, with their cluster of little bells, plunging her hands deep into the
moist shaded sides of the ditch where they would be sure to thrive. In
ancient times, Nonna told us, these were called Our Lady's Thimbles. She
had a fascinating store of knowledge about green growing things and
animals.

But even so, the comparison with the stone house of Mamma's sister-in-
law, built by Papa and Uncle Dom in those early years before she had come
to America, was a festering sore in her breast that would not be healed.

We, too, adored Zia's house, but without envy, and took turns visiting it in the summers. Mostly we loved Zia herself. As a young girl Zia had seen the white horses of Vienna and she would tell us about them so vividly that I could close my eyes and there they were, there in that place that Zia said was like the opera house, with its balconies and flags and crystal chandeliers. There they were, behind my closed eyes, the graceful white horses of Vienna, with their ballet rhythms, their prancing dancing feet, their tails enchantingly swishing like the long hair of prima ballerinas, back and forth, back and forth, swish, swish. The white horses had become a part of the enchantment of Zia's house on Rockland street, where there were other fine houses made of stone that Papa had helped Uncle Dom to build.

"I will not be like those Irish on the hill," Mamma would say, referring, of course, to the Laceys. "I want to live like a human being!"

"Are you not being uncharitable, Donna?" Papa would say in his mild way. "You are not, as the good Lord says, loving your neighbor."

"How right you are, *caro!*" Mamma answered, nothing daunted. "Except for one thing. Have you not heard that cleanliness is next to godliness? Or is this only for the *Protestanti?* The Laceys may be good Catholics but they will have to do a little scrubbing before St. Peter will let them into *his* house, I'll bet!"

Papa had his vulnerabilities too. But only two things threatened his natural amiability—our neighbor, Mr. Leopoldi's, insistence that he and Papa were true *paesani,* and the factual evidence of our indifferent progress in school as shown on our regular report cards.

"What is this 'B'?" Papa would rage, flinging his hands to high heaven in a gesture of total despair. "What is this 'C'? *Mamma mia!* Disgraceful! The top mark is what I expect, *demand,* of you. Your father in school was 'A'—all the way! *This* I expect of you, too, nothing less!"

By nature a scholar, Papa believed passionately in *La Educazione*.

When Mamma insisted, finally, that Trina leave school in the seventh grade and go to work in the knitting mills in Germantown, Papa was horrified, even though Mamma pointed out to him, with admirable patience, that Trina was naturally indifferent to formal schooling and that no amount of prodding was ever going to change her. A book, to our Trina, was something to be used for a doorstop. So, with Papa's bitter disapproval and to Trina's evident relief, Trina went to work in the knitting mills. But, as if in defiance of something she wasn't quite sure of, Trina cut off her hair. It happened the night before she went to work, while we were all asleep. Mamma didn't speak to her for a week, not even on her first payday, when she silently accepted the envelope Trina handed her without giving her the agreed-upon allowance of two dollars in return.

Diana Cavallo

Diana Cavallo was born in Philadelphia in 1931 and attended public schools there. Upon graduating from the University of Pennsylvania, she worked briefly as a psychiatric social worker. She has taught at colleges in the U.S. and at the University of Pisa as a Fulbright Teaching Fellow. She has been a MacDowell Colony Fellow and is the author of *A Bridge of Leaves* and *The Lower East Side: A Portrait in Time*. She is married to the German artist Karl Hagedorn and they live in New York, where she is completing a new work entitled *Juniper Street Sketches*.

from A Bridge of Leaves

When I got up this morning and looked in the mirror, I was not in the least surprised to see my reflection, as I always do. It seemed a perfectly natural thing to be confronted by a picture of oneself that doesn't actually exist, or that exists only in relation to other things, perhaps they also assumed. But the whole thing must be got started in the first place, and just by acknowledging that image without controversy, we are already off—so why not?

After all, we believe quite thoroughly every external form. If I tell you I am within months of thirty, am average-sized, have dark hair, deep-set eyes—even embellish it a bit to say what *kind* of dark hair and *how* my eyes are set in my invisible but omnipresent skull—you are very likely, with only that much, to begin to draw a picture of me yourself. If I am skillful enough, I may even convince you of my reality, and we would get along quite well, you feeling satisfied that you already know something of me, and that being far from the case! It would be totally false; you would know nothing of me, and I want more than anything to impart my presence beyond the form of it, although you hardly expected company the moment you sat down with a book, presumably to be alone. And yet, I will be content if you know relatively little of that external me, and satisfy yourself more with those parts that I would not readily show if I did not feel we were as alone as you thought when you settled down to hear me out.

I should warn you, so that you will not misunderstand when I wander off course, that I intend to talk about things quite as they strike me, but with a purpose all my own. You see, despite everything, I am trying to understand myself, a very ambitious undertaking, especially when I am so contradictory. I am sometimes tiresome, stuffy, and the next moment incredibly poetic or surprisingly humorous. It is very confusing to my friends, and so doubly so to me, who must maintain a semblance of order all the same.

I like to talk and I like to write, and I have such an enormous store of impressions and ideas that I feel weighted down with the load of it. Some of them are not meant to be passed on in conversation. Who nowadays talks about the manifoldness of life and death waiting? It would be considered embarrassing, self-conscious, more than a little naïve. Not that I am going to say such things, not outright, in any case, but I plan to go ahead and say what touches me at the moment or what I am reminded of, regardless of its order or disorder. I don't want to give a mistaken impression, because I want to represent myself and this undertaking in their true light. Yet I want very much to make the right beginning.

Do my intentions seem somewhat indefinite, even contradictory? I am different from what I seem, even here, so different that it is mysterious. The different selves I am are what is mysterious, the ones that I have been, that have been discarded somewhere, until I am so conventionally like other people that there seems hardly a difference between my individual form and theirs.

For I am overlaid with what I have become, and to restore any semblance of the past, I must try to enter it as best I can from this present state, incorporating as much of those other selves as still persist somewhere. It becomes all the harder because thoughts and moments sometimes become so separate from one another, and from what I now am, that I barely remember they belong to me. They vaguely resemble some other that was never me, the one that I imagine myself to be, that is fast disappearing even as I try to fold it into the page.

It is off again; perhaps it has lighted somewhere in these musings, re-membrances, or more than likely, it will pass from page to page as my pen does, impressing a little of itself on the rough sheets; but that tiny insect, it will fly the cover. It is nowhere tied fast, secure, not even in these poor

pages where I hear his faint buzzing and follow the meandering sound into
the night. . . .

1

The amazing thing is that man wants to live, that he does not actively wish
to die, that he would rather breathe in foul air, propagate imbecile children, spread contagion to his neighbor, and not rebel against such unnat-
ural acts. As for me, I am surprised that, all things considered, I do not find
it more pointless than I do.

Certainly, I have expended much less energy and interest in the matter
than its importance warrants. But perhaps I think I will have an excess of
such feeling when I am old, and should experience it for myself. But then,
the old people that I know seem so reluctant to die. There is my grandfather, for example, an incredible old man of eighty-six who is mortally
afraid of death. He suffers the most intense pain in his arms and legs, but
prefers it to any thought of his eventual demise. He complains that he is the
only one left of his generation; each year has taken one or the other of his
friends; he feels out of place and alone in a strange world of youth and
activity. Does this move him to a monumental death wish? No, he clings to
life as though it were a precious thing, too valuable to resign. Fear makes it
so, but still, I doubt that I shall have such spirit or such capacity to be afraid
when I am old. I even feel a little cheated. It seems young people like
myself have less of everything—less contentment, less pain, less serious
ambition, less pride of achievement. We have too much of some things, but
too little of these others. We do nothing to acquire the worthwhile ones; we
only resent not having them. I wonder—if my grandfather had not worked
at his trade for fifty years, would he have had them, anyway?

When I stop to consider what my grandfather has to live for, I am at a loss
for reasons. What precisely goes on in his mind I can never know. Certainly
I cannot ask him. In the first place, he looks at me, already intractable when
I address him, surmising that I am an unintroduced stranger or a tax collec-
tor. He has become very sensitive about money, and has felt since he was
eighty that his Olympian age entitled him to be tax-free. In any case, it is
not until I am with him for an hour or so that he realizes I am one of the
family. Then he insists I am Lily's older boy, and when I insist that I am
David, Helen's son, he sputters that Helen never married. To convince him
otherwise is hopeless.

He has lost all his teeth and refuses to replace them. He eats soft foods and
becomes so irritated with their taste and texture that he splatters them about
the table like a child. He insists conversation helps to pass the time, but he
dozes every few minutes, napping fitfully through the day, so there is no

continuity to his hours. But at night, when he is alone and weary, he is afraid to close his eyes and sits heavy-lidded in a faded armchair, stamping his foot or waving his arm to deter death and convince himself he is still alive.

In his wakeful afternoon hours he can never find what he is looking for. He accuses his daughter-in-law of hiding his things, and has driven her voice up to a shrill pitch, so that her presence is intolerable to him. In between all these exasperations, he has a traveling pain that attacks a different limb or vital organ each day. It is not localized, so he can never complain of his poor stomach regularly, releasing his antagonism on a single malady. He frequently writhes or moans as the pain traverses his frail body, so that it has become intolerable to all of us, each one hoping he will depart quietly in his sleep that night. This is precisely why he will not go to bed or close his eyes at evening. He fears death in the darkness of his vigil, as though it never comes at noon. He is like some parents who take all precautions to safeguard their daughters in the evening, as though illicit love were banished by the daylight.

I almost prefer the intense striving after death of the early Christian martyrs, the blessed release, the marriage with God, the return to the eternal womb, and all of that. Of course, with such religious zeal for death, it would be hard to rule out suicide as the Desert Fathers did.

It seems that one is always confronted with that choice—one either wishes it fiercely or fears it intensely! Surely, there must be a middle course, some ground that someone as modern and conventional as I might tread—somewhere between a prayerful St. Anthony and a senile grandfather—without feeling one has avoided the issue entirely, stupidly pretended it does not exist. And yet, it is supposed that people who are not religious give the matter no thought, and that those who are young do not actually conceive it.

I know I speak only for myself, but I insist such reflections are bound to occur. Can one really pass to manhood without some jolt, some jar, that places it squarely before him? One must dislodge the nettle, whatever the means.

Perhaps, then, my first reaction was hasty and untrue. We are involved with it whether we wish it or not. Having put aside those questions which answer themselves, and those answers which frame the next question, one must prepare to ponder death with questions unformed, let alone answers, and that takes the greater effort. Perhaps here the largest number turn back to old paths once abandoned.

And I fear we are burdened too long with an incomprehensible morality, remonstrated too soon for acts unknown and thoughts unfelt, filled with vague fears for the world's transgressions, not yet knowing our connection with the world, Yes, I knew that exaltation as a child, of being dipped in the concrete of penance, sinking in the swamp briar of confession, disappearing beneath the sin-filled lake, arms outstretched in supplication. To be reclaimed at the bottom of the sea, to be disengaged from the morass of the flood pain, to reappear in the pure waters of the baptismal font a cleansed soul, a purged heart, a resurrected body! But once frame the last question, and all the waters of the world flooding the cavity left bleeding by the moon cannot cleanse our limbs of doubts encrusted by purposeless life. Baptismal fonts run dry, send rusted water, tepid and brown, to drown the unalterable stain fashioned by manhood. Confession consoled the unquestioning child; penance redeemed his sinless heart. They fail the man. . . .

8

This is the very present. Rain falling that has fallen for hours, heard now when the monotonous *tap-tap* destroys itself in a sudden hurling against window, and I look up.

I sit in my room, aware my thoughts have been trailing off, the most recent past tapering until, imperceptibly, we are living the new moment, and some rushing against window, some stir in the room, wakes us to it.

Yet the rain was here when I woke, but exiled to that part of morning which says: it is Saturday, it is drizzling, it is a day at home. It blended so inscrutably with the past that the newness seemed continuous with it, remained unnotable, until a lunging like this forced the head up: this is the very present.

The wind gathers, blowing and stamping on rain; the sky sinks from its gray to a blackness; a thunder roll drops from its midst. Somewhere people are running, seeing skies darken, rain quicken, hearing a dreadful thunder. They scatter, searching skyward for a yellow flash that, even expected, comes over-soon, lighting heavy pockets of cloud. Streets, returning to nature, become rivulets; walls are washed clean. Trees tremble for plumage wind has whipped loose. Between sky and earth no margin; all has become one moist descent.

I saw it close, that blurring of forms, horizon slipped so far, it has soaked in the earth. A boy, I lay by a lake, throwing in pebbles, twigs, watching them cut water, drown in rings their splashing had made. Wind blew against water, rippling wide circles, as if an invisible hand, far larger, stronger than mine, were discharging lightly its fistful of stones. The clouds sank as low as they might, horizon dropping, fading before my eyes. One might sleep in it.

But I heard sound: water fallen on water, welcoming its own, the first growl of thunder, and ran with the rain falling, woodward, to reach the clearing beyond, some roof. So many trees. Overhead a bridge of leaves, pelted, borne down upon by this shower of stones, swayed, holding off sky, imprisoning rain. Underfoot those that had fallen clung to the step. The woods darkened; the birch trees became their heavy, black bands. Boughs, whipped loose by the rain, crashed; my own fear that came to my lips dissolved into that single tremor of forest sighs, earth rumbles—my cry indistinguishable from theirs.

Tripping on swollen root, slipping on perished leaves, where was my sound? In the progressive silence I heard it—the *tick-ticking* of feet, like the beating of an insignificant clock in the immeasurable time of the universe. I stilled it to meet the sudden hush that was spreading. Hardly a bird called or cried or sang. There was barely a movement of leaves. The wind abated. Wood voices stilled . . . trees tenantless . . . shrubs unrustled. Only the echoless, the silent, the void.

Then it burst from the heavens—the thunder clap potens—rumbling and rolling, a giant roar and a mighty quake, a lusty reverberation tumbling a yellow sky into forest darkness. There was a flutter among trees; a quiver ran through them in a common swaying. Only the ash tree was still; nothing of it moved or bowed to break its dark silence. I saw an angry finger of light part its leaves, crackling in deep fury as it sundered that majestic head and plunged itself forcefully into its bowels. I saw it die. In an instant the tallest, loftiest tree in the forest—no more, instantaneously disrobed, shorn of its leaves, clipped of its boughs, stripped of its bark. It remained blanched and naked, gripped by a deadly pallor, a corpse already, and I could see the black disfiguring scar where it was disemboweled, gleaming in its chalky flesh. Yet it remained rooted in earth, as though it were yet forest, still of its world, though less tree. Another monstrous crash of thunder shook the sky, and with it the storm lost force, dissipating as quickly as it had struck.

How many trees in the forest are reclaimed by the Nature that made them? Standing without, who sees them, those blunted tops, broken boughs, hollow trunks that fill the forest? There they stand, covered with the sores of a painful blight, still rooted to the fertile earth that conceived them, no less forest for their passing. Their hulks endure until the forest can cremate its corpses, sometimes hundreds of years after death, when they have, at last, worn away all evidence; disintegrated, they are ground back into the earth where they had lain as seedlings, returning to the conception bed to father new life in their turn.

The moist earth that slides through the fingers, how many lives has it been, how many forms has it taken, while histories mix their silt with the river? Bits of root and flat stone, they underlay the forest: ocean beds grow on them. They have become the soft clay of generation, womb of the universe.

Each single life a small instance, each moment an eternity that cries out against the measuring palm. Who is it counts time? The wind flings sand, grinds boulders, incises mountain faces, takes those captive grains and buries them into the earth, or carries them to the soft underside of clouds where they drop unseen in raindrops to the place where the wind sought them. The river bends trees, strips twigs, dissolves roots, lays them at the foot of the forest, where they had dreamed to be in final union with the earth.

The claim of death, how short a thing, almost as short as life. We fear its violence, yet it has what we seek. The crimson berry glitters in the sun, wishing to stay always crimson, always plump, always berry; yet what is there to fear from the bright-eyed bird sent to pluck it from the bough, warming it in the soft belly? The common rosemary knows: she grows more beautiful, luminously white, exposing a bare head to the approaching foot that crushes its life juice.

I am that berry, that sturdy rosemary, that buffeted grain, that tender root, that lofty ash. We live, yet fear not. It is all the same to us. We have loved what we have been. There is no terror in becoming. Let other men struggle, let them deny, resist. I live, hearing the stilling tread, seeing the quieting finger, not cringing at its dark step. I will be ready. My neighbor, screaming, is welcomed; my father, unfulfilled, is beckoned; my son, unborn, is taken. I wait.

Octavia Locke
(Octavia Capuzzi Waldo Locke)

As her name indicates, Octavia Locke is an eighth child. She was born into a talented Italian family in Philadelphia. She graduated with honors from the Tyler School of Fine Arts at Temple University in Philadelphia and was a Fulbright Fellow at the American Academy in Rome in 1949–50. She has also been a Breadloaf Fellow and a resident at Yaddo. She is an artist as well as a writer, and her work has appeared in shows and is in private collections. For many years she taught art in Washington, D.C. Her novel *A Cup of the Sun* (1961) appeared under the name Octavia Waldo; other work has been published under the names Octavia Capuzzi and Octavia Capuzzi Locke. She and her husband, Norman Locke, have collaborated on writing about art prints. They live in California.

The Rocks

Scott Claus had a way of confusing the day of the first blasting with the day of the first blessing. Maybe he never heard himself. The words would tangle in his mouth and it took a fine ear like Dinney's to tell them apart. But that was before the rocks.

Long before.

On the day of the first blasting Claus witnessed the last sweep of red earth in Marrow County. He thought not of his father or of his father's father who had once owned the land but of a city, conceived and executed as one—brought to light complete in all her parts like Venus from the sea. With nothing less than a smile, Claus watched a time of fields and forests crumble beneath the bulldozers and the dynamite and fold into the past. Futures were not in wheat and not in fruit but in concrete. Urban planning was all Claus could talk about.

Claus couldn't take his eyes off Model City. You'd think he was playing god, working his way toward the seventh day. The seventh day did come, and on the eve of it, when the work was done, Claus borrowed a tradition of the Mohawk Indians and had himself lifted by a crane to wave the American flag above the pinnacle of the Municipal Building. The city stretched beneath him, a vast monotone of concrete and aluminum, as desolate as the city of the dead on the eve of a national holiday. But Claus didn't see it that way. Even when all the cars pulled away, when the doorways were dim and the escalators did not move and no water gushed from Sumpter Fountain, when Claus was standing alone on the highway, watching the sun set over the quiet, he did not see his city that way. He breathed in the last moment of peace ever to touch that place again, and he wept. He wept not for what he had destroyed, but for what he had created. It was the moment he would always remember as the time he touched God's hand.

Dinney told him it was the sunset.

Claus insisted he had seen an image. Maybe that was where the trouble started. Because after Model City was settled and all the TVs were going at

once and all the patio broilers were burning steaks at once and the kids
were running wild and the parents were taking tranquilizers and sleeping
pills so as not to worry about Mary Jane in the schools or the war (even
though NATO kept reassuring them that they were in their 20th year of
peace) or the riots or the next Madison Avenue campaign for President, the
newspapermen began writing that Model City had everything. "Everything," Dinney said. "Except some saving grace to nourish the soul."
Churches weren't the answer. He never expected Claus to listen to him.

In retrospect, Dinney said, it was that image in the sunset that sent Claus
to Columbus. Because the next thing Dinney knew, Claus had convinced
the Columbus School of Arts to open a branch in Model City, and he
returned with a middle-aged lady with twinkle eyes and silver bangs to
direct it in mini skirts and red stockings. She wore a pink rose in her watch
band, and one look at her told Dinney that Claus had met his match. When
she said, "My name's Millah. Miz Millah," with all the lilt of the South
playing on the words, Dinney was certain that Claus had met his match.
"Millah," she repeated. "M-I-L-L-E-R," letting Dinney shake her hand.
His eyes settled on the rose in the wide red watch band. It wasn't plastic.

Claus gave her everything she wanted from art supplies to discount
tickets. The art school opened its classes to eighteen students inside the
Municipal Hall, and when Miss Miller asked for water to spray sweetly from
Sumpter Fountain, by Claus! she had it. Any hour of the day or night.
People began talking about Living Involvement Through Color, saying
things like, "Paint Municipal Hall pink and violet," using words like *kinetic
colors* and *ambience* as if they were tooth paste. It was alive fun, and Claus
never questioned the vitality of it.

That was how Claus came to approve of the *Fall In*. He didn't know what
a *Fall In* was. Nobody did, that was what was so appealing about it. Because
Claus wanted what nobody had ever had. He advanced Miss Miller a check
for $5000.00 and told her to "think big"; and she said, "Man, will I!" and
began structuring a June week-end, alfresco, that promised to give Model
City an avant-garde send off, guaranteed to lift it to the moon. From Canada
to California people began reading about Model City's *Fall In*, which according to the art commentator of the *New York Tides* was to be "a percep-
tual happening, a psychedelic rendezvous with the kings of polar syncopation and electronic raison d'etre." Claus was tickled silly to see Model City
in print, and if you asked Miss Miller how things were moving, her twinkle
eyes flashed wide open and she said, "Swinging', Man, are they swingin'."

It was hard to know whether it was a question of design or accident that
swung the rocks into her head. All Dinney knew was that she had driven to
Cashew County one day and told the chief engineer of Gain Construction
Company not to worry about stock piling the rocks from the hill he had

levelled, but to *carry* those rocks to Model City and dump them in the fountain.

"Carry them on down," she said.

"Lady," said the the chief engineer. "How many you want?"

"All of them."

"You're joking."

"Nope. All of them."

"Lady," he said, "if you'd just look them over and mark the ones you want with your lipstick," he laughed, "I'll be glad to oblige."

"I want them all," she laughed, and for a good while they laughed at each other till she flashed him one of those special cards Claus had given her to authenticate her position in Model City, and he complied. But he thought she was out of her mind.

People looking down from the office windows of Sumpter Plaza couldn't believe their eyes when they saw five and six trucks pulling into the Plaza and emptying their loads of rocks. They telephoned the City Council, the Traffic Department and the Fire Marshall to find out what the hell was going on. Nobody knew a thing. Scott Claus was out of town till Sunday. But there was Miss Miller in beach hat and owl glasses, directing the men to "Pile 'em high."

"Lady, you tell us how you want 'em," the men said.

"Just dump them. We'll have a delicious incandescent structure, no matter how you do."

Well, they laughed at her and dumped them and she laughed right back. That was Friday night.

By Saturday morning the Mayor's office had issued a statement to the effect that the rocks were part of the *Fall In,* and by noon different trucks were seen zooming into the Plaza carrying people in bands of six and seven, all equipped with electric guitars and zithers and xylophones. One truck was filled with tanks of helium and three electronic chambers and men in lustrous hug-me-tight leotards. It wasn't long before the groups had set up their booths on stilts and the Plaza took on the look of a circus.

A girl from the press drove into town with a camera. She wore bell bottoms with patches all over them, and squinting through the eye of her camera, she followed the heart of the new metropolis with a steady click click click, talking while she focused her attention on the movement. "Looks like you're having a show," she said.

"A *Fall In,*" someone corrected her.

"What the hell's that?"

"Stick around."

She did.

Then the carloads of people began heading down the main streets and they were followed by the usual traffic of a city's Saturday. Everybody took one look at that heap of rocks and wondered if they were real.

Rocks, mind you. Blue-black and salt-grey with dark striations. The fountain's mist sprayed them and when viewed from the distance of a city street, they resembled a picture post card of Tivoli. Except neither the urban planners nor Scott Claus had ever been to Tivoli. The girl from the press narrowed her eye on them and clicked her camera, and when someone told her that the rocks were part of the *Fall In*, she asked, "What part?"

"The art part," said Miss Miller.

"Come again," said the girl from the press.

"The art part—you know, they're earth forms. You've heard of found objects?"

"Sure."

"Well, these are *found forms* created by the earth."

"Isn't that rather obvious?"

"Well, I never take things for granted," said Miss Miller. "They're the earth's art, the art of the earth."

"I know," said the girl from the press, "Like 'Fruit of the Loom.' What are you going to do with them?"

"Look at them," said Miss Miller.

"I have," said the girl from the press, grinning at her.

"Pretty, aren't they?"

"If you like rocks."

Miss Miller's mouth opened in a wide O, but the girl from the press said, "When is someone going to do something to them?"

"Like what?"

"Like carve them."

"Do they need it?"

"Well, don't they? Aren't you going to sculpture them?"

"They are sculptured."

"Where?"

"Look at them."

"I am. I don't see anything but rock."

"Don't you?"

"Now look," said the girl from the press. She let her camera swing from the strap around her neck and folded her hands behind her, and with her feet firmly planted on the ground she said, "Don't pull my leg. When is someone going to get up there and cut them so I can get a picture?"

"Scar them?" said Miss Miller, outraged.

"Well, put a chisel to them—a little work."

"Destroy them?" said Miss Miller. "They've already been scarred by dynamite and bulldozers and the ugly hand of man, and they're sculptural as they are, thank you, quite sculptural, and you can just go . . . help yourself to your pictures."

"I have."

That night huge plastic sculptures, inflated with helium, were seen floating above the spot lights in kidney shapes of hot pink and orange. The fountain was strung with Christmas tree lights and the water sparkled like quick silver. Things had the look of a real fiesta. Even the rocks seemed to belong there and people began saying how they understood them now, sitting on them.

Then the electronic boxes began reacting, only people didn't realize it at first. They just kept hearing voices. The boxes would light up like computers whenever someone crossed their paths and they began hissing at people, and the air would fill with whispers of "I see you, seeyou, seeyou. Scared you, didn't I? Scared you. But I caught you at it, caughtyou, caughtyou. Caught y o u." Imagine copping a feel of somebody's wife and that voice sneaking up on you!

At nine o'clock sharp the bands began to play. Although "thunder" might be a better word, because to hear the press tell it, the bands let out one hell of a roar that blasted Model City from there to Kingdom Come. It was so convulsive, the dignitaries went home to put on suspenders.

Four or five bands played at once while singers sang with all of their strength. Their voices whooped into the larger clash of brass against brass and drums and electric strings—forever lost—while mouths opened and closed in measured time, working the motions of sound.

The men in hug-me-tight leotards glowed in the night. Their bodies lighted to the music, their muscles stretched and flexed and trembled like fluorescent beams pulling love to the ground. The crowds thickened and the music rocked them. If you wanted to hear your neighbor, you had to press your ear against his screaming mouth.

Only the electronic boxes kept their equilibrium. They lit up their square faces and the coils of color blushed and ricocheted in neon tubes while a whim wham blurt blip of noises and little voices came out from under the rocks. "I saw you doing what you did. I caught you pickin' your nose."

"Sweet Jesus," Dinney said. "You couldn't make up your mind whether to laugh at them or swat at them. The trouble was they were more real than real. Like the FCI."

But the young people liked them, and the young came from everywhere—from Crystal and Colebin too. Caravans of them, with their long hair and long skirts and long strands of beads and feet looking like the long roots of trees. They came carrying flowers out of the dust. At first sight of them one of the city councilmen hawked, "Lordgoddahosts," and when

Miss Miller began burning incense, he nearly panicked, thinking it was pot. One lady with milkweed hair passed out.

Miss Miller had to seize the microphone to announce that the incense was non-carcinogenic pine and eucalyptus from the woods of Alabama before some people would breathe deeply. But there was nothing she could do to keep the very embodiment of *haute monde* from wagging its head at the love *pavimenti* which the Children were painting in the streets. You might think those representatives of fashion were witnessing words like HATE or SLUT or SNOT. These same people had never batted an eye at the aluminum nipples all over the undersides of Municipal Hall's archways; but now suddenly LOVE and SODA conspicuously offended them. They just stood there on the curbs, wagging their heads as if they were watching their last diamond slip down the drain, not once seeing themselves or each other—the women in see-through tops and the men in gossamer pants.

For a while it seemed that a competition was meeting under the stars, and it was hard to know where to focus your attention: on the Children or on those who watched.

Just when the hoopla had reached its loudest, someone took it upon himself to be literal. A *Fall In* was a fall in was a fall in, he said, squirting detergent into the fountain, and watching till the suds foamed and then he fell in, right into the cool bubbly basin in the night. One by one the Children followed. In and out. They stepped from that fountain like water babies, offering soap bubbles as gifts from the gods. Then dazed and delighted they returned ten times over for more while those prurient sons of Adam, afraid of a handful of bubbles, shrank back on the sidewalks and watched, distorting what was right and innocent into a boiling hell of misplaced dreams.

That audience in all its chic—the fake diamonds set in platinum gold, the poison-ring watches, the 20 years good service buttons and keys to Bentleys—why, they had everything and nothing, Dinney said, while those Children with their hands full of soap bubbles had nothing and everything.

A mist began to fall and the soap bubbles drifted lightly through the air. But the bands kept on rocking and rolling and the Children kept on tumbling in the suds, and the crowds on the curbs watched. Even when the mist thickened and turned to fine rain, people watched in mute fascination as they might have watched the late late show. There was something so compelling about those lithe wet bodies in a night of deafening music and soap bubbles. Nobody saw the rain.

But someone in the crowd began clipping the Children's hair. At first it seemed he was clowning—as if he were part of the show. He slid in and out of the audience with playful speed, and then he stood right out in the open— high boots, brass buckles, a wide chain dangling from his shears to the ground. He began charging after those Children like a lion tamer while the crowds on the curbs didn't budge. They laughed and the Children went crazy running in and out of the snip snip snip of those garden shears while he lunged after them singing, "Three Blind Mice." He snipped off their hair and he snipped off their beards and he sang as they ran, "Three Blind Mice."

When one of the Children took a swing at him, all hell broke loose and the kid with the shears seemed to multiply right there before you in ten, twenty, thirty replicas—all with garden shears and chains and brass buckles. All with the same beef build and faces as distinguishable as un-baked bread. Miss Miller called the police who came and tucked the Children safely into jail. That's how the night ended. As abruptly as a circus, with a huddle of bright booths abandoned in the rain.

When Claus returned from New York and took one look at the morning newspaper and read THE SCANDAL OF THE ROCKS, he nearly called the police, fire squad and sanitation department to Miss Miller's apartment to not only lock her up but to wipe her off the face of Model City. He never read past the first page that told of "a mass swim in and love in" in Sumpter Fountain. Claus's mind was tormented with visions of bubble dancers and daisy chains and pot. He picked up the phone and called Columbus and woke the director of the Columbus School of Arts right out of his Sunday double bed and told him he was sending Miss Miller right back to him. Then he phoned Miss Miller and told her to start packing.

"Where are you taking me?" she said.

"I'm sending you," he said.

"Where?" she said.

"Have you seen the papers?" he said.

"No," she said.

"I'd love to rub your nose in them," he said, breaking the connection in her ear.

Dinney brought her the newspaper. That girl from the press had smeared the *Fall In* with all sorts of inferences and had ripped the heart out of the fun. The Children were still in jail, booked on charges of disrupting the peace with disreputable conduct in the water and on the rocks and flooding the public domain with pornographic suggestions fed through computers.

"Pornographic?" said Miss Miller. "The Children had their clothes on!"

"In the water," said Dinney. "That's the trouble: in the water. And on the rocks."

"Nobody did a thing on the rocks, except sit on them."

"*A scandalous evening of do-nothing-constructive-art to the tune of scur-rilous voices,*" Dinney read aloud from the newspaper. "There's the point," he said. "The rocks didn't move a bit. But the voices. . . ."

"The voices they heard were their own consciences," said Miss Miller. "How could anyone accuse those electric boxes of being lewd?"

"I don't know," said Dinney. "The fountain was jammed though."

"Jammed?"

"The detergent dissolved all the grease in the bearings and Claus had to send a repair man to turn off the fountain and take it apart and fish out all the hair and line the bearings with grease again. And that police affair. . . ."

"O God, Dinney, nobody was killed."

"No," Dinney said. "Your head's coming off but nobody was killed."

"Dinney, there was no pot, no pornography, no nudity, no drunkenness. Just rain and soap bubbles and music."

"Loud music," said Dinney.

"Okay, loud music."

"And rocks," said Dinney.

"And rocks." said Miss Miller.

"People can't stand the thought of innocence," said Dinney.

All of a sudden Claus charged through the door. He hadn't knocked. He bolted across the threshold—his straw hat shading his head—and he said, "Get those damned rocks out of there." He was wearing sun glasses, and he didn't lift them or the hat from his face. Neither did he stand still. "Get those damned rocks OUT. . . ."

All Miss Miller could do was look at him and let her mouth hang open. She mustered a faint, "I thought we agreed. . . ."

"We agreed on sculpture," Claus said.

"That's sculpture," she said.

"The hell it is! Don't try to con *me*, Baby, *I* can see straight."

"Then you'd better take another look!"

"Oh, no, Baby. I've done all the looking I'm going to do. Nobody's going to try to tell *me* the hand of creation is in that mess of rocks."

"Well, it's there," said Miss Miller, shouting at him. "If it's anywhere, it's there."

"What Miss Miller's trying to explain . . ." said Dinney.

But Claus cut him short. "How long will it take you to get those rocks out of there?"

"I'll get them out," said Miss Miller.

"How long?"

"How do you expect me to know? I've never moved rocks before."

"Baby, you moved them here; you move them out."

"All right allrightallright," she said.

But of course she didn't move them. She never intended to move them. She just carried herself and her luggage to the train depot and the last anyone saw of her, she was eating a candy bar, waiting for the Southern Sunset Express. And that might have been that, except that the Children were excused from jail and all of them returned to the fountain, taking turns by night and day to guard those rocks.

"Like homing pigeons," Dinney said. You couldn't chase them away. They carried signs: SAVE THE ROCKS. And it was crazy: someone put an ad in the paper, SAVE THE ROCKS. The next day there were two full page ads. By the third and fourth days there was nothing but SAVE THE ROCKS. The *New York Tides* got hold of the news and gave those rocks so much publicity that Model City was caught in the limelight. Claus was silent as a statue in a floodlight. That *New York Tides* art commentator must have liked rocks because he wrote: "Man so cruel and primitive had smashed God's land till it was void of everything real. And now it wasn't a statue that was being idolized or a woman's face or a nude climbing up and down an escalator, but simply a group of rocks that caught in the sun and mist-spray of the June rain."

The curious thing, Dinney says, is that people come from all over to see them. They touch them, run their hands over them as if they were handling a relic. Mostly they just stare at them or sit on them, fitting themselves into the sides of the rock. Up close, Dinney says, you can see the master's touch of color running through them in lines that are never straight because their maker never drew a straight line, although He could have if He tried.

Claus never mentions Miss Miller and Dinney hasn't the heart to ask him if she'll ever come back. But sometimes on a snowy evening when Claus leaves his office and turns away from the aluminum walls of the Municipal Hall, he stops dead for a cold minute right in front of those rocks.

Mary K. Mazotti

Born in California in 1924 of immigrant parents, Mary K. Mazotti says that her childhood, when her father was a ranch laborer, was spent among Italians who came from the same Calabrian villages as her parents. She has been married forty years and is the mother of seven children. Until recently she was a school secretary. She started to write in 1981 and has been published in several small reviews.

La Ciramella

"Nothing in the house to do?" I heard Papa say as I sat reading on the steps of the front porch. He towered before me like a yellow giant. Papa had just finished sulfuring our vineyard across the dirt road and was covered with the yellow powder.

"We did everything you told us, Papa," I answered, speaking for my two younger sisters and myself. He grunted with satisfaction. Idle daughters always set him on edge, as busyness was Papa's way of life. He turned and walked slowly to the faucet trough to wash up for our main meal of the day. I carefully pinched a rose leaf from the trellis to make a book mark and scooted inside to set the table. It was a spring Saturday, 1936, and six long years into the Depression.

Each early spring the sun's bright rising was directly over our vineyard and small house. In spite of the Depression Mama saw the wand of golden rays as a blessing for her and Papa, and their three young daughters born in America. Times in America could never match the poverty of their native rocky villages in southern Italy. And Mama never stopped pouring out words of gratitude for finding a better life.

Papa was famished from spraying sulfur all morning. Now he seemed content that the new grapes were protected from mildew. He sniffed the homemade noodles Mama had prepared.

"*Una festa!*" he spoke through his nostrils. Mama had tossed the noodles with hot olive oil, minced garlic, and fresh basil, and sprinkled over them her grated goat cheese.

"*Pronto,*" Mama said, putting the steaming platter carefully on the round oak table. Making a swift blessing over our food, Mama served everyone.

I watched Mama's flushed cheeks as she ate. I knew she was hungry. Early that morning she had heated tubs of water on a fire pit outside to wash clothes. She stood stooped for hours scrubbing bed sheets and towels on the scrub board, twisting and twisting out suds and rinse water, and then pinning them to wire lines strung on the sunny side of the house, where carnations and hollyhocks bloomed.

Needless to say, I and my sisters, Lomena and Pina, felt hunger rumbles also from doing housework and picking up around the big yard like Papa told us to do.

Papa finished the first dish of noodles and was into his second when he got off on a conversation about how life used to be in his native village of Grisolia where he was born. (Papa and Mama often spoke of their little villages. Mama spoke of San Sosti.) I tried hard to picture it all and liked to share these stories with my sixth-grade teacher, whom I adored and respected. Papa became very nostalgic as he recalled the fun things that happened as he grew up in Grisolia.

"The thing I itch to do most," he said, "is to play a *ciramella* again." My sisters and I stared blankly.

Mama explained, "It's a music instrument—a bagpipe, made of goatskin."

Lomena and Pina giggled. Staring at my father's unshaven face, I scowled, "Goatskin!" What a stinky instrument, I was about to blurt out, and knew better than to make fun of my father.

Papa rushed on, his face rosy, "I tell you, no one could play the goatskin like me." Laying down his fork rolled fat with noodles, he pretended playing one. With both hands uplifted, he made droning bagpipe sounds come from his nose by wrinkling it upward and humming through his teeth.

This time I laughed till the tears came. "I didn't know you were a musician, Papa," I said with amazement.

"By the saints!" he answered. "I think I'll just make one for old-time sake. It will take the place of the one I left behind in Grisolia. What a pity I was talked out of bringing it to America by *cara* Mama. I let her load me up with dried sausage and her bread instead."

My mother stopped eating. She pushed a loose hairpin into her hair bun. "*Ma*, Nichole," she teased, "what do you know about bagpipe making?" Flinging her right hand upward, she went on, "When was the last time you've seen one?"

Papa stuck out his chin and huffed, "Elena, I can remember a sack of things! What is needed? What is needed?" he repeated, and answered for himself, "Just the skin of a young goat and pipes for playing. That's all!"

"*Sì, Sì*," Mama argued back, with twinkling eyes and still teasing. "What little I remember the skin has to be peeled off carefully—like a sock, not slit down the middle—to make an airtight bag. And curing the skin! It's not something simple, like swatting flies."

Papa couldn't help but laugh. He liked Mama's sharp sense of humor. He then got up to take some food scraps to Primo, his dog, without saying more about the matter. I wondered, as my sister Lomena and I washed the dishes in a pan of hot water, if Papa would really make a *ciramella*.

My mother and father had met and wed in their new country of America, in the early 1920s, when thousands of Italians left families behind and sailed across oceans to find better lives in new lands. They settled in California, in the San Joaquin Valley, where young vineyards, orchards, and farmlands and small shops were already started by friends before them, and by Armenians, Greeks, Mexicans, and French.

Now, in 1936, America was still having bad times called a Depression. People were out of work. Banks were failing and families lost home and hard-worked lands because they couldn't make payments. Worse, crops were not paying much.

Papa and Mama already knew how to make do with little. Fortunately, Papa had his land free of debt before he married Mama. And Nonna, Mama's mother, let them live in the small two-bedroom house rent-free when she moved to San Francisco. There were plenty of fruit trees and vegetables Papa had planted across the road; eggs from hens, milk from the goat, and catches of rabbits and quails by Papa. Sacks of flour and gallons of cooking oil were bought with side-job money Papa made on other ranches. And, Papa was never without a bottle of homemade wine from his own vineyard to help his digestion, and to help him relax from long hours of work.

One evening the whole family walked to the east side of Clovis to visit Papa's *paesano*, Carlo, and family. Carlo and his wife, Amelia, were godparents to Lomena and me. They had a family of twelve children. I liked to visit them because their oldest daughter, Theresa, and I were good friends. We liked to giggle and talk about friends and growing up.

I had forgotten all about Papa making the bagpipe until I overheard him bring up old times in Italy to my godfather. Papa didn't say he was going to make a bagpipe; he just asked clever questions about how to make one. I thought, How wise Papa is. He still dreamed of making one, but wanted to save embarrassment if it didn't turn out right. After our visit, my godfather took us home in his old Studebaker.

As he did every springtime, Papa bought a young goat from a farmer. Besides giving the family rest from eating jackrabbits and chicken meat, the goat provided the skin for the *ciramella*. I was glad that we were in school when Papa did the butchering and skinning behind the chicken shed. Only Primo, the dog, watched. Papa got the dog from a friend and named him after Primo Carnera, an Italian world heavyweight champion boxer a few years back.

Papa had removed the skin as he wanted it—whole, except with openings at top and bottom, and where the legs stood. Then followed many weeks of scraping off the hair, and rubbing and soaking the skin to make it soft.

One day Mama complained to Papa, "*Mamma mia!* What strange things I'm putting up with these days, Nichole. You have used my washtubs to treat your *ciramella* skin and my clothes are drying an ugly smell."

"I didn't know," said Papa. "*Basta*. That's it. I'm finished with the treatments. I'll scour the tubs with wood ashes for you—that is, if you write a letter for me."

Mama pulled her black-and-white-checkered apron above her plump middle and said, "Let me guess. You want me to write to your father in Italy for the blowpipe and sounding pipes for the *ciramella*."

"Please," said Papa, "you know how poor my writing is." So Mama did. I was proud that she had learned to write in Italian before she came to America. She even went to school in America up to the fourth grade. Papa was still struggling with his writing and I was amazed at how fancy he could write when he made up his mind.

Every night my father pinned the bagpipe skin to the clothesline to air out. Not long after, he was heard yelling, "What happened to it? What's happened to It?!!" We all dashed outside. Papa was red with anger. The line was broken and the skin gone. Everyone searched at least three times, every spot of the yard. Just when the skin seemed forever lost, Papa looked in Primo's doghouse. There it was next to him. Papa shook his fist and cursed. Primo ran and hid behind the woodpile. But I knew it wasn't Primo's fault the clothesline broke.

Late October when grape leaves had turned yellow, and some purple red, and the grapes were picked, Papa brought home a package from the post office. "They have arrived," he said happily tearing open the package. Lomena and I jumped up from doing our homework and Pina from her scribbling.

"Can we watch, Papa?" Pina said, jumping up and down. "Sure, Little Squash," answered Papa as he unwrapped the brown pipes. "And after we eat, I'll fit them into the skin."

That afternoon I carried in cut grape stumps to warm up the kitchen. The stumps threw off good heat to warm up the neat tiny living room, two bedrooms and large, kitchen-eating area. Papa worked on a bench that we kept for company. As Mama toasted fava beans for munching, he marked the skin leg opening that would be used to fit in the blowpipe and valve. He fitted the sounding pipes in the neck opening and bound them in place tightly with twisted hemp. Papa neatly sewed up the bottom and remaining leg openings.

"It looks like a giant flat pear with horns," I whispered softly in Lomena's ear. She bent over with laughter.

"What's next, Papa?" said Pina, pulling on the elastic of the flannel pajamas Mama had made her.

"Air," said Papa. "Lots of it." He blew and blew into the bagpipe and rested. Then he blew until the bag got fat. He put his fingers on some piping holes and let air gush out of the others. Wails and squeals filled the kitchen. I ran to the bedroom to hide my laughter. Lomena followed.

"What terrible music," she gasped, laughing and holding her side.

"Shhh, not so loud," I warned. "Papa will think we are disrespectful."

Before supper, each day, Papa went down to the cellar, pulled on the overhead light string, pulled down the double doors, and practiced on his *ciramella*. He played the old tunes of the old country until they came out like he wanted them to. Within days *paesanos* and friends knew there was a *ciramella* in the Bono household.

"Yes, yes," Papa admitted, "I have made a *ciramella*."

"Well, play for us," they begged.

"At Christmastime," Papa promised. So he kept them waiting until then.

School was out for Christmas vacation. My sisters and I took turns wheeling chopped wood to the kitchen door for Mama's baking. First she made the wine and honey cookies and fig bars drizzled with white frosting; then came the pretzel-shaped bread sticks with anise seeds; finally, the fried dough puffs stuffed with preserved sardines and dried red peppers that had been soaked in boiling water. Mama hummed and sang Christmas songs along with the old Philco radio in the living room.

Lomena and I made fringed napkins from bleached flour sacks as gifts for Mama. Lomena drew sweet litle violets on a corner of each napkin and we embroidered six napkins each.

The time was right for Papa. He visited friends and personally invited them for a night of *ciramella* music and Christmas joy. We decorated the living room ceiling with chains of red and green construction paper. A small red candle was lit and placed by the picture of the Christ Child upon Mama's treadle sewing machine. The bare floors had been mopped clean earlier in the day by Mama.

That evening lights shone in every room of our house. They glowed a long ways down the road. Friends with their children walked or drove up in their secondhand cars. The December air stung noses and ears as bright stars speckled the valley heavens. Our walls shook with laughter and chattering.

"Nichole, come on now! How much longer do we have to wait to hear your *ciramella*?" hollered Rocco, who had left the old country with Papa.

"Sì, Nichole, let's see this secret project you kept from us for so long," begged Pietro, the bachelor.

Papa brought in the *ciramella* from the screened-in porch. He held it high over his head for all to see.

It's just like the ones in the old country," marveled my godmother, Amelia.

"Sì, sì," they all agreed. "Exactly!"

The men enjoyed sipping Papa's best wine, and took turns blowing air into the bagpipe, laughing all the while as it grew fatter and fatter.

Then Papa took his *ciramella*. As he blew through the bagpipe, his fingers moved over the piping holes. Gentle wailing sounds became folk melodies of a long-ago homeland. Men and women sang songs they learned before they ever dreamed of seeing America. Tears slid down their cheeks and it became hard for them to sing.

Suddenly Papa stopped playing. "*Basta!* Enough crying!" he shouted. "We are not at a funeral parlor. We are in America! Time to be glad. Time to dance!" He began playing one tarantella after another. Women spread wide their skirts and danced around their husbands—back and forth, hands on hips, round and round each other they danced. Children found partners and did the same in corners, copying.

"*Bravo*, Niccolò! *Bravo!*" friends yelled.

That night Papa appeared to me as one gigantic happy glow. I never wanted the night to end.

Winter passed and then spring. As summer moved into July, a heat wave hit the valley. A terrible odor began to hang in the house.

Lomena complained loudly, "Mama, my stomach wants to throw up from the smell."

Papa sniffed his way to a shelf in the screened-in porch. "*Dio!*" he groaned. "Can it be—no, it can't be!"

"I think your bagpipe is beginning to rot inside," said Mama, holding her nose.

"What a waste," said Papa. "We could have had more fun with it."

We felt sad for Papa. Who could ever forget that Christmas night? Without another word, Papa ripped out the pipes from the *ciramella* and took the skin to the backyard. He grabbed the shovel standing upright in the dirt by the water faucet and dug a deep hole. He plopped in the skin and filled up the hole, stomping on the dirt with his shoes to seal in the odor. I watched as Papa put the shovel back where it stood before; without looking up, he strode across the road and into the vineyard.

Alma R. Vanek

Alma Rattini was born in 1906 in Telluride, Colorado. After graduating from Colorado College, she taught for several years, and then became a social worker. When she married Edward Vanek, they moved to California; they now live in Berkeley. Their two children are married and the Vaneks have four grandchildren. Retired as a social worker, Alma Vanek helped develop classes for the Berkeley Senior Center and has herself attended the classes of writer Dorothy Bryant. Her first writing was a Depression story called "The Debt," which was published in the *National Jewish Monthly*. The story which is printed here, "Zio," also appeared in the collection *True to Life Stories*, volume 1, published by the Diana Press in 1978.

Zio

Alma hated the snow when it melted into waters that ran wild down the mountains, because it kept her friend Zio from coming to see her. Next to Mama, she loved this man she named Zio, best in the whole world. Alma was happy when he rode down from the highest mine in Colorado. Zio had a red smiling face and hair like melted copper pennies. He always looked too big for his horse.

When Alma was small and Zio was still boss at the mine, he would swoop her into his arms, and the rough wool of his red plaid mackinaw would scratch her face. From high on his shoulder she would announce with glee, "Mama, Zio is here, Zio is here."

Mama was always busy with a houseful of boarders and the care of the baby, who was often sick; but she would stop what she was doing and welcome him with her glad smile. Big Sister would come running and Baby Brother would bang his high chair to show he was happy, too, that Zio, their best friend, was here.

Zio would laugh and say to Mama, "Anytime you don't want these kids, I'll take them with me."

It was Zio who helped Alma build a tree house by the fern-edged pool, where the biggest lady slippers fitted the feet of her smallest doll. He even came to Echo Rock, to listen to the funny distorted sounds, where his big laugh boomed back accented with her giggles. Zio was the only one who wanted to know what new names she had discovered and given herself, because she didn't like her own name, Alma.

"What's the new name this time?"

"Ecuador."

"Now where did you find this one?"

"In Big Sister's geography book."

"I like this best so far."

When Zio came alone he brought candy and always had time to play games and listen to Alma's adventures. But after his heart trouble, he opened a saloon, because he couldn't work in the mine anymore.

Then everything changed, and when he came down his wife, Sorina, came with him. Sorina was almost as big as Zio and her hair was jet black as the inside of a lump of coal. She never smiled and she wore black because a brother was killed in the World War that was going on in Europe.

Sorina always brought her pack of greasy fortune telling cards and laid them out for Mama. They never showed anything but bad luck. Then Sorina wanted to see Mama's Italian dream book. They would turn the brittle ragged pages carefully, and always Mama's dreams would spell disaster. Mama would be sad for days, sure that something terrible would happen.

Sorina was having bad dreams about Giorgio, a gambler who had just built a saloon, right above theirs.

"This devil Giorgio sees we're doing good business, so he sneaks around and gets The Mine to lease him the ground right above us. I tried to stop him. I knew all his slops and the water would come down on top of us. I saw trouble right away in the cards and now it's bad in the dream book."

Zio didn't like the cards or the bad dream signs and told Mama. "Cards are pieces of paper. How can they tell what is going to happen?" But Mama believed anything Sorina predicted.

Like the time Baby Brother was real sick. Sorina laid the cards and predicted. "Somebody here is going to die soon. Like I always say, we can't escape our fate." Mama began to cry. Alma stood in front of Sorina. "Why do you make Mama cry with your bad cards?" Mama slapped her.

Alma ran to her hiding place in the attic. Hours later, when Zio found her he told her he had brought the doctor and Baby Brother was feeling better. He wasn't angry with her and seemed just the same until the last time they visited.

That last time they had come down to see the doctor, because Zio was having trouble with his heart again. He didn't play games and even his smile seemed far away.

Sorina was rushing him. "You know we have to get back. I'm afraid what that devil Giorgio will do when he knows we're gone. I had a big fight with him, when he dumped his slops in our yard. He called me a witch and ordered me off his property, when I called him a devil. He's so jealous of our business, he'd do anything."

Zio interrupted. "I don't want these fights. We have to get along or it'll get worse."

"You bet it will get worse. Just wait till the snow starts to melt and water runs like crazy down the mountain and into the saloon."

"It didn't run in the saloon last year, when I made the ditch."

"Last year we made the ditch where we wanted, because that devil Giorgio wasn't on top of us. Remember this year the ditch starts on his property and he'd like to wash us right off the mountain."

"Don't worry I'll fix the ditch."

"Doctor told you. Take it easy, no more hard work."

"I'll work it out with Giorgio about the ditch. No fights."

"You can't work with that devil. I told you when he came that the cards showed bad trouble and now the dreams are worse."

"It's always the cards or the dreams with you. Let's go."

Alma was trying to tell Zio her surprise. She was right on his heels. She touched his sleeve and let the words tumble out. "I'm the only one picked in the second grade to play a part in the senior class play. I'm a pony."

Zio bent down and smiled right at her. "They were smart to pick you. You'll make a fine pony. Stand big, so you'll see me right in the front row. If you do fine, I'll treat you at the ice cream parlor. I promise."

"How do you know you can come? By then the snow will be melting and the water running wild."

"Don't worry. We'll have the ditch fixed and everything will be fine."

"You always think everything will be fine. I know there will be trouble. You better not make any promises to her."

"Don't look so sad, little Pony. Remember, I promise, I'll come to see you."

Saturday morning, a week before the play, Alma woke up happy and excited. Today was the day to pick up her new Mary Jane slippers and go to the dress rehearsal. Feet first, she jumped out of bed into a pool of sunbeams. She paused a minute to warm her toes in their rainbow fire.

After rehearsal, Miss Moran, the coach, sewed ostrich plumes on her headgear. Alma confided that Zio was coming down to see her in the play.

"All that way to see you? He must really like you."

"Oh, yes."

"He'll be proud of you. You're my best pony."

Usually Alma was bubbling over with words, but this time she was so overwhelmed with the praise that she couldn't utter a word. She felt happy enough to fly.

All the way home Alma skipped and flapped her arms to make believe she was flying. She lighted for a second to peek into the ice cream parlor, where Zio promised he would take her after the play. She had never tasted a sundae or soda, just ice cream cones. She skipped on, savoring this delicious choice; but remembered in time not to step on the cracks in the sidewalk. Big Sister had warned her not to break her mama's back. She would never do that, she loved Mama so, and had such important things to tell her today.

Alma burst into the kitchen shouting, "Mama, Mama."

But Mama wasn't there. Baby Brother was crying and Sister was trying to feed him. The boarders were standing like statues.

Alma began to cry too. "Where is Mama, where is Mama?"

"Mama went to help Sorina. Zio was killed dead."

Alma screamed, "Zio, Zio. . . . Dead? No, no, not my Zio."

"Yes." Big Sister was crying too, "Zio's dead."

"Why?"

"A fight about the ditch. Giorgio cut a hole in Zio's head."

"Please I want to see my Zio. Not dead . . . Zio promised to come to see me in the Play. I told Miss Moran he was coming."

Sister was trying to quiet Baby Brother who was screaming and choking. Alma was sobbing so hard she began to shake with hiccups. "Zio, Zio. . . ."

One of the boarders took Alma into his arms. He fed her sips of diluted *tamarindo* and whiskey to stop her hiccups.

When Alma awoke Sunday morning she was in Mama's bed with all her clothes on. Her eyes hurt and her mouth was sawdust dry. Then she remembered.

Mama had found Sorina covered with Zio's blood. She had sat in the running ditch holding Zio in her arms, until the Sheriff came to arrest Giorgio. Sorina refused to move until Giorgio was handcuffed and brought down to jail.

Mama brought Sorina back to stay for the funeral. She was sick with a cold.

Sorina kept repeating the story of how Giorgio had chopped a hole in

Zio's head to kill him. When Sorina had gotten up Saturday morning, water was running through the saloon. Sorina ran out and began to mend the side of the ditch that had been cut. Zio had fixed the ditch on Friday and the work had hurt his heart. Sorina didn't want Zio to come now, but he came anyway. When Giorgio came out with a pickax, Sorina called him bad names and accused him of cutting the ditch. Giorgio knocked the shovel from her hands. Zio lifted his shovel to protect her and at the same instant Giorgio brought the pickax down on Zio's head.

Sorina never stopped crying and talked until her voice was a croaky whisper. Alma felt too tired to cry anymore, but around Sorina the crying never stopped.

Alma was glad Mama let her go to school Monday morning so she could tell her teacher about Zio. "I can't come to school tomorrow, because it's Zio's funeral. Could I tell Miss Moran that I can't practice today or tomorrow and that maybe I can't be in the Play?"

Alma confided to Miss Moran that she didn't want to see Zio dead with the big bloody cut that Sorina kept talking about.

Miss Moran asked if she could come home to talk with Mama. Alma stayed in her room until Mama and Miss Moran had finished talking. Mama called her. "You don't have to go the funeral. Miss Moran says it wouldn't be good for you to see Zio dead. You can still be in the Play. Miss Moran says you practice good and she needs you."

How Alma wished Zio had been there to see her when she pranced out on the stage, right down to the front. For a second when the footlights blinded her, she thought she saw Zio. She was wishing so hard. But if Zio had been there, Mama wouldn't be crying.

Then school ended.

One day Alma asked Mama, "Where is Zio now?" Mama began to cry so hard she had to sit down. Big Sister scolded Alma for making Mama cry. Alma never asked about Zio again, but when she was running through the wet meadows or scrambling up the mountain slopes she began to think-talk with Zio. She only did this when she was alone out of doors. First, she would look into the sky, where she believed he might be. To think-talk she didn't even have to move her lips. It was like saying prayers in church where she wasn't supposed to whisper or move her lips.

Alma forgot Sorina, until Sister told her she had moved from the place where Zio was killed. She was living in the Dalla house on the edge of town, across the river.

One night, Mama made them hurry with supper, because Sorina wanted them to come. Alma begged not to go. She was afraid because Sister told her that Sorina had a row of lemons in her cellar, with rusty nails stuck in them. They were for people she hated and would bring them bad luck, or make them die as the lemons rotted. "She stuck thirteen rusty nails in the lemon that's for Giorgio, who killed Zio."

Sorina's house was across the old bridge. In the daytime it was fun and scary to play on the bridge. But every child knew that the bridge was haunted at night.

In the Spring, the massive waters of the river would explode against a giant boulder to lift and catapult it against the bridge. The bridge would shake and groan as if every timber was breaking. Alma would shriek, "A giant!" and cling to the railing with all her strength. Sometimes Alma and her friends would dare to close their eyes and pretend they were riding a great ship to the end of the river. But when the river was in flood, a momentous force of rolling waters would sledgehammer the banks, clawing out rocks and pulling down trees, as a foot of water poured over the floor of the bridge. Then Alma and her friends just watched from a safe distance.

Alma tried to tell Mama that she was afraid of the bridge at night. Mama said it was safe now and Alma would have to come.

Sister was just a step ahead of Alma, carrying the lantern. The feeble, shifting light made the black shadows from the heavy timbers move like palpable shapes ready to jump out at them. Alma screamed, "Look out," when shadows like long waving arms reached out to her.

"Shut up. You almost made me drop the lantern." Mama, carrying Brother and walking a step behind, scolded, "Be quiet." Now their footsteps rang out so loudly they sounded like the three Billy Goats Gruff trip-trapping across the bridge. The noise would certainly wake the old Troll, "with eyes as big as saucers and a nose like a poker."

The bridge creaked and a chill wind moaned through the old timbers. Alma's whole body shook.

Sorina's house looked dark and deserted, hunched back in the shadows of the bridge. Alma could hear and feel the power of the river as its heavy waters rumbled in the darkness.

Sorina opened the door, holding a candle. The flickering light from the candle made her face look all wavy, like a moving mask. Alma was so frightened she grabbed a handful of her mama's coat. They moved forward in silence to put Brother to bed. The only light in the bedroom was from the candle Sorina now placed before the statue of the Virgin Mary. Alma stayed close to Mama, still holding on to her coat. Sorina broke the silence to scold, "Get away from under your mama's feet. Let her put Baby down. You're not a baby."

Sorina pulled Alma's coat and cap off and shoved her out into the large dining room, where a dim light bulb hung from a long cord, directly over the round table. Tonight Alma would have to sit at the table. Since she was small, Sorina placed Sears, Roebuck and Montgomery Ward catalogues under her. They were slippery and hard; her feet dangled and the books cut into her legs.

Sorina ordered Alma to put her hands on the table and stretch her fingers to touch Sister's and Mama's. Sorina turned off the light and said the table would move and there would be knocks and maybe voices from the spirits. No one was to talk except her.

The room was shivery cold and almost black. Alma pressed her hands hard on the table to keep it from moving. Her neck hurt and soon both feet were numb. There was a wavering speck of candle light from the half open bedroom door. Sorina sat hunched over the table, wrapped in her black clothing, mumbling a kind of chant.

Alma thought of Zio. He wouldn't have liked this any more than he liked the fortune telling cards or the dream book. He liked bright cheerful colors and hated to see Sorina dressed in black. He always wore his red plaid jacket and colored shirts.

The first time Brother coughed, Mama started to get up. Sorina muttered, "Don't move. You'll break the spell."

Finally Brother was quiet and Sorina stopped mumbling. Alma squirmed and Mama and Sister pressed their fingers hard against hers to warn her to be quiet and stay awake. She opened her eyes wide and began to look around the large room, so she wouldn't have to watch Sorina and could stay awake. Everyone was still. Alma stared into the stillness.

Suddenly there was Zio, clear across the room. He looked so big, standing there. He didn't move. She watched him with all her might. He began to come slowly toward the table. It took him a long time. When he came closer, she could see he was smiling, as if he were happy again. Slowly, slowly he came until he was across the table from her. Then he held out his arms, as if he were going to pick her up and swing her.

Alma cried out, "Zio, Zio," pulled her hands from the table and threw herself toward him. The chair slid, the catalogues slipped and she fell.

Alma was shouting, "Zio is here, Zio is here," even before Mama could pick her up. "Look, Mama, look." But Sorina turned on the light and Zio wasn't where she pointed. The smile vanished from her face, as Sorina took her from Mama, shoved her shoulders back with hurtful hands and forced her face up.

Sorina demanded, "Did you really see him?"

"Oh yes. Zio came clear across the room to see me."

"Liar!"

Alma pulled away from Sorina and turned to stand against her mother. "Mama, Zio was here. I really saw Zio."

From the way she smiled and held her, Alma knew that Mama believed her.

Julia Savarese

Julia Savarese was a 1950 summa cum laude graduate of Hunter College in the city of New York. She did graduate work with The New York Times School of Journalism and held editorial positions with various publications. She held a Ford Foundation grant for playwriting and has written several plays of which *Nest of Echoes* was produced in New York. In addition, she has written for television and received the Hallmark Television Award in 1968. She has written two novels. *The Weak and the Strong* (1952) is a novel depicting an Italian American family's misfortunes during the Depression years from 1930 to 1934 as they try to eke out an existence in New York. Her second novel, *Final Proof*, was published in 1971.

from The Weak and the Strong

There did not seem room enough in the whole world for the noise that filled the streets of the 79th Street market. It was as if the blocks from 79th down to 72nd formed the vacuum of a giant airless bubble, as if the noise would grow and grow until the bubble could contain it no longer, and then it would burst. The noise would cascade into the air and then flow unchecked down and up the side streets where it had never before gone. The hot, unmoving day added to the smothering noise. It was always the same, Gino thought, the same old carts of rough, splintered, water-soaked wood, with tattered, celluloid-framed licenses bearing small, odd pictures of their owners tacked on the sides, the same healthy, round-faced woman who called, "Nice string beans today, honey!" and was always smiling as her plump arms delved into the contents of her cart or through the sagging pockets of the faded apron she wore. In the winter the apron would be a

torn lumber-jacket, and the green string beans might be potatoes or frost-
bitten apples, but the smile, the "honey," the sagging pockets were always
the same.

Fortuna thought they might find some cheap peppers that she could fry
for supper, but so far the only ones they had seen were three-for-a-nickel
and no bigger than shriveled little lemons. But the prices would get
cheaper as you moved farther into the market, where the heat was the
strongest and the noise heaviest. They passed the corner where the old Jew
always stood, wearing the same black hat, the same heavy coat winter or
summer, selling long black shoots that looked like jointed fingers, poking
upward to where the Second Avenue El rattled slowly along. Musty Italian
stores, whose floors smelled of soaked-in oil and sawdust and mice, and in
which open barrels of greasy black and green olives floated oil-drowned
flies, leaned against tiny American shops, the ones that never lasted but
were always changing from candy stores to hardware shops to garment
stores. A house dress, size sixty, billowed like a tent from a hanger above
Sam's Department Store, and pushcarts glittered dimly with buttons and
bloomer elastic and faded sequins. It was a Bagdad of two-for-a-penny.
Rotted cantaloupes like fractured yellow skulls spilled their seedy brains
into the gutters. Watermelon slices in glass cases, wilted white with the
heat until the seeds looked like black flies burrowing into the mush. An old
woman sold tiny bottles of lavender perfume, sickening with sweetness.
The gutters next to each cart slushed with the ooze of decay and rot, but
nothing was given away. Brown, wilted lettuce leaves were stuffed into
horses' nose bags, while bare, naked children with dark eyes and swollen
bellies poked into the gutter's sludge, until a turned-on hydrant swept away
any possibility of food from their filthy fingers and swirled it down a churn-
ing sewer.

While his mother stopped to pinch some tomatoes, Gino stood looking
into a small, glossy store whose shelves were lined with greasy, lustrous
boxes and cans. A bland, lubricious young man stood leaning his foot on
an unopened crate, cleaning his nails with the long nail of his right
thumb, which he occasionally flicked across the sleek surface of his polished hair.

The tomatoes were rotten, Fortuna told the huckster, who cursed her as
she walked away. Besides, she thought, tomatoes were not supposed to be a
meal. They were served with the antipasto that came before the meal:
large, oval dishes of crisp romaine salad and tart capers, fresh tomato slices
and, nestling between, an occasional anchovy or pickle cube, with a season-
ing of fine garlic and imported oil. And after that came the roast and the
spaghetti. No, tomatoes alone were not a meal.

The fifteen cents she held was sticky in her palm. The faces and noise and smells made her hungry and then nauseated, and each was part of the other. Then the hunger took the upper hand, growing and spreading within her, until the child inside her belly seemed not a substance but a cavity, a hunger in the womb.

They were coming to 72nd Street now, and the blocks seemed to be aware of their proximity to shameful trade, seemed to shrivel up toward downtown, losing identity and personality in the fear of contamination. It was almost the end of the market; they would have to find something for supper soon. Gino held onto Fortuna's hand, but they had not spoken a word since they left their house; it was too hot to talk and their eyes were like those of hunters stalking an invisible prey. It was ugly, Fortuna thought, the rot of mankind, and you had to pay for it.

Gino hoped that they would walk back through the market instead of crossing over to First Avenue. A small isolated cart near the corner was a mass of green peppers, separated into three sections as irrevocable as any caste system. The lowest sign read: Cheap! Bargain!! 2 for 1¢!!! Fortuna and Gino approached the cart. No word was spoken during the transaction. A fat, hairy man, whose black armpits spewed a vile odor, pushed open a paper bag and Fortuna dug through the pile, one at a time, until twelve undersized peppers lay in the bag. She put the sweated dime in the hard, outstretched hand, and waited while it delved into the pocket like a derrick, bringing forth a handful of change. The man picked four blackened pennies out of the silver mass and dropped them into Fortuna's hand. There were nine cents left. They needed bread to make the peppers taste like a meal; there would be no milk, no eggs, no cheese.

The bakery store was hot and steamy but smelled wonderfully of bread. There was a small, day-old pumpernickel that the lady let them have for four cents. Fortuna stood in the store, physically unable to move. Her hunger now was a large, lumpy mass, pushing against her throat, against her eyes, swelling waterily in her mouth. Inside, her body seemed empty except for the lump that pulled and dragged. The stout blonde woman who had sold her the bread watched anxiously as Fortuna tried to gather strength enough to leave. The woman seemed frightened, almost sick herself. Finally, Fortuna pointed to a tin tray of shelves, on the top of which there was half of a thick pie, lushly yellow at its gash, its thin, soggy crust almost as white as the cardboard sliver on which it lay.

"How much for the piece of pie?"

The yellow-haired woman seemed surprised at Fortuna's having spoken. She started and then stared for a second. "Oh, the pie's half. Six cents. 'Leven cents a whole one it sells. It's a—" she bent down before the yellow half-moon— "a custard, cocoanut-custard." She stood with her hand resting under the cardboard dish.

"Eleven cents? Not five cents for half? I thought—"

"No, it's supposed to be six. But you can have it for a nickel, I guess."

Fortuna laid the nickel down on the sticky marble counter and stared as the woman sprinkled the pie with powdered sugar and twisted a piece of greasy white paper over it.

Outside, it seemed even hotter than before. "Stop a minute, Gino. Here, hold this."

She pushed the bread and peppers into his arms, and tore the string from the pie. As Gino watched, her strong yellow teeth bit into the quivering jelly. Her throat moved quickly and her breast heaved with a desperate roll. She did not stop until she seemed exhausted from furious energy.

And then she looked down at him, as if before she had not known he was there. "Oh, Gino—" She thrust the chewed remains at him, snatching the two bundles from his arms.

Then they started to walk slowly back. From the window of the bakery shop where they had stopped, the plump blonde woman stood watching. Her fat, red arm lay protectively across her stomach.

Dorothy Bryant

Dorothy Bryant was born in San Francisco, in 1930, the second daughter of immigrants from Northern Italy. She has an M.A. from the University of California at San Francisco and taught for many years, including creative writing at Contra Costa College in San Pablo. She began writing in 1960, and her first novel, the very successful *Ella Price's Journal,* was published in 1972. She formed her own publishing house, Ata Books, and has since published six other novels and two works of nonfiction, *Writing a Novel* and *Myths to Lie By,* a collection of short pieces. Dorothy Bryant and her husband, Robert, who creates her book covers and assists in her publishing enterprise, live in Berkeley, California, in a house they built. They each have a son and a daughter by former marriages.

from Miss Giardino

"Ah, good, you're awake." A stout nurse with red hair stood over Anna. "Supposed to take your blood pressure again before I go off." She wrapped Anna's arm and began pumping. "How are you feeling?"

"Is this Saint Paul's Hospital?" Anna asked.

"That's right. You're that accident case, aren't you?"

"My mother died in this hospital. Eight years ago. She was almost ninety."

The nurse nodded indifferently as she read the gauge, then unwrapped Anna's arm. She did not realize Anna's accomplishment: catching, pinning down, placing a memory.

After she left, Anna turned to look toward the window again. Perhaps I am dying, she thought, and, like Mama, will see a vision. "Nonsense," she muttered aloud. She would see no visions, being neither patient, nor saintly, nor believing. And she was not dying, only lying here, wondering what happened, watching the window as if the light rising outside it would gradually reveal her past, her life, herself. *Window. Stay by the window and watch for Papa. Look down the muddy road, up the hill, to where he comes from the mine. I must watch, must see him come over the hill, tall and pale under the coal dust, dark, with an angry face, angry even when it smiles. I wish he would never come. Watch. Soon as I see him, I must run, run up the road to meet him, take his lunch pail and carry it home. If I don't watch, if I read or daydream, he will come crashing and shouting into the cabin. "No one meets me? No one cares if I come home? I should just send the money to feed all of you? I might as well stay in the mine?" He will shout until he starts to cough. He will cough until his face turns white and his black eyes dart around the cabin, like the rat Mike caught last week, eyes looking for some way out, some little slit to slip through and escape its death.*

Mama says I look like Papa. Tall and thin like him, with his black hair and black eyes. I wish I didn't. The others, Mike and Alfonsina and Victorina, all look like Mama. Golden hair and wide blue eyes and small bodies that go soft when there is enough to eat. There never is. Enough for Papa to drink, Mike says. That bad smell Papa has sometimes when he comes home, that bad smell means he will shout and fight with Mike, and Mike will run out. Papa says he works so we can eat. But he leaves the money in the saloon, Mike says. Mama washes for miners who are alone, whose families are still in the Old Country. She hides the money under the olive oil can. "Don't tell Papa." When the food is gone, Mama takes some coins from under the can, enough for another sack of polenta.

The others say, "Mama, let's go back home." They tell me about home, but I don't believe them. Home is, the world is, a cabin on a muddy road up the hill to a mine. It is called Illinois, Colorado, Utah, Montana. We move, but it is always the same cabin, road, mine. We move west, going to California, always going to California. But it stays the same, always the cold, the pot of polenta to stir on the stove, the muddy road between the cabins, the men on the road, walking, coughing. I know them all by their cough. There goes Mr. Santucci. I know without looking, by his cough.

"No sign of Papa?"

"No, Mama."

She sighs, and we do not look at each other. We know where he is.

I try not to think about him. I think about the other end of the road, down the hill, the long house where the thin lady rang the bell to open the school. She taught us all to write our names. I draw my name in great swirls over and over again. Everywhere, with my finger, in the mud outside our cabin, in the dust on the pipe of the wood stove, in the soap suds of Mama's tub of clothes, steaming, always steaming, on the frosted window while I wait for Papa. But the teacher has gone away. No more school till another thin lady comes. But I can read. Somehow I have learned to read. At first I only held, hugged, smelled the books, but now I can read them. I am the only one in the family who reads English. I hold the book the last teacher left with me, but I do not dare to read now. I must watch out the window. Watch for Papa.

Then it is dark, and Mama says not to wait anymore, come and eat.

I am in bed when he stumbles into the cabin. I wake up hearing the muttering, rumbling words, like the growling of the mine guard's dog. I crawl over Alfonsina, over Victorina, out of bed, and I go to the doorway. Mama sits at the table, a blanket wrapped around her. Her eyes look sleepy but afraid. She stands up, offers Papa some food. He does not answer. She sits. He says she does not want to feed him. She gets up again, gets the plate of food she has kept for him. He pushes it away. "Cold, not fit to eat." He stands over her, over the table. He swells up with anger, and his swelling chokes me. I see the fight coming, the fury. Nothing can stop it. He wants it. He needs it.

Mama is already crying.

"Stupid woman, stupid!"

Now everyone is up. Mike puts on his clothes and goes out, slamming the door. He can do that, he is a boy, almost a man, already working in the mine. He can walk out, go to a friend, even go to the saloon. Alfonsina hugs

Mama, they cry together. Victorina yells, "Leave Mama alone! You're drunk again!" She grabs the heavy iron that always sits on the stove waiting to be heated and then pushed across the wash Mama does for the miners. "If you touch Mama, I'll kill you!"

Papa chases Victorina around the kitchen table. She dodges him and laughs when he stumbles and gasps. He cannot move fast without gasping and losing his breath. He grabs a knife from the sink and throws it at her. She ducks. The knife sticks in the wall behind her. Alfonsina and Mama wait. Victorina screams. Papa stands leaning on the cold stove, shaking his fist, at Victorina, then at God, looking up at the ceiling.

I stand in the bedroom doorway, watching. He turns to me, stops and looks at me. His black eyes look into my black eyes. I don't let him see I am afraid. I show him nothing but fierce black eyes like his. I don't believe what Mama and the others say about the Old Country, about how he sang and was happy. I don't believe in that man. I only know this one, this cruel, mean man who sleeps in our cabin, this monster like the giants in the book of fairy tales the last teacher gave me.

"And you! What are you looking at!"

I say nothing.

"The hard one, eh? Hard and skinny, eh? You don't cry!" He almost smiles, to give me a small opening, so I can reach in to touch his anger, make it burst like the bubbles in Mama's wash tub. But I don't move. I make my own eyes narrow and fierce, the way I have to do on the first day of new school in each town, when I stand tall and pretend to be older and stronger than the bullies.

"Answer me!"

I say nothing.

"Won't talk? Talk! Answer me! I'll make you answer!" He comes at me. Mama and Alfonsina scream. Victorina steps between us, swinging the iron. He pushes her, and she crashes against the wall. I stand still, saying over and over in my head, I hate you, I hate you. I know if I stop saying it I will flinch, fall, even cry like Mama. I won't let him make me cry. I will die first.

He stops in front of me, stands over me, then starts to shake and cough. I do not move while he coughs, breathes great sucks of air, the way I did when I almost died of whooping cough. "Answer me, talk. I'll make you talk." But his voice is already softer. He stands with his hand over me, but does not hit me. His hand hangs in the air over my head. My head bends back as far as it can go, so that I can keep looking into his eyes as he looks down at me, coughs down at me. His hand droops. He shakes his shoulders. "This one is too afraid to talk."

"I am not afraid," I say. Quietly. In English. Somehow I know the words in English will hit his eyes like a whip. He blinks. The new language, the

language of the people outside the family, outside the cabin. The language of the people who own the mines. It is my language too. I alone in the family speak it without accent, read it, think in it.

I will never, never speak to him again but in English. I will save Italian for Mama. All my life, all her life, I will caress her with the easy, good-humored Piedmontese dialect, the tongue of golden sunsets and sweet oranges, of the place that is forever home to her. But to Papa I will speak only the language of this new country, my country, that promised him a new life but instead brings him to a new kind of death.

After a while he does the same, speaks to me only in broken English, laughing and saying, "You think I am a stupid immigrant, eh, but I speak English too." He stops calling me Anna. To him I am "the skinny one" "the stick" or, more and more, "the American."

"Miss Giardino?"

Anna opened her eyes. It was a different nurse this time, a pale, empty-eyed girl, pregnant and very tired-looking.

"You have a visitor."

Anna looked at the old woman who stood by the side of the bed. She was fat and fierce looking, as if puffed up with anger. Her hair was dyed reddish brown and her face was covered by a mask of makeup. Red lipstick ran into the wrinkles radiating outward from her lips. She wore a heavy brown coat and a matching hat, very expensive looking, very heavy and ugly.

"Do you know me?"

"Victorina."

"They said you couldn't remember anything."

"I remember some things. I was just thinking of you, in fact. Did you come all the way from San Jose?"

"Where else would I come from? Yes, from San Jose. They called me, said you were in an accident. You look all right."

"I'm fine."

"What happened?"

"I don't remember that yet." She felt an uneasy quiver, her first stab of fear, and she wondered how and why she should fear what she could not remember.

Victorina pulled a chair to the side of the bed and sat down. "I just got back from Reno. My feet are killing me."

Anna could not think what she could say to her sister. They saw each other at most once or twice a year since their mother died. Victorina's husband had died at the same time. She had fought with him for nearly fifty years, as if continuing the fight with her father. When he died, she was lost. She turned to religion, not the Catholic Church of her childhood but a small cult devoted to development of occult powers and something called "mind raising." It turned out to be not so sinister as it sounded to Anna. The most important thing it had brought to Victorina was an introduction to a friend, a slot machine addict who was also a medium. When not engaged in seances, Victorina spent her time in Reno, standing for hours before a slot machine, wearing her pink house slippers, her "lucky" slippers, and sipping gin and juice. She was seventy-five years old.

"I'm sorry they bothered you," said Anna. "There's nothing for you to do, no reason to have driven that far."

"I don't mind coming," Victorina said irritably. "You're just lucky you weren't killed. Why you stayed on in that neighborhood all these years I'll never know. Full of those Mexicans and Blacks and . . . perverts! You should . . ."

"It's a very nice neighborhood and I like it," snapped Anna.

"It's not safe!" Victorina persisted. "Things have changed. It's not the same like when we were girls. You don't have to live there, you could live in one of those nice apartments out of town, San Jose, Walnut Creek, Marin, any of those nice complexes. You can afford it, you . . ." Her voice trailed off. She seemed to know that Anna would not listen, would not argue with her.

"I've thought of many old things today," said Anna, looking off into space. "I've been remembering things."

"Remembering things? What things?"

"I started with thinking about Mama, in the hospital, at the end. You know she saw visions?"

"It was the drugs they gave her. Made her see things. She was getting senile anyway."

"She was not! She forgot things, but she was quite rational to the very end." Another argument starting. Anna sighed. It should be possible to talk with Victorina without arguing. "I lived with her, after all," Anna insisted more quietly, "up to the last few weeks in the hospital. She was just the same as always . . ."

"Afraid, superstitious, weak . . ."

Anna shook her head. "Sometimes I think you hated her more than you did Papa. I don't understand."

"Easy. Easy to understand. Do you think I ever let my husband lay a hand on my children? Do you think I would put up with any of that? Of course, we had our differences." Anna smiled at the thought of Victorina's long battle with her husband. Even when he was dying, she nagged him, accused him of not trying to stay alive. "But I would never let him treat the children the way Papa did us."

"What could she do?"

"Walk out! I'd have scrubbed floors on my hands and knees to raise my children, but I'd have left that man."

"So would I," said Anna, suspecting that she would have left while Victorina would have stayed and fought. "But Mama wasn't like us. She couldn't. It wasn't possible for her even to think of leaving her husband. Surely you can forgive her for that. I got the worst of all from Papa, and I don't blame her."

"You got the worst? You were always the favorite. You were the smart one, you went to college. What do you think he said to me every time I saw him, why aren't you smart like your sister?"

"He did? Yes, he would. He knew how to be cruel. Do you realize he was only fifty-three when he died? We've lived so much longer than he did. I'm old enough to be his mother."

"And just like him."

Anna nodded. "The older I get, the more I look like him."

Victorina shook her head. "I mean inside. I don't know what it is. Something driving you. It makes you not need people, makes you do things, like go to college, to make a place for yourself above us, above . . ."

"You still see it that way!"

"Yes, why not say it? Better than others. I still remember his funeral. You, coming back from the university, just graduated, everyone so impressed, talking about you, not about him, talking to you, asking what you were going to do now, the college graduate."

"They were just being polite. They were Mama's friends, not his. They couldn't say a good word for him, so they showed interest in his children."

"Hypocrites. There must have been nearly a hundred people there, none of them who'd speak a word to him if he was alive . . ."

"All there for Mama's sake, and for ours."

"For ours? What did we care? I was glad he was dead. I wasn't a hypocrite, like you."

"Like me? What do you mean? I was as glad as you. I never tried to hide it. Even if he'd been good to us, with his sickness he was better off dead."

"Then what was that scene all about, the great act when you came in?"

"What act?"

"After the funeral, when we all came home. And those people came to my house, you know the way people used to do, we had them come to my house because you couldn't have them all in those crummy rooms over the store. And it was like a reunion, *paisani* who hadn't seen each other for years, been afraid to visit Mama for years, and everybody more relieved than anything else, relieved it was finally over and he was dead." She moved to the window, staring out on the noisy, smoky street with hard eyes, hard voice, not looking at Anna anymore, not even really talking to her anymore. "And you were listening to old man Rossi, the only one who had a good word to say for him, talking about the Old Country and what a fine, intelligent, handsome boy Papa was in the Old Country, how everyone in the village said he'd go far. And then you were crying, and everyone said what a devoted daughter you were, and so smart too. When all the time, I knew you hated him more than I did, but you had to put on this little act for the crowd. I always respected you before that, but . . . when you did that . . ." Her voice dropped to a grating whisper as she muttered to the window, "You had to have that pose, the dutiful daughter who stayed after Alfonsina and I ran off and married and left Mama. But not you. Not perfect little Anna, who stayed by the deathbed and . . ." *I sit beside his bed, awkward, uneasy, though there is now nothing to be uneasy about, nothing to fear from him. No more rages, no more threats. Little breath in him now, no more than a few whispered phrases between long gasps. He whispers short, carefully chosen English phrases. What makes me uneasy is the strangeness of him. He is not the man I know, not Papa. Without his anger, his fury, his cruelty, what is left? A pale, thin man with thick black hair, gasping for air he cannot use, lying there, his thin, yellowish arms limp on the sheets. An uncertain man, opening his eyes from time to time to make sure I am here. Then, quieted by the sight of me, giving a slight nod and closing his eyes. His face is unlined, gaunt, the ascetic face of a saint. Where is the man I hate?*

For a week I have been sitting here, since he could not get out of bed, since the doctor refused to come and only sent more drugs, since Mama called and said he wanted me, only me. During my four years at the university he had refused to see me. The deserter, the American, dead to him. "You won't see me alive again," he had told me when I left.

But now, at the end, he wants me, only me. I must stay beside him so that when he opens his eyes he sees me. If I move from the rocking chair, he calls, gasping, "Anna," the name he had hardly ever spoken.

"I'm right here, Papa." During the day I sit in the old rocker. At night I lie on the floor on an old quilt. Mama sleeps on the couch in the kitchen.

On the fifth day his breathing grows more quiet. At first it seems smoother, easier. No more gasps. But there are long intervals between the shallow breaths. Longer. His skin turns ivory. His fingers twitch. He opens his eyes, looks at me and whispers, "Ecco," as if summing up everything, as if looking at me and telling me that I am all he has to show for his life, his struggle. He closes his eyes again, and does not open them for hours.

Later that day he speaks again. "The American," he whispers. But there is no sarcasm or bitterness in his voice. "Smart." His tone is even proud. He fixes his dark eyes on mine. "You know," he says, with just a shadow of the old cruel irony, "you . . . are like . . . me . . . or you could . . . never done it."

That night I stay in the rocking chair, dozing lightly, waking with a start when the interval between his breaths grows long. Soon his breathing is too faint to hear at all. I stay awake, watching the slight rise and fall of his narrow, bony chest. Sometimes there is no motion, only the twitch of his fingers to tell me he is still alive.

About three in the morning he opens his eyes and looks directly at me. He is alert, and his breath seems to come easily. He can speak without gaps between words for gulps of air. "How does it go, at the university?"

"Fine, Papa."

"You are now a Bachelor of Arts?"

"Yes, Papa."

"Bene. And now, what do you do?"

"I will get a teaching credential and become a high school teacher."

"What will you teach?"

"English."

"Ah." He nods and tries to smile. "You still read many books."

"Yes, Papa."

Now there is silence again, but he does not close his eyes. He seems to be summoning all his strength to do something or say something. Something very hard, almost impossible. What can it be? I watch and wonder what he must accomplish before he dies, what is it that he must tell me.

"You know . . ." He is back to short phrases again, barely whispered through his blue lips. "I . . . like you."

It is as close as he can get. He cannot say he loves me. Yet, it comes through, like a burst of light, that he does. He loves me. He has envied me and hated me, abused me, resented me. He has projected upon me all his bitterness and disappointment. And yet he does love me. He has always loved me. It is true. It is inescapable. It is terrible.

He watches me, waits for my response. I sit dumb . . . hearing, watching, seeing what I have never seen before. My mind sees that here is a new situation, calling for a new response. But my feelings, so long frozen against him, cannot thaw out at once. I sit, stiff, stuck, unable to respond, unable to give him the words he begs for, the simple, "I love you, Papa." Never mind if it is true or not, never mind if it is impossible. I must say it. To hold back will be cruel, more cruel than anything he has ever done to me.

But the moment comes and goes too quickly. His eyes close. They do not open again.

"I guess," Anna said, "I cried because I didn't hate him anymore." But her sister turned from the window and gave her a blank look. She had obviously forgotten what she was saying and had merely been staring out the window, lost in her own memories. "How are the children?" asked Anna, falling back on her last resort for conversation with people of the married, family world. She was beginning to feel very tired again. Now she would be able to rest while her sister sat down by the bed again and recited her complaints.

Her son lived in Los Angeles. Her first granddaughter had married last year and was pregnant. The other two were in college. But no one ever wrote to her. They were only an hour away by plane, but invited her only once or twice a year, and then she didn't feel welcome. Her daughter-in-law didn't like her. Her daughter lived right in San Francisco and had just divorced her second husband. "I told her, at fifty-three she's not going to find another husband. I blame her for the way all her children turned out, all long-haired freaks, one living like a savage off in Mexico, another raising an illegitimate child like she was proud of it. Oh, I never see her, we just fight. I told her, you're getting old now, we're mother and daughter, but we're just two old women now.

"I'll be honest, Anna, I used to think you missed something not having children, but maybe you did the right thing. No matter what you do with your life, when you're old, you're old, and that's all there is to it. So what did I have children for? No one wants you anymore. It doesn't matter which way we went, we end up in the same place."

Anna did not know what to say. Her head was beginning to hurt.

"I'll stay here, take care of you when you get out of the hospital."

"I don't need taking care of. I'm all right."

"I can stay downstairs in Mama's old apartment. Give me the key. I'll go get things ready for you. I'll stay until you feel strong."

Anna said nothing. . . .

Anna thought again of her father. In her mind, she saw him, gasping and shaking his fist at God. He had made the great effort to change life, to bring hope to it. He had endured the horrible wrench of the emigrant, out of misery to desperate hope. But all hope had been eroded away until only desperation was left.

And how had she differed from her father? At first she had hated him; then she forgot him. Now, finally, she understood him. She had learned to understand him by becoming him. He had a vision of a better life and had strained himself to the utmost to go after it. So had she. He had been used and abused by the forces in which he had put all his hope. So had she. He had become filled with hatred and bitterness and despair, and had vented his hatred on the nearest targets. So, finally, had she.

Anna could barely get up from the rocking chair. She made it to the bedroom, keeping her fingertips on the walls, like a drunk trying to steady herself. She stepped out of her shoes, dropping her clothes on the floor, and let herself down on the bed. It took all her strength to pull the blankets up over her. The weight of them seemed enough to crush her. Maybe now she would die. Enough had happened, more than enough in the past few days, to kill an old woman. This exhaustion might be the beginning of dying.

As she sank toward sleep, one last dim thought of her father drifted through her mind. There was one difference between them. It was a difference in what they knew. Arno was wrong. She must not forget what she now knew about herself. If she forgot, if she dulled her consciousness, she would die in the same despair as her father, without even his hope of a new generation to benefit from his sacrifice.

Tia G. Talamini

At age eighty-four, Tia Talamini, a retired psychologist and teacher, has begun thinking of a new career as a writer. In Cambridge, Massachusetts, where she lives, she attends a Writing Workshop at the Adult Center and has produced a number of short stories. She was born in the Dolomites area of Northern Italy and was brought up in Boston. She holds an M.A. from Boston University, and has never married.

I Learn Three New Words

My stepfather, Dino, who had always been rather frail, took ill. I was then a big girl. I was twelve going on thirteen, so I took care of him. He seemed so very unhappy. He missed his music and so did I. Our friend Alfredo, the phonograph man, lent us some new records and I would play them for him, but when I was at school Dino was very lonesome. So the phonograph man helped me find a little canary—one that sang ever so happily.

Dino and I loved to watch him carry on and we named him Ti-ti-to. We planned the duets they would play together—Capricci by Dino and his Ti-ti-to—when he would be strong enough to handle his violin. But Dino did not gain strength quickly. He worried about it, especially when he had to stop teaching me Italian. He had promised my father that he would teach me at least three new words a day.

One noon my brother Paulie met me on my way home from school and told me not to go home. I became frightened. Paulie threatened me but I ran home anyway. The house was crowded. I heard my mother talking angrily. A policeman was standing by. She was talking to a priest. My brother Tommie grabbed me as I ran into the kitchen. He said, "Ginetta, go way, go way! Paulie, take her away." They didn't have to tell me. I knew. Dino was dead.

But why was everyone there, the priest, the neighbors and the policeman? Everyone was talking and everyone wanted me out of the way. My big brother Tommie said, "You are too little and you will cry and then you will have bad dreams. You better go to Papa." I pleaded with my mother. She put her arms around me, "Please, Ginetta, I have so many worries. *Fa la brava*, be good. It is better you go with Paulie to your papa."

Someone said angrily, "Cover that silly bird so it will stop its noise." I became frightened. I took the birdcage from the hook and ran to the phonograph man. He comforted me, "Dino had suffered much. Now, he will suffer no more." Alfredo gave me a basket of tiny Italian pinks from his garden for Dino's funeral. Paulie came for me. I kissed Ti-ti-to good-bye.

Tommie would not let me go into Dino's room. He kept saying, "If you don't look, you won't dream." I gave him the flowers and he crossed his heart and promised he would put them on Dino's coffin.

Paulie took me by the hand to the station. It was my first train ride that was not a joy. Through my tears, I could see only the telephone poles and one by one they became walking coffins.

Leaving the station, we walked to my father's office and Paulie said to him, "He is dead." Paulie never talked much. My father just stared at him. Then Paulie said, "Ginetta is to stay here."

My father looked funny and said, "Isn't she going to his funeral?" My brother whispered something to him. My father looked shocked, then he shook his head and sighed. He looked from Paulie to me and said, "He was not a bad fellow." My father and my brothers never referred to my stepfather by name.

My father tried to comfort me as we walked with Paulie back to the train. Then my father took me to his home. I did not want him or his wife, Gabriella, to know how dearly I loved Dino so I pretended to sleep and wept alone. I could hear my father's wife talking bitterly as she always did when she spoke of my mother. Usually the litany was, "I work night and day for you but after all she did to you, you still love her. *Stupido*. Don't say *no*. I can see it in your eyes." It was such an old story to me and yet this story somehow seemed different. It had new words in it that I had never heard before. They were three long words and perhaps it was just the way my stepmother seemed to spit them out that made them sound like such wicked words.

I could hardly remember the hard sounds but the very next day I asked her what they meant. She seemed to scream out the words as though she were vomiting all the poison she had wished for my mother these last years. She pounded away, for she wanted me to understand.

She explained. Dino had been a good Catholic. He came from a very devout family. His marriage to my mother, a divorced woman, had broken his old mother's heart and she had died. Dino's son had been shocked and gone away. Dino had pined because of his remorse. But he had not died. He was a *suicidio*, and so he could not have the last holy rites of the church as he had been *scomunicato*. He could not even be buried like a Christian. They would take him to the *crematorio*.

My ignorance of these three words infuriated her but she continued to explain. He had killed himself; the church had cast him out. It was all my mother's fault. She had bewitched him into marriage to spite my real father and now Dino would go to hell, a sinner. First, he would be cremated, but his soul would continue to burn for all eternity in hell.

"Cremated? What is that?"

"Burned—he is to be burned in a fire until he is all ashes!"

I felt a pounding in my ears and a sickish sweet taste in my throat and all mixed up; before my eyes came red and black flames around a swollen mass of burns. Oh, Sweet Mother of God! No, not poor Dino. No, you can't burn to ashes, sweet Dino. I tried to cry out to my father to save Dino but I could not.

When I opened my eyes, I was in my father's arms. He was stroking my hair. "*Povera bambina*," he kept saying. I told him I couldn't bear to have Dino all hurt and in ashes. I couldn't stand it if he didn't have a nice funeral with flowers and a High Mass with lovely music and if he didn't go to heaven. Dino loved flowers and music so he should go to heaven.

"*Povera bambina*, do you think the priest and your stepmother know everything? They don't. Sometimes your stepmother thinks because her name is Gabriella that she'll help Gabriel blow his trumpet on the Final Day. *Carina*, if anyone deserves to go to heaven, he will go. God takes care of that. Do you think only the people that are buried in Catholic cemeteries go to heaven? No, no, my child, all good people go to heaven."

"But why did Dino kill himself?"

"No one but God knows, but perhaps he was so sick he didn't want to be a burden. Maybe it was because he loved you all."

Finally, I fell asleep in my father's arms. Was it only my stepmother's spite that made her repeat those three hissing words? My father did not love Dino, so if he said Dino would go to heaven—well, he would. Now, I could again picture him in heaven playing his violin for the angels and nodding his head and smiling as he always did for me.

When I returned home, my mother hugged me, wiped my tears and told me not to cry. After all I was almost thirteen. Besides there was nothing to cry about. Dino knew best. He wanted to go. He had been too sick . . . So I was afraid to cry.

Only once I cried anyway. That was when Tommie told me they didn't have any flowers because Dino didn't have a regular funeral, but Tommie had put some of my little flowers in Dino's hand just before they closed the casket.

Povero Dino. Just a few flowers and no music. I had even taken Ti-ti-to away. And somehow I could never go back for the gay little canary.

Lynette Iezzoni

One of four daughters of an Italian immigrant father and a mother who was "a farmgirl from upstate New York," Lynette Iezzoni says her childhood was marked by "visits to the Italian grandparents' house," and she is still fascinated by the implications of the immigrant experience, the adaptation of Europeans to America, and the concomitant tensions. She now resides in California, where she has a creative writing fellowship at Stanford, studying with Gilbert Sorrentino. Her work has appeared in the literary reviews *Calyx, Primavera*, and *Jump River Review*.

Window Seat

When I was ten, my family's house bordered a graveyard. The graveyard's stone wall was longer than I could see and much taller than I, and on its top, embedded in sandy cement, were pieces of sharp, broken, colored glass. My bedroom was at the back of our house and its dormer window overlooked the graveyard. This window was so wide that when I knelt on its seat and spread my arms I could just touch each slanting wall. Mother hung dotted swiss curtains at my window and tied them back with satin braids, and for the seat she sewed a velvet cushion and ruffled it with dotted swiss. "A woman must have a place to lie," she said softly, emphatically. So I lay on the velvet cushion, being what Father called "a girl," reading and staring out through the branches of the maple tree at the glass on the graveyard wall. On summer days the glass glittered sea green, coral, and lavender; and the ship I was on rolled in a wave. The captain tipped his hat and smiled. And in winter, when weeds shivered like skeletons against the graveyard wall, the gray, the blood-red, the ice-white glass were the captain's uniform, his teeth, his eyes as he steered through a fierce Arctic storm.

I was intrigued by how, in every season, the gravestones looked the same. Even those tangled in ivy or streaked gray with rain or fallen over seemed oriented, composed. Elegant. Like how my mother folded her hands in her gray silk lap at dinner parties as Father leaned against the fireplace and cigar smoke floated across his eyes and he told stories of India, the lost empire. Father was born in India in a house with terraces and fountains. He told how Indian slaves crept in from jungle fields and hid bamboo in meals prepared by a trusted cook, bamboo which became a hundred knives in a man's stomach. He told how he couldn't tell brown, swarming people from vultures; and how incense like thin strips peeled off a human heart burned so raw that it clouded the sun and dazed your eyes. At every dinner party Father told these stories. My eyes would sting and I'd notice Mother's hand flutter across her lids as if her eyes hurt, too.

The night that my summer vacation began, Father's voice fell to a whisper. "Blue blood is for real. Men are animals without it."

I crossed my patent leather shoes and stared at the pink lace on my ankle socks. Suddenly, I saw Father's cigar lying on the Oriental carpet, and a flame licking gray smoke. Voices became loud and I covered my ears until

Mother grabbed my hand and I was in the kitchen with her and Mrs. Donette. The counter was cluttered with dirty dishes.

"How gallant Peter is," Mrs. Donette said, eyeing Mother. "Of course, that British accent and the beard give him a natural advantage. Still, he has a flair for storytelling." She was wearing a red silk blouse and her dark hair was pulled into a knot below her left ear. Mrs. Donette was new to my parents' dinner parties. She had just moved into a house down the street, near the playground.

"Yes, he tells a good story," Mother said.

Mrs. Donette smiled. "Oh, Judith, don't sulk out here with the filthy dishes just because Peter burned your carpet. A woman who doesn't humor a man's faults loses him."

I leaned against the counter. The door swung shut behind Mrs. Donette. Mother ran the water in the sink. I stared at her nose. It was the smallest, slenderest nose, with such tiny nostrils that I wondered how she breathed.

"Women are cads," Mother said. Her pearls swung loose, dipping into the soapy water.

I turned away from the counter and kicked back through the swinging doors, until I was on my stomach on the embroidered, mirrored pillow near Father's feet and Mrs. Donette's laughter.

That weekend Mr. Aita moved in next door. Father and I watched through the lace curtains as a moving van pulled over to the curb. Two men leapt out of the cab, swung open metal doors, and rolled a flimsy bed, a table, a wooden chair, and several packing boxes into the white brick house with the green shutters and boxwood hedge.

Mother walked into the living room and peered over my head. "He probably just wants to decorate fresh in his new house."

"Not new house," Father said. "*First* house. Diane Donette told me about him. Comes to us from Coaltown, Pennsylvania. An ex-*miner*." He rumpled my hair. "Off to the playground, sweet child?"

"Soon," I said. "Eva's at the dentist."

He turned away, wearing his gardening whites. Father was tending the foxglove and lilies-of-the-valley that he had planted along the graveyard wall. Mother stared after him.

I skipped upstairs. I laid down my book and gazed out the window. A ball was being held on board ship. The pink, purple, soft green glass shimmered into a brocade gown that I danced in, fluttering behind my sequined fan, curtsying to the captain. He seated me on a satin chair; knelt down. His eyes were bright. Weakly, I looked away.

Father was bent over his flowers, whistling. He disappeared down the driveway, carrying a bouquet of red roses from Mother's sagging trellis.

Mother walked out the kitchen door. She held a coffee cake.

"Where're you going?" I called down.

"To welcome our new neighbor."

"The *miner*?" I climbed lazily off the window seat and headed downstairs.

There was a hole in the lilac hedge where I used to hide. Mother and I slipped through. When I looked up, across the green lawn, I saw an old man sitting on the high, stone terrace. He had no legs.

Beside me, Mother stiffened. She called, "Hello," and walked quickly on. He was sitting in a wheelchair. His white hair was bushy and uncombed. His black eyes glittered and his fists were clenched on stumpy thighs.

"Hello," Mother called again. We climbed the stone steps and stopped in front of him. "I'm Judith Anderson. Your neighbor. This is my daughter, Rachel. We came to welcome you."

"Hello," the man said.

"Mr. I-EE-ta—have I pronounced it correctly?"

"Yes."

"I brought you a coffee cake." Mother's hand fluttered to her collar. "Lovely day, isn't it? Late spring is my favorite time of year. It reminds me of being a girl. . . . This is a beautiful house, Mr. Aita."

"It's my son's house."

"Oh. Does your son live here with you?"

"No, I take care of myself," he said, and Mother responded quickly, politely, "How unfortunate."

The old man leaned forward and undid the top button of his faded plaid shirt. "My son is not unfortunate. My son is a doctor. My son used his brains. I am not unfortunate either. My son bought me a house. I am a very fortunate man."

Mother was staring at her feet, rapidly nodding. "Well," she said, "I guess we'll be going. Now that we're neighbors, you must come visit my husband and me."

She handed him the coffee cake and he spoke again, softly, staring at her. "Yes, I saw your husband. Your husband was handsomely dressed in white. He grows beautiful flowers. He keeps a very neat garden. I shall enjoy watching your husband tend his very neat garden. I am a very fortunate man to have such a gardener to watch."

I backed down the steps. Mother was pausing. "Good-bye," she said in a high voice; then she was beside me, and the spring grass seemed very thick and deep and the hole in the lilac hedge was much smaller than before.

"Weird, weird, weird," I hissed.

"Shhh," Mother said. "Keep walking."

Finally, we were in the dining room and I rolled my eyes, giggled, and fell hard against the table. "Gross!" But Mother's cheeks were flushed and her eyes were very, very blue. "I think I like that man," she said. She threw back her head and laughed.

She chased me around the table until I slipped and screamed, then grabbed my hands; and we spun through the hall, shrieking, into the living room.

I lay on my window seat. Spread open was my fourth novel of the summer. I did not turn the page. Mother stood in my doorway, watching.

"I wonder who invented suffering," she said gaily. "Silent suffering. It's June first. Time to air the cedar closet. Check the sweaters for moths and send them to the cleaner's. A womanly chore. Let's get you"—she pointed—"in practice. I refuse to raise a bookworm."

I slammed closed the book. I followed her.

A bright, naked bulb hung from the smooth beams of cedar. The closet smelled musty, like brown, mildewed flowers. Mother closed the door behind us.

"I was just at the good part," I said.

"Oh." She laughed, pulling sweaters down off a shelf. "Now I see! The handsome hero was just about to take her in his arms and . . . kiss her."

"None of your business. You don't know everything."

"About romance I do."

"Liar!"

She looked at me, tossed a sweater into a plastic bag.

"You don't know that I tortured a girl in the playground today. Tortured her because of a BOY. The girl stole Amy's boyfriend. She made him *feel her up*. We captured her in the jungle gym and bombed her with pieces of paper that had 'slut' written on them. Eva thought it up."

Mother stroked her neck.

"Eva said I should grow up. She said life is war."

"Everyone for himself," said Mother.

"Yes!"

"Repay betrayal with cruelty."

"Yes!"

"Make the other suffer. Demand that he do what you want."

"Yes!"

"*Demand* that he stop hurting you."

"Mother!"

"It's simple."

I pressed my head against the door.

"Simple. Easy as pie. A pie in the sky."

Behind me she was unwrapping something, opening a box. "Look. Rachel, *look*." Mother held up a pink lace dress. She pressed its shoulders against her own. She held to her waist a belt beaded with white seed pearls. "This is my wedding dress."

"It's *pink*."

"Our wedding was informal. It was . . . hurried. Your father said I was divinely beautiful. He could not wait. He said I was the most gracious woman in the world." Mother cocked her head, staring into the corner above me. "What he mistook for graciousness was that it never occurred to me to raise my eyes to his." She uttered a sharp, brittle laugh. "Rachel. I *do* believe in graciousness. That and kindness." The stiff lace brushed my arm. "Kindness holds you together. It keeps life from being a mess."

Suddenly, Mother smiled. "Look!" She dropped the dress onto a pile of blankets. "My hatbox. Here, Rachel, my orange hat. My old pillbox hat. That sexy bow. Try it on."

She tugged the hat down around my ears. "Pretty. Why don't you surprise your father and wear it to dinner tonight?" She turned her back. I reached out to touch the wedding dress, but it slipped off the blankets onto the floor. "Go let the hero have his kiss," Mother said firmly.

When I finished the book I lay gazing out my window. The shadow of our house fell across the graveyard wall and the glass was dull and empty. Then I saw her. She was sitting next door, on the stone terrace with Mr. Aita. Their two heads were like one. Mother's hand waved in the air. She leaned back, laughed.

I swung around. My feet slammed to the floor.

I ran and sank beside my tea table. I arranged the cups and saucers, but did not serve tea.

Crystal tinkled downstairs and I knew Father would be talking of India. I knew how the chandelier would rain white drops of light upon the women's hair and the men's faces and how delicate a knife sounded upon china and how the women would gently toss their heads back and touch their wineglasses to their flushed cheeks and their laughter would seem soundless in the gracious, noisy room. Mother sat opposite Father, at the end of the table near the kitchen door. A dark curl would be sculpted over each ear and her eyes would carefully roam and she would be up and down without anyone noticing and no one would notice her eat and then her hands would fold in her gray silk lap. Mother often said that Father trained her well. Father would raise her chin with a finger and kiss her when she said this.

"Rachel!" Father was calling from the foot of the stairs. "Come down. A young lady must learn to socialize!"

I pointed one foot after the other down the carpeted stairs. I entered the living room.

The crowd stood in a blue haze of smoke. Mother was kneeling on the Oriental carpet, her hair in her face. She was putting pieces of glass onto a napkin. Above her, Mrs. Donette lit a cigarette and swayed into Father's arms. "Peter, you big *lug*," Mrs. Donette laughed.

Father stroked his beard, rolled his sparkling eyes. "We men lack the delicate manual dexterity of the fairer sex." He pulled an iris from a vase of fresh flowers, closed her fingers around its dripping stem.

"Judith," he cried suddenly. "You'll cut yourself!"

Father lunged forward, knocking Mrs. Donette's drink from her hand. It splattered, staining the carpet red. A cocktail cherry rolled toward Mother. Mother wiped her eyes.

"Men are such lugs!" Mrs. Donette said.

The room exploded with laughter. The fire was spitting ash.

Father gestured for silence.

Mrs. Donette held her glittering necklace to red, parted lips. Smoke from her cigarette curled around Father's head.

"I've wondered if this is also true among ape couples," he said. "Or if it's a blessed difference reserved for us higher forms to keep us bloody infuriated and coming back for more!"

Mother stood up. In a low voice, she said, "Peter, please tend to the fire. A fire anyway—in June? Our guests must be *burning up*."

Gravely, with a flourish, Father bowed.

Mrs. Donette giggled. "Judith," she said. She tapped her chest and cleared her throat. "I've wanted to compliment your taste. This room is . . . *extravagantly* furnished. All the pillows, flowers, mirrors."

"Peter likes to surround himself with beautiful objects."

"Your wish is my command," Father said to Mother.

Mother walked out the door.

"Judith," Mrs. Donette cried. "Judith."

Back in my room, I lay curled on the dark window seat. Laughter came from downstairs. My ears seemed to beat like hearts.

Finally, there was silence. They were coming up the stairs.

"Why can't you just relax and have a good time? You should see yourself," Father said. "Not a woman. A little girl."

On Independence Day I was tired and stayed home. The neighborhood was alive with noise. That night, when I put down my book and leaned to one side of my window, I could just see the golden fireworks bursting against the dark sky.

The next morning Eva called me on the phone. "Howdy, stranger. Ever heard of the Fourth of July? America?" she said. "Listen to this." I heard the sound of rushing air, growing louder, rushing—bang! The receiver shook. "What did I do?"

"You popped your gum," I said.

"Good, Rachel, good. Now come over to my house. My mom bought me a pair of fishnet stockings. They're *red*. She says I'm becoming a woman."

"I'm *reading*."

Silence. The sound of rushing air—bang! "Nerd," she said, and hung up.

I ran down the stairs. Mother was lying on the living room sofa. One arm covered her face; the other hung down, her fingers tense like a spider on the Oriental carpet. I flew out into the backyard. The sun was burning just above the graveyard wall and in its yellow glare the sharp glass glittered like a hundred eyes.

"Slut, slut, slut," I whispered, my chest hurting, bursting with strange, terrible energy. I ran back and forth along Father's garden. I kicked a stone. It broke a flower stem, ricocheted off the wall.

"Come here."

Mr. Aita was sitting next door, on his stone terrace. His voice echoed across the lawns. "Come visit an old man."

I ducked through the lilac hedge. Chin high, I walked quickly. I stopped a yard away from him. His face was sliced with deep, brown lines and his black eyes glistened like wet soil.

"Are you playing?"

"Well, *school's out*."

"Nothing useful to do?"

I made a face.

He laughed. "Not even any boys to hold hands with?"

"I don't care about boys," I answered loudly. His head nodded to one side. His eyelids drooped. "Though I tortured a girl over a *boy*," I said.

He gave a little snore.

"And I wasn't punished!"

Mr. Aita smiled and picked a piece of lint off his plaid shirt. His mustache twitched. "Why do you think you did something wrong? And even if you had, what makes you think you'd be punished?" He swelled back in his wheelchair, laughing. He caught my eyes with his. "Let me tell you a story. I often tell this story. It comes in handy.

"You see, I am a thief. A thief who grew up on a shabby farm in Italy, who couldn't tell his brothers and sisters from the chickens and the pigs. The stoop of our house was worn from sons and fathers and sons and fathers sitting on it and never lifting their feet out of the dirt. Because it is the duty of strong men to stand up, pretend they're God, and *walk*, I took action, the only action possible. One night I stole the key to my father's wine cellar from where it hung beside his bed. I packed up all his wine in his sturdiest cart, harnessed it to his best mule, and ran off to Naples. There I sold everything for a good price and bought passage to America. I knelt before the Statue of Liberty and, since this is the land of opportunity and freedom, went right down into a coal mine. For forty years I labored in the dirt. But when a beam fell and crushed my legs, I didn't need them anymore. My son was a doctor. A wealthy doctor. And all because I had seen and done my duty. I had been a thief.

"Do you understand?" he asked.

"Yes," I lied.

He laughed. "There is no justice. It is up to you. Only the very strong see and act. The majority paw away at life like animals."

I backed down the steps.

Suddenly, his arms flung open wide and he shook them as if embracing the sky. "Blue, blue. There is blue sky above the brown earth. Go now. I can tell you are a good girl. You have a good mother. Tell your mother she is a strong woman. So to be a strong woman." His arms fell, his eyes darkened. "Get out of here," he said. "I am just a brilliant old thief talking a useless game, playing God."

By late July I had read nine novels. I never went out. I lay on my window seat. It was so hot and humid that my eyes stung and my skin itched. Mother spent all her time with Mr. Aita. She neglected the house. When I pointed this out to her she ignored me and mumbled something about Mr. Aita, her mouth twitching, happy. "His wisdom is so brutal." She giggled like a baby, clawed her white throat. "So . . . selfish."

I got into the habit of taking cool baths. I ran the water and lay with it lapping my chin. I made my hands rise to the surface, palms up, and tried to keep them afloat so my fingers wouldn't pucker like an old hag's. I asked Mother for bubble bath. She said bubble bath wouldn't be good for certain parts of me. She said I might get infected. When she came home from Mr. Aita's and I was still in the tub, she would point her finger and say, "You're becoming a fish."

One night Father did not come home for dinner. Pork chops hardened in the oven. At nine o'clock Mother said Father had called and would be staying at a hotel in the city to be near work. She pulled the pork chops out of the oven and folded her hands in her lap. She left the table before I finished eating. Carefully, I put our plates side by side in the dishwasher.

Two nights later Father came home. When he entered the kitchen Mother shivered, clapped her hands wildly, and walked out. "Jesus Christ," Father said. He tickled me under the chin.

Mother began spending her days on the living room sofa. She lay with an arm across her face, a hand clenching the rug. I stayed outside, wandering along the graveyard wall.

Mr. Aita watched as I wandered. Often he called, "Come here, Rachel." I sat at the foot of his wheelchair. He told stories. He used strange words—grief, betrayal, wisdom, courage—and everything sounded complex and beautiful. He told me stories about men with rusty picks and axes tunneling through a black stone earth. "In darkness a man becomes only a smell, a pair of hands and legs, a sound of hoarse breathing," he said. "Flesh . . . and blood." He asked after my mother. He said she was doing something useful. Often I stopped listening to Mr. Aita, and daydreamed to the passionate sound of his voice. Vaguely, wistfully, I gazed up at him.

One day at the end of August, Father sat down on my window seat. He ordered me onto his lap. "I'm too big," I said. "You're never too big to sit on your old dad's lap," he pouted. "Come here."

Father told me my mother is unhappy.

Father told me she has not been happy for a long, long time.

Father has tried to protect me from seeing this, because it is not pretty.

A girl should see only pretty things.

Father told me my mother says she is alone and wants to be left that way.

Father is going away for a while, but not leaving me.

I will never be alone.

Father told me that since there is no tear on my cheek I am a young lady.

A young lady doesn't cry, she understands, and her understanding and happiness make others happy.

Without women's love, where would this crazy old world be?

Where would a man like Father be?

I walked down the stairs. The grass in the backyard was yellow and dry, broken by patches of dirt. Mother's trellis leaned against the graveyard wall, littering Father's flowers—the naked, tangled stems—with moldy brown roses. I felt dull and vague, as though I would suddenly laugh. I ducked through the brittle hedge, and approached his house.

"Mr. Aita!" Arms spread like wings, I ran up the wheelchair ramp and flung open the screen door. I entered the house. The large, white room was empty.

I walked through a doorway. Eerily, my footsteps echoed.

His profiled head did not turn. Yellow light filtered through a bay window. Mr. Aita's wheelchair glittered. He sat facing an empty wooden chair. "What do you want?" he said.

"Where's your furniture?" I said.

"The kitchen."

"The kitchen?"

My cot is next to the stove."

"You sleep beside the *stove*?"

"I have all a man needs. Food and a bed."

"Why are you staring at that empty chair?"

"Sometimes my son forgets. The visiting day comes and goes and he forgets to visit his brilliant father. The one who sacrificed his life for him."

"He's probably just busy."

"Yes, my *girlfriend*, you are certainly right. Please sit down and tell me a story."

"You tell."

Mr. Aita wheeled slowly toward me. "Me? But I am just an old cripple with garlic for blood, and my son's wife says I talk too much. She calls me 'Big Mouth.' She says I have 'delusions of grandeur.' Do you think I have 'delusions of grandeur,' Rachel, or do you believe I'm a man like God?"

His finger cocked, gesturing me near. "I'll give you a hint," he whispered. "They're the *same thing*. Now you tell *me* a story."

"I don't know one."

"Yes, you do."

"No."

"Coward. But you are beginning to understand. That all stories are corrupt, just blasphemies to fill ourselves with."

Mr. Aita kissed his fingertips. Gently, he touched my cheeks with them. "Go home," he said. "Go home."

"Mother!"

I called at Mother's door.

She answered, "Rachel, please make your own supper."

I awoke in darkness. My face ached with horror and to cry.

I had climbed out my window onto a branch of the maple tree. My hair flew in the wind. Only moonlight guided me.

I crawled far out on a thin limb. I lay just above the graveyard wall. The shards of glass glittered into an enchanted room. The room was filled with mirrors and velvet chairs and satin pillows and vases of lovely flowers, flowers every color of the rainbow. Women's fiery eyes burned, inflaming the gestures of bowing men. I reached out, and slipped. With one arm I caught myself, but the glass ripped open the flesh of my feet, my legs, and I bled, a bright, luscious, terrible red. My blood coated the glass and flowed slowly down the wall into the graveyard.

The next morning I got up early and was at the library when it opened. I chose a new novel.

When I returned home Mother was standing in the kitchen. She was naked except for red satin underpants. Breasts hung heavily from her chest and her brown nipples were thin, like twigs. Her puffy eyes looked at me: slits. She leaned against the counter, steadying herself.

"The idea, dear girl, is to be a noodle," Mother said.

I laid my book on the table.

"Noodlebrain." Mother opened the cupboard and stared as if deliberating. She chose a can of beets. Her shaking hands knocked the can opener onto the floor. I bent over, picked it up, wanting to get away, upstairs, to my window seat.

"A noodlebrain looks in the mirror and sees what others tell her to see. She never grows up. She spends her life in a continual state of self-beautification, trying to please others. *Not* because she has a big, generous heart, but because this is how she gets her head patted. This is how she is told she is sane and kind and good. This is how she makes the world a gracious, a happy place to live in. But do you know the catch? The catch, Rachel? Rachel?"

Juice slurped from the can of beets and Mother bent so close that her breasts brushed my shirt.

My teeth chattered. "If you tell me, can I go?"

"The catch, Rachel, is that after a while noodlebrains *become* noodlebrains. Just bundles of lies. God knows how to begin separating a woman from her illusions." She gave a little cry, and turned away. "Of course you can go," Mother whispered, her head against the refrigerator. "This is a free country, isn't it?"

Anna Monardo

A 1983 graduate of Columbia University with an M.F.A. degree in creative writing, Anna Monardo continues to live and work in New York. She has been an editorial assistant at Random House and *McCalls* magazine, and has taught in the New York City public schools and at LaGuardia

Community College. She won the 1982 Ella Grasso Memorial Award sponsored by UNICO National Foundation for the best story submitted in their
literary competition. The story, "Roman Ruins," first appeared in *Redbook*,
and her articles have also been published in *McCalls* and *Seventeen*.

Roman Ruins

Weekdays, Leah brings coffee to the office in a melting cardboard cup from
a nearby deli, then pours it into a mug, a gawky, earth-colored piece of
ceramic with a brush stroke letter "L" glazed on it. The mug was a gift from
her high-school boyfriend. He later became a potter. They only once said, I
love you.

Over the back of her chair in her cubicle at work hangs a sweater, waiting
for a day when Leah feels chilly. Knitted by her mother in a surprisingly
inoffensive, in fact a pleasant, combination of reds and pinks, it is a good
background for Leah's wild spread of tan hair. For all the other young editors
at the publishing house, as well as for some of the more important editors, the
old sweater constant on its peg is a comfort. It calms them to think that even
in the midst of the impossible business of putting forth literature there is
room for something made by someone's mother and maybe, by extension, for
their own soft spots and quirks, their slight imperfections.

The coffee, the mug, the sweater: these are all very important. They are a
few of the touchstones Leah is depending on to feel her way from one day to
the next.

There was a time, right after Matt left, when sadness took over Leah's life
with the persistence and skill of a charismatic lover. It lured her to bed
early. In the morning it would not let her leave. Whole nights through,
sadness kept her from sleeping, touching here, touching there, in deep
regions of emotion, places where she had never had feeling before. Leah's
longing for Matt, ignited each night by his monstrous absence beside her,
was the strongest desire she had ever known.

Leah thought Matt had the loveliest hands—sharp bones, fine veins,
chiseled from the tautest skin; hands that made her think of art history class
and anatomical drawings by Leonardo da Vinci. College was less than one
year behind her when they met, so that world was still her most immediate
reference. Matt was four years out of college and, because he hated working
for people, was trying to live as a freelance journalist. "I'd rather be on my

own at any cost," he said when they first met at a party. To Leah this had sounded noble and she'd told him so.

When two years had passed and she was alone, Leah became obsessed with trying to separate the features of Matt's face and reassemble them into some graspable vision that would prove he existed and had loved her: the deep slope of his nose, his sharp green eyes circled with dark lashes. All she saw before her, though, were those hands, resting patiently on tabletops as she and Matt tried to decipher what had happened to them.

The view out of Leah's bedroom window is of recently renovated brownstones, formerly abandoned tenements that sagged in a row. One May night, a few years back, not long after Matt was completely moved in, an arsonist's benzined rags sabotaged the old buildings and left them smoking for days. Their stale cinder smell whipped through Leah's small apartment, robbing Matt's possessions—the beet-colored couch, his alphabetized collection of jazz, a splintery desk and boxes of files—of their own unique scent, making them indistinguishable from Leah's in a way that was strangely exciting to her. Love had never, so completely, encompassed her before.

Each night that hot summer, they fell asleep to the sound of vandals picking through the rubble across the street as if through a fruit orchard. During the day, workmen arrived with bulldozers and cranes to chip away the burnt interiors and haul away the debris. At his desk in the living room Matt was doing proofreading between article assignments. When he could find no reason to call Leah at work—no new article ideas, no good-news or bad-news mail—he'd call to report on the work across the street.

"They just knocked out a partition so we can see straight through now. You should see the exposed brick in there," he'd say. Or, "They're stringing scaffolds along the sides. I think they're going to start scrubbing it. Yeah, they're wearing raincoats. Hey, Leah, you should come home and watch them doing this." Once or twice she did go home. Matt began research for an article on tenement renovation. "You know," he said once, "those old heaps over there are incredibly strong structures."

With their stone skins washed white, the scrolled pediments and ornate facades of an earlier time, some classical time, reappeared. Completely gutted, with patches of flat, blue sky filling their gapped windows and doors, the old buildings stood as solemn as ancient ruins. Roman ruins, Leah called them.

Mornings, she would roll away from Matt's chest where she spent the night, ease one thin arm from beneath the quilt, to pull away the long striped curtains, to look.

"Little boy, look," she would say, "we're in Rome."

Into the back of her neck Matt would whisper, "We are, my sweet," and then they'd make love.

From the start Matt was intrigued that Leah bled only when the moon was full. "Are all women like that?" he asked her. She told him, No, every woman is different. It was a natural embellishment of the conceit of those times for Matt to imagine Leah's body as the cycle from which the rest of the universe took its cues.

One year passed, then several more months, then waking in the morning—pulling away from Matt, placing the two of them in what went on beyond the window—began to feel like climbing out of an abyss. By then, Leah and Matt, convinced that together they formed some absolute, were hibernating in a dark and private intensity. An intensity which was, at first, exciting in its exclusiveness. An exclusiveness which turned terrifying in the way it consumed them and was inescapable.

Matt said he had to buy a newspaper before he could sit down to work, and each day, with that excuse, he walked with Leah to the subway. Leaving him at the newsstand, Leah would hesitate a moment before crossing the street, balanced on the curb, feeling anxious as a child waiting for a chance, the right second, to jump onto a carousel or into a spinning jumprope. Filtered through Matt's constant presence, as distorting as a prism, the world, to Leah, had begun to feel strange.

One morning she caught herself reflected in a shoe store's large window. She was shocked. The hem was torn and hanging from the back of her badly-wrinkled skirt. In the center of her white cotton shirt Leah noticed a gap instead of a button, and a pinch of pale skin. All this time, she thought, I felt really lovely. Matt had said she was.

That second summer, July's moon filled, then ebbed. A new quarter appeared and still Leah wasn't bleeding. They thought she was pregnant.

"Go to the doctor," Matt said.

"No, I'll feel stupid if it isn't true."

"You're not making sense. You're being illogical. How can you go on not knowing for sure what's going on in your body? Listen, if you'd like, Leah, I'll go with you."

"Why? Why should you go with me? You think all of a sudden I'm not capable of doing anything without you?" But Leah knew she had lost that ability long ago.

A few days later, one night in her sleep, Leah felt her stomach cramped and distended, felt the muscles across her back tighten like tourniquets. She held onto sleep for as long as she could, but the pain grew and spread and finally woke her. When she reached the bathroom she was bleeding.

Rocking slightly, Leah wandered through the apartment. The living room at five in the morning looked disconcertingly useless. Usually if she found herself alone by Matt's desk she would linger there, examining his fountain pen sketches on the desk blotter: complicated series of interconnected cubes. She would proofread and make notes on the pages piled around the desk. Matt was getting many good assignments. "Can't talk, Leah," he'd say when she called him from her office. "I'm in the middle of something." Glancing at the page inserted in the typewriter that night, she saw he was working on something new, an article he had never mentioned to her. So things are happening to him, too, she thought.

Passing his desk, Leah walked into the kitchen, found aspirin, orange juice. Then, half way through that act of curing herself, Leah stopped. Sitting on a low stool, she was spotlighted by one naked lightbulb hanging high above her. A pale, oversized nightgown hung around her like a loose skin, barely touching her own skin, a casing for the pain. The grain of the kitchen table was magnified in the bottom of her empty juice glass. Into the glass she said softly, "I wouldn't have had it."

That thought did not feel blasphemous to Leah. Two aspirins were turning gritty in her hand. The cramps were sharp and everywhere, pouring out of some small spot where a baby did not exist, never had. She realized that. Realized, too, that a child would have grown and grown there, all out of proportion, as Matt had throughout the rest of her, and then she, Leah, would have been lost. Instead, she had her aching middle. Leah's pain: private, her own. She dropped the aspirins back into their bottle. Greedily, she wanted to hold onto it.

When she told Matt that her body, unlike the moon, had simply skipped a few beats, he said, "Leah, did you know I would have wanted it? I think the whole time I wished it was true. I wanted us to have a baby." He said that, he admitted later, only because having a child seemed the one act of faith that could bring them, together, back into the world.

They lived on together for a few ambiguous months, slowly drifting apart, yet also, out of habit and fear, looking to one another for comfort and direction. Sometimes, staring across the living room at Matt reading on the couch, Leah willed him to look up. A few times he did, smiled, stood and walked towards her. But the desire in his narrowed eyes looked more like curiosity and Leah felt betrayed: already he was seeing her from a stranger's distance. Later, in bed, they'd move against each other in new ways, dissonantly. Matt's face below her looked so far away, above her he looked savage and too close.

Then, on Sunday night, lonely and hollow as only Sunday in the city can be, Matt's glass coffee pot slipped from Leah's wet hands and broke.

"I can't believe you dropped it," Matt said.

"I'm sorry," Leah told him. "My hands were soapy. It slipped. Hey, besides, I thought it was *our* coffee pot."

"I've had that thing for years. What happened? Couldn't you catch it?"

"Matt, I said I was sorry. You know I'll buy you a new coffee pot. I'll buy two. What do you want?" She was crouched down, picking up the larger chunks of glass. "It was an accident. I'm sorry. I'm sorry."

"O.K. Let's forget it, Leah." Holding his hand on Leah's shoulder for balance, Matt stooped down beside her, leaned over to kiss her.

"Don't" she said and pulled away.

Matt's hand still rested solidly on her back. "Leah, why are we fighting?"

Crying, she turned to face him. "Because we're making each other crazy, Matt. We're not happy together anymore."

Two hours later she was standing, shaking, in the shower with the water turned on hard so she wouldn't hear him packing or the sound of the front door closing when he left.

The next day, he came back. For three days. Then he left and returned again twice. Finally, when it seemed he was gone for good, Leah emptied all the drawers and closets into the center of their—her—bedroom floor, knelt into the pile and wept.

It was February when Matt left, melting into a timid spring, as it had been when they met. Breezes from the river still skidded old newspapers into Leah's ankles in that ruthless winter way, but the air was turning softer, kinder. Walking alone each night from the subway, Leah sifted through, listed, her grievances against the world. She cursed Matt for saying their parting was a good thing—a generous and cautious parting, he had said, because they had given each other time; a respectful parting because they had never been unfaithful. Leah knew better. She knew they had failed. She hated herself for having lost Matt. And she cursed herself for having given so much that in loving him she lost herself. Now she felt alone. When she walked down the street it was with her face raised, her head slightly tilted, as if she were ready to walk into a hug or hoping to catch a kiss from some gentle stranger.

These days, though, Leah climbs up from the subway tunnel at the end of the day, turns toward distant New Jersey and walks home watching the sky. On nice evenings, an apricot sunset might be slipping into the bruise-colored Hudson. Above her knee socks and boots and beneath her wool skirt, Leah's snagged nylon slip licks the back of her knees; this is a pleasant secret. Life seems good. She passes neighborhood kids sitting up on mailboxes. The music they play in their cassette players makes Leah want to spin her sack of manuscripts one, two, three full times, loose it to the wind, and dance, dance. When it feels like hard work to keep from swinging herself down the street, Leah knows she is getting better.

Finally arriving at her apartment, she calls out, Hello. It is not a greeting, because no one else lives there, and not really a warning in case someone has entered. She just wants to hear her own voice in the stillness, throw new air into the home that keeps breathing while she's gone.

Later, through one side of an Earth, Wind & Fire album, she does sit-ups, leg lifts, and sustained body stretches over her knees, while her dinner—chicken, liver, or a nice piece of fish—simmers in a cast-iron frying pan beneath a new aluminum lid.

During dinner she reads the Sunday paper, slowly, all week long. When she sees articles about renovations, architecture, independent business people, jazz clubs, Mexican restaurants, French movies or the Pittsburgh Steelers, Leah knows, for sure, that Matt has read them. Once she saw his by-line and though she thought of calling him she never did. She knows, as he does, that probably another whole year must pass.

Afterwards, she goes to her bedroom and her bed becomes a small universe. She leans back on four lilac pillows and covers herself with a forest-green quilt—soothing is how Matt described the effect of those two colors against each other. Eventually, a red-trimmed bowl of lukewarm cereal and milk will be balanced on the bed. And a manuscript—one stack of down-turned pages which she has read, and another stack of upturned pages to be skimmed the next day on the subway. Rubber bands which held the manuscript together will be bracelets on her wrist. By midnight Leah will be surrounded on the bed: the telephone, pencils, the jewelry she wore to work that day, her checkbook, hand lotion, an aqua chenille robe, the mail, orange peels, her hairbrush, a grocery list, her appointment book, a few magazines, a glass of melting ice, and her purse. More than the luxury of lying amidst the jetsam of the evening, Leah enjoys the organized feeling after she's cleaned it up.

Before clicking off the light when she is ready to sleep, Leah billows up the top sheet and quilt so she can see clear to the bottom of her bed. If you were watching, this would seem a casual enough gesture, but Leah knows she is looking for things that crawl and sneak. Things that shouldn't be there. The night a small mouse skimmed the floorboards in the living room is when this ritual began. (Too often while making this inspection, Leah remembers a man falling asleep next to her—Ben somebody—who said, "That's some phobia you've got there. We should cart you right off to Vienna." Unable to sleep beside him when he began to snore, Leah went into the living room, taking a manuscript with her. Ben has not been invited back.) Then she bunches and positions a pillow so she can lean her back into it, for company, during the night. In the dark her eyes stay open until she sees how the shadows have settled around the room.

On Sundays now, Leah often makes dinner with friends, almost always women. One friend, Hilary, suspects it is time for her to leave her own boyfriend and each week she presents further evidence in her favor. Hilary might say, "I feel he's grown a lot through our relationship. He's less shy, more confident. Isn't he? Everyone says so. But I feel stagnant, as if I haven't grown at all through him."

And then someone, usually Amy, says, "Hilary, it sounds like you know exactly what you want to do. Make a decision and get it over with."

Listening, chopping green peppers and onions for spaghetti sauce, Leah wonders what Matt told his friends when he moved out.

"I'll probably never meet a man who cares about me again." This is Hilary's worst worry.

"It's true, Hilary," Amy says, "you probably won't."

By the time the dishes are done and everyone has left, Sunday has passed with a minimum of pain. Leah takes a book, she reads a chapter, billows the sheets, sets the alarm, clicks off the light. The darkness. The shadows. Eventually Leah falls asleep.

Mornings, she still has problems getting out of bed. It is not depression or sadness holding her, but a covetous instinct to possess the early morning, to give length to a moment of perfect peace. When the windows are clean, the plants on the sill look greener. On the sculpted ledge outside, a few pigeons might be perched, making those throaty noises, those deep, trilled gulping sounds.

Looking out above the brownstones (her new neighbors are less interesting than the ruins were), Leah knows now that although love can be as random and elusive as an intuition or a lucky streak, it is always hoped for and always possible. And she is almost convinced that in a single morning, in the simple shifting of one day to the next, the world, so tired and old, can be born again, even out of sadness.

Rose Carmellino

Rose Carmellino, a Brooklyn resident, is a graduate of Vassar who went on to get an advanced degree in creative writing at Columbia University with the help of a Claire Woolrich Memorial Scholarship. While a student, she was awarded the Transatlantic Review Award in 1981 and was also the recipient of an UNICO literary award. In 1984 she was granted a

residency at the artists' and writers' colony in Woodside, California, run
by the Djerassi Foundation, where she plans to complete her novel in
progress.

---

from a novel in progress

Pigeons gathered at Grandmother's feet. Their necks crooked forward as
they snipped crusts of bread. Iridescent colors bristled among the gray
feathers. They reminded Nina of grease slicks, the kind she saw floating like
sheets of ice on puddles in the street. Grandmother called them "earth
rainbows."

"Yes," she would say, bringing dried heels of bread out from the deep
pockets of her housedress, "God gives even the poorest pigeon a fine coat to
wear. And today, on the holy day, they all wear their best necklaces."

It was the feast day of the Assumption, and leaving the house at ten
o'clock they had walked across the long avenues to the church. Nina knelt
quietly against the marble altar railing and bowed her head. The black
mantilla that she wore fell about her face. Only points of light were discern-
ible through the lace eyelets. Watching her hands clasped in the posture of
prayer, she listened for her grandmother's breathy exclamations.

"Ah, God . . . I fear your church, filled with old women . . . and the
priests always sending poor souls to Hell. . . . But yet, your world is so
beautiful."

She would cross herself hastily, jabbing her fingers from forehead, to
heart, to shoulders, and hearing the smack of her lips against the folded
knuckles of her index finger, Nina knew they would be leaving soon.

They did not go home. They continued walking, passing open markets.
"Fish, fish . . . live and fresh . . . What, too expensive, Signora . . . then
scarola . . . Sardines for the frying pan . . ." the vendors barked in raspy
voices. Muscular boys in T-shirts carelessly unpacked wooden crates. They
sang, *"Femmina, tu sei una male femmina . . ."* Onto piles along the stands
they jostled vegetables, and musty-smelling melons, and they shouted out
their prices. "A good buy, the best buy . . . Fish . . . Apples . . . Sardines."

Taking Nina's hand as they came to four lanes of traffic, Grandmother
turned a cold eye upon the streets behind them.

"These are holy hours. On this day we would always go to throw our sins
in the water."

Once across the avenue they followed the uneven path that ran alongside
the chain linked fence of the Dyker Park golf course. Slowing her pace to
match Grandmother's, Nina watched her small feet in their black boots

move with careful determination among broken glass and ruptured cement. Grandmother had told Nina Italy was the shape of a "boot, kicking Sicily away," and she imagined it to be like her shiny black shoe, with the stout heel and wiry taut lace.

Running ahead, Nina leaned up against the railing which separated the walkway from the rocks, holding the wet metal in her hands. She gazed out at the water. It was calm and continuous in its splashing against the littered and stunted shore. Soon Grandmother caught up with her. She spoke above the lulling tide, and highway traffic that raced behind them.

"Once a Gypsy woman came to my town, and everyone was afraid of her, because it was said she could cast the evil eye. One day as I was out gathering twigs for the fire I found her resting upon a stile. Seeing me, she called me by my very name, and told me I would cross much water. There were so many streams and brooks up in the hills, I did not think much about her words. And though I crossed the ocean only once, with each new day, each year, every dollar in my purse, I traveled farther away from the knoll that was my village. And was it all my sin of pride? Did I become a pilgrim, only to wear the face of a signorina? I remember the first time I saw these shores. I had two children pressed to my legs, and a year-old promise that your grandfather would be waiting. So many women had their husbands swallowed up by America. At first, letters full of plans and money, and maybe a photograph at Easter. With time . . . less news, little money, and finally nothing. Deathless widows, yet lower than widows. No respect, only pity and half-smiles. I prayed to Saint Joseph every day, each free moment, while threading a needle, scattering grain for the hens, rocking my babies. 'Noble husband, Saint Joseph, preserve me and mine.' " Tears glistened in the creases of her eyes, and Nina knew she was remembering the girl, who had grown to be her mother, and the boy, who had died wearing the uniform of a country he did not belong to in the faraway land he would not belong to.

"We sold everything. Everything we had went to buy three certificates on the black market. The boat was going to Argentina, but stopping in New York. The whole time I kept the papers hidden to my breast. Men would kill for them. America had laws . . . they did not want any more immigrants." Grandmother pointed left, out to the tip of Coney Island.

"You could imagine, after all those days when we first saw land, how happy everyone was. First it was a faraway dot. Almost nothing. Some said America could not look so small. But then it got bigger and bigger, until finally we were coming right through these Narrows."

They began to walk with their backs to Coney Island, retracing the path of the boat, as it voyaged toward Manhattan.

"I was so afraid. I could hardly breathe." Grandmother beat her chest three times, as if in response to the holy chimes. "Afraid that the men to take us off the boat would not come, and that the officials on Ellis Island would know our papers were false. Everyone was on the deck when we passed into the harbor. The children were taunting each other, 'Who will be first to find Papa?' We had not seen him in three years."

Grandmother sat down on a bench. Reaching into her pockets she brought forth scraps of bread and sprinkled them on the ground.

"So many people were at the dock. All cheering and shouting . . . words I could not understand. I looked and I looked, but I saw not even one familiar face. The children were quiet. I was silent. I looked at us three, me in a dowager's rags with my mother's cameo pinned tightly at my throat, and the children in sailor's suits I thought were American. We wore strained masks. We were all afraid. Then, Lucia began to jump and cry, and shout, waving her fists. 'Papa . . . Papa.' On the dock wearing a black-banded straw hat of white, and shaking brown paper bags filled with chocolate kisses, was my husband."

Hands clasped in prayer, eyes turned downward, Francis led our evening grace. Uneasy, he stumbled over the words quickly. Mother smiled approvingly and patted his hand.

"My son . . . blood of my blood," she whispered with pride. *"Figlio mio."*

At the head of the table Father's chair stood empty. Three salt shakers within a furious grasp and a stack of crusty bread surrounded the plate that for the past two nights had been untouched. Mother and Grandmother exchanged furtive glances, and Nina watched their faces, eager to share their confidences. The clock, the door, the plate, the chair: they were careful to turn their heads and avert their eyes from them, as if a bold stare could somehow summon Father to appear.

"And so, Francis," directed Mother in a cross tone, "I already told your sister Lucy, and now I'm telling both of you. I don't want Nina left alone in the house. This afternoon as Mama and I were coming down the street, we saw Nina open the door for two strange men."

"Oh, Nina." Shaking his head, Francis reached out to catch one of her braids.

Nina's face reddened with shame. She could not understand how Mother and Grandmother could turn away strangers, humbly pleading *"non capisco,"* or pretend to them no knowledge of the people next door.

"Not another word." Mother was impatient, and she looked coldly upon Francis.

"Who was at the door? Insurance men? Jehovah's Witnesses?" Lucy lifted hurt eyes from her plate.

"*Non lo so,*" answered Grandmother in grim Italian. "Men in raincoats with briefcases."

"Remember the time Mrs. DeLessio was looking for someone to rent her basement?" continued Lucy. "A man with red hair and a red beard came to her door, and Mrs. DeLessio thought he was Christ. She started crossing herself and praying."

"If the man had a devil's wit, he could have stolen even the cheese from her mousetraps," Grandfather smiled.

"Enough of this." Mother made another impatient gesture, as if to clear away her children's laughter. "Francis, did you tell Grandma that the monsignor wants you to assist him for Easter High Mass?"

Francis scowled, his pale face darkening with irritation. "Only because this is my last year," he said without looking up from his plate, then adding, "The younger kids always mess things up."

"The holy days will be here soon. Who eats on Shrove Tuesday, starves on Ash Wednesday," instructed Grandmother in Italian.

"Yes, the holidays," agreed Mother. Her eyes darted around the table, brushing past each face, and finally rested upon her hands. Everyone was silent, eating quickly and noiselessly, and shifting in their chairs.

"My first holiday in America I was all alone," began Grandfather with renewed vigor. "I was living in a boardinghouse on Mulberry Street. During the day I worked digging the subway tunnels, and at night I'd go to this rooming house, have a glass of wine and maybe a plate of *scarola* and some bread dipped in oil, and then go to sleep in a room with eight or nine other men."

" '*Cca nisciuno è fesso,*" Grandmother interjected.

"Yes . . . on the wall someone had written in Neapolitan, 'No fools here.' Every man would write something—if only the name of the town they left. Anyway, I was going to spend Christmas Eve with some second cousins, who lived way up in the Bronx. I had bought two enormous eels at the fish market, and I carried them in a burlap sack. After work, I got on the elevated train, sat down holding this bag at my feet, and after a while I fell asleep. Before you know it, the bag had slipped from my hand, and the eels had slithered out onto the floor. 'A snake! A snake!' women were screaming, people running and somebody pulled the emergency brake. Waking up I didn't know what was happening. I couldn't speak two words of English, but I ran out of there so fast, cursing the loss of those eels. They came with fire ladders to get the people down."

"*È vero,*" nodded Grandmother. "*È vero.*"

They laughed with a forced gaiety, and then finding themselves suddenly relieved of the oppressive silence, they laughed clamorously, senselessly.

"Your father comes," whispered Grandmother.

Father stood at the doorway of the kitchen, uncertain whether to enter. He was tall, with an angular face and bristly hair, and his clothes hung crookedly on his thin frame. Sitting stiffly in his chair, his eyes searched each one of them, studying them with a piercing gaze.

Nina thought he had winked at her, his right eyelid opening and closing with a cold protracted sweep. Only Grandmother glared back at him, the one savage eye of the cameo pinned at her collar joining in her reproach.

His plate before him, Father folded his hands and with his lips moving wordlessly said his prayers.

"Thank the Lord you don't find the lock changed." Grandmother hissed.

"My food has turned to stones," Father gasped, holding his forehead with great anguish.

"Vincent, where have you been?" Mother's voice was a shrill soprano.

"Tenafly," he gulped awkwardly.

"*Dov'è* Ten-a-fly?" muttered Grandmother, shrugging her shoulders. "*Che cos'è*"

"Jersey . . . I was in Tenafly, New Jersey," Father cried fretfully with a nervous twitch of his lips. And then overwhelmed, the palms of his hands turned up in supplication, he grieved, "I had the newspaper. I was going to find a job. I was in Manhattan with the newspaper. Everthing was black and white," he moaned, "and I walked down the street . . . brick upon brick, but in my home not two stones left together. I went into an office. The man looked at me, 'You unemployed?' White shirts everywhere. White shirts and black shoes. Suddenly I couldn't breathe. I felt dizzy, *stordito*. I went outside and I saw a bus."

"Three days? What did you do for three days?" Mother shrieked incredulously.

There was a long silence as Father, his eyes unblinking, his face stony, considered the past days. "I walked . . . I looked. There were trees and hills."

"This *cap'ombrell*. Wasting his time when he should be feeding his children. This *pazzo*," Grandmother railed.

Father turned toward her, shaking a slender bony finger in her face. Dark with rage, he shouted with venom, "You put the *malocchio* on me. You're the one! Ever since you came into this house, your black dress at my table, black stockings on the washline, you've put a black curse upon me. It's you twisting Lucia's mind." He pounded his fist, and wailed in a voice overcome with grief, "Am I not the man of this house?"

"*Sì, sì*, Vincenzo," Mother hushed. "You'll make yourself sick." Placing a finger to her pursed lips, she signaled Grandmother to say no more. "Eat your dinner, Vincent. You are tired. You need to rest."

"*Una bella figura*," Grandmother sneered.

Una bella figura, a fine figure, was what Lucia first saw when she met Vincent Savino. Newly arrived in this country after World War II, he was tall and slim, with a graceful pallor on his face. Unlike the roughhewn men in her neighborhood, she saw in Vincent's gauntness a religious asceticism, in his nervousness a sensitivity, and she was impressed by his fine *alta* Italian. In reality, his thinness was the scar of his poverty, and his nervousness the result of the bombings of his town. "I would roam the streets like a hungry dog, yet quicker than a dog, looking among the rubble for a bit of bread," he would say bitterly. "And if I found a scrap it was as poisonous as the gall forced between Christ's lips. And the bombs, always coming when you thought you were safe. *Dio Mio, Madonna Mio*, whimpers of the dying in the night."

Vincent had received some training in architecture, and Lucia, the only high-school graduate of her circle, was convinced that this intelligent man should be her husband. She was proud of the fact that he could work with *matita a mano*, pencil in hand, for Lucia's special dream had been to go to City College and become a schoolteacher. Lucia was bitterly disappointed when she found herself working behind a sewing machine, but she tenaciously hoarded her one dollar each week, her share of the earnings, tucking the money in her shoes, between the pages of her missal, under the statue of Saint John. Now, with the chance of marriage to an educated man, Lucia began to plan for the future she had been promised. She would have the neat house and well-schooled children, the kitchen where only the costliest oil and best cheese were used, the dining room with the ornate chandelier. Although there was no one to recommend Vincent, neither was there anyone to speak against him, and Lucia, who was not young, married.

"He's of no use to you, Lucia," began Grandmother, once Father had gone upstairs. "You should turn him out." Grandmother cleared the dishes off the table, leaving only a half-filled glass of wine before Mother. She worked at the sink and spoke with her back to Lucia. "He's crazy."

"No." Mother shook her head. "He just needs a job."

"Lucia, Lucia, don't you too deceive yourself. In all these years has a job made any difference? Always coming and going as he pleases, and finding his soup waiting hot too. And what work can he do? This fine man with his business suits and English newspaper under his arm. Always lamenting over his town—the fountain, the church, the whorehouse, the garbage heap—as if his Godforsaken village was paradise."

"What can I do? What would become of him?"

"What will become of these children?" Grandmother waved a hand in the air, throwing droplets of water as a blessing across the three faces. "He's week, bloodless. Turn him out. There would be no shame. The shame is in this poor comedy. His wailings and posturings."

Nina wanted to run upstairs into her bedroom and hide. She edged toward the door, dropping her dishrag on the tabletop.

Mother, seeing that, pushed her wineglass toward Nina, offering her a sip. "*Basta*," she said, giving the final word of every argument.

Nina rested against Mother's side and she was comforted to have an arm around her waist. They drank in turn, until there was no more wine left in the glass.

Tina DeRosa

Tina DeRosa lives and works in Chicago, where she has been a guest lecturer in the Italian American Studies Department of the University of Illinois. From 1977 to 1982, she was a writer in residence at the Ragdale Foundation in Lake Forest, Illinois. There she began work on her first novel, *Paper Fish*, and worked on subsequent short stories. She has just completed a second novel. The publication of *Paper Fish* by The Wine Press in Chicago was made possible, in part, by grants from the National Endowment for the Arts and the Illinois Arts Council. Upon publication in 1981, *Paper Fish* was nominated for the Carl Sandburg Award.

from Paper Fish

The family plot was purchased as soon as they had any money, before any of them had decent clothes. It is big enough for all of them, they will be buried on top of each other like layers of a wedding cake. The family name is carved into the stone, and the negro grave attendants can not pronounce it. The stone is so large, it is visible a good distance away, so that any living member of the family who visits it never gets lost. On Sundays, they pack a picnic lunch and go to take care of the grave. On the way to the cemetery, in the summertime, they stop at a specialty store that sells monuments and wreaths and small plants for the gravesite. Inside the store, stone angels with blank eyes and a look so forlorn it will tear your heart out if you are five years old are lined elbow to elbow on the wall. The angels sit with their legs crossed, their eyes have no pupils. They sit with their heads in their hands. There the family buys plants green as artichokes, flowers red as blood. In the wintertime, they buy an artificial black wreath and set it in the snow. But in the summertime, the entire living family spends Sunday afternoon at the gravesite.

Marco and Sarah help Grandma Doria out of the blue sedan. Grandma is wearing her old straw hat to protect herself from the sun; stuffed under her arms are the long loaves of Italian bread. Aunt Katerina, Aunt Josephina, Aunt Rosa carry straw picnic baskets filled with tomato, with onion. Uncle Salvatore stuffs into his large pockets the bottles of wine. The blue sedan pulls up silently to the curb by the gravesite, the sun shines on them as they all tumble out of the old blue car, tumble out onto the gravesite, telling each other to keep quiet, helping Grandma and her proud old hat, settling Doriana to sleep in the car's back seat, striating the vigorous cemetery grass with their baskets, their wine, their own healthy bodies.

Set into the stone are the small framed pictures of the dead; their faces are set so that they always look directly into the eyes of anyone who looks into theirs.

Carmolina is five years old. She sits and eats tomato sandwiches with Grandma Doria while the family laughs and talks and digs little holes into the face of the grave to plant the flowers. Grandpa is under the flowers; he does not eat tomato sandwiches. Carmolina runs, when she is asked, to fetch water from the pump at the corner to water the new plants. She is careful not to step on any graves when she does this. She stands, holding the heavy watercan over the family grave and watches the cool water spill out over her tennis shoes, wetting them, watches the holes just dug by Mama for the plants eat the water up. Inside the grave Grandpa listens to them sing, but he does not get water on his face. Inside the grave Grandpa Dominic is glad they are there, is glad the old woman Doria his wife and his children are there with the tomato sandwiches. Grandpa had a white mustache; it's with him in the grave. Carmolina sings the Italian love songs which Grandma taught her, *O rosa! O rosa! O rosa gentillina!* her small mouth opens and sings, and Grandma looks up at her from where she is slicing the onions.

The skin of the onion squeaks in Doria's hand when she pulls it away from the white body. The thin yellow paper of the onion makes no sound, but the

first layer of skin squeaks. She watches Carmolina singing in her small
broken Italian; she is growing up with the music tooled inside her brain.
The sound of Carmolina's growing is filled with music in her head, of the
laughter and quick tears of her large family around her. The sound of
Doria's time was quiet, was patient, the sound of her growing up was slow
and deliberate. The time of Doria's growing was marked by usual, small
events, but her people had their own way of remembering. They sat in the
dusk of Italy and they made their lives slowly, measuring out the days like
milk or salt. They kept picturebooks of their lives, and in them they pasted
likenesses of themselves. The pictures were bound in corners of black
paper. The people in the pictures had skin the color of onion; they were
dressed in shades of brown. Their smiles were fixed and faced forward
toward the man under the black hood who with his great funny puff of white
smoke would seize them. Their skins were not truly the color of onion; their
clothes were not really shades of brown.

On the day that the first family picture was made, Doria wore a white
dress which was made for her by her mother Carmella from the wool of
sheep. It was a heavy dress, much too heavy to wear in the sun that day, but
it was her best dress and her mother insisted. After the picture was taken,
Doria wiggled out of it and gave it to her sister Sabatina who immediately
undressed and got into it while the family looked on. On the day the first
picture was made, Doria was eight years old. She lived with her family on a
small hill in a town near the city of Naples which they visited on holidays if
the year was good. Their town was a small one; the furthest border was a
graveyard whose markers went back to the sixteenth century. The white
stucco house was Doria's house. It was buffed white by the sun of Italy;
there was no glass in the windows. In the summer the glad weather washed
through the windows; the trees became part of the family. In the wet season
the rain washed into the house; it dripped down the walls. Then Doria's
mother set out after the great black waterbugs with her straw broom.
Sometimes Doria and Sabatina found a waterbug in their bed and they
snapped it open between their fingernails. Outside was a small garden; this
garden was the joy of Doria and her mother. The two of them, dressed in
black dresses, sat under straw hats and weeded the grasses away from the
small green plants. The mother spat into her hands for luck before she
began to work. From the garden came sharp white radishes and lettuces for
the salad. Sabatina did not like the garden; it dirtied her hands. The mother
said that Sabatina was the child of royalty, that she was kidnapped by
gypsies who wore golden earrings and stole children. She said she found
Sabatina in a basket in the garden, and that Sabatina was a princess who
would never do a lump of work in her life. Doria laughed when her mother
said this, because in her heart she knew it was true that Sabatina was lazy as

the sun and would never amount to anything if she did not wake up soon. It was true that there were gypsies. They roamed the countryside and played music on their dulcimers, they shook tambourines in the dark. The cries of the strings and of the little silver bells enchanted the children. Doria had seen them, the black eyes and black souls of them. The breasts of the women were large, like the udders of cows; they swung under bright red dresses. Their bodies were dressed in golden jewelry; they wore silver combs in their hair. They were beautiful; they were terrifying. They frightened goats in the night so that their milk turned sour; they terrified the chickens so that they went barren. Whenever Doria and Sabatina passed the gypsies on the dirt roads, they crossed themselves and called upon the Madonna for protection from the evil eye. At night the two little girls lay in their white bedroom, on the clean sheets beaten white in the river. Outside the moon was a blue hole in the sky, washing the world blue-black, making the trees black as ash or as death, making the trees stick all out of the world like the broken brooms of witches. Outside the world turned blue from the moon, its enchanted light made the bedroom blue, and the sheets and their toes sticking out from under the sheets turned blue along with the world. It was then that Doria and Sabatina heard the singing of the gypsies, heard the cry of the dulcimers and the strangled chatter of bells, heard the laughter and songs of the gypsies reaching up out of the ground. The gypsies ride black horses, Doria said, and Sabatina curled into her side of the bed, pulled her feet away from the pitiless blue light, hid her face in the pillow. The gypsies ride black horses that once were devils, the devils grew tired of hell and changed themselves into horses. The gypsies find them and ride them, and the horses run faster than the horses made by God. The teeth of the horses are like knives, they can bite through the walls, Doria said. Sabatina buried her pretty brown face in the bedclothes and her legs were stiff. The horses run faster than the wind, faster than the rain, and if a gypsy wanted to catch you, you could never run fast enough, Doria whispered. Outside their windows the trees were black as matchsticks; a gypsy could set them on fire with his curse. Outside the window the trees looked into the bedroom with twisted faces. The voices of the gypsies travel through the ground, Doria said. The gypsies can reach up out of the ground and grab you with their teeth. The devil gave them special power. Sabatina screamed into the pillow and Doria scared herself. The sound of the dulcimer and of the thin tambourines travelled through the night hills. It was magic music, and sad. The gypsies were sad because they had been cursed by God to wander the world; they must live forever in tents, pitched by lonely fires. They sat round the fires dressed in their devil's gold, with gold at their ears and at their breasts, with gold at their waists and in small beautiful rings round their toes. The gypsy women sat with their long black hair and sang out of throats which burned. The men with their hard gypsy muscles listened and wept and grew angry. They revenged themselves. They stole children. They twisted the life of the animals so that goats vomited and chickens gagged. Sabatina rushed to the window, slammed the wooden shutters shut. She slapped out the blue light of the moon and the evil arms of the trees. Under the sheets, she still heard the music and Doria laughed at the way she scared little princess Sabatina. In the dark room, Doria watched the small slip of blue light under the shutters, clean and swift as a fish. She watched the shadows, stuffed like thick milk into the corners. The shadows only seemed to move. When she grew up, Doria would run away to the circus. With her blue eyes and black hair, she saw the circus and loved it. She loved the humped little dwarf with the yellow teeth, she loved the old wagons. There were green babies, flat and floating in bottles. The people of the circus dressed in clothes like jewels; Doria with her laughing blue eyes would be a part of them. The people in all the towns the circus passed would call out, there is Doria run away. Sabatina would grow old and fat; she would be forced to make large dresses to wear; no bracelets would fit her fat arms. But Doria would be beautiful, with slim ankles. She would lead the elephants, smiling.

In their small bedroom, his children were still asleep. Pasquale glanced for a moment at his daughters. He was a rough man. He had learned all he knew at the side of his father now rotting in the graveyard. The skin of his hands was almost as thick as the wood he worked; his eyes and the world they saw were the same. He wrestled with the world and forced it to yield to him all he demanded. He spat in the face of anyone who would steal from him that which was his. Carmella his wife was his; she had been given in proper ceremony. He had taken her properly in bed. She had yielded him two children though neither, curse God, was a son. He hammered and nailed and chiseled the wooden world into place. What would not yield he placed in a vise and then shaved off or sawed off what would not submit. His hands were black from his work; the palms were scarred by small tears in the skin which would not heal and by slivers of wood which were fixed parts of his flesh. His eyes were not the eyes of his brothers the farmers. His eyes were not marked by days spent under the yellow sun. His eyes followed the narrow grain of wood, followed it closely so that it would not deceive him and crack at a vital point. His eyes watched the fine shavings give way to correct proportions. His eyes ran over countless beams, ferreting out failure. The earth and its rooms, its fields and gardens, its houses and sheds, smelled of varnish and turpentine. He had long since lost the smells of his wife's kitchen, of the dishes set before him. Long ago he surrendered the delicate feast of anise in his coffee, the smell of honey in his cakes. The world smelled of turpentine and of sharp black varnish. His hands he had trained to know a slab of wood as a lover's hands know a woman's sex. They were hands fine in their work, and from them came the cabinets, tables and chairs which enabled him to marry Carmella his wife. His work had given him his family and this small house. He would not, like his father, become a broken doll, lose his trained eyes. He had taken care of these eyes and hands, the tools given him by God to make his way on the earth a man and not a shrivelled worm.

He did not know if his children were beautiful. He knew that they were his. He had made them, he continued making them the way he made a ladder or stool. When he walked into his daughters' bedroom on the morning when the pictures were taken, he noticed only that they were asleep. His eyes were trained to see the joints and pinnings of the world, and not its luster. Behind him, the black hills of Italy were filled with spectacular creatures, with creatures of myth, of legend, of dreams and nightmares, squirming out of people's minds, leaping out of their souls. The restless people looked up from their cooking, from their seeding, working the pulp of fig against the soft skin of their mouths like squirrels, looked out from their eyes and seduced from the humps of stone images which nourished them as the earth could not. They supplemented what the earth failed them. They provided the mysteries which God in his haste had overlooked. Thus the hills were peopled by bandits who slit human throats with the ease with which mothers slaughtered chickens; who slit open and spilled human life while glancing at the stars. Their taste was for swift and splendid death, their hands were bruised with blood, and they licked them clean. Headless bodies floated in the streams, suspended astonished in the water. The air was rich with the smell of their blood. Travelling through the hills was never an unconscious act. The people's eyes filled with what they expected to see; their irises were moist with the blood they might shed. Waiting, the people believed their bones lacked marrow, like birds. But more than the thieves filled the heavy pockets of the hills. The unborn, the never-seen, populated the trees, the small stone paths, and the stories of these astounded Doria. Creatures which had never existed lurked in the tales of her mother, Carmella, lurked in her words, in the catches of her voice. They peered out of their red eyes at the small child listening. The mother stirred beans in the pot on her stove, shredded the cheese and told Doria of these, the unseen creatures. The mother's face was deeply olive and her eyes sought the truths outside her kitchen window, as she prepared the meal. The souls of the unforgiven dead walked the hills at night. They held their hands before their faces, hiding their rotted features. They marched in a hard blue line and the sight of their faces could shoot you into madness, could spit you into hell. On a hill outside the town they gathered in a blue-black circle and chanted their prayers for forgiveness. They set their faces towards the stars, searching out the fingers of God which would hold them safely once again. They dressed themselves in leaves and danced. In the rain, they turned silver as pond scum, in the rain their secrets were revealed. It was true according to Doria's mother that each man is given a secret when he is born. He is meant by God to protect his secret, to hide it like a jewel throughout life. Each secret is different, and only God knows them all. The telling of secrets is forbidden. They must be held close to the body all through life, because they are the only treasure. Without them, a man is a snail. You must never, Doria, squander the secret. You must, Sabatina, be careful. Do not tell.

Sabatina is one of the faces on the family stone. Her eyes look out from behind her glasses; her smile is quiet on the stone where Carmolina is watering the grave. Her quiet dead eyes smile at her sister Doria. She looks like Doria who is slicing the tomatoes open so that the seeds will spill into her hands, but Sabatina is slimmer, and she is dead. She does not have little whiskers on her chin.

Because Grandma Doria is the only member of the family who has little whiskers on her chin, like a goat. The whiskers float in the air when she talks to Carmolina, Carmolina stares at the whiskers, they are like the antennae of a gentle insect. She laughs from her stomach; Grandma's laugh has a wheeze in it. It is as though she uses up too much breath, laughing, and Carmolina is frightened of the wheeze, let God never take Grandma's breath away. Her skin and her teeth are yellow. When Grandma makes lunch, it is cheese on Italian bread, or tomatoes on Italian bread, or just Italian bread. They sit together at the formica table in the kitchen, the whole world is burning from the heat of the summer, but coolness is on the table and Carmolina and Grandma talk:

When Great-Grandma Carmella died, she was sick a long time. Then Grandma was just a little girl and she sat with Great-Grandma who was dying, and everyone else was asleep. Deep in the night, Great-Grandma screamed and sat up in bed. Grandma saw a woman dressed in white crawl out from under the bed; she was a skeleton; she was Death; only Grandma saw it. Grandma screamed and ran out of the room; Great-Grandma died instantly. There is a mountain in Italy filled with candles. Some of the candles are tall and white. Some are short and sputter with the blue flame. Each person has his own candle. When he is born, the candle is lit; when the candle goes out, he dies. You can see this mountain, Carmolina, only in your dreams, but God will not let you see your own candle, even in a dream. If there is a mistake, and you see your own candle, you will die. This is how people die in their sleep. Great-Grandma, knock wood, did not die in her sleep.

Grandma keeps food on the back porch. She hangs long red peppers from the line with wooden clothespins. She keeps white lima beans in jars of salted water; she keeps them there until they grow juicy and bloated; then

she salts them more and feeds them to Carmolina, who loves them.
Grandma keeps trays of seeds from the pumpkin to dry in the window.
When they dry, she salts them and cooks them in the oven until they are
brown.

Grandma stands by the window on a hot summer day; the air is yellow
outside. She is laughing, she is fat in her black cotton dress. The sun makes
her little whiskers precise and obvious; they are white. She is smiling at the
little girl called Carmolina and lifting the screen from the window. The sill
is cement and the birds are nowhere to be seen, but Grandma breaks the
day-old bread and places it on the cement sill. The sun is making her face
beautiful. It is doing magic to her face, and here, in the corner where
Carmolina sits, the shade is gray and peaceful and Grandma is standing in
the spotlight of sun that someone is shining on her because she is feeding
the birds. The old woman laughs, she throws bread out the window. The
little girl Carmolina can not reach, the grandmother picks her up, holds her
high against the sun so that she can feed the birds too. The circle of sun
shines on the little girl, she is laughing, her grandmother owns the sun and
is calling the birds:

In the sun the sand was hot like nothing else could be hot under her feet, so
that her body did little jumping motions when she walked and she looked
like she was flying, but she wasn't, she was walking on the hot sand that sent
her up and jumping into the world. In the shade the sand turned cool. It
was gray there and small things grew with quiet rocks and red lady bugs
that flew in the air and landed on her skin, and all that made it cool.
Carmolina left the land and went walking off into the water, and before the
water began, the sand was ripples, it was rippled by the wind and was
packed hard, like a bed sheet, and she went walking into the water, which
was blue like an egg, which made long soft breaking sounds out there where
it struck against the world, and spilled over. Standing in the sand, she could
hear the water breaking from far away, it sounded like thunder only it was
sweet and she wanted to go out into it and she did, she ran out, she ran into
the blue water and it was cold around her feet and the water was eating her
body up, like a little rock or a fish, and she jumped up and down in it, she
put her feet into the bottom of the water and she stood on the world and
laughed. When she looked back at the sand, she could not find the blanket
with her family on it, she could not see her grandmother with the lunch
basket filled with sandwiches, she could not find the right colors in the
sand, none of the colors were hers. She splashed her hands in the water and
her toes dug themselves into the sand, it was packed hard, with little rocks
in it, the rocks bit her feet, they were small mean bites under the water,
like angry fish. Then a voice called her from the sand, one of the colors was

moving, she watched the color float across the sand, it had no feet, but moved towards the water and was calling a sound like her name. Her toes dug into the water, something was coming to get her. The color came into the water, it was big like a tree, it called her name but she could not find its face and the water no longer was cold, the warm skin lifted down for her, in its hands she was warm, and she was lifted from the water and carried back to the sand. Then she rode the horses of the merry-go-round. The horses were painted red and gold and green and black, they had separate saddles and the reins were real leather, the bit was metal. She climbed up on the horses and she was as far above the ground as she would be on the second level of the monkey bars. The merry-go-round started slowly, it made slow circles of light in the hot summer air, and slowly she moved past her mother and father behind the mesh fences. They were small figures, smiling, and she smiled back at them as the horses moved past. Then they turned into quick little blurs of colors, whisked by air into pure colors which were smiling at her. And her horse rode up and down, it carried her up closer to the top of the merry-go-round where she could see the fantastic iron works which made the horse move, the iron bars pumping steadily up and down, making the horse dance. And the music of the merry-go-round was sad, it was the sound of the ball park where people stood straight and sang to the flag, where the wind was so gentle it was like a hand on your face, and sometimes you saw the moon over the grass until someone moved it and you had to watch the game instead. It was the sound of the men at the ball park whose voices called Coke and hot dogs and beer and peanuts, it was the sound of the men running out there. The feel of the wooden horses between her legs was cool like the sand on the beach when the sun is going down and it's time to go home. It was the feeling of the fun house where everything happened and moved and exploded and disappeared in the half-light; it was the sound of her mother calling, calling to her where she drew chalk pictures into the bricks of the alley to come home, because the sun was going down and dinner was ready but she never wanted to leave because she loved it and this was the last day of summer before school started because tomorrow was September. And the music of the merry-go-round slowed down and the funny fat colors turned into her mother and father, and they were smiling because she was laughing so hard on the horses, and when she got off the ride, she couldn't find them for a minute because she was so dizzy and everyone looked like maybe they could be her mother and father and she looked back at the merry-go-round, at the horses, at the man who stood by the lever, the giant metal lever that made the horses move, and he was lighting a cigarette and his face was sweating, he was wearing a dirty T-shirt and one of his front teeth was missing. And the horses were hard like wood, like all the other rides in the amusement park, like the wood of the roller coaster where they strapped you in so you wouldn't fly out and bump into the clouds or blow across the ocean to the other side of the world. And the music of the merry-go-round was the sound of young voices calling at the beach to pick up the blankets and wrap up the sandwiches, to shake the sand out of your clothes and the rocks out of your shoes, to run to the water to wash the sand off, to splash your feet in the water, to watch a bird fly away, to do everything quickly.

Nancy Maniscalco

Nancy Maniscalco was born in Queens, New York. Her father was a bricklayer and her mother a housewife. She holds a B.A. in creative writing from Goddard College and has taught in writing workshops and at Manhattan Community College. Her novel *Lesser Sins* was published in 1979 and she is presently at work on another. Nancy Maniscalco divides her time between an apartment in Greenwich Village and the island of Ibiza.

from Lesser Sins

Confessions of a Venial Sinner

In psychoanalysis the mental condition of the patient is important but still more important is the mental condition of the doctor.
C.G. JUNG, *ABNORMAL PSYCHOLOGY*

The closest I ever came to a psychiatrist-patient relationship were my weekly bouts with the supreme white-collar worker: my friendly neighborhood priest. Unless, of course, Nurse Telby puts in a word for me at the psychiatric ward when ol' Father Debenedetto (Uncle Nunzie's friend's priest, no doubt) decides I'm a hopeless case and leaves.

The Most Immaculate Heart of the Virgin Mother is a really old church. All the bricks and the marble were shipped here from Italy. The ceilings are about two hundred feet high. There are these paintings of angels and saints and the Holy Ghost all over them. Along the side walls they have paintings of the Stations of the Cross. They're the story of the crucifixion of Jesus. They have *The Agony in the Garden,* when Jesus got scared and God came down and put a crown of thorns on his head. Boy, I really scream if I pick a rose and one tiny thorn pricks my finger. Then there's the three times he falls with the cross, and Saint Veronica puts this towel over his face to wipe him. Frankie told me that the Pope has the towel with the imprint of Jesus's face on it at the Vatican, and when the end of the world comes he's gonna show it to all the people, right before the Russians drop the bomb.

You should see all the genuflecting I have to do. When you walk into church, you have to dip your fingers in Holy Water (it's water blessed by the priest, but it's right from the faucet) and cross yourself and say, to yourself, "In the name of the Father, the Son, and the Holy Ghost," and bow your head each time you say a name. While you're crossing yourself, you have to kneel down on your right knee. Then you get up, and head toward your pew. When you get to the pew, you have to genuflect again, and cross yourself. After Mass, or even if you get up to go to Communion, you have to genuflect, whenever you come in or out of the pew. Plus, when you reach the center isle in front of the tabernacle, where the host is, you have to do it again. I almost forgot, you have to do it three times when the priest takes the sacrament out of the tabernacle for Communion and the altar boys ring their bells. Only, then, you have to pound (not really pound, but that's what they call it) your heart and say, "My Jesus, have mercy." If you don't it's a venial sin, and you'll be punished.

My favorite pictures are the ones on the windows. They're called *The Joyful Mysteries. The Annunciation* is the best. It shows this angel coming down and he tells Mary that she's with child. There's a bunch of doves flying around and she's grinning like crazy. The next picture is *The Visitation.* That's when Mary visits her cousin Elizabeth, and they're sitting around having coffee. Elizabeth's husband, the rabbi, tells Mary that she's going to have the King of the Jews. They're all very happy.

In the back of the church, there's a statue of Mary, it's called *The Immaculate Conception.* She's always dressed in pale blue. Sometimes when people get married, the bride gives her bouquet to the statue. It's really very dramatic, and I usually get the chills, unless the bride is really corny about it.

The candles on the altar give the church a waxy smell. My nose gets clogged up when I wait on line for the confessional. We have to stand, girls on one side of the confession box, boys on the other. The priest sits inside the wooden box on a little stool. He turns from side to side, boy, girl, boy, girl, all day long. The confessionals are dark, so you can't see the priest, I guess. He's supposed to be taking the place of God, so if you saw him close up, you'd be dead or in heaven. Frankie says the confessionals look like coffins standing up.

The First

There was a girl in my class named Lynn Krutz. She pissed on the floor of the confessional. It was the day we were making our first confession for our first Holy Communion. The fat ladies who take care of the priest's house had to bring buckets of some green stuff to clean it up. I was waiting to go to confession, and started laughing. I knew I'd have to confess laughing in church; that's a venial sin. Catholics are not too big on laughing. I remember thinking, I have so many spots on my soul, it must look like the sift, that's short for syphilis, the disease you get from sex, and dirty stuff.

Wouldn't you just know I had to go to Father Benchslinger? He is the oldest, dumbest priest in the world. He talks real loud, and can't hear a thing. It must have been him and not poor Lynn who pissed on the floor, I thought, and then giggled. But Lynn was the type. She threw up at least three times a week in our classroom. She wets her lips and sits there all sick-looking, while the nun glares at her real nastily. Then, blah! She vomits all over the place.

Then the next Sunday, after our first confession, on the day of our first Holy Communion, Lynn fainted in church. She was sitting in front of me, and all of a sudden I heard a thud and looked over the bench. There she was. First I thought she was dead. Her crinolined white dress was standing up over her face. The whole church could see her panties. I started to laugh. Three nuns came over. They genuflected and picked her up. Then they genuflected again, still holding Lynn. Lynn's hoop hit the floor and her dress flew up. They got up and carried her up the aisle and out. Boy, was she pale. She probably got yelled at for making a loud noise when her head hit the pew. Catholics don't like noise.

Anyway, back to the confession box. I was whispering, so ol' Bench-slinger says, "What? Speak up!" He screamed so the whole damn church heard.

"I lied!" I shouted, and it echoed through the church.

"Your penance will be two Our Fathers and three Hail Marys!"

When I came out of the confessional, my friends were laughing like crazy. I went up to the altar, knelt before the Blessed Mother, and said my penance. I knew then that I wasn't going to like this confession stuff.

The general consensus of my fellow confessors was: all you have to do is say, "I missed Mass. And I lied." The priest never asked what the lie was, so it could be that you cursed or some mortal sin like that.

The Foremost

The most traumatic test for my swiftly moving mouth came each year on Good Friday (to this day, I can't figure out what's so good about it). Between the hours of 3 and 6 P.M., all good Catholics are supposed to observe Christ's demise on the cross by silence. I'm still counting my lucky stars I wasn't hanged for being a traitor, what with my inevitable snickers, whispers, or coughs during the Pledge of Allegiance every morning. Not to mention my anxiety at not wanting to offend God on the day his son was killed (by the Jews, or was it the Romans?). You see, to speak during this time is a mortal sin. For the nonbelievers, a mortal sin is the sin of all sins. If somebody dies with a sin of this kind on their soul, they go directly to HELL. You do not pass purgatory, you do not collect two hundred dollars, and you do not have hope of salvation. Catholics are very unforgiving.

I would have to sit in church with my classmates and the nun in charge, in total silence. On one occasion, I managed to remain close-mouthed for two hours. I kept repeating the "Gettysburg Address" to myself. I was up to "testing whether this nation or any nation so conceived and so dedicated can long endure . . ." when Diane Proccocino nudged me. She mumbled something I thought at the time was important, and I lost my senses, once again, and spurted, "What?" Next thing I heard were Sister Veronica's rosary beads clinking together. Nuns are like cats; they saunter and stalk. When we were still wearing taps, they had rubber "souled" shoes. My ears were attuned to the clink of those beads. Thank heavens, 'cause the way they come up on you, you could have a heart attack.

As a matter of fact, I know at least twenty people who still stutter at the sound of clinking rosary beads. Sister Veronica proceeded to grab my ear and pull me up from my seat. She gave me a deadly look, dragged me over to her pew, pushed me down on my knees and, still holding my ear, went on with her prayers. Eventually she let go. I wasn't sure, since the pressure had numbed my ear, but I saw her make the sign of the cross. I don't believe this, but I once heard of a nun who moonlighted at a jewelry store. The owner claimed that her method of pinching was far better than any anesthetic in numbing ears for piercing.

At six o'clock on the dot, she turned to me and said, "Miss Mauceri, you will have to go to confession tomorrow."

"Yes, Sister," I said.

She then advised me of my rights. "If you don't go to confession, you will not be able to receive Holy Communion on Easter Sunday."

I stood perfectly still as she towered over me. I nodded at all the right times. Then I did it.

"Sister, I was supposed to go shopping for my Easter shoes tomorrow . . . maybe?"

She had the kind of complexion that became Crayola crayon red when she was angry. She spoke in a whisper, and her voice had a steady terrifying hum.

"You cannot receive the Holy Sacrament on Easter if you do not confess. You want to buy Easter shoes?"

I nodded, thinking there was hope.

"Christ's feet were nailed to the cross on Good Friday, for you and your sins."

I peeked up long enough to see the vividly painted feet of our church's Christ on the cross. It was like a childhood nursery character, like Winnie-the-Pooh. She shook her finger and her head, then went on.

"And you are concerned with shoes? Our God, Jesus (she bowed her head, then continued), died for your sins, and you want to buy shoes."

I retaliated with tears. "No, Sister, I'm going to confession . . . tomorrow, first thing."

She made one last gesture (just in case), "If you dare not receive Communion on Easter, you will be excommunicated."

I stuttered, "Yes, Sister, thank you, sis . . . ter" She turned, and I watched her walk all the way up the aisle. Then she genuflected, splashed herself with Holy Water, and vanished.

I knew my Holy Saturday would be spent standing in line with all the old people who went to confession once a year, on Holy Saturday. The church was like Macy's on Christmas Eve. The last-minute confessors dressed in black, all the statues draped in purple, and me. I thought of not going. Then I thought about the repercussions such an act would have for me. Such rebellion could mean only one thing: instant, irrevocable excommunication. I could imagine myself having to write on employment applications, under religion: EXCOMMUNICATED. So there I'd stand, my feet aching, my sinuses clogged, in the stuffy church, waiting to be absolved.

Father Debenedetto's head is hung. He's praying like crazy. Every time I glance over I catch the reflection of the lamp on his scalp. I've never seen a perfectly bald priest before. He probably never took his vitamins. At least that's what Aunt Dora would say.

Looking at him, sitting there with his head shining and his hands clasped, and his lips moving, I feel sorry for him. And, as usual, I feel like laughing.

The same year, while I was still in Sister Veronica's class, I got more trouble. There was this rumor going around about this gang, the Baldies. I didn't start the rumor—Frankie did! He told me they were coming around to our neighborhood, and they were going to take over the school. He said they carved their names into girl's chests, and raped nuns. Well, at first, I didn't believe him. I thought he was trying to scare me, like when we watched horror movies, and he'd make me scream.

The next day I was sitting in class, and Sister Veronica looked real nervous. The Mother Superior, Sister Mary, came into our classroom, and called Sister Veronica out into the hall. Diane Proccocino nudged me, "I don't think it's really Sister Veronica . . ."

"What do you mean?" I said.

"I heard that gang, the Baldies, are gonna take over the school. I heard they're kidnapping the nuns, and dressing up in their habits, and taking over the classrooms!"

"Don't be . . ."

"No really, did you see her face today? She doesn't look like Sister Veronica," she said, her eyes bulging out of her head.

My stomach started doing tumblesaults.

"Yeah, the way she was facing the blackboard all morning. Like she didn't want us to see. Oh, Diane, I'm scared. We'd better tell the other kids."

Diane started crying, and my eyes began to fill up. The lunch bell rang.

"Let's get out of here," I screamed. "Sister Veronica isn't Sister Veronica! She's a Baldy and . . ."

The entire class scrambled, and ran out into the hall, and down the rickety steps, and out into the street.

"Yeah, that's right they kidnapped her . . ." I pronounced. The kids ran off in all directions. "Run!" I screamed, completely out of control.

When I got home I told my mother about all the trouble at school.

"What kind of story is that?" she said.

"Mom, it's not a story, it's true. Please don't make me go back there. Please, Ma."

My mother grabbed my arm, and before I could swallow my peanut butter sandwich, she carted me off to school. As we turned the corner, I was shocked. The streets were packed. It looked like open school day. Frankie was standing on the corner. He ran up to my mother.

"Ma, Denise got the whole school in an uproar! None of the kids want to come back. All the parents are here. Sister Veronica and Mother Superior want Denise in the auditorium right now."

"You liar!" I screamed. "I didn't start anything! You did!"

"I'm not even in your class. How could I?"

"Stop! Denise, come with me. You too, Frankie."

The auditorium was full. Sister Veronica and Mother Superior were on the stage. They were standing by the flag. Mom dragged us up to the stage. Everybody was whispering and talking.

The nuns ran backstage as soon as they saw us. "Well, young lady, what do you have to say for yourself?" Sister Mary, the Mother Superior, said.

I was crying, "I didn't start the whole thing. I just . . ."

"You better not lie, Denise. You'll have to go to confession," Sister Veronica said.

"Well . . . I . . ."

"Denise, you'll have to go out onto the stage and conf . . . I mean . . . tell the children you lied."

The next thing I knew my mother had me by the arm, and Sister Veronica had my ear. They carried me out onto the stage. I was crying like crazy.

"Denise has something to say," Sister Mary said, pushing me to the front of the stage.

I stood, knees knocking and tears flowing, I looked out into the crowd of faces, especially Diane's, and said, "I lied!"

The Last

On the Good Friday before my nineteenth birthday I made my last confession. It wasn't in the form of last rites, obviously. I was attending night school and learning, via Mr. Biasi, in Social Psychology 101, what constitutes an attitude. He informed me that of all minority groups, women are the most easily recognizable victims of prejudice. Mr. Biasi had an uncanny grasp for the obvious. I was an apprentice bohemian and boarding with my best friend Tina Caralanza.

I got off the bus on 57th Street in Manhattan and walked up the stone steps to the big apple of churches, Saint Patrick's Cathedral. Why would a budding existentialist go to confession? Don't ask. I told you, they had me. I tiptoed past the wax mannequin of Pope Pius something or other. The lines at the confessional were short for Good Friday. Anyone who didn't confess today would be excommunicated. I strained to disregard my new-found moral affiliations, and to remember my sins.

I stammered over the Act of Contrition and spoke:

"Bless me, Father, for I have sinned. My last confession was . . . ah, one year ago." I caught a glimpse of his face; he looked like a hardened criminal through the thinly barred partition. I imagined myself as a gun moll, visiting her lover. Preferably, James Cagney or some good bad guy like him.

"I missed Mass." As I waited for a response, I felt a twitch in my privates. It reminded me of my unclean thoughts and how I put my fingers down there. I knew it was wrong, but it felt so good. I'd never done it before I moved away from home. I guess I didn't think it was so bad after all.

"I prolong kissed," I said, fighting a battle against an insane urge to laugh. I thought of Tom breathing heavily and grinding his penis. How good it feels, I thought. I suddenly felt ridiculous. I started grinning.

He shouted, "You're all alike."

I wondered how he knew I was Italian. Must have been the orange kerchief. He couldn't mean what I was thinking. How could he know?

He roared, "Women are the root of all evil!"

I was mesmerized by the sheer contempt in this man of God's eyes.

"All alike, shameless! Tempting men, sinners."

I was paralyzed.

"Leave this confessional!"

Unconsciously or self-consciously, I crossed myself. I stumbled out of the confessional in time to hear the echo of his last words:

"Leave this confessional!"

For the next few months I dreaded opening my mailbox for fear of finding a very formal, gold-embossed, handwritten scroll proclaiming me EXCOMMUNICATED. When it didn't arrive, I realized the full concept of excommunication. It's from within. You excommunicate yourself. And I did. Every time I felt the twitch.

DRAMA

Introduction

In the last decade, there has been a vigorous and notable burst of dramatic works from young Italian American women playwrights, some of which have been presented by companies like New York City's Forum of Italian American Playwrights and Il Teatro del Rinascimento, whose stated interests and aims are to showcase playwrights and theatrical artists of Italian American heritage and to stimulate interest in and exploration of the Italianate identity. Both groups have been receptive to the work of women, and Cleveland resident Rosemary Terango's *October Bloom* and *Her Mother's Daughter* have been staged in New York, as well as work by Anne Paolucci and dramatizations of John Fante's fiction by actress Rosemary De Angelis.

Dorothy Fields's *Poppa* was one of fifteen plays (out of thousands of entries) which were selected to be staged at the National Playwrights' Conference at the Eugene O'Neill Theatre Center in Waterford, Connecticut. Born Dorothy Gentile in the Italian community of New York's East Harlem, Fields has written a warm and humorous tribute to growing up Italian in America.

Rose Grieco's tribute to her heritage was the three-act play *Anthony on Overtime,* staged to critical acclaim at the Blackfriars Theater in New York during the 1961–62 season. This was followed by *Daddy, Come Home* at the same theater in 1962–63.

Donna DeMatteo is an active playwright and teacher of playwrighting at the HB Studio in New York. Among her plays are *The Silver Fox, Rocky Road, The Ex-Expatriate,* and *There She Is, Ms. America.*

Anne Paolucci is a talented writer who has worked in every genre, including playwriting. While she was a Fulbright Professor at the University of Naples, her three-act play *The Short Season* was produced in Italy; a one-act play, *Minions of the Race,* was staged three times and in 1972 won the drama award of the Medieval and Renaissance Conference.

Rosemarie Caruso's play *The Suffering Heart Salon* won an award and was showcased in Los Angeles in 1983. Her first play, *Shadows of the Morning Moon,* was written while she studied with playwright Karen Malpede. It is Rosemarie Caruso's feeling that the activity in drama by women of Italian American background is due to their grounding in the real and the tangible—they like to see and hear what is going on between people; they like the clash of dialogue; they like the sheer relief of expressing their feelings *aloud.* After the silence, they want to be heard. Men, she says, present points of view, and then rebuttals. But women want to explore and probe into feelings, and dramatizing them feels natural to them.

There does seem to be a natural attraction to the theater on the part of Italian American women: Virginia Giordano is a theatrical producer, and Nina Faso was coproducer of the spectacular and enduring *Godspell.*

Michele Linfante

Michele Linfante was born in New Jersey and has lived for fourteen years in San Francisco, where she has worked with the SF Mime Troupe and Lilith Theatre as an actress, playwright, and director. In 1981 she was awarded a National Endowment Playwrighting Fellowship. Most recently she has worked as a playwright-in-residence with the Dell'Arte Players Company, and for the Improvisational Theater Project in Los Angeles. Her one-act play *Pizza* was published by West Coast Plays, a project of the California Arts Council.

Pizza

GRACE INNOCENTI: A woman of thirty.
PIZZA LADY: A pizza deliverer.
LENA INNOCENTI: Grace's mother.
SADIE PETRILLO: An older lady and crony of Lena's.
BONSEY: A punk in the original fifties style.
PERLA THE EXOTIC: A Latin nightclub performer.

SETTING

The play is set in Grace's San Francisco apartment in the present, with flashbacks to a pizzeria in Paterson, New Jersey, in the fifties and sixties.

The apartment, which occupies one-third of the set, stage right, is realistic, whereas the pizzeria, which takes up the remainder of the playing area, is more suggestive and dreamlike.

The apartment is created by two walls with an entrance to the extreme stage right. On the upstage wall are houseplants, a case full of books, a cassette recorder, assorted objets d'art. A faded Oriental carpet is on the floor and some tasteful, handpicked wall hangings serve as decoration. A homey armchair sits in front of the bookcase and a low coffee table holds the telephone. The room is studious and comfortable.

The pizzeria walls, abutting those of the apartment, are suggested by a skeletal structure of metal bars strung with small, colored Christmas-tree lights. A larger-than-life, cartoon-style pinball machine and juke box are along the upstage wall. A shelf above the pinball machine is covered with baseball trophies. Left of the juke box is a curtained doorway to the kitchen. The metal framing angles away from this door to create the storefront. The large window holds a bright, neon "PIZZA" sign which faces the street.

Downstage from the window the metal framing creates the open door to the street. Below the "PIZZA" sign is a counter which holds all the trappings of a fifties' pizzeria: telephone, pizza trays, chrome napkin dispenser, large pepper shaker, etc. In the center of the pizzeria space is a table flanked by three chrome-legged chairs.

While the pizzeria remains in blackout the lights come up on GRACE *who is sitting alone in her apartment. She's dressed in layers of clothes including a robe and slippers. In the opening moments she's holding a pad and pencil and is anxiously mulling something over. She finally puts down the pad and dials a phone number, long distance.*

GRACE: Hello, Richard. This is Grace. I've been thinking . . . well maybe it's not such a good idea to send ma all by herself on the plane. I mean, she's a sick woman, you know. Yeah, I know you know. But the idea of sending her with a note pinned on her dress is kind of callous, don't you think? It's a long way. Can't you arrange a business trip or something and bring her yourself? . . . Or maybe you can convince daddy to take a plane and he could come too. . . . Yeah, I know he needs a rest. How's he doing, anyway? That's good . . . Yeah, well make sure she brings the note from the doctor about her medicine, and remember to pack some warm clothes. It's not that sunny here , you know. And tell daddy not to pack any dented cans or anything, I've got plenty of food . . . I guess that's it. Er, are you sure there's nothing else I need to know, because I might unplug the phone and then you won't be able to reach me for a while . . . Uh-huh, well I guess that's all, then. All right, Richard, good night.

As she is saying goodnight the doorbell rings. GRACE *goes to answer the door and there is a* PIZZA LADY *there holding a pizza. She's dressed in black trousers and a short-sleeved white shirt. She's wearing a cap with a winged pizza emblem and on her back is the same emblem in an oversized appliqué with a considerable wingspan, giving her an almost angelic appearance when she turns around.*

PIZZA LADY: Here's your pizza. It's $6.50.
GRACE: Oh sure. (*She goes to get the money.*) You know, I don't know what came over me tonight. I haven't ordered a pizza in years.
PIZZA LADY: Well, the moon must be in pizza tonight 'cause we sure got plenty of orders.
GRACE: (*Nervous smile.*) Maybe that's it. I thought maybe it's because I'm a little nervous. I'm one of those people who eat when they're nervous. I also eat when I'm not nervous. I eat when I'm depressed. I eat when I'm happy . . .

PIZZA LADY: Can't complain. Keeps us in business.

GRACE: It's awful cold tonight. Are you sure that jacket's warm enough?

PIZZA LADY: I got a truck full of pizzas to keep me warm.

GRACE: (*Finds her money and hands it to the pizza lady.*) Keep the change.

PIZZA LADY: (*Already out the door and offstage.*) Thanks. Good night.

GRACE: (*As she carries the pizza to the coffee table she is giving herself a lecture to calm herself.*) Nothing to be nervous about. I'm a grown-up person of indeterminate youth. My rent is paid. I have no cavities. My mother is coming to stay with me, but I can handle that.

GRACE *puts the pizza box down on the coffee table and arranges the few things beside it in an elaborate gesture of meticulousness and composure. She then goes to the bookcase and activates the tape player and we hear the strains of Erik Satie's "Trois Gymnopédies." She then sits down, composes herself, and opens the pizza box. As she opens the box the telephone in the pizzeria starts ringing and the chorus (composed of* LENA, BONSEY *and* SADIE) *is singing "Sh Boom." During the opening bars of the song the lights have also come up on the pizza set.* BONSEY *is animatedly playing the pinball machine.* LENA *and* SADIE *are seated at the table playing with a larger-than-life deck of cards.*

CHORUS: Life could be a dream. Life could be a dream.
        Life could be a dream
           Sh Boom. Sh Boom.
        If I could take you up to paradise up above.
           Sh Boom. Sh Boom.

LENA: (*Calling to* GRACE *over the sounds of the song and the telephone.*) Gracie. Gracie.

GRACE: (*She has gone first to the doorway then to the tape cassette to discover where the music is coming from. She responds to the call inadvertently in the annoyed voice of a twelve-year-old.*) Whaddaya want, ma?

LENA: Gracie, answer the telephone.

CHORUS: (*Continuing.*) And tell you darling you're the only one that I love. Life . . .

GRACE *finally suspects the music is coming from the pizza box and slams it shut, freezing the action in the pizzeria. As she opens it again the sounds and actions continue.*

CHORUS: . . . Could be a dream, sweetheart. Hello, hello again. Sh Boom and hoping we'll meet again.

LENA: Where is she? (*The phone keeps ringing.* LENA *goes to the counter to answer it and the song fades out during her conversation.*) Lena's Pizzeria. Yeah we got some pies left but we can't deliver anywhere tonight. We close in half an hour if you want to come down and pick up your pie. Yeah, that's right. Dominick is here, but the car got stolen. No, we didn't call the police yet. No, my son can't drop the pie off. He's the one that stole the car. (*Hopeful.*) You think so? When does the drive-in get out? (*Whining voice.*) Oh. I don' know. That car is such a junk it wouldn't make it to Hackensack. I'm afraid the engine'll blow up or somethin'. Yeah? Well why don't you call your sister and have your nephew Raymond call me as soon as he gets home. And if you want any more deliveries tell my husband to buy his son a car. All right. Yeah. Good night. (*Calling out the front door.*) Gracie!

GRACE *responds to this last call and enters the scene as a twelve-year-old.*

SADIE: (*Using all her willpower not to peek at* LENA's *hand.*) Lena, come on. Finish this hand.

LENA: (*To* GRACE.) Where were you?

GRACE: Down by the dye house.

LENA: Down by the *river*? I *told* you not to play by the river!

GRACE: Aw, ma, nobody could drown in the river, there's too much junk in it.

LENA: Look at your clothes. They got all holes. What happened to your clothes?

GRACE: I dunno. We were just playin' with this box a rags. And then we saw our clothes were gettin' all funny. Kind of eaten up.

SADIE: She looks like a swiss cheese.

LENA: It's the *chemicals*! Go wash your hands!

GRACE: I already washed my hands. Doreen took us to her father's store and let us wash. Then she gave us ice cream and let us look at the comic books.

LENA: Why do you play with that girl Doreen?

GRACE: Is Richie back yet?

LENA: No, and I'm worried sick.

GRACE: I brought you a Chunky.

SADIE: Look, Lena. You gonna finish this hand or not? I gotta go before Sam gets home.

LENA: What are you afraid somebody's gonna steal all your money? Don't go yet. Dominick will walk you home. (*To* GRACE.) Where's your father? (*To* SADIE.) Stay and have some pie. (*Phone rings. She runs to answer it.*) Yeah, this is Lena. We only make one size. A dollar ten. We got a

half-and-half pie with anchovies and a combination with peppers and
sausage, or peppers and mushrooms or mushrooms and pepperoni . . .
or you can get a garlic pie with just tomatoes and garlic or a zombie with
everything on it, that's two and a quarter. (*Pause.*) Yeah, well I'm sorry.
We're closin' for the night. We only got two pies left and we're gonna eat
them. Call back tomorrow.

Towards the end of the phone conversation, GRACE, *who has gone over to
the pinball machine, gets into a fight with* BONSEY *which overlaps the last
part of* LENA's *conversation.*

BONSEY: Get your elbow off the machine.

GRACE: I didn't do anything.

BONSEY: I was hittin' sixty-five thousand on the fourth ball. That coulda
been the week's top . . .

GRACE: Not a chance. Deeker got the week's top. Ninety-five thousand.

BONSEY: Who aksed you, pimple brain?

GRACE: Except for Richie. He got ninety-eight thousand but that don't
count 'cause he lives here.

BONSEY: You busted my streak.

GRACE: I didn't do nothin'.

BONSEY: Tell your mother to give me another dime.

GRACE: I'll tell her you won last week 'cause you put a matchbook under one
a the legs.

BONSEY: Shut your mouth, half pint.

GRACE: Who you callin' a half pint? Ya half wit.

LENA: Shaddup, both a you. Bonsey, you go home now.

BONSEY: Come on, Lena. I was on a streak till a certain adolescent messed it
up.

GRACE: You're crazy.

LENA: (*Shouting and shutting them both up.*) *No more games tonight!*

GRACE: (*To* BONSEY, *sheepish and conspiratorially.*) She's in a bad mood
'cause Richie's missin'.

LENA: Aaaaaa . . . (*She bites her hand in a rage.*)

BONSEY: Awright. I'm sorry, Lena. I'm goin'. I'm goin'.

LENA: (*To* GRACE.) What do you fight with that moron for?

GRACE: (*Quiet and angry, wronged.*) I wasn't doin' anything.

LENA: (*Going over to* SADIE.) There's men fightin' and dyin' in stupid wars
all over the world and these kids are gonna wind up just like them and
there's never gonna be any peace unless people learn how to talk to each
other.

SADIE: These kids today are no good.

LENA: I got no more patience. I see them fight and I want to break their heads. (*Phone rings.*) Dominick. Is he still upstairs? (*Phone keeps ringing.*) Gracie, you better get that.

GRACE: (*Answers the phone, singing to the tune of "Bella Ciao."*)

It comes with sausage and pepperoni,
and extra cheese if you please,
on your pizza pie.
It's hot and tasty
That's why we're crazy
About our pizza pies.

(*Lena turns to look at her.*)

Oh yes we're crazy.
Our future's hazy.
But there's one thing for sure
That our sauce is pure.
My mother made it.
Sometimes I hate it.
And I'd like to run away.*

She hangs up the phone ready to run as LENA *gets up and goes towards her.*

LENA: What did ya do that for?

SADIE: Look, Lena, I gotta go.

LENA: Don't go yet. Dominick will walk you home. (*To* GRACE.) Where's your father? (*To* SADIE.) Stay and have some pie. Gracie, put a pie in the oven with a lot a garlic like Sadie likes.

SADIE: No, I shouldn't stay. I dunno if I want any pizza.

LENA: Come on. You want a little glass a wine.

SADIE: No . . . Well, maybe just a little glass.

LENA: And a slice of pizza.

SADIE: Well, maybe just a little slice.

LENA: With a lot of garlic.

SADIE: And some anchovies, maybe?

LENA: (*Calling into the kitchen.*) Put some anchovies on the pie, Gracie.

SADIE: And some peppers?

LENA: And some peppers.

*© 1980 by Marga Gomez.

SADIE: (*Calling into the kitchen.*) And don't cook it too crispy 'cause I can't eat it so good.

LENA: (*Returning to the table with a glass of wine.*) You know, Sadie, as much as you eat, that's too much work for one tooth. Why don't you take some of that money from under your mattress and buy yourself a set of teeth. (*Phone rings.* GRACIE *appears from the kitchen and answers it.*)

GRACE: City Morgue.

LENA: (*Frantic, thinking it's the city morgue calling about her son.*) What?

GRACE: You kill 'em, we chill 'em.

LENA: (*Shouting at her daughter for fooling her.*) Shut up!

GRACE: Actually this is Lena's Pizzeria. Home of the world famous Zombie Pizza. Oh, hi, Raymond. Yeah, she's here. Ma, it's Ray Donato.

LENA: (*Grabbing the phone.*) Raymond, were you out with Richie tonight? (*Pause.*) Was Gabe with you? . . . What about Gene Cherini? . . . When was the dance over? And you didn't see any of them? . . . You wouldn't lie to me would you, Raymond? (*Curtly.*) Yeah. All right, never mind. Yeah, goodbye.

GRACE: You think we should call up Missing Persons and they could send out a search party?

LENA: *Be quiet!*

SADIE: (*Now she's getting mad.*) This game's no good anymore. You don't want to come and play 'cause I'm winnin'.

LENA: You probably got all my cards memorized by now. Why don't you finish the game yourself?

SADIE: You can't talk to me like that. What are you mad at me for? You think you can buy me off with a piece a pizza.

LENA: (*Coming back to the table, nervous and distracted. Whining.*) I don't wanna finish the game. I can't concentrate. Maybe Gracie wants a finish or we could play three-handed scope.

GRACE: I don't feel like it.

LENA: (*Nervous, as if stalling for time.*) Why doncha tell us your story, then?

SADIE: What story?

LENA: What story? Your one story. The one about the devil. (GRACE *ad-libs a grimacing remark and attempts to go back to her chair but her mother pulls her over.*)

SADIE: Oh . . . in that case, lemme see. Are you sure that pizza's not gettin' too crispy?

GRACE: I just put it in.

SADIE: Jeez. The time I saw the devil. Can you imagine? It was after my first son was born and my mother was still alive, God bless her. My mother was a saint. I still get masses said for her. How she suffered, poor woman. She never liked Sam, you know. He's the one person she called an *imbecile*. (*With an Italian accent*.) She never said that about anybody. She was such a good woman.

LENA: (*Prompting her*.) Go ahead. Tell us the part about the devil.

SADIE: I'll get to that part. Where was I?

GRACE: Your mother was callin' Sam an imbecile. (*English pronunciation*.)

LENA: It was after your first son was born.

SADIE: Ohhh. An' I got so sick. And in them days they didn't have any medicines like they do now. An' I swelled up like a gourd and I couldn't get outta bed. An' I couldn't eat to save my life. Er, are you sure that pie won't burn?

GRACE: I put it on the top shelf and turned the oven off.

SADIE: An' there was snow outside higher than the doorway. And the wind was bangin' at the windows.

GRACE: (*Incredulous*.) I never heard the part about the snow before.

LENA: Shhh.

SADIE: An' I had such a fever I got so I couldn't see nothin' even with my eyes open. An' I closed my eyes for a minute and I opened 'em an' that's when I saw him.

GRACE: The devil.

SADIE: Standin' at the foot a the bed no farther away than you are now.

GRACE: What did he look like?

SADIE: He looked like a man who was too handsome to be any good. An' he was wearin' a red suit and his hairy arms were reachin' out to me.

GRACE: How could you tell his arms were hairy if he had a suit on? Did he have a pitchfork?

SADIE:No, I don't remember seein' no pitchfork.

GRACE: What did he do?

SADIE: He told me to come with him. He said "Veni qua," and pointed his hand at me. I said, "No," and he got mad an' he said it again. "Veni qua," an' he looked right at me with his black eyes like a couple a coals an' I tried to reach my throat for my crucifix but my arms wouldn't move . . . An' then he opened his cape an' he was naked as a red devil.

GRACE: I thought he had a suit on.

LENA: Shhh.

SADIE: An' I said, "Go away, devil." An' I closed my eyes and started to pray but I felt myself gettin' pulled by my feet to the foot a the bed an I musta wet my pants 'cause I felt wet—down there, y'know—an' I heard a sound like spit on a hot stove. And I made the sign a the cross inside my mouth with my burning tongue an when I opened my eyes I looked right at that devil an' said "*No*." The bed shook but he started movin' away an' the last thing he said to me was, "Tu sei più forte di me . . . you're stronger than me."

GRACE: I never knew the devil spoke Italian.

SADIE: Sure, what do you think?

GRACE: Did the sheets get burned?

SADIE: Black as coal, an' they never did come clean, either.

LENA: Get the pie outta the oven Gracie.

> GRACE *goes to get the pie while* PERLA *enters to the sound of a low wolf whistle from outside. She's in spiked heels and flamboyant clothes.*

SADIE: Speak of the devil.

PERLA: Aren't they a little young to be hangin' around at this hour?

LENA: (*Goes to the door and calls out.*) Bonsey, go home before I call your mother.

PERLA: Are you still open?

LENA: We're closin' up but come in. We were just goin' to have a pie.

PERLA: I thought I'd see if I could get a pizza to take upstairs and maybe rest a minute.

LENA: (*Motioning her to sit down.*) You want a soda? (*Calling back to the kitchen.*) Gracie, bring a couple a sodas, too. (*To* SADIE.) This is the new neighbor from upstairs.

> *At this moment* GRACE *enters with the things from the kitchen and as the action slows down or freezes for a second she acknowledges this new memory, quietly, with a half laugh, as she reminisces.*

GRACE: You too, huh, Perla?

LENA: (*To* PERLA.) What's your stage name again?

PERLA: Perla the Exotic.

LENA: This is Sadie Petrillo from across the street.

PERLA: Pleased to meet you.

SADIE: (*Very close-mouthed and disapproving of* PERLA.) Hello.

LENA: Perla's a dancer. She toured in South America and everything. (SADIE *lets out a whimpering harrumph. To* GRACE.) Did you put the cheese away? (GRACE *nods.*) We gotta put the sauce away too. An' take out the garbage. Where's your father?

GRACE: Last time I saw him he was upstairs calling in the numbers.

LENA: (*Giving* GRACE *a high sign with her face behind* PERLA's *back to be quiet.*) Sta zit. (*Which means "be quiet" in Italian. Then to* PERLA *to make sure that she didn't understand.*) Er . . . you don't speak Italian, do you?

PERLA: No. But a lot of people think I look Italian. Do you think so?

LENA: Oh yeah, yeah, you could be. But you're not, huh?

PERLA: No. My father was Spanish, Castilian. My mother is Puerto Rican. (SADIE *lets out another disapproving whimper.*)

LENA: (*Brusquely, to* SADIE.) Well, what are you doin' just sittin' there. Eat your pie.

GRACE: Eugene next door is Spanish.

PERLA: Oh.

GRACE: He never goes out anymore since the time he tried to drown himself in the river. But he had on t his bulky jacket that made him float until they fished him out, right, ma?

LENA: (*Reminded to be anxious again.*) Don't talk about the river. Look what time it is and your brother's not home yet. Go get your father. (GRACE *leaves to go upstairs. To* PERLA.) Have a piece of pie. Go ahead.

PERLA: Well I was thinking of ordering one.

LENA: Have some of this. It's for us. It's got peppers and garlic. You like garlic?

PERLA: Yeah, sure. Have you got any forks?

LENA: Forks? Eh, sure, if you like. I'll get you one.

PERLA: No. Don't get up. I'll get it. Where are they?

LENA: There are some on the counter back there. (PERLA *gets up and sashays back to the counter.* SADIE *leans over to look at her ass.*)

SADIE: Guarda che culo. (*Loosely translated, "Look at that ass."*) Pizza with a fork like a real American. (*Said with an Italian inflection.*)

LENA: (*To* SADIE *curtly.*) So, what's the matter with your pizza? Is it too crispy, or what?

SADIE: (*Tartly.*) Yeah.

LENA: Then dip it in your wine. Or eat the middle part. It's soft in the middle like the brain of an old woman. (PERLA *returns with a fork and sits down.* GRACE *returns.*)

GRACE: Daddy fell asleep listenin' to the baseball scores. Not only that, but Richie is takin' a shower and the car is parked across the street.

LENA: (*Incredulous.*) No! (GRACE *nods.* LENA *goes to look out the door for the car.*) He musta sneaked upstairs. (*Angry whine.*) Oh, I could kill him. He had me so worried.

SADIE: (*She is starting to grill* PERLA *before* LENA *swoops in.*) Do you let your mother see you dressed like that?

PERLA: My mother knows I'm in show business.

SADIE: You Catholic?

LENA: (*Bustling.*) You finished with your wine, Sadie? You finished with your pizza?

SADIE: (*Still to* PERLA.) You married?

LENA: (*Hustling* SADIE *out.*) Here, I'll wrap up a piece for you to take home with you. Gracie, bring some wax paper for Sadie.

SADIE: (*Putting her sweater on.*) You told me Dominick would walk me home.

LENA: Yeah, well I don' wanna wake him up now or he'll get started with Richie and wake up the whole neighborhood. (*She looks out the door*.) Hey you, Sheik? What are you still waitin' around for? You walk Sadie home and I'll give you some free games on the pinball machine tomorrow.

SADIE: Lena, you wanna gimme another little piece a pie for my breakfast tomorrow?

LENA: (*She rushes to wrap up another piece of pie from the tray*.) Sure. You want one or you want two?

SADIE: Naw, one's enough . . . er, well, all right. Two. Maybe one with anchovies.

LENA: Yeah, I got it. (*She brings the pizza to* SADIE, *who is still hanging back at the door*.)

SADIE: You sure it's all right to go home with this kid?

LENA: What are you talkin' about? I know these boys like I know my own son. (*Thinking of her son immediately inspires her whining anger again*.) Oh that lousy punk! Wait'll I get my hands on him.

SADIE: All right, I'm goin'. I'll see ya tomorrow. (*She goes out*.)

LENA: Good night, Sadie. (*Calls after her*.) Don't forget to dip it in your milk if it's too crispy.

SADIE: (*Off*.) Go on.

LENA: (*To* PERLA.) You want to hear some music? Put the juke box on, Gracie, and lock the door. (*She comes to sit down*.)

PERLA: You look as tired as I feel.

LENA: Yeah, I'm always tired lately. Anyway, I think I was born tired. My mother used to call me sheep-eyes because I always had such dreamy eyes. An' my husband still jokes about when he used to come and take me out and he'd hear her yell, "He's comin'. Go wake her up."

PERLA: You do have beautiful eyes.

LENA: Oh, you should have seen them when I was a girl and I'd put on makeup, you know. And with my dark hair, it was long then. Once at the World's Fair in New York they gave me a card to take a screen test.

PERLA: No kidding? Well, I can believe it. What did you do?

LENA: I didn't do anything. I was stupid. Backwards. You know. I never called up.

PERLA: Have you still got the card?

LENA: What for?

PERLA: You could still call up. It's never too late.

LENA: (*Titillated, opening up in a big smile*.) Go on.

PERLA: You got to follow all those leads. You never know what somebody can do for you 'til you find out. I've been in a few movies myself, kind of like an extra.

GRACE: You know how to cha-cha?

PERLA: Yes, but that's not the kind of dancing I do in the shows. I do this special act with fancy costumes. Feathers and sequins. They cost plenty, let me tell you. And I sing, too. Would you like to be in show business when you grow up?

LENA: Gracie, do your Jimmy Durante impersonation for Perla.

GRACE: Maaa, I haven't done that since I was little.

LENA: Then do the Sid Caesar, or the Bette Davis. "Peter darling." Go ahead. She does it so good. (GRACE *shakes her head no.*) Come on, Gracie. Do it for Perla. She does stuff like that all the time in front of the mirror on the cigarette machine. Come on, Gracie. You do it so good.

GRACE: (*To* PERLA.) I wrote a poem, if you want to hear it.

PERLA: Why sure.

GRACE: Life is a two-pronged fork
     With space in between
     Life is a cold butter knife,
          rather dull
     Life is a napkin ring
     An eternal type thing.

PERLA: (*To* LENA.) She's very bright, huh?

LENA: Yeah, she got skipped once, already. And she draws, too. (*To* GRACE.) Go get the sketch you did of Pinochle with his big mustache. And the comics. (GRACE *goes off.*) My people are all intelligent. Two of my sisters finished high school and they're both teachers. My mother always used to say, "I'd rather be bad than stupid. If you're bad, you can always move to another town. But if you're stupid, people know it as soon as you open your mouth." (GRACE *comes back with various pizza boxes.*)

GRACE: (*Showing* PERLA.) There's comics in this one and this one. This is the little match girl and this one's a story about Niccolina; she's a wicked girl scout who's mean to everybody all the time and she gets hit by a car. See, these are her legs under the car. I've been practicing how to draw cars. This one's an Impala. This is old stuff, the animals in the movie house and the talking peppers. And this is a paper doll I made and these are all her clothes. They don't fit so good now 'cause I got mad one time and ripped her in half and now she's got all this Scotch tape around the waist and she can't really wear two-piece outfits anymore.

PERLA: You're really good. I should have you design some of my costumes sometime.

GRACE: No. I don't know. I don't design clothes anymore really. I'm getting ready to throw all this stuff out.

PERLA: Are you sure? I'm working on this new act and I've got to come up with something really special, you know. (*She is pulling them in to her with her energy.*) It's got to be a costume that when you come out on stage in the nightclub you can hear their eyeballs fall in their glasses. Now it's a challenge to design a good costume when all the clubs really want to show is your body, let's face it. But I got this idea for a number and the costume is going to be important.

LENA: Well, what do you need? Maybe I could think about it too?

GRACE: Yeah, she's good at that stuff.

PERLA: Well, you know Sonja Henie the ice skater, right?

GRACE: I *love* her movies.

LENA: She's got a fat face though, doncha think?

PERLA: Well, it's going to be like a Sonja Henie number, except without the ice.

GRACE: (*Excited.*) Oh, I do that all the time. (*She jumps up and "ice skates" around.*)

LENA: Yeah, that's how I get her to polish the floors when we wax 'em.

PERLA: Then you got the idea perfectly. I want to come out as an ice queen. I want to look so cold that they will have to put on their fur capes and order hot toddies. And then the number will be so *hot* that the costume will start to melt and by the end of the song they will be fanning themselves and ordering rum coolers.

GRACE: What's a rum cooler?

PERLA: You don't need to know that.

LENA: (*Thinking.*) So you want something like a big ice cube maybe.

GRACE: What's the song going to be like?

PERLA: Here, I'll show you. (*She takes* GRACE's *hand and takes her to the middle of the pizzeria. Then she goes to get* LENA *by the hand.*) You too, Lena. Play these. (*She takes maracas out of her bag.*) And when I tell you, you sing the chorus, it goes "Turn up the heat." You got that?

LENA: (*Sheepishly.*) Oh, I don't know.

PERLA: Come on, you can do it. (*She poses, readying herself for the song. She skates forward.* LENA *and* GRACE *join in and eventually get carried away by the end of the number.*)

> My story is sad.
> But I don't feel so bad.
> Romance was a thrill.
> Now it gives me a chill.
> I'll be icy 'til I meet
> Somebody who can turn up the heat.
>
> CHORUS
> Turn up the heat.
> Don't let me shiver.

Turn up the heat.
When I can quiver,
Turn up the heat
And raise my temperature.

You better get lost
Or you'll turn into frost
Unless you are sold
On a passion that's cold.
I'll be icy 'til I meet
Somebody who can turn up the heat.

CHORUS . . .*

LENA: Come on, Gracie. Why don't you do one of your impersonations now. Do the Jimmy Durante.

PERLA: Yeah, come on. I'd like to see it. (PERLA *and* LENA *seat themselves and* GRACE *fusses a little and then goes into her act.*)

GRACE: (*As Jimmy Durante.*) I was takin' a bath when the telephone rings . . . And I gets up and I goes to the phone . . .

LENA: I get such a kick out of this one. She looks sort of like him, don't she? She does those funny parts so good.

GRACE *hears what she says and stops, distraught. Then she runs off, back to her chair in the present. The light darkens on the pizza set and* PERLA *walks off.* GRACE *is left breathing hard, remembering this incident.*

GRACE: Don't think I'm ever gonna forget that, ma.

PERLA: (*Notices* GRACE *has run away.*) Gracie, Gracie, come back.

GRACE *finally gets up and walks back into the scene. She talks in her adult voice.*

LENA: Why did you run away like that? Why did you get so mad?

GRACE: Because you said I was ugly.

LENA: I never said you were ugly. What are you talkin' about?

GRACE: It's when I was doin' Jimmy Durante and you told Perla I looked like him.

LENA: No I didn't. I just meant you did it so good.

GRACE: I am ugly.

*"Turn Up the Heat" © 1980 by Marga Gomez.

LENA: You're not ugly. Don't talk like that. You got nice features.

GRACE: Perla's beautiful and you were beautiful and I'm ugly.

LENA: Who says I was beautiful?

GRACE: You say it all the time. Daddy says it.

LENA: (*Sheepishly.*) I wasn't so beautiful. I just wore a lot of mascara. You shouldn't think so much about beauty. Do you think beauty is everything? I got news for you: a lot of beautiful people are unhappy.

GRACE: Yeah, well as long as I'm gonna be unhappy, I'd rather be beautiful and unhappy.

LENA: You got brains. That's more important. And you got a good personality.

GRACE: That's what you always say about people who are ugly. You hate me because I'm not beautiful like you.

LENA: (*Crying.*) Don't talk like that. That's not true.

GRACE: And I hate you. I didn't ask to be born. I'm gonna die and you'll be sorry.

LENA: Don't say that. Never say that.

GRACE: Die, die, die, die. I wish you'd drop dead. (*There's a gasp between them.* GRACE *reverts to her twelve-year-old voice.*) I didn't mean it, mommy.

LENA: I never wanted to hurt you.

GRACE: I'm sorry, ma. I didn't mean it, honest. (*She goes over to* LENA.)

LENA: I'm sorry, Gracie. I didn't mean nothin'. I just meant you did it so good. I love you so much. You gotta believe me. I love you more than anything in the world.

GRACE: I know, ma.

LENA: Put the lights out, Gracie, and put the juke box on. (GRACE *goes to put the lights out.*) Come and sit by me. I like to sit here sometimes with just the light from the juke box on and the sign light from outside. It's cozy. (*Opening strains of "In the Still of the Night" can be heard faintly.*)

GRACE: Richie wants me to massage his arm. He's gotta pitch tomorrow.

LENA: Keep me company a minute. (GRACE *goes over to her.*) Gracie, let's have a Halloween party here. We can turn the lights out like this and have a stuffed dummy over in the corner. We'll make it scary. I kind of like that. To scare people, you know. Even when you and Richie were in the baby carriage I used to make those big scary eyes at you. You think that's normal?

GRACE: Probably not.

LENA: Is the oven off, Gracie? (GRACE *nods.*) We better go upstairs or I'll never get you up for school in the morning.

GRACE: (*Going into a subtle performance.*) Oh yeah, that reminds me, ma.

You know I had this funny dream that I was hit by a truck right down by the playground on the way to school.

LENA: (*Scared; the anxious voice again.*) What are you saying? You're kiddin' me.

GRACE: No, I just remembered. I think it was a Wonder Bread truck.

LENA: Don't go to school tomorrow! I'll write you a note.

GRACE: I really ought to go. I got that editorial due for the paper.

LENA: You can take it in on Monday.

GRACE: Well, if you say so. I think I feel a little sick anyway. You think I got a fever? Feel my face. (LENA *feels* GRACE'*s face with her face.*)

LENA: I don't know. You feel a little warm. But you were back by the oven.

GRACE: Maybe you can make me some tea and toast tomorrow and some Lipton soup and I'll take my blankets and go lie on the couch in the living room . . . and you can help me write my editorial.

LENA: I thought you said you wrote it.

GRACE: It's almost done. I got the idea . . . And we can watch the afternoon movie on Channel 5. It's a Fred Astaire movie.

LENA: I don't like Fred Astaire. He's got no sex appeal.

GRACE: Then we can play cards, and I'll draw your picture. Or we can play Modern Art.

LENA: What's that one?

GRACE: Tessa and me invented it. I'll show you. (GRACE *wraps herself around* LENA *in a bizarre pose, then shouts.*) Modern art!

LENA: (*Laughs, but acts annoyed and tough.*) You're chokin' me. (*They poke at each other playfully.*)

GRACE: Gimme a kiss. Oh, let's play the kissing game and see if I can catch you. (LENA *shakes her head slowly from side to side and* GRACE *moves her head until she zooms in and plants a kiss: This is a game that they are obviously familiar with.*) You're gettin' too slow. See if you can get me.

She starts shaking her head while LENA tries to plant a kiss. When they start the kissing game the sound of "In the Still of the Night" drifts in while the lights fade and LENA backs out of the scene. As the song fades out GRACE slams down the pizza box and dials the phone again.

GRACE: Hello, is this Suicide Prevention? This is Grace Innocenti. I used to work there, answering the telephones? Oh, you're new. Well I've got this pizza over here that I can't eat and I thought maybe I could bring it over to you. No, it wouldn't be any trouble . . . You did, huh . . . Oh, yeah, that's all right. I could always freeze it or something . . . No, this isn't the kind of mood I feel like sharing with a friend right now . . . Oh no, I've just been reading too many psychology books. You read them and you start thinking about how messed up your parents were and then you start thinking about how messed up you are and how messed up the world is and you get to feeling how you just want to crawl into somebody's armpit and feel safe, you know. And then you start thinking about all the people you've ever loved and wonder where they all are and you wonder who's going to care if you die and then you get mad and think about dying just to spite everybody that doesn't care, and you start thinking about how nobody needs you. But as soon as you find out somebody needs you you start worrying about your freedom. You know what I mean? . . . (*Repeating what the other person has said.*) You hear what I'm saying, huh? (*Sharply.*) Of course you hear what I'm saying, your phone's working, isn't it? Anyway, I just thought you might like some pizza. I better let you get back to your phones. Good night.

During the last two lines the doorbell rings and it's the PIZZA LADY *with another pizza.*

PIZZA LADY: Here's the pizza you ordered.
GRACE: (*Slightly bewildered.*) Thanks. (*She goes for her money again and brings it back to the* PIZZA LADY.)
PIZZA LADY: You know, it's a good thing you don't like pizza or we're liable to run out tonight.
GRACE: (*Smiles weakly.*) Yeah. Look, I'm sorry to make you come all this way again.
PIZZA LADY: It's all in the line of duty. (GRACE *pays her.*) Thanks. (*She exits.*)
GRACE: (*Calling after her.*) Be sure to lock your car door. (*Then, coming back into the room, she talks to the pizza box in a whining tone.*) What did I say that for? (*As she carries the pizza box over to the table she talks to herself in the voice of an Indian guru.*) Nostalgia is a dangerous thing. Too much mooning over the past, like too much mooning over the future, may not leave enough time for living in the present. (*She sets the pizza box down delicately and then speaks in a normal but dreamy voice to herself as she goes to open the second pizza box.*) One must, however, acknowledge certain modes of receptivity where the slightest provocation . . . a melody, a scent, the look of your own aging hand, a wad of tissue in your pocket . . . brings on the deluge.

The lights come on in the pizza set while LENA *summons* GRACE. *This is a quick and delicate change.*

LENA: (*Quietly.*) Gracie.
GRACE: (*From her apartment.*) What, ma?

LENA: Something's wrong with me, Gracie. I can't remember how to make the dough. (*A bowl is on the pizzeria table in front of her as if she were standing over the dough.*) I don't remember what to do. My mind is trying to tell me but it doesn't work. (*There is crying in her voice.*)

GRACE: (*Slowly enters the scene as a fifteen-year-old.*) Don't cry, ma. Maybe you're just nervous or something.

LENA: No, it's not that. That's what Dr. Pellicone says. He thinks I'm just nervous, but it's more than that. Something's happening to me, Gracie. I don't know what it is.

GRACE: Well, maybe we ought to take you to another doctor.

LENA: You think maybe I had a stroke? Is this what happens when you have a stroke?

GRACE: I don't know, ma.

LENA: They think I just complain. Nobody understands. Nobody believes me. Your father doesn't believe me. Take me to the hospital, Gracie. Something's wrong with me.

GRACE: I took you to the hospital last week. They said they couldn't take you, that you had to go through a doctor. They can't tell what's wrong.

LENA: Take me to the state hospital, Gracie. I think I'm losing my mind, Gracie.

GRACE: (*Nervous, trying to cope.*) Come on, ma, you just forgot how to make the dough. It can't be that hard. I'll help you. You showed me before.

LENA: I got this terrible feeling I can't explain. I don't understand. I'm scared.

GRACE: Don't be scared, ma.

LENA: Take me to the state hospital, Gracie. We'll get Katy's son from across the street to drive us. I've got five dollars in the underwear drawer.

GRACE: Ma, I don't want to go to the hospital again. They're shitty. They ask you all these questions and then they say they can't do anything for you. Anyway, you can't be so bad if you remember you got five dollars in the underwear drawer, right?

LENA: No, something's wrong, Gracie. You gotta believe me.

GRACE: I believe you, ma.

LENA: Promise me you'll take me to the state hospital, Gracie. Make them do something for me.

GRACE: I promise, ma. We'll take you to a specialist.

LENA: I can't make the pizza anymore. I never feel good anymore. Who's going to make the dough?

GRACE: I'll help you, ma. (*As she says this she starts backing out of the scene towards her apartment.*)

LENA: I can't clean the house anymore. I get this lousy nervous stomach all the time, I can't do anything right anymore. (*The lights eventually fade to a blackout on* LENA *by the end of their exchange.*)

GRACE: Don't cry, ma.

LENA: Do something for me, Gracie.

The lights are up on GRACE *standing behind her chair. She is shaken, not wanting to cry, trying to look tough. She crosses her arms in front of her and looks down at the culprit pizza box.*

GRACE: For six lousy dollars you'd think they'd at least sell you a pizza that makes you forget. (*To the pizza box.*) People pay to forget. Who wants to remember anything anymore? Who wants to feel anything anymore? What do you think I'm a chump? (*She has sat down nervously and is giving sidelong glances to the pizza box as a real enemy. Petulant and trying to sound tough.*) A person could starve trying to get a bite to eat around here.

She goes through an elaborate strategy of trying to sneak a piece of pizza out of the box. As if stealing something, she has sneaked her hand into the pizza box and sneaked out a piece of pizza. As she raises it to her lips we hear the strains of the first lines of "Mama," a sappy Italian-American song that Connie Francis used to sing. A look of comic despair and defeat crosses over her face through this first bar of music and as she opens the box to replace the slice of pizza the second "Mama" swells out.

The lights come up on the pizza set, but the lighting is different to indicate a change in the place. The colored lights are dark on the outlined pinball machine and juke box, leaving just the bare construction show-ing. There is a large James Dean poster over the pinball machine, a cloth over the table, a colored spread over the counter to give the place a look of abandonment, of a closed resort, besides indicating that it is GRACE's *living space now. There is a typewriter on the table. Some books and cardboard packing boxes are scattered about.*

*   LENA *is standing, leaning on the table. She is stooped, aged; one arm is bent and her leg drags. She's wearing a soiled housecoat, slippers, and stockings drooping around her ankles. She has a handkerchief or a wad of paper towel in one hand that she twists nervously during the scene. It is obvious that she is sick and has deteriorated from the first scene. She has a certain bright-eyed, tic-like animation because of the medication she takes.*

LENA: Gracie, where are you? You in the bathroom? Don't squeeze your face. What are you doin'? Where are you?

GRACE: (*Entering the scene as a twenty-year-old.*) Ma, you know you're not supposed to come down the stairs by yourself.

LENA: You wanna come upstairs. Daddy bought some cold cuts.

GRACE: Not right now, I'm busy.

LENA: What are you doin'?

GRACE: I'm getting some of my things together.

LENA: "Animal Kingdom" is on.

GRACE: Yeah, so what?

LENA: Put it on and watch it with me.

GRACE: I don't want to watch "Animal Kingdom."

LENA: You know I like to watch it when the animals fight. You think that's normal?

GRACE: (*As if in disgust with the human race.*) Probably.

LENA: I like the way you got it fixed up here now, Gracie. Like Picasso.

GRACE: What do you know about Picasso?

LENA: I know. He's a painter, right. What do you think I'm stupid? (*She has been walking around, crotchety and childlike at the same time, looking at things like a visitor.*)

GRACE: All right, ma. I want you to sit down here, okay? So you don't fall down. I want to talk to you. (*She guides* LENA *to a chair.*) Did you take your medicine?

LENA: Yeah, but it don't make me feel so good anymore, this new medicine.

GRACE: Well, I was reading about it. It's all experimental, you know. They don't know that much about it. It's important that you don't take too much or you get these weird side effects.

LENA: I got to take the medicine, Gracie, or else I can't do nothin'.

GRACE: I know, I know.

LENA: Daddy got some rolls, too.

GRACE: All right, all right. I'll come up and eat later. I want to talk to you first.

LENA: Put the television on, Gracie.

GRACE: (*Getting a little angry.*) Not now, ma. In a little while. I want to have a talk with you, ma.

LENA: What's the matter? Somethin's the matter.

GRACE: Nothing's the matter, ma.

LENA: Gracie, you wanna make me a sandwich?

GRACE: That's one of the things I like about you, ma. Your dedication to the à la carte school of philosophy. "I eat therefore I am."

LENA: Yeah go on. What do you want to talk about?

GRACE: My friend Jay found me an apartment in New York.

LENA: What are you talkin' about?

GRACE: I found this great rent-controlled apartment and I'm gonna move to New York.

LENA: *You're crazy*. What do you want to move to New York for?

GRACE: Lots of reasons. I got my friends there . . . and, and there's lots of museums and lots of theatres and . . .

LENA: Lots of murders.

GRACE: Yeah, well I don't plan on getting murdered.

LENA: You're crazy, Gracie. All the relatives used to live in New York. We all left. Now you want to go back and live in New York. It's stupid, stupid.

GRACE: (*Petulant, angry.*) It's not stupid. Living in *this* dying, polluted city is stupid. Living in this dying neighborhood with its boarded-up, broken-down corner stores and its broken-down pizzeria is stupid.

A light comes in on SADIE *in a corner of the set. She's an apparition. Only* GRACE *sees her.*

SADIE: A girl ought to stay home and take care of her mother.

GRACE: You shut up. You're dead already.

SADIE: The devil's gonna get you.

GRACE: He should be so lucky.

LENA: (*Who hasn't acknowledged this interchange.*) Don't go, Gracie. Stay here. You don't have to pay any rent.

GRACE: Ma, I gotta live my own life. I need to . . . gather my rosebuds, sow my wild oats.

SADIE: What's she gonna do? Go live on a farm?

GRACE: I can't stay here living in a closed-up pizzeria, reading old magazines, writing letters to dead authors.

LENA: But you got it fixed up so nice.

GRACE: I want to *do* something with my life. (*Quieter, half-assured.*) I want to be a beatnik.

LENA: What do they do?

GRACE: (*Shrugging her shoulders.*) Nothin' . . . (*Brusque and defensive.*) I don't know. They write, they paint. They make love.

SADIE: She's gonna get in trouble and then she'll come back.

LENA: What do you want to move to New York for? It's so expensive. It's so much trouble.

GRACE: Give me a break, ma. Nobody sticks around here. Even Perla moved back to New York.

SADIE: At least she got married. She's respectable.

GRACE: (*To* SADIE.) She's bored.

LENA: There are no jobs. What are you gonna do? You can't find a job.

GRACE: I'll do something. Anything. You think I can't live on my own.

SADIE: She thinks she's better than everybody here in the neighborhood.

GRACE: (*To* SADIE.) Just different.

LENA: You can stay here. You don't have to pay any rent.

GRACE: Look, ma. Nobody said anything when Richie left us, right?

SADIE: That's different. He's a man.

LENA: He's got his own family.

GRACE: He got married and got his ass outta the ghetto and nobody made a fuss. He wasn't around when your brains started leakin' and we didn't know what was happening. It was me you used to talk to, right? Well my brain is leakin', ma. I've got to get out of here.

LENA: (*Whining voice.*) You won't come back. You just want to be with your friends. You'll never come back.

GRACE: Ma, it's only thirty minutes away. I can come back a lot. Or you can come and see me.

LENA: (*Still whining.*) Oh, it's so much trouble. You got to take the bus and the train.

GRACE: (*Blowing up.*) Jeezus. Life is too much trouble, right? Let's face it. I'll go turn on the gas on the pizza oven right now and we can stick our heads in it. Is that what you want?

LENA: (*Angry, sullen.*) All right. Go on, go on, go on.

GRACE: I'll come and see you a lot. I'll take the bus. . . .

LENA: Yeah, sure, sure.

GRACE: Jeez, ma. You could be happy for me.

LENA: (*Still sullen and sarcastic.*) Sure, go ahead. I'm happy.

GRACE: You don't look happy. Why don't you try and get happy about it?

LENA: (*Curt and standoffish.*) I don't feel good. I feel lousy. I never feel happy. I feel lousy.

GRACE: (*Trying to get through to her mother, who is sitting there rigid and angry.*) If you just think about it and try to accept it . . .

LENA: (*Angry and sharp.*) I don't think about nothin'. I feel lousy, that's what I think about. I think about nothin'. I feel lousy. (*More quietly.*) I'm gonna die. (*She whines on the last line and rocks back and forth in a series of short moans.*)

GRACE: (*Blows up and swats her mother impetuously on the head.*) I'm gonna die. Everybody's gonna die!

LENA: Go on, hit me. Like your father. Like your brother. Everybody hits me. (*The juke box starts playing "Mama" again; GRACE goes over and kicks it. It stops and SADIE disappears, too.*)

GRACE: (*Trying to get through to her mother, holding her shoulders.*) Ma, you're not gonna die from the Parkinson's disease. Especially now that you're taking the medicine. You just got to help yourself.

LENA: Go on. You sound like your father.

GRACE: You're just afraid to die because you never lived enough, ma. I got to go out and live, ma. I gotta find out about things. Why didn't you tell

me anything, about anything? About girls. About boys. About getting
married or having babies. Or being normal.

LENA: I never knew much.

GRACE: I can't stay here like this, ma. Afraid to leave the pizzeria. Being
sickly all the time. Never leaving the family, like the girl next door. Like
the whole family next door.

LENA: (*Whining cry.*) I want you to go, Gracie. I know it's no good for you
here. I only care about you. I don't want you to be like me. I want you to
go and have a good time. I want you to be happy.

GRACE: I want *you* to be happy.

*GRACE and LENA repeat this phrase, each in her own inflection, simulta-
neously as GRACE backs away. Lights fade on LENA. We eventually hear
only GRACE's voice as she returns to her set.*

GRACE: I want you to be happy. I want you to be happy. I want you to be
happy. . . . Is everybody happy? That's what I want to know. Because it
seems I can't be happy unless everybody's happy. (*Looking over to pizza
set.*) I know you're not happy. But it's you who got sick. I didn't make you
sick. Why are you making me sick? You're making me sick, ma. I'm
supposed to have it together by now. I had to leave you. Can't you see
that? I couldn't hang around trying to keep you alive with every breath I
take. I still do it. I keep everybody alive with every breath I take. (*The
doorbell rings. She thinks it's another pizza delivery.*) Oh no. Cancel my
order. No more pizzas tonight.

*The bell still rings incessantly until GRACE gets up to answer it. As she
moves to the door LENA enters from the kitchen door in the pizzeria and
crosses over into GRACE's apartment. She's an apparition of a younger
LENA, more youthful and graceful than we have seen her in preceding
scenes. Her hairstyle may be different and she is dressed in heels and a
stylish, classic coat suggestive of a twenties' style. Her opening lines
startle GRACE, who's standing at the open doorway.*

LENA: Hello, Gracie.

GRACE: (*Stunned.*) Ma?

LENA: What a nice place you got. Real cozy. (*She turns to GRACE, who is
still dumbfounded at the doorway.*) Gracie. You should close your mouth
or you might catch a fly.

GRACE: (*Starts to look suspiciously at LENA while she closes the door.*) All
right, who are you?

LENA: I'm your mother.

GRACE: You are *not* my mother.

LENA: I surprised you, didn't I?

GRACE: This is crazy. Come on, who are you? What is this?

LENA: I'm telling you. I'm your mother, Lena. You were thinking about me and waiting for me, weren't you? Who, then?

GRACE: How come you're not drooling?

LENA: (*Indignantly*.) I don't feel like it.

GRACE: You're not moaning. You're supposed to moan. You're sick. You feel lousy. There should be food stains on your clothes. I don't know who you are, but you are *not* my mother. *What did you do with my mother?*

LENA: Look at me, Gracie. It's me. You want to see the mole on my neck? Remember how you used to want to bite it off?

GRACE: (*Grilling her suspiciously*.) Where were you born?

LENA: The Bronx.

GRACE: How many miscarriages did you have?

LENA: Two.

GRACE: Who won the World Series in 1955?

LENA: (*Sharply*.) How do I know? The Dodgers probably lost is my guess.

GRACE: Where do you keep your money?

LENA: Well I used to keep it in the underwear drawer but I got it all with me now. I thought maybe we could go shopping.

GRACE: (*Shouting, beside herself*.) What are you talking about? We haven't gone shopping in twenty years.

LENA: (*Calmly*.) That's why I thought it would be time for something new.

GRACE: (*Whining cry*.) Where's my mother?

LENA: Gracie. You shouldn't get so upset. I hate to see you agitated like this. What are you making a big deal about? You wanted me to be different all these years, didn't you? You're the one that always used to say anybody can be anything they want to be. If you don't peg people a certain way anything is possible. Right? Isn't that what you always say?

GRACE: Yeah . . . but *this isn't possible*. You're not like my mother.

LENA: How do you know what I'm like? Besides, I'm not all that different, I'm just more like I was before you knew me. Isn't that what you always wondered about? Who I used to be? Who I could have been? Well, here I am. And maybe tonight we could go dancing?

GRACE: *Dancing?*

LENA: Yeah, I love to dance. Before I knew you I used to like to go to Roseland Ballroom. You got someplace like that out here?

GRACE: But you're sick. You moan all the time.

LENA: Jeez, I wish you wouldn't be so morbid. I came all this way to see you and I went to all this trouble so you could see me looking good.

GRACE: (*Still stunned but wanting to accept it*.) It's a miracle.

LENA: (*Casually and skeptically*.) Maybe. Whatever you think.

GRACE: (*Dejected, skeptical*.) It's no miracle. (*Hitting on in*.) It's jet lag. That's what it is. It's some kind of cosmic jet lag . . . (*Getting anxious*.) You better go and lie down, ma. Don't you want to lie down? I'll fix up a bed for you. Don't you want to lie down and watch television?

LENA: No, I don't feel like it.

GRACE: Now look, ma, I'm gonna make your bed and I want you to lie in it.

LENA: What I might like to do is go out and take a walk, look at the sunset.

GRACE: By yourself?

LENA: And why not?

GRACE: But you never like to take walks or look at sunsets. You've never been alone in your whole life.

LENA: That's not true. Sure, I lived with my family until I got married, but when I was a girl I used to like to take long walks in Crotona Park, right near my house, especially in the winter when the snow made everything so clean and quiet. I used to wear this big brown overcoat that I loved and it was like I could look down from above and see myself standing there against the snow and think, "This isn't just the second-born daughter of the shoemaker, or the pretty one, or the lazy one, or the girl on the end of the line at the candy factory that got all the jokes a little late." I'd think, "There's a part of that girl that nobody knows. That nobody will ever know."

GRACE: (*Stunned and then grumbling*.) Yeah, well this neighborhood is kind of tough. Maybe you'd better not go out by yourself.

LENA: It don't look any worse than the Riverside. I can take care of myself.

GRACE: You might fall down or something. (LENA *is walking around the apartment and* GRACE *is following right behind her with her arms out as if waiting for her to fall down*.)

LENA: (*Turning to her daughter abruptly*.) I feel fine and I'm not gonna fall down.

GRACE: (*Whining voice exactly like her mother's in the first scenes*.) Nooo, I don't know what's going on but you're really old and sick and sooner or later you're going to fall down. (*Last lines are especially wimpy*.)

LENA: Stop it, Gracie. Stop it.

GRACE: (*Same whining voice*.) And I'm going to have to pick you up.

LENA: Yes. But why don't we worry about that when the time comes?

GRACE: (*Sits down*.) What's the matter with you? I'm worried. I'll call this friend of mine. She's a doctor. (*Picks up telephone*.)

LENA: (*Sarcastically, crossing to* GRACE.) Good, ask her if she wants to go for a walk. (*Still behind chair*.) And you should·come too, Gracie. You look a little pasty.

GRACE: (*Slams telephone down*.) What are you so anxious to go for a walk for? You just got here. I've been thinking about you all this time. I've been worried sick.

LENA: What for?

GRACE: Worrying about you. I don't know. I worry about you all the time.

LENA: Well what good does that do? You should worry about yourself. Or better yet, you shouldn't worry at all. And do me a favor, Gracie. Quit thinkin' I want your blood. Just because you're a bleeding heart don't make everybody else a vampire, you know.

GRACE: (*Looking at her mother mildly, quietly, incredulously*.) Who are you anyway?

LENA: Come on, let's not go through that again. Listen, Gracie. I smell pizza. Is that a pizza you got there? Maybe we could have a piece before we go for a walk, huh?

GRACE: You are my ma, aren't you?

LENA: That's what I been tellin' you. You got some with sausage?

They lean down towards the pizza box together.

BLACKOUT

POETRY

◆

Severina Magni

Severina Magni was born in the Tuscan town of Lucca in 1897, came to the United States in 1921, and apparently had a hard life as a worker in a flag and banner factory. Her only known book of verse was *Luci Lontane*, written in Italian. She died in Detroit on May 30, 1954.

In the June 1954 issue of *Il Compasso*, an Italian-language weekly of literature and art published by Rodolfo Pucelli, he made this comment on the passing of Severina Magni: "She was our gentlest and most spontaneous immigrant poet. Reading her verses in *Luci Lontane*, I was always moved to wonder how a poet of such fresh sentiment, so openly expressive in such few melodious lines, could live and work so assiduously among the flags, and all for a bit of money. Wouldn't her life have been less melancholy in Tuscany among the sweet countryside which renews mind and body? How did it ever happen that a woman so fragile, and born to sing, could find herself in a country like this, so adverse to poets?"

The only other known details of her life are that she was married to John Magni and contributed her poetry to several Italian-language periodicals, as for example, *Stella di Pittsburgh*. Nothing more is known of Severina Magni, but she is emblematic of many Italian women of sensibility who came to this country, lived hard lives, wanted to express themselves, and died all but unknown and unheard. Only one poem of Magni's—translated by Rodolfo Pucelli from Italian into English and reprinted in his *Anthology*

of Italian and Italo-American Poetry (Boston: Bruce Humphries, 1954)—
remains. It is in a different vein from the work of other Italian American
poets of earlier years who wrote in a vainglorious, superchauvinistic, and
self-congratulatory way and produced nothing lasting.

Poetry

When in my heart resounds the tone
Of poetry, so dear and sweet,
I'm like a beggar to whom someone
Offered a necklace in the street.

I'm like a sleeper in a garden
Who wakes up at the fall of white
Petals that whisper, dance, and wander
Lightly before they, tired, alight.

I'm like a prisoner full of grief
To whom one a love-letter hands.
The jail is no more dismal, if
With harmony my heart expands.

Pacé Nicolino

Born in Barre, Vermont, in 1917 of Italian immigrant parents, Pacé
(named for peace by her Socialist father) Nicolino has lived in that
region of the Italian granite workers all her life. Orphaned at an early age,
she went to night school for drawing lessons, put herself through college
teaching cake decorating, and has worked as a speech therapist with handicapped children. She is married and has four children. Pacé Nicolino has
been a member of the Poetry Society of Vermont for many years and is

represented in the society's anthology of poems, *Second Harvest*. She has also published poetry frequently in the review *Troubadour*, often accompanied by her artwork.

Goodbyes and Hellos

My consciousness quietly
unfolded in the super market
as if
by remote control.

Two gray heads
one, Silver Pearl No. 17
simultaneously turn,
handshakes that set
the pressure soaring,
aeronauting as if
I were handing out
my flaming heart;

That last night
of adolescent youth,
the moon ballooning,
dip-needling the clouds
spanning the cosmic display
of hidden destinies
flooded with expectancy.
We almost did—
but didn't—

Carriages filling
with beans and carrots,
honey and forbidden fruit
as we exchanged pleasantries—
the distance between
two parts of the brain
controlling them forever
on different planes
but still back-tracking
forty years.

What if we had?

Dandelions

Out of the rain-sopped ground
I dug
enough for a salad
while
the May-like sun scorched
and
the March-like wind chilled.
In proper time
I'll brew my wine.
From gold to gray
leftovers by the millions
I'll puff away
childhood fantasies
now grown
to old necessities
rounding out a circle.

Kathy Freeperson

Born Kathy Telesco, she chose a new surname that reflects her rebirth as a feminist. Freeperson is on the National Steering Committee of the Feminist Writers' Guild. She has published her work in *Chrysalis* and *Kalliope*, and from 1971 to 1981 she wrote for, acted in, and directed a women's theater troupe. Freeperson lives in Gainesville, Florida.

Italian Bread

Exorcise the little Italian
devil who makes fat and
mucus.
As grandma and ma
shove it towards me
in a paper wrapper still warm
from the local Italian
bread pushers.
The monster emerges from its
long envelope and rears its
ugly but beautiful crispness
and smell
warm and sweet like
blankets of childhood.
Dad rips off an end.
It heaves a visible sigh and
gives
with the sound of crisp
spilling little brown
bits of gold around the
wrapper like sand.
The white soft center yields
stretches like the soft
olive thighs of a plump
Italian.
I am trying to reduce.
This loaf has a (w)hole like a
mouth saying "oh"
like the tongue's response
when it hits slice
after slice
the hole continues
but in a little different size
dunked in gravies, juices

it gets sloppy drunk and
wavers before the
open mouth bent close to
receive it.
Soggy with the taste of whatever
else is served
and somehow against
what I know is right it
makes its way to my mouth
and the mellow ballet my
lips and teeth play
has nothing to do with
the sermon with the fishes.
These flour clouds
cannot reproduce unaided.
The last sound is the heel
of the bread that crunches like
soft glass
and that hand that pulls the rest
away before your nose
gets stuck in its shape.
My willpower disappeared like
rising dough after a poked finger.
The pillow fight is finished.

Elaine Romaine

Elaine Romaine (née Romagnano) was born in the Bronx, New York, and has lived in various communities of Westchester, currently in Hastings-on-Hudson. Her chapbook, *The Molly Bloom Poems,* was published in 1977 under the name Romaine Murphy, by which she was also known as one of the editors of *Gravida*, a poetry review. Elaine Romaine has published widely, has been part of the Poetry in the Schools program and a guest at Yaddo, and has finished a new collection, *Double*. Her muse, she says, is her son.

---

fan letter

---

ah marcello marcello I love you because you are Italian. No.
I love you because I am Italian and you wear it better
than me whose only green growing plant in the kitchen is a
clove of garlic suspended in water, hanging by toothpicks and
that is not wearing my Italian melancholy well if I can't laugh at
the irony and Yes I do love you and your weary mouth, your
sallow skin, your heavy-lidded visions that finally
make me laugh/love that garlic for now it can green my days,
and I can love that risible miserable symbol, that goddam
garlic. I love you marcello. you wear our Italian well. send
a glossy. I will hang it above my plant.

Song and Dance Lady

Next to her dance of snare drum and tap
What's stillness but a minor scale?
Now eighty, still the high stepper
jiving across her backyard, this is
her way to raise hell: on its haunches
ready with the kick of a spit-and-polish
hoofer who hears the drum, the music roll,
a harmony she's not forgotten.

To the last beat she's quick with
a rowdy buck-and-wing, brisk
on the stone path, circling her yard.

This is a game where time is her rule,
where she tests like an explorer
each stunt of the heart, refusing pause,
storming the dance that arrives
from the neat center of death.

---

you were always irish, god

You were always irish, god
in a church where I confessed
to being Italian.

But then St. Anthony
had a feast and lights ringed
the street as sausage and peppers
steamed in booths, gambling wheels spun
as the tenor held his stomach, pushing
a note higher. Behind a booth my brother
pitched pennies with a priest, rolling
deep fried bread sprinkled with sugar
in his mouth. The processions began.
My father and his brothers shoulder
the statue through the crowd, hymns
and feast bless the air.

And all the sights of you, god,
were wine-filled.
For these sins we took communion
the next morning, sleeping on each other
in the pews until the altar bell rang
and we filed up to the railing,
opening our mouths for your blood
and flesh. O god,
god, I confess nothing.

Grace DiSanto

Born in Derby, Connecticut, in 1924, Grace DiSanto was a journalist before moving to North Carolina in 1961. She is a graduate of Belmont Abbey College in Belmont, North Carolina, and lives in Morgantown, North Carolina, with her husband and three children. She has studied with James Dickey in his poetry workshop and has published over 160 of her poems in various publications. *The Eye Is Single,* her first collection, was judged the best collection of poetry published in North Carolina in 1982. She teaches poetry at Western Piedmont Community College and in the Poetry in the Schools program.

In Defense of Plath, Berryman, Sexton

I used to wonder
how they lost it,
how desperation
got so deep
they overdosed,
jumped the bridge
into fire and ice,
ribboned their brains,
unpetalled their hearts;
now as I salute pain,
the claw and pull
and snarl,
rabid clutch devouring,
understanding starts:

As soon as one does not
kill oneself, one must
keep silent about life.
First, they locked
their ears against screams
of survivors;
then they sewed up
their tongues to dumb
speech; next
they gouged out their eyes,
tucked them,
potato stubs, beneath
the soil to grow the
horror out of light;
last, at the stage
where their guts
spilled out each to each,
they began to choose how
and when: week, day, hour

Last Supper

In memory of my grandparents

In your chiesa-large kitchen,
at the oak table where
with praise for one another,
we celebrated,
Lord have mercy
Christmas, Easter,
we believed,
believed you would breathe on
with time, believed
you would not die.

As we knelt, gave your
ropeveined hands the kiss
of reverence, windowglass blushed
beneath the warm sun.

From the cup,
elevated high,
we drank wine:
blood of Concord grape,
sweat of Nonno's hand;
with each other
we broke Nonna's bread,
panis, panis angelicus.

And happy we were
called to that supper.

Today years after your deaths,
in Milano, where Leonardo's
"Last Supper" amazes a wall,
I enter the ristorante,
find spread before me,
ritual of the past,
and an old couple,
ropeveined fingers outstretched,
approaching.

I ache to genuflect,
kiss their hands,
but then I realize
that supper,
the bread and wine of childhood,
was long ago consumed.

The Eye Is Single

---

for Mother, July 2, 1896–August 28, 1977

1.
Mother
I want you young
when
your flesh was unused
tissue,

your eyes Balinese bells,
your hair crackled
wheat
and your mouth spilling
merlin-
magic, kings and knights,
queens and wizards, fairies
and elves.
Mother
I want the time
we both thought death
a unicorn.

2.
Mother my eyes quiver,
my heart stares.
Like an umbrella
death stays a net
above your head.

Anne Paolucci

Born in Italy, Anne Paolucci studied at Barnard College and received her doctorate from Columbia University. She is currently a university research professor at St. John's University and chair of the English Department there. She is also an astoundingly prolific writer of fiction, plays, poetry, literary essays, scholarly articles, translations, and books, including *The Plays of Edward Albee* and *Pirandello's Theatre*. Anne Paolucci is president of the Pirandello Society of America and, as founder and editor of the *Review of National Literatures*, devotes much of her time to finding ways of integrating Western and non-Western literatures. She had a panel show, *Magazines in Focus*, on television, and has been honored many times for her professional attainments and for her contributions to education in the Italian American community. She is married to Dr. Henry Paolucci, professor of government and politics at St. John's University, and they reside in Beechhurst, Queens, New York.

Party Overlooking the Narrows

To Robert Lowell, who wasn't there

At my age
A party is a routine sacrifice.
Incognito
I stand Olympian
In the midst of critics,
Hounds from printing houses,
Girls from Ohio
Learning how to live,
Professors stretching myopic egos
To the social test.
I wait for food
Wondering if editors
Have time to brood.

Miss Gotham
As delicate a bird-lady
As ever wore a flowered straw
Stands listening to bearded lore.
O beautiful young man,
What's love to birds,
To ladies raised on Schraffts?
Do they write poems
Sit on grass
Roll over on the lawn
Wait under umbrellas until dawn?

At my age
I'm just a peevish guest.

To My Fat Friends

A simple theory, mine:
The soul in us
Circles in ever-widening orbit
Until drowsy, tipsy, tired,
It drowns.
Our puppet lines grow limp;
We raid the freezer then
For ice cream
Rip into pretzels
Potato chips
Watch Perry Mason
(The fat-idol of our waste),
By slow stages soothe our flesh.

Or, in Wordsworthian fare:
We brood first, refuse to eat,
Then all our energies burst through,
Find hooks, fly high, and spin
Around our youth!
Falling in love is but a passing feast,
The morning after tells us just how brief;
And when we glance behind
To apple cores and orange peels
Chewing gum wrappers, Glad bags—
The history of our intentions—
We circle sleep to rest
In that point of no dimension
Where Satans burn their blessings.

Acuto

I am afraid I shall not know
The place, unless it is

Mountains crowned in a mist,
Clean morning sounds,
And the friendly donkey
Struggling up the narrow path
Under my window.

Here in the cold light
Of habit I thread my days,
Smoothing the snags that catch
On inconsiderate memories:
The sun does not reach down
Deep enough here
For recognition. But
In the purple morning
Of Angel-donkeys carting
Fresh apples to market,
I shall know my way:
A child
Running across the busy square,
Down the path below
The open fields,
Past stalls and sheds
To my father's house.

Back in the Old Country

Back in the old country, a white beaver coat
Would be presumptuous, even in a dream;
I'd dress in black or in a cotton print
And bless the Lord for a warm shawl
On Sunday. In the evening, I'd sit
By the fire, knitting caps and sweaters,
Listening to the scratch of pens
Over notepaper as the children add up
Their days, conjugate the past in two
Neat columns, and dream of the future.
Back in that other world, I might have been
A country girl, singing my mornings
To the fountain's tune, carrying a pail
Of water effortlessly on my head.

In my father's village, shabby urchins
Stare at me and young girls smile
As if they knew me. Among my people,
In my own place, I feel secure—as though
I had not come on a visit from afar
In a magnificent white beaver coat,
An American with a familiar kind of face
And a nostalgic look around the eyes.

Phyllis Capello

Phyllis Capello writes that she is a single mother of two children and engaged to remarry sometime soon. She is self-taught, with some study of poetry writing at New York University with William Packard. She is also a musician and craftsperson and "a rather strange mixture of traditional Italian mama who loves to cook and sew and do for kids and home, and maverick thinker, philosopher, writer." Her poetry has appeared in little magazines and in the collection *The Wind in Our Sails*. She is currently writing fiction dealing with working-class Italian Americans in Brooklyn, New York, which is where Phyllis Capello was born in 1950 and still lives.

getting my jazz down

sliding around that thin ebony neck
fingers looking for strings
chord position into chord position
a seventh lays back into a sixth
a major sneaks into a minor

oozing out those thick sweet melodies
that make the air smell like pastries,
skimming the nape with the left thumb
feeling the rosewood hum

fingers jumping like a gymnast on the beam
smoothing it out—playing it until the hands know
reaching for those faraway frets
getting the note clear before the muscle stabs
in the back of the hand

listening for those sweet, rich sounds
getting my jazz down

at my breast

his hair is a velvet phrase
a brown nap on his round head,
he drinks
and is drunk in my arms

my nipple like the nib of a pen
writes a poem inside him

his hand
rests in my palm, a tiny starfish
brought in by the tide
to the shore of my skin

Camping Out

Stars watch us undress;
his face is the moon between my knees.
He is creeping prick first into
my sleeping-bag cunt;
we cling zipped together.

I envelop his penis;
my vaginal canal is lined
with goose-down quilted silk.

Like wolves we sniff each other,
nestling in fur and flesh—
we see-saw rocking horse on our buttocks,

and warm wet orgasms
fall down in me like clitoral dominoes.

Rita Valentino

Born in New Jersey and still living there, Rita Valentino says she's not going to apologize. She has been writing poetry since grade school and is also a painter. Her work appears in the collection *The Wind in Our Sails*, published in 1982.

---

o walt, I had no idea

---

o walt, I had no idea
it was your world
that I made die inside of me
your tears that rolled down my cheeks
as I expressed thru your hills
in some air-conditioned bus
there was no way of knowing

you were the father
of my unborn children
breaker of my bread
piler of my wood
starter of my fires
how could I
who barely knew your name
know it was you
who leaped out of every blossom
patted every dog
smiled at every child
hugged the earth's equator
tell me what should I do
with your outdated clothes
that have become part of my skin

the funeral parlor's in brooklyn

I'll get it ma
ma jeanette wants to know
if louie's going to take us to the funeral parlor
no jeanette, uncle lenny said he's taking us
but one of us will have to go with jo ann
ok I'll call you back
hello jo ann
yes I know maryann's car is broke
but she decided to go with bill didn't she
now I told jeanette
o alright I'll call you back
yeah ma I got it
yes maryann jo ann called
but why didn't you . . . O I didn't know that
when did this happen
uhhh. . . . maryann I hate to interrupt but
jeanette and jo ann are waiting for me to call
and I have to find out what's with bill
hello bill

you're not going, well that's nice
put your wife on the phone a minute
at the beauty parlor, of all the
well tell her if she wants to go with me, jeanette and jo ann
to meet us under the big clock at two, got it
you what
are you crazy I haven't the
but I have to
O alright, what are they
go to tenth because there's no eleventh ave, got it, then what
then when I reach ft. hamilton
make a right
for only half a block?
alright I'll try to call you back
hello angela
no bill has to work
but he gave me the direct . . . . .
uh angela, call me back
the dog just ate them

Maria Mazziotti Gillan

Maria Mazziotti Gillan won a New Jersey State Council on the Arts creative writing fellowship in poetry in 1981, and has taught at numerous colleges. She is a Ph.D. candidate at Drew University, director of the Poetry Center at Passaic County Community College, and editor of *Footwork* magazine there. Her poetry has appeared in over a hundred publications and received several awards. In addition to publishing a collection of her poetry, *Flowers from the Tree of Night*, she has given many readings of her work. Other publications of hers include *Thomas Hardy: A Critical Perspective* and *Thomas Wolfe: A Critical Analysis*.

Petals of Silence

The softness which comes to me at dawn
has petals made of silence.
Upstairs, my husband, my children sleep,
dreaming their own shadows.

In these moments, stolen from the night,
no one needs me. I have my own quiet joys.
My notebook page is clean and white.
My pen moves across it almost by itself.
Even the cat sleeps content in the corner.

I collect the edges of myself around me,
curl in the flowers of my stillness
where I find the strength to emerge
into the world of this house,
your bubbling lives.

It is not that I love you less
or would wish you gone;
it is only this need
to gather my forces,
to drink from my own fountain
that causes these retreats from you, my loves.

Someday, perhaps my daughter will read this poem,
see her reflection in its glass,
as she sits alone, in the clarity of early morning,
with the sound of the crickets and her ghosts
and the place inside herself
that nothing, nothing can shatter.

1980

Public School No. 18: Paterson, New Jersey

Miss Wilson's eyes, opaque
as blue glass, fix on me:
"We must speak English.
We're in America now."
I want to say, "I am American,"
but the evidence is stacked against me.

My mother scrubs my scalp raw, wraps
my shining hair in white rags
to make it curl; Miss Wilson
drags me to the window, checks my hair
for lice. My face wants to hide.

At home, my words smooth in my mouth,
I chatter and am proud. In school,
I am silent; I grope for the right English
words, fear the Italian word will sprout
from my mouth like a rose.

I fear the progression of teachers
in their sprigged dresses,
their Anglo-Saxon faces.

Without words, they tell me
to be ashamed.
I am.
I deny that booted country
even from myself,
want to be still
and untouchable
as these women
who teach me to hate myself.

Years later, in a white
Kansas City house,
the psychology professor tells me
I remind him of the Mafia leader
on the cover of *Time* magazine.

My anger spits
venomous from my mouth:

I am proud of my mother,
dressed all in black,
proud of my father
with his broken tongue,
proud of the laughter
and noise of our house.

Remember me, ladies,
the silent one?
I have found my voice
and my rage will blow
your house down.

Elizabeth Marraffino

Elizabeth Marraffino lives and works in New York, where she does free-lance writing, editing, and reviewing. In the seventies she was a student of the poet John Logan. Her work has appeared in many publications and anthologies, and her most recent book of poetry is *Blue Moon for Ruby Tuesday*, published in 1981 by Contact Two Publications.

Blues After 35¢ Beers in St. Louis

Frank is probably home in Ottawa
It's damn hot here in Memphis
2 hour bus delay

Air sticks deep
    to the soles of my feet
Elvis Presley postcards glow in the dark gift shop

Omens are less frequent
except I wore white again
    last night
Slept in Jobo's room
        surrounded by monster games
          HOW TO BE THE INCREDIBLE HULK
& lots of Indian history books

Was nearly dreamless first time in months

I'm scared I'm pregnant

Would abortion in this case be murder:
Wayne is in Minnesota with his wife populating his future

A couple of years back
    driving home from Great Barrington
I got lonely
    because I was going extinct

Night after night light after light

Night after night light after light
goes on in Canaan across the hill
from my house where hours later
dawn will turn on the sky with
a hundred beautiful colors.
I want to believe in unhappiness
but each day there is this joy
beginning out my window
& I find going on alone
is no less no more separate
than being with you.
That the spaces in my life
are not holes but entrances
& I begin at last
to be brave to slowly one by one
step through.

Claudia Menza

After many years in the publishing world as general editor and production manager at Grove Press, Claudia Menza has formed her own literary agency and works from her apartment in New York's Greenwich Village. She also participates in a literary salon, and has done readings of her poetry. She is an intensely literary person, which derives, perhaps, from having parents who were college educated and teachers.

Poem for Miles Davis

"Didn't your mama ever tell you that hanging out with Negroes and
listening to jazz music ain't gonna bring you no good?"
—a friend

Used to be I couldn't sleep at night,
could not keep worry from my mind.
But I found the cure for bad dreams
when I discovered sweet cream
at my door . . .

In the welcome hands of midnight,
I turn on a tape
when I turn out the light.
I spread like butter beneath the sheet . . .

I got Miles to go
before I sleep.

Oh Creator of star-touched sky lines,
more facile than a lover's rime,
I'm strung in the plexus of 4/4 time,
your dawn . . .

Make me your melody,
your note to be slid upon, hit upon.
Encourage me with variations—anticipation—
blow sweet nothings in my ear . . .

When you're close,
I hear "Funny Valentine,"
I taste those full-blown lips swallow mine,
then you're gone . . .

I'm expecting resolution,
but you hit a blue one:
you're on the ceiling—revolution!

I got to jump up
from the bed,
reach as high as I can

I feel your hand:
the light engage of fingertips

then you rip

pulling me
trip and stumble
thru the percussion,
over the bass,
we leap the sax

down dark, wet streets
lit by the dusky sparkle
of your horn

We're starting toward rooftops
bound for galaxies

We're up
and we never hit ground.

When the vibes come in,
we're gone . . .

miles and miles and miles away . . .

We hit home with moon rocks,
the fiery streak of meteors:
the bed is alive with syncopation—anticipation—
that triple tonguing up and down my spine,
no more bad dreams,
only sweet cream . . .

Come blow your horn
between my thighs—
I'm under your starlit tune, Miles!
but you must come soon, Miles!

Anna Bart

Using a combination of her mother's and father's first names, Bernadetta D'Arcangelo Gorski arrived at Anna Bart as the pen name under which she publishes her poems and has done a reading of them. She was born in Buffalo, New York, and is a graduate of the University of Buffalo and the Buffalo School of Fine Arts. Under her real name she has established a reputation as a designer, and in addition to being exhibited widely, her work is represented in many books on textile arts. She is married to an artist and has two grown sons. Presently she teaches at the Paier College of Art in Connecticut.

Ravioli

Grandma's long black dress   black iron stove
narrow windows on a narrow alley
the Roma Street kitchen a shadowy cave
but the back door opens to a sunny yard

She breaks eggs into a flour volcano-crater
mixing, kneading, rolling it smooth on the dough board
cutting circles with a coffee can lid
spooning ricotta in each circle
folding them into half-moon pillows

At five I can press the fork tines round the edge
crisp bird tracks in the dough
press my thumb to make a dimple
in the powdered skin

Cover them with a towel
they need to rest awhile
Let's go out and feed
the Pee-Pees

Bouyant air bright with sunny ferment
jostling each other hungry chicks
lift red wire legs beaks stretched
in frantic Pee-ee-eep!
Pee-ee-eep! Pee-eeep!

Preserving

after school as I near home
pungent smells spice the air
red paste drying on a board

propped up netting makes a tent
to keep the hungry flies away
    backyard altar of *conserva*

mother, aunts have worked all day
call out "come down here and help!"
in the cellar summer kitchen
bushels of tomatoes   peaches
quart jars to be washed and scalded
overflow the laundry tubs
    copper boiler's steady chuckle

golden peach halves firm and slippery
pack them down in clean quart jars
pour in sweetened juice to cover
fit the tops with rubber jar rings
twist the metal cap just so
    the sealing twist comes after boiling

and one bleak day in February
"get a jar of fruit for supper!"
in the cellar dark the light bulb
shimmering on rows of jewels
bounces off the grey stone crock
    storing dried tomato paste

---

c. 1896

Ermelinda, young wife with two small boys
leaves the mountain village in Abruzzi
    muleback to Naples
    steerage to America
a month it takes
    but Luciano her husband is waiting.

Ellis Island confusions
New York's bewildering mass
endless train ride across that wide state
the blaze of newness stuns
    but Luciano her husband is waiting

Sister, cousins, brother-in-law will ease
the way: Benedetta, Ortensia, Persabella,
Giovanni   how they welcome her! They
have their own land, small house and garden.

Where is Luciano?
      Ah, of course, at work
      Thank God he has a job
      Tonight he will come for them
      Dominic, Donato, play in the yard,
      Papa comes tonight.

Then in swoops grim Ortensia
and roughly drapes a black shawl
on Ermelinda's shoulders,
      Piangi! Piangi!
      dear sister   cry!
      your husband is dead.

Giovanni   1854–1940

All that remains, this saddle model rifle converted to percussion
    with brass patch box
a J. H. Merrill, patented 1858, bought for $2.00
    from *paesan* Desiderio
immigrant entrepreneur of Vesuvius Paving Company.
    Unskilled laborer
Giovanni never hunted, had no time for sport. What did he
    want with a gun?

A quiet man. I remember him sitting on the porch, resting a lot
    in old age.
Came to America in 1887 with promise of a job. His life
    shaped by jobs.
From Roma Avenue he walked six miles each way to Williamsville
    stone quarries.
In 1900 walked west to Delaware Park to dig for the
    Pan American Exposition.

Walked to Lake Erie, 5¢ ferry ride to Canada, then walked
    to Ridgeway quarry.
Back home again at night, dug his garden. He learned about gunpowder
    in the quarries.
Fourth of July mornings Giovanni stood in his yard, aimed his rifle high
    and fired in celebration.

Maria Iannacome Coles

Born in the Abruzzi region of Italy after World War II, Maria Iannacome
Coles immigrated to the United States with her family at the age of
fifteen. In Rochester, New York, where they settled in the Italian American
community, she says she "came to know immigrant life, its toil, its whole-
ness within, and its marginality to American culture." She studied at the
State University of New York at Buffalo but says that her literary education
was arrived at independently of institutions of higher learning. Her poetry
has been published in many literary reviews and has also appeared in an
anthology entitled *All We Are Saying*.

Millinocket, Maine

To repay for their passage
with their aged skills, the weightless treasure
    theirs to bring across the seas,
the fathers built the mill on the Penobscot River and
scratched off the numberless twelve-hour days
        on the towering mason walls.

The sons reproduced unfancifully
up to this son who knows his parents' life
the way a soldier knows the country he fought
the places he bombed with accuracy
the people he shared rations with afterwards.
On the bare spot above the end table
hangs the photograph
a big-shouldered man in *carabiniere* uniform
pushes out his chest like priceless medals.
He was among the hundreds picked up for the mill
right from the Boston Harbor.
On the side of the rushing river stands the white cross still.
It marks the death of the "unknown river driver"*
for all men with see-through aliases
who took refuge on the slippery tree trunks
driven down the wild water to the mill.

The mothers brought dry *camomille*,
handfuls of seeds
in bright handwoven kerchiefs.
Their backs powered the passing
of everyone's season.   Nurtured
in gardens.   Built
no standing walls.   Their names
had the meaning of their days forever gone,
offered up
like the steaming baskets they carried to the mill at noon

*The "river drivers" were the men who in the earlier part of the century accompanied and pushed timber downriver. The job was particularly dangerous because when the logs got jammed one of the river drivers would be asked to dynamite the jam and often be unable to run away fast enough. Since men running from the law were attracted to the isolation in the woods, many of these lives were particularly cheap to the paper companies for whom they worked.

Gray Waters and Geraniums

She raked up some orange leaves
with her bare hands
and dropped them

over the gray waters of the river
where they shined bright, warm.

   walking and leaning
her head for the sounds at her feet,
hearing as many thoughts as there are leaves
and with the same promises,
   she returns home
   the kitchen, the smells,
   the spices next to the stained volumes of poetry
and begins the ceremony maintained
although the kids are gone:
washing the breakfast dishes,
cleaning the counter top,
sweeping the floor.
Against silence
she recognizes in the rasping of the broom,
the sound of festive cleaning,
hears the voices in the language become foreign to her,
and the women in clothes made colorless by time
clean house to house, medieval dwellings some,
somber, haunting, brightened with geraniums,
spices hung to dry, embroidered tablecloths.
There was the smell of woman made spring there.

She looks up.
The front door,
the full length window precisely framed
in the corridor of rooms and doorways
faces her. The front yard tree framed still.
A few leaves hang on it like old christmas toys.
The tree trunk stands defined again, its
leaves are gone.

Taking a book between the palms of her hands,
she sits at the refinished table,
opens to a marked page.
One hand holds the book on her knees
like a piece of cloth,
the other hand inside her blouse,
around her breast as she reads.

Rina Ferrarelli

Born in the Sila area of Calabria and orphaned at a young age, Rina Ferrarelli was sent for by relatives in Pittsburgh in 1954 and educated here. She has an M.A. degree from Duquesne and is presently teaching at La Roche College. In addition to writing and translating poetry which has appeared in numerous small magazines, her activities include directing a series of poetry readings and workshops for the Mount Lebanon Public Library and teaching Italian in the continuing education program. Rina Ferrarelli, whose full name is Caterina Ferrarelli Provost, lives in Pittsburgh with her husband and their three children.

Fictions

It's raining hard.
The cat has invented a mouse
to chase across the living-room floor.
She lopes
        hides under a chair
               crouching
then pounces   lets go
               pounces again.
With as much gusto as if it were real.
We sit next to each other
the way we do almost every evening.
Absorbed in our books.
            You have your fictions
and I have mine.

On the Outer Banks

To the Wright Brothers

And life sometimes is on the fringes
a fringe of sandbanks strung along a coast
what relief there is is man-made
the shapes of man's work
the shapes of man's leisure

blending with the pebbles and coarse brown sand
you plover your way in and out
constant motion one way to survive

or you forget about all that:
singleminded about your needs
you incubate your dream in a drafty barn
until it grows wings
then watch it rise above the low landscape
soar higher than gull and sea hawk

A Georgia O'Keeffe Bloom

The hawthorne hedge by the school
parking lot is in full bloom
tonight, throbbing in the blue of dusk,
blue-white, its aura electric, the scent
a current that pulls me across the street.
                              Early today
I woke with lines to a new poem
running through my head, again
after a long fast, and now this,

and as if it weren't enough, the moon
has just come up above the neighbors' roof
large between silhouettes of pines,
and it, too, seems to glow from within:
a Georgia O'Keeffe bloom
pinned on the breast of night.

Jacquelyn Bonomo

Born in 1948 in Bayonne, New Jersey, Jacquelyn Bonomo has a Sicilian heritage from both sets of grandparents. She has been a serious poet since her undergraduate days at Clark University, where she graduated magna cum laude and Phi Beta Kappa. Her doctoral work was done at Rutgers. Since 1972 she has been teaching a broad range of writing courses and has led numerous poetry workshops through the Kilmer House Poetry Center of New Brunswick, which she helped found. She also founded and directed Writers' Weekend, a conference of nationally known writers held in 1979 and 1980 and funded by the New Jersey Council on the Arts. Her current position is as publicity coordinator for the School of Continuing Education at New York University, and her avid interest is running.

Patience in the Endless Rain

Always to kneel like this at the porch edge
With one hand cupped for rain,
The small reserve in my mind filling,
Leaves alert and unalterably patient with the rain.

Days and days of it,
Long grass swaying back and forth
Like a woman's head gone wild with passion.
I think of the rain I must see in your smile,
The alterable truths spilling down
On my naked body in the warm bedroom,
How difficult and necessary the patient yielding to rain.
Always to kneel like this,
Not to judge too much or too little,
To have the right kind of strength,
The long muscles of a swimmer.
"Patience," Grandmother said,
And for once the old seem rightfully wise,
The old one in me from the island seems wise.
There's a sensible way to walk across the road,
To stand above the filling valley until the earth gives way,
To swim above the gravestones.
Patience in the endless rain
That rains on both of us this night.

Hens

Dry thunder.
Rasp of the hotrod driving the sun to perfection.
10 A.M.
90 degrees.
The heat sits on my body with the cumulative weight of my dream men.
All night they climbed on and off
Yelling at me in panicky whispers,
"No babies!"
Outside the hens are clucking in crescendoes,
Like crickets who have evolved bourgeois mentalities.
Who asked them anyway? my men might say,
To lay their eggs so punctually, so prolifically,
Making such a job out of instinct?
Every day the fussbudgets get me
To set out their corn, their mash,
The water they desperately gobble with their clipped beaks

So they may brood on eggs some don't seem to know
Will never hatch.
This is what a hen does and has to do,
Cock or no.
I'm ashamed to spite their bodies,
To pry one out of her nest with a stick.
Handling her eggs, white, hot,
Even I am tempted to think that soon
Something would have to break through with a life of its own.

The Ninth Life

Like an old woman searching for the one change
In a house she could walk through blind
Again and again,
You search your life.
Have the homemade constellations on the mantle
Shifted positions in the last second
Before you came down the stairs?
Coming down the stairs! What work!
Eight invisible black cats
Now retrace your footsteps
In every shoe of every size you've ever worn.
It's the ninth life,
The only one that has to make good luck for itself,
God knows.
God crosses the bad luck lines of centuries
To the seeming magic of stardom.
By now he leaps as high as Nijinsky,
Dies with Pavlova's grace,
Defies gravity like Astaire.
One clear-hearted turn from the bed to the window
And your mind's night stars
Dance into view.

Delaware-Raritan Canal, on a walk with
a friend.

The Flashlight

Trained on the towpath
Makes a light tunnel we can walk through
Without fear of stepping in shit.
It's as if we're underground driving from New York to Jersey.
Every hundred yards I look back for the pale figure
That wants to stay in the city,
Hoping to turn her to salt.
Now the office fluorescence interrogates the night
And my heart still hurts from asking of watches
"What time is it? What time is it?"

I am efficiently bored with thinking
I know what I see.
The flashlight is a bad habit.
When we come to a dimensional darkness
I can say, "It's just a tree root.
It's just shit."
I don't see the spirits caught in the trees
That can't feel when the wind makes them touch.

We are discussing our mothers and fathers,
How you have come to some peace with them,
How you stayed up all night
To hear your father say he was relieved to know
You were not stupid as he had thought.
This is what I too want of the night,
To hear the voice of the owl admitting its ignorance.

Still, I say it's impossible for me
To be free of mourning my parents' marriage,
As if each turning away from my own contentment
Would map out the place and time when their broken trust
Civilized, then buried my feelings.
And I again pull the files, seeming to make the final report
Using the diction of deadlines for two people I saw just once

Kissing at the foot of mahogany stairs, the richest wood of all,
To say this is not worth an investment.

Shit and roots, shit and roots.
The flashlight exposes what's waste,
What's grown away from its source.
Better to imagine in the dark two tree spirits,
One like this one, split to the roots by lightning,
And the standing one it's gashed in falling.

Between husband and wife they call this cruelty,
Because of the giving, the feeling of pain.
I try to think another way,
Hearing how my father always said
Even after the lightning bolt,
"Don't think so much. Don't worry so much.
You'll grow old before your time."

All night the flashlight searches the world
For the mahogany staircase ripped out of the city house
By the new owner.
Who knows where it is? Who cares?
Who who who cries the owl.

Jennifer Lagier

A second-generation American of Italian descent, Jennifer Lagier is a California born and educated writer of prose and poetry. She currently reviews for *Hard Row to Hoe*, published by the Seven Buffaloes Press, and is a member of VOICES, a writers' cooperative which sponsors readings and anthologies. Jennifer Lagier holds two master's degrees, one in English literature and the other in library science, and works as a children's librarian in Manteca, California.

second class citizen

for mom

we laughed
calling it latent wop syndrome
the compulsive addiction
that triggered your spending
week after week
using layers of i. magnin clothes
t-birds and two hundred dollar a pair shoes
to eradicate the shabby shame of
growing up foreign and poor
being born to farm laborer parents
in a contractor's shack
using bank books to balance
your cheated childhood
that scrawny immigrant's kid
who still squirms uneasily around
behind the elegant vogue dressed facade
scared that someday this
middleclass masquerade
will crack down the middle and fall away
letting a squatty italian fishwife with a
broken womb in black
wearing fat nun's shoes
climb through and escape
you with one foot planted
on the skidding skateboard
of near country club status
the other nailed
back there on ellis island
stuck in quarantine
and waiting official permission
to be let off the boat

Janine Veto

Janine Veto has an Italian side from both her natural father (born near Milan) and her stepfather (Calabrian), while her mother is of French, English, and Sioux descent. She is a 1971 graduate of Northwestern University, has worked in radio, television, public relations, and advertising, and is now development director for Poets & Writers, Inc., in New York. Janine Veto's poetry has appeared in small magazines and her first novel, *Iris*, was released by Alyson Publications in 1983. In 1979, she was the recipient of a grant from the Chicago Council on Fine Arts and the National Endowment for the Arts to stage *The Dream of a Common Language*, based on the poetry of Adrienne Rich and produced by Quicksilver Theater in Chicago.

Body Wisdom

for Donna Brookman

out of unknown bodies
        we come
slippery from moist spun space
an echo across light years
from the tunneled silence

we come
out of unknown bodies

our own and its opposite
alien as first breath
grappling on the grave of wonder

out of unknown bodies
we become   our own
unknown body
crying across
                a loop of time

Naturally, Mother

1.
I looked for you
spinning the wheel of my horoscope
I lied for you in court chambers
I performed for your benefit in Catholic charities

But you were always with me

every time I loved and left
each time I put my life in suitcases

as I watch the coupling of friends
and know I can not follow

envying the simple faith of the world's majority

with the clairvoyance of daughters
I wrote you five years ago

knowing even then
I was writing myself

2.
No wonder you now wear watches
synchronize every clock
panic when someone seems unconcerned

We are all fleshed out pivots of your time

I am here
but only because discreet phone numbers
were not yet published in underground papers

My sister you sold to Miami Jews
for red shoes and a purse to match

The boys you kept
hoping it would be easier
not to raise your own reincarnation

and the nameless one
decomposing somewhere in North Africa

the final ticking under your heart
before your racing timepiece
was disconnected

Freud aside, all our fathers
do not matter
A woman bleeds through her mother

3.
So tempting to stop sailing

retire to a Zen simple room
washed ashore on contemplative rocks
safe from the question of waves

It is not us

We get sweaty from grappling with this life
there is no hope of approval
no safe drydock

I forced your gaze back, mine inward

But we will not drown

We are buoyed by our own messy faith;
we love

Theresa Vinciguerra

The founder and director of Poet Tree, Inc., in Sacramento, California, Theresa Vinciguerra was moved to do so by her urgency to share and her need to break the isolation she found herself in as a writer. Poet Tree, Inc., has become Sacramento's most visible literary cooperative, hosting literary events and regular readings, and putting out the monthly *Poet News*, a literary calendar and news and reviews. Aside from Theresa Vinciguerra's outstanding service to the literary community, she is a free-lance writing and editing consultant, a mother of two, and a candidate for an M.A. in creative writing. Her poetry has appeared in *The California Quarterly* and *Hard Pressed* and in 1982 she won the Bazzanella Award for Poetry from California State University.

Aftertaste

About this morning lingers
the thin, round sheet of moon,
the aftertaste of you, an apple
cooked down
till the skin thickens and bubbles.
I am full to the sugared rim
from the midnight fruit,
have no appetite
for ordinary breakfasts
and lick the sweetness of peel
and core that circles the moons
and arcs of my fingers.

This Small Universe

1. *The Twenty-eighth Day*

Our belly swells,
the twenty-eighth day of its cycle colliding
with the full white circle in the night, and
as we look aside in our mirror, its lunar shape
glares at us, its gravity tugging our flesh,
our very expectations.

We wish
we wish to dam this female tide,
push the waters back,
protest aloud the harshness of it
making the bright clots like constellations
shower from our body.

Wearing all the full moon's vestments,
singing the ocean's pitch
this same red-black orbit consecrates itself
the inviolate gift.
We look again with more than a sidelong glance.
We wonder: Can we attend with nothing less than
acceptance to this small universe of mystery?

Rope

I pull on the rope of your body drawing you in
at the center where there is no struggle
where the unbraiding begins at the tip of the spine
and we unravel strand by strand
the thick twine in the spiral of pleasure
where there are no ends
no letting go.

Kathryn Nocerino

Kathryn Nocerino is a poet and a critic who lives in New York. Her first poetry collection, *Wax Lips*, was published by New Rivers Press in 1980. A second collection, *Candles in the Daytime*, will be published by Warthog Press. She has been a writing fellow at Yaddo and at the Ragdale Foundation, and reports that she's broken a long writer's block regarding novels and is now near completion of her first.

El Sueño

for Frida Kahlo, Mexican painter,
1910–1954

one woman, asleep, sees flowers
  start purple from the rib-cage of her
skeleton.   at the foot of the
  bed are tap-roots;   around her hair,
dark water pouring from the pillow,
    bowers of green leaves.

another woman stands at height of
  day before her mirror.   her own hand,
bearing a cloth, rises slowly to her face.
  she erases one eye and then the
    other.   mouth, nose, contour and
expression disappear.   when she screams,
    the sound is made of dust.

345

Maria Dominica Lazzari, "L'Addolorata," a Miller's Daughter, Who Received the Stigmata in 1835

Herodotus, in his description of a temple of Hercules in Egypt, wrote that it was unlawful for the authorities to capture runaway slaves who took refuge there, if they received certain marks on their bodies, devoting them to the deity.

> she awoke
to the morning of the ploughed field;
>   scrub-brush; washing pail;
to shoes kept on a shelf till Sunday,
>   to the black dress that a woman wears:
her earth!

>   mysteries
made their home in the sky:
>   the saved flew up to heaven, or they rode the chariot.
>   the priest's voice:
"dust thou art, and unto dust thou shalt return."
>   sometimes she woke from a dream, crying.
she had been lying down, hands crossed;
>   earth
had filled her mouth until she could not breathe.

>   rise, then,
like the woman in blue robes, or else be doomed.
> eyes up,
she saw the ladders of the prophets
> being lowered for her, then withdrawn.
her smile of secrets brought her gifts of oranges and olives
>   from the village boys.

she saw no one.
she was a spring field waiting for first fruits;
she was thorns and roses:
she was not earth.
she was not merely earth.

Empty Factory, N.J.

the train passing and passing these buildings,
a view persisting long enough to slow our wheels

beyond the shattered panes,
business in night is booming.
the painted legend on the brick,
M—s—n Ma-h-ne-y Co.

the broken windows say, "death"
the still freight car in the loading-yard,
beached in sand, says "death."
death walks the roof-spine,
cocking its head at foreign movement.

volumes of silent air
carry a glittering suspension of dust—
gold coin of forgetfulness.

an instant more,
and we will rest before these walls
forever.

the forward pull begins at last.
rounding the bend,
we thrust it into memory.
the motion of this great, wheeled scythe
parts two halves of spoked earth.

Sandra M. Gilbert

Sandra M. Gilbert is a widely published and critically acclaimed poet and author. Her important feminist criticism appears in the collections of which she is co-editor, *The Madwoman in the Attic, Shakespeare's Sisters,* and *The Norton Anthology of Literature by Women.* Her published volumes of poetry are *In the Fourth World: Poems, The Summer Kitchen,* and *Emily's Bread,* and her poems are included in several anthologies. Born Sandra Mortola in 1936, she grew up in Jackson Heights, Queens, New York, and married Elliot Lewis Gilbert, a professor of English. They have three children and reside in Berkeley, California. Sandra M. Gilbert got her doctorate from Columbia and is an associate professor at the University of California at Davis.

Mafioso

Frank Costello eating spaghetti in a cell at San Quentin,
Lucky Luciano mixing up a mess of bullets and
calling for parmesan cheese,
Al Capone baking a sawed-off shotgun into a
huge lasagna—

are you my uncles, my
only uncles?

Mafiosi,
bad uncles of the barren
cliffs of Sicily—was it only you

that they transported in barrels
like pure olive oil
across the Atlantic?

          Was it only you
who got out at Ellis Island with
black scarves on your heads and cheap cigars
and no English and a dozen children?

No carts were waiting, gallant with paint,
no little donkeys plumed like the dreams of peacocks.
Only the evil eyes of a thousand buildings
stared across at the echoing debarcation center,
making it seem so much smaller than a piazza,

only a half dozen Puritan millionaires stood on the wharf,
in the wind colder than the impossible snows of the Abruzzi,
ready with country clubs and dynamos

  to grind the organs out of you.

Doing Laundry

I am doing laundry in my laundry room
the washing machine grinds and pumps like my father's heart
it is sick   it is well
sick again   well again

behind the round window your shirts
leap and praise God slowly like gentle souls
and my old brassieres bound like the clean breasts
of antelopes

I am doing laundry in Africa
and overhead the parrots shriek
they encourage me to beat harder
beat the dirt out of the flowers

I am doing laundry in Indiana
my husband the insurance salesman comes in
wanting to know if I would like to buy his new
insurance against laundry

I am doing laundry in the river Styx
I pound and I pound
the shirts disappear
the brassieres dissolve to nothingness

I am a heart doing laundry
and I beat and I pound
until I no longer remember
the color of dirt

The Grandmother Dream

My Sicilian grandmother, whom I've never met,
my Sicilian grandmother, the midwife, who died
forty years ago, appears in my bedroom.
She's sitting on the edge of my bed,
at her feet a shabby black bag,
and she speaks a tangled river of Italian:
her Sicilian words flow out like dark fish, slippery and cold,
her words stare at me with blank eyes.

I see that she's young, younger than I am.
I see her black hair gleam like tar as
she draws from her small black midwife's bag
her midwife tools: heavy silver instruments
polished like doorknobs, polished—misshapen, peculiar—
like the knob of an invisible door.

The Thoreau Pencil

Thoreau's father was a pencil manufacturer, and young David Henry improved the Thoreau pencil in several important ways.
                                                        —Arnold Biella

I am not writing with it
right now   you can't buy one
for ready money
anymore   but
I dream   dream of it
(who has not)
the steely graphite
at the center
rock-dark
black-night-lake-surface-dark
inscribing   scribing
the wood around the outside
a fir-tree   a birch-tree
—I don't know the details—
pared down to size

what characters it must write
what clean Romantic
hieroglyphs
pebbles from the shore of Walden pond
(beyond the trailer park)
nut shells   mosquitos wings
tangled branches intricate
and indiscreet
"to glorify God and enjoy him forever"

they say Thoreau could pick up twelve
Thoreau pencils at a time
without looking
like picking up a year   all at once
in a minute

The Summer Kitchen

In June when the Brooklyn garden
boiled with blossom,
when leaflets of basil lined the paths
and new green fruitless fingers of vine
climbed the airy arbor roof,

my Sicilian aunts withdrew
to the summer kitchen,
the white bare secret room
at the bottom of the house.
Outside, in the upper world,

sun blistered the bricks of the tiny
imitation Taormina terrace where fierce
socialisti uncles
chainsmoked Camels and plotted politics;
nieces and nephews tusseled

among thorny bloodcolored
American roses;
a pimply concrete
birdbath-fountain dribbled ineffectual
water warm as olive oil.

Cool and below it all,
my aunts labored among great cauldrons
in the spicy air
of the summer kitchen: in one kettle
tomatoes bloomed into sauce;

in another, ivory *pasta*
leaped and swam;
on the clean white table
at the center of the room
heads of lettuce flung themselves open,

and black-green poles of zucchini
fell into slices of yellow
like fairytale money.
Skidding around the white
sink in one corner

the trout that Uncle Christopher brought back
from the Adirondacks gave up
the glitter of its fins
to the glitter of *Zia* Francesca's
powerful knife.

Every August day *Zia* Petrina
rose at four to tend the morning:
smoky Greek chignon
drawn sleek,
she stood at the sink.

Her quick shears
flashed in the silence,
separating day from night, trunk
from branch, leaf
from shadow.

As the damp
New World sunrays struggled to rise
past sooty housetops,
she'd look suddenly up
with eyes black as the grapes

that fattened in the arbor:
through one dirt-streaked window
high above her
she could see the ledge of soil
where her pansies and geraniums anchored.

Higher still,
in tangles of heat
my uncles' simmering garden grew,
like green steam swelling from the cool
root of her kitchen.

Leslie Scalapino

A reviewer of her collection of poetry, *Considering How Exaggerated Music Is*, wrote that Leslie Scalapino "may well be the most original young poet writing in America today" as she "explores . . . dislocation and confluence between her public and personal selves." Scalapino grew up in Berkeley, California, and went to Reed College, then got her M.A. on a Woodrow Wilson fellowship at the University of California, Berkeley. In 1976 she was the recipient of a creative writing grant from the National Endowment for the Arts. She has taught at New College of California in San Francisco and is presently doing editing work.

In sequence

We cross India in a train, our feet on a cake
of ice which our father buys in a train
station.

We take a train which stops at a village by rice when a Chinese girl is killed on the tracks. The villagers come out to the side of the track. I thought they didn't like female children; but they bend over and are crying sounding as if they are laughing.

I see a man who is starving lying holding out his cup to beg from me.

In Calcutta my parents are in a building while we sit outside in a horse-drawn cart waiting for them. My grandmother who sits in the cart with us doesn't give money to the beggars because there are too many and they have begun to push holding their hands on their bellies and hands stretched out to take the money. My grandmother is wearing a heavy corset and occasionally removes her hand from mine in order to fan herself.

An Indian doctor examines us at our hotel and thinks that we have smallpox, though he is not sure and a day later we are well. We take the ship from Bombay and Indian women on the ship become ill with smallpox because they have not been vaccinated. The ship is segregated by race and a dance is held but the white people stay on the upper-class deck and listen to the music. We sit by the dance floor on the second-class deck with Indian families who do not dance even if they are married.

We dance with two African men—so that we are the only couples on the floor. My partner's legs shake violently while we dance; my parents sitting beside the empty dance floor with the Indian families, their heads nodding every once in a while.

The Indian women who have smallpox get into an ambulance which is like a wooden paddy wagon. An Indian man goes down the ship's gangplank—his brother has come to Mombasa for him—our parents sit in the car also, and they take us for a ride in the countryside going eighty miles an hour to cool us.

Later we meet them again, drive up after we've been travelling for a while and have come to the town where they live and they're under their car working on it.

We stay with a family. Their servants fan us at the dinner table. We go out for a drive around Manila with the daughter and she buys us ice cream bringing the cones back to the car.

My sister is embarrassed and gives her cone to the chauffeur but then the daughter is angry and the chauffeur refuses to take the ice cream cone. We go by ship to the southern islands, sleeping on deck. A herd of pigs is on the lower deck. The pigs slip to one side of the deck when the ship rolls, then slip back again. It is hot and our parents talk to the ship's mates. Later the daughter visits us, comes on Thanksgiving bringing a dinner though we have already prepared it, and she occasionally addresses my mother as "auntie."

The students in the class are black, a student asking to go to the toilet but the teacher not letting her—then he lets her, calls me up to his desk in front of the class asking me to look under the toilet stall to see if she went there.

I say she was there after I go into the hall and wait. I don't realize that I can say I won't do it and the other students don't either. I talk—try to kill myself because I think that I don't have enough ability but I have to continue in school—and so the principal comes to observe our class, the teacher getting fired and the principal is made a math teacher the next year.

We get to know a friend even though her father will not allow her to go anywhere usually.

My mother asks the father if we can go to the movies and we walk to the theatre where in front of the doorway a beggar who has no legs wheels himself on a cart like a sled. Our friend speaks in a flirtatious way to my mother and us and the movie starts. It is called *Mother India* and the heroine in it sings wading in mud up to her waist after a monsoon. The son has lost his legs, the husband is crazy so the audience and our friend weep during the movie but my sister and I react by laughing. We laugh wildly. We go back to America and go to school. One of my sisters has a boyfriend and he stays in bed with her by climbing up to a balcony on the second floor.

We go to the coast on the motorcycle. We have a minute weaving before the motorcycle turns over since there's a blowout. There aren't any cars anywhere, it's Thanksgiving, and my friend says to hold on so I am on his back when we're thrown from the cycle, sliding several yards. He isn't hurt. People who tell us they are missionaries drive up. They run over to me and take us to the hospital in their car with the cycle lying beside the road, the doctor saying that I should take off my clothes.

I pull off the clothes very slowly since my arms are twisted and she remarks about it when I've removed them.

A boyfriend and I are wild about each other but don't get along, break up and then home on vacation I come in my sleep. I am in school, my father advising a president the other students and I not agreeing with his views— they slam their books on the floor making sounds when I'm talking about something else.

A man who has been hit by a club climbs a pole when I am walking back from class; then later an instructor asks our class to think of any women scholars—an instructor skips me and I decide not to go back to school.

I get married our families coming with us, sitting in the pews in the chapel in Reno with people in wedding clothes outside in line for their turn. I want to laugh when the minister is a holy roller yet my husband almost cries at the ceremony although later we are divorced, my sisters get divorced, my father sees my uncle in a museum embracing a woman other than his wife.

The museum has ramps rather than stairs so my father crouches afraid my uncle will be embarrassed, will turn and see him so he goes up and waits.

I sit in the car in a parking lot of a market, hold up a bottle of wine for a sip, two old men sitting in the front seat of a car facing me—they each take drinks out of cartons of milk with their chins up as they drink the milk. I like music playing on the radio in the car and a friend comes out of the market.

We go back, get into bed, come—I'm entirely concentrated on this—I think everything is the country.

I sit down to write about a man's mother who is killed in a car accident but I make tea before the telephone rings. I hear that my grandmother has been killed in a car and I leave and go there, finding my father in a motel sitting with her clothes hanging up, frantic, and he eats a date out of a package because he is hungry so I take the clothes down and wring the sweater to make the blood and rain water fall into the bathtub in my room.

We get back. Later they go to Java where my mother is carried in a chair on a mountain because she can't walk since the accident and people there sing,

"Americans have gone to the moon. Now you have come. We are glad you are here."

I go with a friend to Las Vegas. He and I gamble at the slot machines people gathering around me as money pours out of my machine. I like Cleopatra's Barge in a casino floating in water with gold leaf on the woman's body and we go to Colorado—I realize I have never thought about money—see a man who pumps gas where there are no people who gives us his newsletter and it is all about things like baby shoes dipped in bronze.

We bring a painting to someone's house and are asked to stay to have lunch my friend saying no by mistake and leaving so that we get in the car. We drive and I have a dream when we sleep for a few minutes, reclined in the car seats.

I left, was in New York, people came up and told me how to get to the subway; since they saw I was looking around standing on the street—I thought that people have an inner world, associated it with architecture and monopolies.

I have various jobs—I make a mistake at the soda fountain and a milkshake doesn't catch on the blender, flies off splashing the counter where the old white-haired men and women have come to have lunch.

I walk looking at clothes hanging in windows—the weather is hot—and sit in a restaurant by myself. A woman is loud at a different table but she throws a bottle of perfume at me all of a sudden and it breaks on the floor—I had been angry hearing her though not saying anything and there are only a few people in the restaurant—the staff standing behind the counter.

In autobiographical sections

Our parents go to Mandalay leaving us with missionaries who say we shouldn't go around by ourselves.

Water pipes have been bombed, we have a barrel of water to drink from that's in our house, and we take a ricksha around the city getting out near shops. Then we take one back but the man knows where we live—we didn't see him before—pedals very fast not wanting to hear our address and calling to other ricksha drivers who race with him.

Driving down to Los Angeles a man who was in the lane on the freeway beside me began talking to me out his window.

The wind blowing, he went over onto the soft shoulder of the road to get me to drive into the fast lane—since my window on the driver's side wouldn't roll down and he was going very fast. My window—on the passenger's side—being rolled down. He didn't do it just having a sense of liking me, for that reason alone, since he'd just come up very fast beside me—me answering him although not going into a rest area; so he'd then continue his trip.

People were speaking emotionally, in Peking with my mother, and finally she asked you mean that you were the ones who paraded the professors in public—and they said yes we were, upset; another one there says she's one who was turned in front of a stove—she hadn't had clothes on—and then thrown outside; this not being done by ones sitting there.

I had a job, possibly then I got an injury, of working in a restaurant with boys who were the other dishwashers. I washed enjoying it. A boy had been dismissed for being late and two who were there asked me how old I was—I was much older than they—when a friend came back into the kitchen wanting to talk though I had this work.

I woke in the morning—my fingers on one hand wouldn't separate—perhaps beginning prior to this work.

I didn't associate it with injury—I couldn't continue the job—yet I associated it with some people who upset me then.

The weather was hot and I took a job at a soda fountain, the hands not ready yet to clear dishes though time had gone by, above the sink at the soda fountain there was a long window and a house where one of the people lived could be seen from it. I looked out sometimes seeing them going in the house.

I rode—seeing pigs on the farms, of surprising size—and six hours away from where I started I feel warm going into the cafeteria where several people are. Coming at someone's invitation, I then perceived that his son is hurt and therefore this meant that the father sees women, the wife isn't there, and I dropped him off in the car as he asks me to do a ways away from their house but not driving there, driving back again instead in the heat with the farm animals on the road sides again; it is getting late and I return after it's night though it is summer-time then.

We'd been in bed and then on a ride stopping in front of a record store where there were adolescents standing near some motorcycles, a thought occurring from seeing a man intermingling with the adolescents just in walking by them, only without his having facial wrinkles, and seen to be probably in his thirties. Us having come (sexually) earlier—it having just occurred really—and then being outside there anyway in the particular situation.

I was enjoying weeding some of the weeds very tall on a strip of a road. Of the passengers in cars a few looked at me or didn't attend to that, the cars going by very fast up a hill, and someone began speaking to me who lived near there, asking if I were paid indicating the work I was doing.

Jean Feraca

J ean Feraca grew up in New York in a household where her father constantly recited poetry and told her her true identity was Italian, and "not
Yankee-Doodle." She tested this after she graduated from Manhattanville
College in 1965 and spent two and a half years living and teaching in Rome
and traveling extensively throughout the south of Italy. In 1976 she was
awarded a grant from the National Endowment for the Arts for publication
of her poetry collection, *South from Rome*. In addition to teaching she has
had extensive experience in the communications field. She did her doctoral
work at the University of Kentucky and is now working in Madison, Wisconsin, where she is humanities coordinator for Wisconsin Public Radio.

Memorare/8

Maratea, Lucania, 1974

1
Sleepless he rages, fists on the rails
howling for hours . . .

This, the old dream to be martyred
the calling denied
floats up, a kidney in a bowl
carried to the altar, St. Agnes's breasts
Ophelia's face

the procession of Virgins advances, she carries
a candle
she wears a white dress

a thimble rolls out of my grandmother's coffin
I am bound on the hoop sewn into my hem

This is the way, each moment
I mount
ever higher, the life
of the flesh
falls away

knock knock knock

upstairs, the invalid thumps with his cane
from the bed

knock knock knock

in his three-legged
crib, the infant stands up.

2
I live alone on the edge of town
I keep my father's house

Remember, O most gracious virgin mary
never was it known that anyone who fled
to thy protection
was left
unaided . . .

Skull-bald, these mountains hang over us
massive and terrible
leaning like great-aunts over an infant's crib.

3
teeth descend from the cave roof in rows
Mouth
under the Mountain

O mother of the word incarnate
before thee I stand
sinful and sorrowful

a tower extrudes from a hill
salt
laps at the edge, uneasy

my darling, I'll croon to you, I'll coo
I'll carry you for hours
your wails
splash my sides like a tide of acid
you wear me away all white

the sea sucks up, shudders
subsides to a hiss
starfish slide
dead crabs float
belly up
the moon spins upside down

I'll croon, I'll coo, I'll carry you for hours

all the rock pools give up their ghosts
in the sun
white algae heaps up in pockets
petals on the altar
airy
weightless
I drift, I rove, I carry you for hours

O Mountain, O Rose, O Gold

knock knock knock

pocked, pitted, this blister of rock

white algae heap up in pockets
despise not my petition
hear me, O mother
answer

Scirocco/12

At noon, bells crack the air. I climb
into light
clattering on the rooftiles.
Above the slamming of shopfronts, wet sheets
slap like sails. The smell of fishhead,
flower-stem, sweeps up in gusts.
In this dirty wind, I hold
a steady watch
wary as a whore in steerage, traveling alone.

Vision in the Grove/6

> ". . . *and this is the sixth month*
> *with her that is called barren.*"

1

Driving to Roccella Ionica, east across the boot
through a forest of hair
rank
as pubic growth. Prickly-pear
erupts along the rockwall, a red cancer of thumbs.
Lizards clash, geranium jetting over the edge like blood.

Suddenly I am sick of it: this harsh landscape
running to extremes
the south, the struggle to survive—
Agave thrusting with its horn
gores
its way out of my side;
honey-coy, the locust hides its thorn.

Let me unlearn these hills
I have loved,
scogliera needling the shore; my ancestors
saracen-faced, with your thick black speech
how you tongue me, your eyes brooding under cliffs.
I carry the itch of those looks
under my skin for days.

2

It's april in North Atlantic States, the maples
pushing out their sticky leaves like scouts.
Here, the honeysuckle already brown
the mouth of the rose
blown wide,
it hurts. I close my eyes
dream my way back to olive groves
we passed at dawn:

Gioia Tauro, Laureana, Taurianova
old hags, old crones
I call you like a congress of great-aunts
your crooked trunks unhook
a universe of moss
and rime
that drifts, sinewy smoke. Your wrinkled
rippling flanks unleash black rain
to nets below. You grow like scars
beyond yourselves you dream
you're young again wandering the grove
loose as snakes
weaving each other's necks and waists.

Lulled by the haze, I stay
a long time.
The grove fills. Calves brushed
by dew, I move through dawn-soft air,
wet light mews in the leaves
I pick my steps
with care, until my walk
becomes a kind of swim
through long wet grass
I am drenched
newborn
swimming in a sea without a name.

Diane di Prima

D iane di Prima grew up in Brooklyn but has now lived many years in San
Francisco and is part of the core faculty of the Poetics Program at New
College of California, where she teaches the esoteric traditions in European
and American literature. She studied Zen with Suzuki and is also a teacher

of the healing force (prana) at the San Franciso Institute of Magical and Healing Arts. She is a steady and prolific writer and has published twenty-one books of poetry and prose. She was one of the founders of the New York Poets Theater, a co-editor with LeRoi Jones (Amiri Baraka) of *The Floating Bear* literary review, editor-publisher of the Poets Press in New York and then of Eidolon Editions in California. She has had grants from the National Endowment for the Arts and other foundations for her work in writing, editing, and publishing. Of her the poet Robert Creeley has written, "It is some act of essential clarity I value—which in these initial occasions of her writing is already moving to declare itself: food, places, friends, nights, streets, dreams, the way. She is an adept and flexible provider of the real. . . . She is true." She is the most important woman poet of the counterculture which grew out of the 1960s.

Lullaby

Rockabye
baby-o
nothing is strange
your daddy cut
for Baltimore
your mommy's
making
songs

Rockabye
baby-o
no one's to blame
your daddy lives
with wife and child
your mommy
doesn't
cry

Rockabye
baby-o
nothing will change
your lunch is hot
your bed is made

your daddy
sends
his
love

Marriage

This husband of mine thinks the sea is to visit
In the summer
Whereas I find it the thing to live beside
Desiring as I do to step into it every morning: cold & grey
Or not, as the sun
Rises, before the tasks start,
That my skin and hair should taste salt & I
Could easily live on seaweeds, clams
Breathing that air.
He says it would give him arthritis.
Yet we are better matched than most, we recognize
This as a thing of value, a bone of contention
Between us

Letter to Jeanne (at Tassajara)

---

dry heat of the Tassajara canyon
moist warmth of San Francisco summer
bright fog reflecting sunrise as you
stop out of September zendo
heart of your warmth, my girl, as you step out
into your vajra pathway, glinting
like your eyes turned sideways at us
your high knowing 13-year-old
wench-smile, flicking your thin
ankles you trot toward Adventure
all sizes & shapes, O may it be various

for you as for me it was, sparkle
like dustmotes at dawn in the back
of grey stores, like the shooting stars
over the Hudson, wind in the Berkshire pines

O you have landscapes dramatic like mine
never was, uncounted caves
to mate in, my scorpio, bright love
like fire light up your beauty years
on these new, jagged hills

To My Father

In my dreams you stand among roses.
You are still the fine gardener you were.
You worry about mother.
You are still the fierce wind, the intolerable force
that almost broke me.
Who forced my young body into awkward and proper clothes
Who spoke of his standing in the community.
And men's touch is still a little absurd to me
because you trembled when you touched me.
What external law were you expounding?
How can I take your name like prayer?
My youngest son has your eyes.
Why are you knocking at the doors of my brain?
You kept all their rules and more.
What were you promised that you cannot rest?
What fierce, angry honesty in the darkness?
What can you hope who had preferred my death
to the birth of my oldest daughter?
O fierce hummer of tunes
Forget, eat the black seedcake.
In my dreams you stand at the door of your house
and weep for your wife, my mother.

Prayer to the Mothers

they say you lurk here still, perhaps
in the depths of the earth or on
some sacred mountain, they say
you walk (still) among men, writing signs
in the air, in the sand, warning warning weaving
the crooked shape of our deliverance, anxious
not hasty. Careful. You step among cups, step out of
crystal, heal with the holy glow of your
dark eyes, they say you unveil
a green face in the jungle, wear blue
in the snows, attend on
births, dance on our dead, croon, fuck, embrace
our weariness, you lurk here still, mutter
in caves, warn, warn & weave
warp of our hope, link hands against
the evil in the stars, O rain
poison upon us, acid which eats clean
wake us like children from a nightmare, give the slip
to the devourers whom I cannot name
the metal men who walk
on all our substance, crushing flesh
to swamp

Backyard

where angels turned into honeysuckle & poured nectar into my mouth
where I french-kissed the roses in the rain
where demons tossed me a knife to kill my father in the stark
        simplicity of the sky
where I never cried

where all the roofs were black
where no one opened the venetian blinds
O Brooklyn! Brooklyn!
where fences crumbled under the weight of rambling roses
and naked plaster women bent eternally white over birdbaths
the icicles on the chains of the swings tore my fingers
& the creaking tomato plants tore my heart as they wrapped their
      roots around fish heads rotting beneath them
& the phonograph too creaked Caruso come down from the skies;
      Tito Gobbi in gondola; Gigli ridiculous in soldier uniform:
      Lanza frenetic
& the needle tore at the records & my fingers
tore poems into little pieces & watched the sky
where clouds torn into pieces & livid w/neon or rain
scudded away from Red Hook, away from Gowanus Canal, away
from Brooklyn Navy Yard where everybody worked, to fall to pieces
      over Clinton Street
and the plaster saints in the yard never looked at the naked women
      in the birdbaths
and the folks coming home from work in pizza parlor or furniture store,
      slamming wrought iron gates to come upon brownstone houses,
never looked at either; they saw that the lawns were dry
were eternally parched beneath red gloomy sunsets we viewed from
      a thousand brownstone stoops
leaning together by thousands on the same
wrought-iron bannister, watching the sun impaled
on black St. Stephen's steeple

April Fool Birthday Poem for Grandpa

        Today is your
        birthday and I have tried
        writing these things before,
        but now
        in the gathering madness, I want to
        thank you
        for telling me what to expect
        for pulling

no punches, back there in that scrubbed Bronx parlor
thank you
for honestly weeping in time to
innumerable heartbreaking
italian operas for
pulling my hair when I
pulled the leaves off the trees so I'd
know how it feels, we are
involved in it now, revolution, up to our
knees and the tide is rising, I embrace
strangers on the street, filled with their love and
mine, the love you told us had to come or we
die, told them all in that Bronx park, me listening in
spring Bronx dusk, breathing stars, so glorious
to me your white hair, your height your fierce
blue eyes, rare among italians, I stood
a ways off, looking up at you, my grandpa
people listened to, I stand
a ways off listening as I pour out soup
young men with light in their faces
at my table, talking love, talking revolution
which is love, spelled backwards, how
you would love us all, would thunder your anarchist wisdom
at us, would thunder Dante, and Giordano Bruno, orderly men
bent to your ends, well I want you to know
we do it for you, and your ilk, for Carlo Tresca,
for Sacco and Vanzetti, without knowing
it, or thinking about it, as we do it for Aubrey Beardsley
Oscar Wilde (all street lights
shall be purple), do it
for Trotsky and Shelley and big/dumb
Kropotkin
Eisenstein's Strike people, Jean Cocteau's ennui, we do it for
the stars over the Bronx
that they may look on earth
and not be ashamed.

Minnesota Morning Ode

for Giordano Bruno

The City of the Sun is coming! I hear it! I smell it!
here, where they have made even the earth a jailer
where not even the shadows of animals sneak over the land
where children are injured & taught to apologize for their scars
the City of the Sun cannot be far now—

(that's what you said then, brother, waiting in prison
eight years to be burned, to find the sun at last
on the Campo de Fiori—FIELD OF FLOWERS—yes)
how could it be far?
isn't evil at its peak?
(you asked 300 years ago) has not
the descent into matter reached a nadir? & here
5000 miles later, Northern Minnesota
a forest once, now wasteland
where they mow grass, rake leaves:

I vomit lies like the rest, not knowing
whom to trust, here where betrayal is taught as virtue
I weep alone for the words I would like to say
& silently put the faces of the old gods
into the hands of the children; hope they recognize them
here in this Christian place, where Christ the Magus
& Christ the Healer are both forgotten, where the veil
of the temple is rent, but no resurrection follows. . . .

THE CITY OF THE SUN comes soon, cannot be far
yes, you are right—what's a millennium
or two to us, brother? The gods can wait
they are strong, they rise—the golden tower
flashing the light of planets, the speaking statues
that guard its four gates, the holy wind
that carries the spirit of heaven down thru the stars

it is here! it is here!
I will build it
on this spot. I will build it at Attica
& Wounded Knee
on the Campo de Fiori, at the Vatican:
the strong, bright light of flesh which is the link
the laughter, which transmutes

Minnesota Home School
Sauk Centre

Ree Dragonette

Called by fellow poets who knew her one of our finest "undiscovered" poets, the bulk of whose work remains unpublished, and an audacious original, Ree Dragonette (Rita Marie Dragonetti) was born in Philadelphia in 1918 of Italian immigrant parents and died in 1979. She came from an artistic family which also produced the singer Jessica Dragonette, and was, for those who knew her in the years she lived in New York's Greenwich Village, a legendary figure—poet, teacher, and mentor for young writers, social and political activist, and devoted mother to her children. As did Diane di Prima, Dragonette made her children and her home a deep and abiding focus of her life, and all her work is dedicated to her three sons and one daughter. To support her family, she worked at many jobs, including typing, and had long periods when she could not write at all. In her apartment at Westbeth, a subsidized artists' residence in Greenwich Village, she held readings, workshops, and ran the Calliope Poetry Theatre and co-edited a poetry publication called *Voice Media*. She is remembered as an exceptional jazz poet of the fifties and sixties and performed her poetry in concert at New York's Town Hall in 1962. Her published works, virtually unobtainable, are *Remember Zion* and *Parable of the Fixed Stars* (1968).

The prose poem *This Is the Way We Wash Our Hands* was first read on radio in 1974 and then privately published in 1977 with a foreword by D. H. Melhem.

This Is the Way We Wash Our Hands

Side by side we sit in a café as if in a trough. Uneasy after long absence we have almost forgotten who we once were. We reach out our hands; our lips touch; our smiles gather ashes. You ask how my life is.

It is season of gale wind. From unimagined parsecs the quasi-stellar clocks unwind, rise on their pulses. It is the hour struck by inexplicable transitions where midnight crosses morning; the hour poised unreal between births and deaths. Moment when the moon, nicked, shudders among its winter phases. Time of sun glittering cold in Capricorn; time scaled faster than light-months, than the familiar order of our days piling and sinking.

A waitress comes to the table; we greet her. You gaze at her, gaze; measure each contour. A look of proud birds overtakes you; you straighten, puff into feathers as if into mating regalia from pebbled arena. The waitress repeats and marks down the items we chose from the menu. She is tall; she displays before us her fluent, delicate body. Her thighs are exquisite, her hips curve flawless between the links of a silver chain belt. In cordial understanding, although unlike one another, she and I become telepathic, our glances and perceptions islanded together where no man can follow.

Her skin is ivory; tinted pale it pales and deepens. Her hair ripples brown, yellow-brown, gold. It sparks under the lamps, under stuttering neon. She is wearing a silk dress, fringed, silvered with flowers. The flowers sigh when she stretches over the table to set glasses and spoons into place. The blouse of her dress ruffles low, almost to her nipples. She is Piscean; her feet make no sound on the floor; she walks filmed. Her shoulders seem ultramarine and lapped with reflectors.

I am mildly jealous of what, palpable, occurs between you. You are quick to conceal it. She and I let it surface. We are calm and ironic, bearing each other no malice. Considerate, we look away from you. I train my mind inward to attend nova explosions; to examine fiery lines in the Crab Nebulae. To read scrolls freezing and fanning out in the spaces between galaxies. On awful summons I return. On sudden arrival of

faces which I recognize, which come into my sight in splinters and
clusters, nearing and receding.

They are brown faces, gray, orange ochre; with cheeks gnarled and
shrunken on their bones. I dream them. Women and children shot out
of huts, out of hovels. They run over fields, over hilled cities. Some of
them stand still, open-mouthed; arms outstretched, bleeding. They push
through my sides, my swelling veins. Their lips are cracked, pressed
together crooked and like insects. Some have mouths which dangle from
gashed jaws. Many of them are infants or babies just learning to walk,
unsteady as foals on their legs. They are not dressed in silk or in flowers.
Rags cover their sexes. Their backs are laced with sores, dried rusting.

You are drained away from me, your conflicted demands yielded up
beyond my concern. I witness plague now. Wars, wars; blaze on blaze,
the whirlwind. Sibilant return of reptiles! I have fallen out of time; I
lodge mesozoic on slime. Fallen on petals and ripped branch blowing
seared; on burnt limbs blowing into red leaves. I have received lost life
to eat unholy eucharist sweated into drops, into glistening brine soaped
under naphtha.

You call me back, aura of you slanting imperative along my being.
Inquisitor, now, you hold me, rake my flesh.

We speak of the present—how glad we should be that we have met
again. We laugh; our laughter casketed, embalmed fragrant. We ask each
other why we parted; why our best plans fell away. Why we were
broken from rapture—our joys redolent and canceled in rain, dissolved
in strict circumstance. Memory coffins us, fills us burdened and contrite;
tugs our senses until arced. Until changed, longing ceremonial, we start
awake, astonished as ancient mummies trying to shake off griefs, to cast
off quivering scarabs. We reach out our hands, stiff to fathom one
another. You ask why we cannot be joined again close, as once we were
close.

We ascend raging to face one another polar over walls, righteous
through impenetrable barriers.

You turn in your chair, hold back tremor, halt the twitch of nerves,
nerve's ache. You turn guarded, cognizant to decipher signs, avoiding
dire surprise. You study my face for omens. You cull your thought to
manufacture a charm, to build gemmed recess in which to catch me and
arrest my thought. You kiss me.

We move apart, linger safely in clearings beyond pull from our
opposite magnets. You are circumspect, unimpeachable with gestalts.
With dry airs, you comb the world's affairs.

I hear you criticize the play you saw last night; ask you if your wife is
well. We share speckles from a text on modern metaphysics. We ridicule

our feckless, rambling statesmen. We deplore judicial systems, rising prices, national elections. I call for God's wrath to come down and smite the consciences of those who jail devoted nuns for saying nones, for their practice of soft mercy. God's wrath upon tycoons who stifle honest workers' tongues. Who compensate skilled laborers with pity-pennies for daily struggle in airs of vinyl chloride fumes; laborers who tread assembly lines whose floors are carpeted in arsenic or braided deep with thick carcinogens. God's wrath to fall on those who murder minstrel-priests; who silence poetry.

We debate each raw new filament in theatre, in massage emporia and sensorium of pseudo-therapies. With eyebrows raised you skim green scented gardens, approve palaces of flesh and fuming necromancy. How sad it is, I say, that anyone must shatter old inhibitory rules by copulating foolishly on stage, cheered on by drums and giggles. Must wash their grime of hell-fire guilts in scald of oiled pornography.

You beam, applauding Youth Culture, that it rocks the nation. You praise the young, their somnambulism, their night rise over cliffs in thick migrations luminous as penguins crossing pack ice. You call them pagan and gloriously free. Watching their revelry I weep: see their lives snared, descending between webbed feet, snared! My mind reels on squalls; my nostrils hurt pinched on fossil fuels, on odorous cannabis and on cocaine.

Your cigar chokes me; I cough. Your smile twists into grimace.

I tell you our children are in thrall; are seduced by wizened hawks who sell them apathy. By panderers who cover them in studded shrouds which bury sexual identity. Who nourish them on spiked drink, on bread stuffed with submolecular nightmare. Who tell them loudly *live, dance, flash* like flashing comet tails. But really mean to tell them *die, burn out* too soon.

You ravel and unravel platitudes about American democracy. Tally its treasure troves of goods and services, its generous opportunities. You do not lament as I do, famine spreading pandemic. Do not notice tantalus of abundant orchards denied the poor, blighted by official ill-intention. You are placid; you gloss over whoredom of politics and bureaucracy. Murder by isotopes; the massive, inverted magic show accelerating on human sacrifice, led by satanic cohort.

Tell me, how do you relieve humiliation of black men, of Caribbean slaves? How do you comfort the innocent, deranged and roaming the planet in search of clean meadows? Are you never seized to consider prisoners mocked by miscarriage of justice? Adolescent boys who hang themselves, their spirits fierce and wanting to stampede; narrowed eyes colored topaz, Indian copper, colored striped marble; eyes fixed sardonic, dull and no longer supplicating.

No, nothing seems to prod you, nothing stabs your vision so that you anguish. So that you sympathize with mothers wailing against indifferent fate, their bodies caved like pathetic shields over dying offspring. Mothers of discourteous sickness—cancer, sickle cells, malnutrition of lead-paints. They walk like draft horses. They pray; they keep their children alive by clawing and scrubbing, by shrieking through salt-tears; by mystical wishes. Have you seen them in welfare centers, in courts and detention pens? Waiting in hospitals, trying to lick away gunshot wounds; pawing at needle holes in daughters' skins, where morphine and meth-crystal have chewed? Or leaping into chasms where rapists have bitten, have snarled and plundered.

In our city of discothèque, of thug and transfixion, of radiant carousels, have you embraced wives of killers? At autumn of fire and transhumance, have you known girls kept from first bloom, made into concubines for men who judge themselves bestial? Thieves, procurers, peddlers of powdered death who enjoy only the supremacy of their lust. Self-devourers taught that to be male is to pillage, to slay or be slain.

You bid me hush and have hope. You weave and shimmer. I cannot glow in your glow.

We stare at one another; perish under neon's glare. We lock our trembling hands together. You drowse in rivering warmth, whisper to me how much we need each other, but I say to protest how much we love is not enough.

The skies fall. Among cold winds they fall into the spaces between our skulls. Far away, double stars fly. Blind they tumble, dying in upon each other. We freeze to the sockets of our eyes, our wrist bones, to the masks and visor of our smiles. I say:

The world is at shine point near crest before it crashes, before humanity drops into stillness. Governments are run by men. Diabolical, they want us docile and grinning under masquerade. They want the peoples dull, stupefied, if not stupefied then smoothed fat for bathing in the endless baths. Want us washed into sepulchers, winking under coined eyes under degenerate brahmins.

The male of the species has studied conquest, has instructed his sons to study conquest. The folly of women is that we have surrendered too long, tarnished our nature; let men, monumental with idolatry, tarnish our children.

My voice drops, my words dwindle into your senses as a snowflake fades in hard sunlight. I notice that you have aged since last summer.

You are old in your clean, polished fingers, at the top of your spine
where it is bronze and tucked to your neck between bones and
meninges.

The waitress passes our table, goes to sit among friends at the far end
of the room. I watch her closely, catching her unawares. You watch her,
too. We see her through steam and through smoke wreaths. We see her
shadowed auburn into mirage, waving her mutable arms among the arms
of her playmates. Her neck inclines supple on its lengthening stem. You
lean on your elbows impacted, shot with desire. The future descends,
folds in stealth through our foreheads.

You grow tranquil, stretch, drink your coffee. Planning in casual
posture, seeming at ease, you are alerted exact as a gunfighter. I watch
you gaining time rehearsing, hiding battle plans. I read your mind's
blueprint, can predict that, tomorrow, the waitress will become yours for
a time. You can wait.

Tomorrow, in her room filled with incense and enchanted trinkets, she
will jewel your life. Give herself to you for an hour or two, without
pledges or passion. When next you wish to possess her she will refuse
you. Bearing a fresh scar over old scars you will be left hankering, as on
reflection of certain flowers blue and drifting beyond reach. As on the
wake of lake birds wavering, stirring unseen.

Your sorrow veils me, brushes me with small stones.

We are lonely, busying ourselves at dipole moment, breathless with
gesture and abstractions. So that truth will not bolt us into gape, into
dismay. We rest, give off faint resonance. Perplexed, we are beached
surfers trying to understand what force once drove us to ride out huge
waves, to fuse into each other.

You smoke, inquire how I am feeling; have I taken a lover?

You are vain, yet I cherish you. Agonized, dizzied with ambivalance,
fettered with biology and outworn traditions we remain trapped
together. For all our glimmering insights, our needs and ventilations, our
will to converge in pure love is worn effete; is mechanized and debased.
Residual, we inherit our fathers. Will we ever become serene and equal!

Being man among men; among those who, until now, have owned the
world, why do you make no effort to transform it? Privileged since birth,
you are self-absorbed. Placated by rich rewards, by baubles and
indulgences, are you grateful? Blessed by women generous to kindle
your self-esteem—your mother, your wife, loyal and content to bask in
your shadow. Graced with friends, with ardent lovers, do you notice the
misfortunes of others? No, and so I love you but judge you wanting.
Love you, but cannot forgive that you do not labor in vineyards; that

gifted with talents you stint and work only for material profit. Only to bolster your ego; to satisfy your appetites.

Night chimes around us. It ends on muffled clocks, in radio quiet and dead stars.

A young man enters the café. He walks slowly and unsteadily. His eyes hollow his face; he scowls and smiles. I have known him since he was a small child. If you were not with me I would go to him, cushion him with my body. But as he passes our table, I ignore him; do not look up or speak his name.

He is old enough to vote, to compete in business, to be summoned into armies. He will not maturate in peace; if he sires children he cannot promise them they will escape neutron bombs or ecological disaster. His mother abandoned him long ago. She is very glamorous; drinks too much, vacations too much, changes partners too often. His father despises him because he does not want to be an industrialist or a super-athlete. Rich in money, alienated, the young man is dying of heroin addiction.

I avoid his glance. I do not want to acknowledge him or expose him to your phallic scrutiny. I tell you I would like to go home. Cunning, you delay me, question me about the boy; how long I have known him and what he means to me. You put your palm to your chin, your voice is dry-husked.

No, he and I have not slept together. But in a realm you will never even visit he is, indeed, my dear love.

He sends me a message, silent, solitary as a ginger flower, as a wood anemone. It is a wisp, easily erased, but it scourges me. Ebbed, dragging himself through existence, he can still think of me, offer himself should I need him.

Reading your unspoken thoughts I remind you that you never seem able to transcend your combative gender. Paternal, you will be chastised. Male, you will meet nemesis; inexorable women. Male, you have made war, have made numerous poisons. Have ravaged those who live dreaming, who will not worship your fierce image.

Dawn has come. I stare into your eyes, rise and leave the café. You follow me. The streets outside are flushed with light, but not light rinsed or opalescent. Dawn struggles through clouds, through grained layers as alien as alloys, as cobalt rare earths . . .

We walk together, thin on thin bearings. We meet late troubadors. They are pallid and smell of orange trees. They smell of weed-smoke, of loss and patchouli oils. I take your hand. You and I walk like stilted birds, careful not to fall.

Daniela Gioseffi

The most publically celebrated author of Italian American background, thanks to the profusion of national performances, readings, appearances, interviews, and publications in which she has participated, is, perhaps, Daniela Gioseffi, a poet, novelist, musician, and performer of birth dances. Born in 1941 in Orange, New Jersey, Gioseffi now lives in Brooklyn with her teenage daughter. She writes prolifically, teaches dance, and teaches creative writing in the Poets in the Schools program. She holds an M.A. degree in playwriting and acting from the Catholic University of America in Washington, D.C., and has continued her studies in dance, yoga, and holistic healing. Daniela Gioseffi has been repeatedly featured in anthologies of women's writing. Her novel, *The Great American Belly Dance*, was published by Doubleday in 1977. A collection of her poetry, *Eggs in the Lake*, with an introduction by the poet John Logan, was published by Boa Editions in 1979.

from American Sonnets for My Father

Written in Edna St. Vincent Millay's studio at Steepletop, New York

1.
You died in spring, father, and now the autumn dies.
Bright with ripe youth, dulled by time,
plums of feeling leaked red juices from your eyes,
pools of blood hemorrhaged in your quivering mind.

At forty, I climb Point Pinnacle, today,
thinking of you gone forever from me.
In this russet November woods of Millay,
I wear your old hat, Dear Italian patriarch, to see
if I can think you out of your American grave
to sing your unwritten song with me.
Your poetry, love's value, I carry with your spirit.
I take off your old black hat and sniff at it
to smell the still living vapor of your sweat.

Bicentennial Anti-Poem for Italian-American Women

"You are one of only two or three Italian-American women poets in this country," said the professor. "You are a pioneer. There are fewer of you than Black women poets."

On the crowded subway,
riding to the prison to teach
Black and Puerto Rican inmates how to write,
I think of the fable of the shoemaker
who struggles to make shoes for the oppressed
while his own go barefoot over the stones.

I remember Grandma, her olive face
wrinkled with resignation,
content just to survive
after giving birth to twenty children,
without orgasmic pleasures or anesthesia.
Grandpa, immigrant adventurer,
who brought his family
steerage passage to the New World;
his shoemaker shop where he labored
over American factory goods
that made his artisan's craft a useless
anachronism; his Code of Honor
which forced him to starve
accepting not a cent of welfare

from anyone but his sons;
his ironic "Code of Honor"
which condoned jealous rages of wife-beating;
Aunt Elisabetta, Aunt Maria-Domenica,
Aunt Raffaella, Aunt Elena, grown women
huddled like girls in their bedroom in Newark,
talking in whispers, not daring
to smoke their American cigarettes
in front of Pa;
the backyard shrine of the virgin,
somber blue-robed woman,
devoid of sexual passions,
to whom Aunt Elisabetta prayed
daily before dying in childbirth,
trying to have *a son*
against doctor's orders
though she had five healthy daughters;
Dr. Giuseppe Ferrara,
purple-heart veteran of World War II,
told he couldn't have a residency
in a big New York Hospital
because of his Italian name;
the mafia jokes, the epithets:
Wop, guinea, dago, grease-ball;
and the stories told by Papa
of Dante, Galileo, Da Vinci,
Marconi, Fermi and Caruso
that stung me with pride
for Italian *men;*
how I was discouraged from school,
told a woman meant for cooking
and bearing doesn't need education.

I remember
Grandma
got out of bed
in the middle of the night
to fetch her *husband* a glass of water
the day she died,
her body wearied
from giving and giving and giving
food and birth.

My Venus Fly Trap Is Dying

because it frightens me.
I've tried to remember to water it.
I keep saying I'll buy it a new pot,
furnish it with fresh earth.
After all, it is a plant and I do love
greenery. But it's carnivorous,
ingesting raw meat, living
insects, engulfing them in heart-
shaped leaves. Other plants wait
for death to give flesh to roots.
I resolve to become a vegetarian.
I've loved and envied plants
for their peacefulness,
their quiet conversion of the sun,
that first all contingent link
between solar energy and animal.
But this Venus Fly Trap
is too much for me.
It will have to die
tossed into the waste can
with the bright red lipstick,
the blood red nail polish.
I no longer wear.
This Venus Fly Trap doesn't
photosynthesize peacefully.
It's trying to become an animal
and I
trying so hard to be a tree
can't bear it.

Peace Prospect

Too many people scribbling on each others' tongues
gagging the cities.
Politics muddle the nature of bodies.
Sexual energy, a force confused, wasted.

While sleep plays out the pain in me,
I have a pleasant dream,
a land inhabited by bright animals
who refuse fire
and eat nothing but leaves.
I count the people I have tried to touch;
my hands melt sand into glass.
We can't manufacture food like vegetation
standing in the light. Photosynthesis
is the trees making love with the sun.
A vague intuition blossoms in my stomach,
a chance for a finer love.
We are a mind-ridden race, incompatible with earth.

A better race will come. I feel
bright animals waiting
for the right genetic moment.

Lorraine DeGennaro

orraine DeGennaro lives in Valley Cottage, New York, in the Hudson River Valley, with her husband and their eight-year-old son. She has published poetry in many small-press publications throughout the country and her first chapbook, *Brushfire Publications*, came out in the spring of 1984. She is presently working on her first novel.

Table Manners of an Only Child

I covet
The six chairs around your table,
The crumbs you sponge away
After every meal. I am neat,
Leave no crusts behind
No drops of Cabernet
On yellow linen; yet you
Complain about the mess,
Dishes in the sink, brothers
At the door demanding plates.

I unfold my napkin,
Trays pass from hand to hand.
I enjoy the clash of covers on pots,
Opinions on statements
That you find ordinary.

I barely eat, my eyes are
Nourished by connecting lives.
I could grow fat on them
Without ever tasting foreign
Aperitifs and sweet tea
Never minding the thickness of my waist.

I carry a glass to the kitchen
Admiring the hill of stoneware,
Silver and wooden spoons.
I caress Brillo in my fingers
Scrub each piece
And hand them to you to dry.

We hear the scrape of chairs pushed
From the table, the fumbling
For coats in the hall.
I wipe my hands when
You lock the door,
Help fold your grandmother's tablecloth.

Maryfrances Wagner

Maryfrances Cusumano Wagner was born and raised in Kansas City, Missouri, and chairs the English Department at Raytown High (Raytown, Missouri), where she teaches writing. She has published in many reviews, done readings and workshops, and co-edited *Missouri Poets: An Anthology*. She has recently started taking Italian lessons, for although both sets of her grandparents were born in Italy, she, like many other second-generation Italian Americans, does not speak Italian. Some of her poetry has been collected and published in two books, *Tonight Cicadas Sing* and *Bandaged Watermelons*.

Ragazza

A good Italian woman
will cover her dust-free house
with crocheted doilies,
bear dark-eyed sons,
know what to do
with artichokes and chick peas.
Her floors will shine.
She will serve tender brucaluni
in her perfect sauce,
make her own cannoli shells,
bake biscottas for every wedding.
Supper will be hot at six o'clock.
She will always wear dresses.
She will not balance the checkbook.
He can doze behind the paper
when she washes dishes.
Because she will never leave him,
he will forgive her bulging thighs.
Because he will never leave her,
she won't notice unfamiliar stains.

Italian men always know *ragazze*
who work the fields in Bivona.
For airfare one will come.
In time she will learn English.
In time they may learn to love.

The Winemaker

Father collects red earth
in the cracked canals
of his paddle fingers.

At dinner the oars,
flat and splintered,
grip his wineglass.

He tells us hard work
fulfills a man,

lifts his wine to the light,
smiles, "Pure. One glass a day.

Good for the blood.
Elderberries for color."

Inhaling the fragrance, he
rubs his fingertips with his thumb

trying to find the right word there,
trying to construct wisdom
on his forefinger.

I notice a sliver of tape
butterflying an open channel.

"Pure. No sugar added."

Acknowledgments

Grateful acknowledgment is made for permission to reprint:

Carol Bonomo Ahearn, "Definitions of Womanhood: Class, Acculturation, and Feminism": copyright 1984 by Carol Bonomo Ahearn.

Anna Bart, "Giovanni 1854–1940," "Ravioli," "Preserving," "c. 1896": copyright 1983 by Bernadetta D'Arcangelo Gorski.

Marion Benasutti, selection from *No Steady Job for Papa:* copyright 1966 by Marion Benasutti. Reprinted by permission of The Vanguard Press, Inc.

Jacquelyn Bonomo, "The Flashlight," "The Ninth Life," "Hens," "Patience in the Endless Rain": copyright 1984 by Jacquelyn Bonomo. "Patience in the Endless Rain" is reprinted from *The Massachusetts Review,* Summer 1981, by permission of The Massachusetts Review, Inc.

Dorothy Bryant, selection from *Miss Giardino:* copyright 1978 by Dorothy Bryant. Published by Ata Books, Berkeley, Calif.

Phyllis Capello, "Camping Out," "at my breast," "getting my jazz down": copyright 1982 by Phyllis Capello. Reprinted from *The Wind in Our Sails,* published by Midnight Sun, New York.

Octavia Capuzzi Waldo Locke, "The Rocks": copyright 1973 by Octavia Capuzzi. Reprinted by permission of *New Orleans Review,* Loyola University, New Orleans.

Bloom" appeared in a slightly different version in the Summer 1983 issue of *Poets On: Celebrations*.

Kathy Freeperson, "Italian Bread": copyright 1976 by Kathy Freeperson.

Sandra Gilbert, "Mafioso," "The Thoreau Pencil," "The Grandmother Dream," "Doing Laundry," from *In the Fourth World: Poems:* copyright 1978 by Sandra Gilbert. Published by University of Alabama Press. "The Summer Kitchen" copyright 1983 by Sandra Gilbert.

Maria Mazziotti Gillan, "Public School No. 18: Paterson, New Jersey": copyright 1983 Maria Mazziotti Gillan; "Petals of Silence," from *Flowers from the Tree of Night:* copyright 1981 by Maria Gillan. Published by Chantry Press, Midland Park, N.J.

Daniela Gioseffi, Sonnet 1 from "American Sonnets for My Father": copyright 1981 by Daniela Gioseffi; "My Venus Fly Trap Is Dying," "Bicentennial Anti-Poem for Italian-American Women," "Peace Prospect," from *Eggs in the Lake:* copyright 1978 by Daniela Gioseffi. Reprinted from *Eggs in the Lake: Poems by Daniela Gioseffi*, Foreword by John Logan, by permission of Boa Editions, Ltd., Brockport, N.Y.

Mary Gordon, "Zi'Marietta": copyright 1976 by UNICO National. Reprinted by permission of UNICO National, Bloomfield, N.J., publisher of *A New Day*, where this first appeared.

Rose Grieco, "The Sunday Papa Missed Mass": copyright 1955 by *Commonweal* magazine. Reprinted by permission from June 3, 1955, issue of *Commonweal*.

Barbara Grizzuti Harrison, "Godfather II," from *Off Center:* copyright 1980 by Barbara Grizzuti Harrison. Reprinted by permission of Doubleday & Company, Inc., from a Dial Press Book.

Lynette Iezzoni, "Window Seat": copyright 1983 by Lynette Iezzoni.

Jennifer Lagier, "second class citizen": copyright 1983 by Jennifer Lagier.

Michele Linfante, *Pizza:* copyright 1980 by West Coast Plays, Berkeley, Calif.

Severina Magni, "Poetry": copyright 1955 by Severina Magni. "Poetry," from *Anthology of Italian and Italo-American Poetry*, edited by Rodolfo Pucelli, has been reprinted courtesy of Branden Press, Inc., 21 Station Street, Brookline Village, Mass. 02147.

Karen Malpede, Introduction to, and Scene 2 of, *A Monster Has Stolen the Sun:* copyright 1981 by Karen Malpede.

Nancy Maniscalco, selection from *Lesser Sins:* copyright 1979 by Nancy Maniscalco. Published by Avon Books.

Gigi Marino, "Angelina": copyright 1983 by Gigi Marino.

Elizabeth Marraffino, "Blues After 35¢ Beers in St. Louis," "Night After

Night": copyright 1983 by Elizabeth Marraffino. Published in June 1980 issue of *Waterways* and reprinted with permission.

Mary K. Mazotti, "La Ciramella": copyright 1983 by Mary K. Mazotti.

Claudia Menza, "Poem for Miles Davis": copyright 1982 by Claudia Menza.

Anna Monardo, "Roman Ruins": copyright 1982 by Anna Monardo. First published in September 1982 issue of *Redbook* magazine.

Pacé Nicolino, "Goodbyes and Hellos": copyright 1982 by the Poetry Society of Vermont. Published in *Second Harvest: An Anthology of Poems by Members of the Poetry Society of Vermont;* "Dandelions": copyright 1982 by Pacé Nicolino.

Kathryn Nocerino, "El Sueño," "Maria Dominica," "Empty Factory, N.J.," from *Head with Hat:* copyright 1983 by Kathryn Nocerino. Published by New Rivers Press, St. Paul, Minn.

Anne Paolucci, "Party Overlooking the Narrows," "Acuto," "Back in the Old Country," "To My Fat Friends," from *Poems:* copyright 1977 by Anne Paolucci. Published by Griffon House Publications, Bergenfield, N.J.

Antonia Pola, selection from *Who Can Buy the Stars?:* copyright 1957 by Antonietta Pomilla. Published by Vantage Press, N.Y.

Elaine Romaine, "fan letter," "you were always irish, god," "Song and Dance Lady": copyright 1983 by Elaine Romaine. Published in *Gravida* and reprinted by permission.

Rosemarie Santini, "An American Dream": copyright 1976 by Rosemarie Santini. First published in the *Daily News Sunday Magazine,* October 31, 1976. Reprinted by permission of William Morris Agency, Inc.

Julia Savarese, selection from *The Weak and the Strong:* copyright 1952 by Julia Savarese. Published by Putnam. Reprinted by permission of William Morris Agency, Inc., on behalf of the author.

Leslie Scalapino, "In Sequence," from *Considering How Exaggerated Music Is,* copyright 1982 by Leslie Scalapino. Published by North Point Press, San Francisco, and reprinted by permission.

Sister Blandina Segale, selection from *At the End of the Santa Fe Trail:* copyright 1948 by Bruce Publishing Co. Used by permission of Glencoe Publishing Company.

Tia G. Talamini, "I Learn Three New Words": copyright 1983 by Tia G. Talamini.

Gioia Timpanelli, selection from "Italian Traveling": copyright 1983 by Gioia Timpanelli.

Mari Tomasi, selection from *Like Lesser Gods:* copyright 1949 by Mari Tomasi. Published by Bruce Publishing Co., Milwaukee, 1949. Used by permission of Glencoe Publishing Company.

Rita Valentino, "o walt": copyright 1982 by Rita Valentino. Reprinted from *The Wind in Our Sails*, published by Midnight Sun, New York. "The funeral parlor's in brooklyn," copyright 1983 by Rita Valentino.

Alma R. Vanek, "Zio": copyright 1978 by Alma Vanek. First published in *True to Life Stories*, volume 1, Diana Press, Oakland, Calif.

Janine Veto, "Naturally, Mother": copyright 1979 by *Earth's Daughters* and first published in *Earth's Daughters*, October 1979. "Body Wisdom": copyright 1983 Janine Veto. Reprinted by permission of the author.

Theresa Vinciguerra, "This Small Universe," "Rope," "Aftertaste": copyright 1980, 1981, 1982 by Theresa Vinciguerra.

Maryfrances Cusumano Wagner, "The Winemaker," "Ragazza": copyright 1983 by Maryfrances Wagner. First published in *Blue Unicorn*, Kensington, Calif.

Frances Winwar, selection from *Poor Splendid Wings:* copyright 1933 by Frances Winwar Grebanier. Published by Little, Brown, Boston. Reprinted by permission of Jerry Warwin.

Index